Doing Feminist Research in Political and Social Science

Doing Feminist Research in Political and Social Science

Brooke Ackerly
and
Jacqui True

First published 2010 by
PALGRAVE MACMILLAN

Palgrave Macmillan in the UK is an imprint of Macmillan Publishers Limited, registered in England, company number 785998, of Houndmills, Basingstoke, Hampshire RG21 6XS.

Palgrave Macmillan in the US is a division of St Martin's Press LLC, 175 Fifth Avenue, New York, NY 10010.

Palgrave Macmillan is the global academic imprint of the above companies and has companies and representatives throughout the world.

Palgrave® and Macmillan® are registered trademarks in the United States, the United Kingdom, Europe and other countries

ISBN 978–0–230–50776–0   hardback
ISBN 978–0–230–50777–7   paperback

This book is printed on paper suitable for recycling and made from fully managed and sustained forest sources. Logging, pulping and manufacturing processes are expected to conform to the environmental regulations of the country of origin.

A catalogue record for this book is available from the British Library.

A catalog record for this book is available from the Library of Congress.

10 9 8 7 6 5 4 3 2 1
19 18 17 16 15 14 13 12 11 10

Printed in China

In memory of Hayward Alker

Contents

List of Key Concepts

List of Boxes

List of Figures

Acknowledgments

We would like to thank our families who have arranged their holidays (and work schedules) to enable us to collaborate.

I (Brooke) would like to thank Seamus and Hugo for teaching Annlyn and Aasha about New Zealand, "Hi-5," and *Charlie and Lola*. I also appreciate you sharing your Mum. Aasha and Annlyn, I still love the story of the snowball down your Daddy's back at Mt. Ruapehu in the middle of summer and the memory of you covered in the black sand of Lake Taupo. Bill, I appreciate the spirit that you brought to New Zealand and to every family adventure. Michael, I will remember enjoying a coffee on the back patio in Auckland under the Pohutakawa tree. Jacqui, I will always remember outlining each chapter while drinking tea in your bach. I appreciate all that you brought to our project and the care you put into making sure that our families had a wonderful experience of New Zealand. Thank you, Jacqui.

I (Jacqui) would like to thank my family, Michael, Seamus, and Hugo for working and playing around my schedule as Brooke and I worked on this book. When we wrote the proposal for this book Seamus was three and Hugo was 20 months, they are now seven and nearly five and a half! I would also like to thank Brooke, Bill, Annlyn, and Aasha who welcomed me as practically a member of their family on my two trips to Nashville. I will remember Annlyn creeping into my bed at 6am, listening to Annlyn and Aasha's music practice, Bill's great salads, and watching girly movies with your family. Sharing day-to-day life and commitment to this project with Brooke across countries and worlds really, has been a privilege and a learning experience. Thank you, Brooke.

We have approached the writing and editorial process of this book collaboratively. Of course, we shared in the authoring and editing of the book; further, we invited many students and colleagues to read chapters that were in their earliest drafts; these include Josh Bezuin, Jadzia Butler, Don Clarke, Stacy Clifford, Chris Desante, Tania Domett, Kevin Duong, Kathy Errington, Nina Hall, Lyndi Hewitt, Farhana Loonat, Sonalini Sapra, Ali Sevilla, Rebecca Todd, and Ying Zhang. We owe a particular debt to Bina D'Costa, Lyndi Hewitt, Sonalini Sapra, Heather Tally, and Sarah VanHooser who shared with us their work in progress and reflected on their methodological choices with us in workshops and personal communications, some of which are included in the book.

Many colleagues have been helpful in enriching our understandings of their areas of expertise. These include Ann Tickner, Roland Bleiker, Morgan Brigg, Tony Brown, Charlotte Epstein, Giacomo Chiozza, Suzanne Globetti,

Christian Grose, Sandra Harding, Marc Hetherington, Lyndi Hewitt, Emma Hutchinson, Megan Mackenzie, Kathy Smits, Barbara Sullivan, and Liz Zechmeister.

Additionally, we have benefited from financial and personal support from many institutions. The University of Auckland Research Committee funded Brooke's visit to New Zealand to meet with Jacqui through a strategic collaboration grant. Research and Study Leave from the University of Auckland also made it possible for Jacqui to have that important face to face writing time with Brooke at Vanderbilt. Mona Frederick and the Warren Center offered Brooke a place to work in a refuge of fellow tea drinkers. The Global Feminisms Collaborative is a group of feminist colleagues who model collaborative partnership in everything they do and provided example as well as intellectual feedback during the framing of the book. Vanderbilt University funded Brooke's Research Leave during which this project was completed.

Throughout the process we have benefited from important audiences at the International Studies Association, American Political Science Association, the Global Feminisms Brown Bag, the Oceanic Conference on International Studies, the Alternative Methodologies Workshop hosted by Roland Bleiker, the Politics and International Relations departments at the University of Queensland, the University of Sydney, and Victoria University of Wellington, and Jacqui's Global Civil Society graduate class.

Our collaboration owes a debt of gratitude to our publisher, Steven Kennedy, who shifted pace with us as our scope of the project became more ambitious. His patience allowed our collaboration to be as fruitful as it could be.

Finally, with thanks we dedicate this book to Hayward Alker. Hayward was a wonderful teacher and devotee of methodology and methodological innovation. He was committed not only to teaching, but also to learning and practiced ongoing self-reflection over all questions of methodology. It is in this spirit that we dedicate this book to Hayward, who, having taught so much to so many, always knew he had much more to learn.

BROOK ACKERLY
JACQUI TRUE

Chapter 1

Introduction to Feminist Research

Introduction

Are you curious, skeptical, persistent, and surprised by the social and political world around you? These are often the conditions of a good researcher. Yet, we cannot be good researchers just by wanting to be. It takes reflection and practice.

In this book, we provide students and scholars from a range of social science fields with a comprehensive, step-by-step guide to feminist research reflection and practice. Before we go any further let us set out our view of feminism explicitly. We think of feminism as that critical perspective on social and political life that draws our attention to the ways in which social, political, and economic norms, practices, and structures create injustices that are experienced differently or uniquely by certain groups of women. Taking this view of feminism in your research does not require you to participate in direct social and political action or necessarily to label or identify yourself as a feminist.

In this book we argue that a critical feminist perspective is expressed (in part) through a feminist research ethic that guides our research decisions and helps us to reflect on and attend to dynamics of power, knowledge, relationships, and context throughout the research process.

Since this book is specifically focused on how to do feminist research, we have assumed our readers will already have a fair idea about what feminism is and its main variants (but see Box 1.1 below for some suggestions on introductory reading). Throughout the book we have tried to summarize and briefly explain our understanding of the main contours of

1

1.1 CRITICAL FEMINIST PERSPECTIVE

There are many kinds of feminist theory (see Box 1.1 for some introductions).

A critical feminist perspective uses critical inquiry and reflection on social injustice by way of gender analysis, to *transform*, and not simply explain, the social order. The perspective encourages opening new lines of inquiry versus simply "filling in gaps" in already established disciplinary terrains. Such a perspective is informed by critical, post-colonial, post-structural theories and neo-Marxist political economy.

This form of feminism is the lens that guides this book, but throughout the book we also cite other feminists thereby exhibiting a broad range of perspectives.

feminism where we feel that this is necessary to ensure you understand what we mean by *a* feminist research ethic and how to apply it in your research.

In order to help those with this critical feminist perspective do research, we make readily accessible much of the teaching and advice we routinely share with our students and colleagues about how to carry out methodologically and ethically sound research. The book is founded on an appreciation for the diversity of feminist studies, their reluctance to be defined, and their ambivalent reception by some researchers and groups, including women around the world. Recognizing that "feminism" around the world has a mixed reception and sometimes faces a skeptical audience, even among women and often from non-feminist professors and academics, the book lays out a theoretically informed methodological guide to research.

1.2 FEMINIST RESEARCH ETHIC

A feminist research ethic is a methodological commitment to any set of research practices that reflect on the power of epistemology, boundaries, relationships, and the multiple dimensions of the researcher's location throughout the entirety of the research process and to a normative commitment to transforming the social order in order to promote gender justice. It is an *ethic* in two senses: it demands that we use critical reflection as a work ethic during research and it points us to recognize and account for the provisionality and contingency of data, the construction of knowledge by way of boundaries and categories, and the need to relate to these categories and boundaries in non-essentialist and transformative ways. (See Chapter two).

Box 1.1   Introduction to feminism: a reading list

Surveys

Rosemary Tong. 1998. *Feminist Thought: A More Comprehensive Introduction*, 2nd edn. Boulder, CO: Westview Press.

Dietz, Mary G. 2003. "Current Controversies in Feminist Theory." *Annual Review of Political Science* 6: 399–431.

Hawkesworth, Mary E. 2006. *Feminist Inquiry: From Political Conviction to Methodological Innovation*. New Brunswick, NJ: Rutgers University Press.

Ackerly, Brooke A., and Katy Attanasi. 2009. "Global Feminisms: Theory and Ethics for Studying Gendered Injustice." *New Political Science* 31,4: 543–55.

Selected critical perspectives

bell hooks. 1984. *Feminist Theory: From Margin to Center*. Boston: Southend Press.

Benhabib, Seyla, Judith Butler, Nancy Fraser, and Drucilla Cornell. 1995. *Feminist Contentions: A Philosophical Exchange*. New York: Routledge.

Mendoza, Breny. 2002. "Transnational Feminisms in Question." *Feminist Theory* 3, 3: 295–314.

Other feminists (and we elsewhere) put forward substantive accounts of feminism (see Box 1.1). Feminists make normative, conceptual, and empirical contributions to their fields. In this book, we focus on the *methodological* contribution that feminists have and can make to social science. We expect that readers will use these methodologies to make their own substantive contributions to their fields and to feminism.

The research that leads to those contributions often follows a non-linear process. This is because social and political research is inherently dynamic. As social scientists we are part of the very world that we are trying to understand, and that world is always changing and affected by our study of it. At the same time feminism requires us to reexamine continually our assumptions as we engage in research, making that research even more dynamic and non-linear. Feminists reflect again and again on the ways in which we approach our work, and on the changing nature of what we study. We focus on the ways in which power affects our assumptions, on the continually revealed exclusions and inclusions of research, on the relationships among its stakeholders (course instructors, researcher-participants, subject-participants, assistant-participants, translators, facilitators, audiences, communities, etc.) in our research, and on the ways in which our own decisions about how to conduct our research are linked to our particular social and political location. The feminist methodology we outline is explicit about the dynamic

KEY CONCEPT

1.3 RIGOR

For a feminist research project, the very concept of rigor is defined from a critical perspective on methodology. Etymologically, the term "rigor" means stiff. However, in social science it has come to mean using "systematic" and accountable methods. While we wouldn't want to argue that feminist scholarship is stiff, we want to show that feminist scholarship has standards of quality which overlap in their key features with the standards of all social sciences: that they can be defended before a jury of academic peers. See for comparison (Mason 2002: 40–1; Yanow 2006b).

nature of social science research and provides an account of research that is true to the experience of most social science researchers.

To convey the diversity, self-reflection, and the dynamic character of research, we draw extensively on examples of local, international, regional, global, and multi-sited research projects. We guide students through the research process in a way that reveals the methodological structure of a feminist research process. And we guide the researcher in the exposition of her project to feminist and non-feminist audiences alike. Making a feminist research project accessible to a non-feminist academic audience is not about concealing its feminism; it is about revealing its theoretical and methodological rigor.

In this book, we redefine, rework, and develop the basic architecture of political and social science research in order to improve it and to create a feminist research practice. You can read this book as feminist scholarship to be evaluated and challenged from multiple perspectives as you would other scholarship. Or, you can pick it up and take it with you on your journey of feminist research. However, even if you take this second route, trusting it as your guidebook, we hope you will treat it as an adventurer treats his favorite guidebook, and develop your own way to do your research guided by your feminist research ethic. The book should give you the tools to do this yourself, and to become an informed critical feminist researcher and evaluator of feminist research.

Key Tools in this Book

To facilitate a linear exposition of the dynamics of the non-linear research process, in this book we use supplemental modes of exposition. Each chapter contains Key Concepts, Boxes, and Selected Sources for Further Reading.

Box 1.2 Doing Feminist Research on the Web

The accompanying website at http://www.palgrave.com/methodology/ doingfeministresearch includes:

- a searchable glossary of terms;
- a set of practical exercises organized by book chapter;
- materials for facilitating interview research;
- guidelines for reviewing and evaluating your own research.

The book's website http://www.palgrave.com/methodology/doingfeministresearch has other supporting materials, including practical exercises for each chapter of the books, a glossary of terms used throughout the book, examples of materials we have used in our own interview research, as well as guidelines for how to use the feminist research ethic to evaluate research.

Key Concepts highlight those concepts that have a developed or contested literature and sets out our use of them. These are brief expositions of concepts that deserve more attention than the narrative of the text allows. Sometimes, we use these key concept textboxes to indicate how we are deploying certain concepts that are the subject of debate.

Boxes provide insights from our experience as researchers and illustrative examples of effective and insightful research in different fields of study. While each researcher needs to create her own research, it can help to see what choices others have made and what constraints others have faced. Boxes give the reader examples from published research, unpublished reflections from our own practice or from that of other feminists. See the "List of Boxes" to help you relocate Boxes that you have found useful.

Selected Sources for Further Reading also appear at the end of chapters to provide the reader with references to key literatures on the topic. Since we offer rich bibliographic references throughout each chapter, we offer the selected bibliography as a recommended starting place.

In addition to the glossary of terms and concepts on the accompanying website http://www.palgrave.com/methodology/doingfeministresearch (see Box 1.2), these are also defined either in the text or in Key Concepts boxes, generally where they first occur.

Doing Feminist Research: A Book for Your Practice

This book is not intended to make you an expert on the *scholarship* of feminist methodology, but rather to help you develop *your practice* of feminist research. Because this book is a guide to the overall research process rather

1.4 METHODOLOGY

KEY CONCEPT

Generally, "methodology" is understood as a particular set of methods or way of doing research. However, a feminist methodology is *not* a series of particular methods or guidelines for research, like a protocol, but a commitment to using a whole constellation of methods reflectively and critically, with the end aim being the production of data that serve feminist aims of social justice. Thus, a feminist methodology is a *way* of using and reflecting on methods, and not a particular set of methods or a particular research design. Rigorous feminist methodologies lead to decisions made during the research process that are to academic peers.

This view of methodology helps us reexamine the basics of the research process in the social sciences.

than an exposition of particular research methods, the text encourages students to make use of the bibliography to explore further certain debates and methods. In some disciplines, feminist methodology is now an area of specialization. Graduate students are examined in feminist methodology. Graduate and undergraduate courses are devoted to feminist methodology. Many feminist courses have a methodological component. Many methodology and research design courses have a feminist component (Chafetz 2004; Hesse-Biber 2007; Hootman 2006). The bibliography will help you pursue the scholarship of feminist methodology on your own.

Methodologies take many forms. For the purposes of introduction, we conceive of methodology as the ongoing reflection that guides research. Feminist methodology encompasses reflections about the relationship among the purpose of research, how we tell fact from belief, theory and conceptualization, research design, ethics, methods, and analysis. In particular, it involves self-conscious reflections on the purpose of research, our conceptual frameworks, our ethical responsibilities, method choices, and our assumptions about what it means to know rather than just believe something. Such reflection occurs *throughout* the research process.

In previous work we refer to this ongoing ethical reflection as a "theoretical methodology" (Ackerly and True 2006). Many readers stumbled over this term and found it jargon-y. In this work we shift terms. We argue that in feminist empirical inquiry, the insights of feminist theory are used as a guide to a research practice. A feminist research ethic is a set of research practices and a normative commitment to using and developing these. Importantly, this is a feminist normative commitment to a research practice. Such a research practice does not involve specific normative

1.5 FEMINIST PRAXIS

Feminists often use the language of "praxis" to refer to the practice of feminist scholarship that is informed by critical feminist normative and theoretical perspectives. Praxis is theory in action and action-oriented theory. Generally, we do not use the language of "praxis" to describe our methodology because we don't think it is concrete enough in its prescriptions.

Although critical self-reflection is not unique to critical feminism, the scope of these reflections sets most feminist contributions apart from the mainstream social science disciplines of politics, international relations, sociology, and human geography for example and makes feminist inquiry an important partner in the more critical endeavors of those fields. Often, but not always explicitly stated, a feminist research ethic (in the sense of a practice and a set of ethical commitments) guides the researcher through systematic reflection throughout the process, from research question to publication.

---

commitments to an ideal world, that is, they are commitments about *how* we study the world even while we may differ on *what* kind of world we would like to bring about. While we respect that for many of us feminist research is an important part of our personal normative commitments, we wish to distinguish these substantive, normative commitments – which may be broad and diverse and important to our research – from the normative commitment to a reflexive research, which should be the focus of your methodological work.

A feminist project is identifiably "feminist" by its research question, by the theoretical underpinnings of the project and by the use of a feminist research ethic throughout the research process rather than by any particular method(s) used or a particular set of normative commitments (Ackerly 2008b; Ackerly, Stern and True 2006; True 2008c). For instance, feminism alerts us to the importance of studying silences and absences in familiar institutions and of studying marginalized and excluded peoples' experiences for understanding our local and global world. However, no definitive feminist method exists because many methods may be necessary for one question or another in order to reveal silences and oppressions and to understand the conditions, processes, and institutions that cause and sustain them. Feminist goals are plural and contested and, as such, feminist research cannot be reduced to a particular normative orientation or political, ideological agenda. Yet, in looking closely at our feminist colleagues' work, we see familiar methods – such as ethnography, oral history, participant observation, semi-structured interviews, and survey research – being carried out in more or less feminist ways.

Box 1.3 Baker and Cooke on the Bronx Slave Market

Feminist empirical inquiry predates feminism in academe. In 1935 two NAACP colleagues, Ella Baker and Marvel Cooke, joined hundreds of African Americans who sold their labor on 167th Street and Simpson Avenue in the Bronx in order to study and reveal their working conditions and to demonstrate the connections between these African American women seeking domestic work and the plight of other workers and families affected by the depression.

"In the boom days before the onslaught of the depression in 1929, many of these women who are now forced to bargain for day's work on street corners, were employed in grand homes in Long Island and Westchester, at more than adequate wages. Some are former marginal industrial workers, forced by the slack in industry to seek other means of sustenance. In many instances there had been no necessity for work at all. But whatever their standing prior to the depression, none sought employment where they seek it. They came to the Bronx, not because of it promises, but largely in desperation ... The general public, though aroused by stories of these domestics, too often think of these problems of these women as something separate and apart and readily dismisses them with a sign and a shrug of the shoulders" (Baker 1955: 330, 340).

Critical Feminist Approaches to Methodology and Research

Students and scholars today benefit from the critical building blocks of feminist scholarship in the social sciences and even before the institutionalization of feminist knowledge in the academy (see Box 1.3). Feminist scholars have paved the way for serious engagement with gender and other categories of oppression and exclusion in previously gender-blind fields of study. For example, feminist scholars have opened the field of economics to a whole new research agenda by revealing the gender bias implicit in the oversimplifying assumption of the household as a unitary and homogenous actor and unit of analysis. Such treatment assumes that resources are distributed equally among household members, and that decision-making is unitary rather than subject to power dynamics within the household (Dwyer and Bruce 1988; Folbre 1984; Tinker 1990). Similarly, in the field of International Relations, feminist scholars have challenged the core concept of security and its association with the state's provision of military security rather than individual human security, such as the insecurity experienced by women subject to domestic violence, rape in war, or chronic insecurity associated with living in a conflict zone, living in poverty, and environmental degradation.

> ## Box 1.4 Create and seek out opportunities for discussion of methodology
>
> The conferences, workshops, and panels we have organized in recent years have confirmed that there is a pressing demand from students and scholars engaging in feminist projects for an explicit methodological guide.
>
> We urge the reader to participate in methodological discussions wherever they happen, during their disciplinary conferences and in small and large multidisciplinary meetings including Feminist Epistemologies, Methodologies, Metaphysics and Science Studies (FEMMSS) which meets biannually in the United States and the International Interdisciplinary Congress on Women which meets triannually.

As a result of path breaking feminist scholarship, students and scholars are continually formulating new feminist research questions and agendas. The articles published in the increasingly voluminous range of feminist journals, illustrate the theoretical diversity, multidisciplinarity, and often global scope of that new research. However, students, instructors and supervisors often do not know the methodological "scaffolding" that frames this feminist research.

Certainly, there are essays and books on methodology, but trailblazing critical feminist scholars have not always left a trail of methodological guidelines. Publishing norms that were established during the process of legitimating a discipline do not generally include encouraging reflection on *all* aspects of a methodology, especially those more awkward aspects that don't seem parsimonious. Consequently, those reflections are not visible in the final design. In this book we intend to make feminist research more doable by making visible all aspects of methodological reflection (Box 1.4).

The impetus for this book is the need felt by ourselves, our colleagues, and our students for a guide to translating normative and theoretical feminist work into successful, ethically-rigorous research on feminist and non-feminist questions. We complement other work on critical and feminist methodology. By offering both *critical reflection* on research from purpose to practice (cf. Davis 2005; Gadamer 1989) and *constructive advice* about how to do and present academic scholarship (Baglione 2006; Burnham *et al.* 2004; King *et al.*1994; Marsh and Stoker [1995] 2002), we encourage the scholar to produce scholarship that challenges, but is accessible to, a wide range of audiences.

In many discussions of social science, including feminist studies, the boundary between methodology and method is fuzzy. In *Feminist Methodologies for International Relations* together with Maria Stern (Ackerly, Stern and True 2006) we followed an account articulated by Sandra Harding who distinguishes between an epistemology – that is, a "theory of knowledge" – a methodology – that is, "a theory and analysis of how research does or should proceed" – and a *method* – that is, a "technique for (or way of proceeding in) gathering evidence" (Harding 1987: 2–3). This typology is not meant to encourage linear thinking, but in practice we have seen scholars misuse it to parse epistemology from methodology and method. Instead, we provide an account of a feminist research ethic that relies on a dynamic epistemology, one that is destabilized by continual reflection *as well as findings*.

Drawing on feminist theories of methodology and research, we aim to provide a practical guide on how to do feminist research, conveying the actual detail of that research from several disciplinary and interdisciplinary fields (cf. Fonow and Cook 1991; Harding 1987; Hesse-Biber *et al.* 1999; Hawkesworth 2006; Hesse-Biber and Yaiser 2004; Ramazanoğlu and Holland 2002). The book guides the student through the research process from research design through analysis and writing while simultaneously introducing the reader to the range of debates, challenges, and tools that feminists make use of in their research around the world, revealing feminist ways of doing research in a broad range of applications. The chapter order roughly follows the order of a dissertation or funding proposal, although typically there is not room in a proposal to display the detail that is required to exhibit the degree to which feminist reflection informs your project. We all need to reflect on the dimensions of our research beyond merely the reflections that will appear in the proposals or publications. This book can be your friendly guide from refining a research topic through to the final writing whether you are writing an undergraduate research paper, an academic monograph, or a dissertation or funding proposal.

The fact that the chapter sequences in this book largely follow the "linear" order of research suggested by conventional social science and its textbooks on methodology is potentially problematic when we intend to convey the non-linear, back and forth process of research that is the actual experience of most researchers and certainly those researchers guided by a feminist research ethic. We also sometimes use scientific metaphors in the discussing research such as "hypotheses," "variables," "validity," "rigor," etc. Many feminists and critical researchers argue that we should resist this scientific order and language that dominates social science and tends to reproduce essentialism and the notion that there is only one model for doing good research (Fausto-Sterling 2000; see also Ramazanoğlu and Holland 2002). From our feminist critical perspective, there is no perspective on research that is above this risk. Any account of research is at risk of relying on and producing its own essentialisms. Our best response is to be alert to this possibility and to attend to it. We use this language as feminists, attentive to the potential power in the habituated meaning of these concepts to constrain our imaginations. Moreover, we choose to proceed in using some scientific language for social science inquiry because we see feminist scholarship as a transformative *part*

1.6 GENDER MAINSTREAMING

Gender mainstreaming is a meta-gender equality strategy (Krook and True forthcoming; True 2009b). The United Nations, the international institution working in a broad range of substantive areas defines mainstreaming as applying "a gender perspective in all policies and programmes so that, before decisions are taken, an analysis is made of the effects on women and men, respectively" (United Nations 1995: 116). The implication of this definition is that gender equality cannot be achieved if policy makers do not consider the gendered consequences of all policies, global, and local. The purpose of the gender-based analysis promoted by gender mainstreaming is to "eliminate obstacles to the exercise of women's rights and eradicate all forms of discrimination against women" (1995 Beijing Platform for Action. paragraph 207, section c).

of social science, not outside it. For instance, in this book we develop ways of talking about and doing our methods that are recognizable to traditionally trained scholars. If after ontological and epistemological reflection on how and what it means to know, you view the purpose of research as to change the world, you will nonetheless need to ask what methods will best enable you to change the world through your research.

In many ways this book puts forward one way of being a feminist researcher, working within the mainstream to broaden its boundaries. For instance, we suggest following the outline of a dissertation proposal or mainstream social science article. We offer tools that would enable you to research and write for the mainstream journals and publishers of your discipline. We discuss the obstacles in Chapter six as individual challenges rather than engaging with their structural dimensions more thoroughly. This book is not revolutionary. However, we do not mean to suppress your revolutionary spirit. Rather we intend to set out a path for transformative gender mainstreaming within social science research in its current instantiation.

In the remainder of this chapter, we outline the structure of the book and the kinds of readers who will find it most useful. We guide the scholar in how best to use the book to help design her research and anticipate challenges she is likely to face in the research process. We lay out the research process in a deceptively linear fashion but do so in a way that acknowledges that the possibility for linear exposition does not come from a linear research process, but rather from careful attention to moments of methodological decision. We guide you to notice and enjoy the nonlinear aspects of research and help you to reflect systematically on them so that you can engage in the research process more consciously and deliberately. Most importantly, this book aims to help you maintain your self-reflective perspective throughout the research process.

The Plan of Doing Feminist Research

The sequence of chapters of this book follows roughly that of a proposal – from question statement (Chapter four), literature review and hypotheses (Chapter five), methodology (Chapters seven through eleven), through to presentation of findings (Chapter thirteen). Around that we frame the research with a feminist research ethic (Chapter two), the tools for sustaining a non-linear research project (Chapter three), the personal and political constraints on research design (Chapter six), the important things that researchers tell each other (Chapter twelve), and review and evaluation (Chapter fourteen).

In Chapter two, "A Feminist Research Ethic Explained," we argue that a feminist research ethic is definitive of feminist methodologies and explore the implications of this ethic throughout the research process. We explain the key elements of this ethic: (1) attentiveness to power; (2) attentiveness to boundaries, intersections, and normalization; (3) attentiveness to relationships among all stakeholders (course instructors, researcher-participants, subject-participants, assistant-participants, translators, facilitators, audiences, communities, etc.); and (4) self-reflection at each stage of the process. This ethic is applied not only to our research but also to our *process* of research. That means that we reflect on our own ways of discerning fact from opinion, looking for our own hidden assumptions, and we reflect on past decisions in our research process, noting that the moments of those decisions were themselves artifacts of the power of epistemology at those moments. Power shifts as we research and with it, our research needs to reflect and shift. This is obviously true for those studying explicitly political phenomena, but it is true for those studying social and cultural phenomena which are likewise affected by shifts in power.

How we present our work does not mirror how we actually do our work. While the table of contents of this book outlines steps in a research process, it does not describe our research process. In Chapter three we set out conceptual tools for thinking about the research process. We offer a number of ways that researchers describe the research process. Although the process itself is not linear, we include in our conceptualizations the linear model. We invite you to offer the appropriate exposition for your audience. We suggest a linear model of *exposition* of a project and findings because we think it can make them comprehensible for both researchers and audiences. However, we also suggest that for those audiences interested in research process, it might be appropriate to share the dialogical nature of certain aspects of the project.

Chapters four and five set out the work of coming up with a good research question and situating that question theoretically, conceptually, and politically. What makes for a compelling research question that both contributes to a field of knowledge and can be manageably researched? How can a thoughtful review of the literature help you to conceptualize your question, making it relevant to existing and future scholarship? We offer concrete advice for structuring a literature review. You may choose to follow an existing typology of your field, or decide that your question is better exposed by setting out your own typology or none at all.

Chapter six serves as an intermission between setting out the methodological scaffolding of our research and actually doing our research. It is a time to take a step back from your project and to situate it in the context of your life. In this chapter we make visible and attend to a range of social, personal, cultural, political, economic, and geographic factors that contribute to research design. Can an undergraduate do fieldwork in the remaining ten weeks of the term? Does a father of small children leave them with a working spouse to do field work? Do partners choose research agendas that enable them to travel together? How can non-indigenous people do research with indigenous people? Can an untenured tenure-track academic pioneer unconventional research methods? Should and how should job market considerations inform a graduate student's choice of research topic? How do contexts that differ by institution and academic culture affect the researchers of those contexts? How do contexts affect research collaborations of scholars from different contexts? These questions that may seem not to be questions about *research*, in fact *do* influence methodology. Of course, many researchers may proceed as if they do not confront these questions. However, *not* confronting these questions is a privilege that only some in academe enjoy. By asking these questions we can make visible the differences among us, including those differences between faculty and students and among students that make each research project face its own invisible methodological challenges. Asking these questions as a methodological precondition of our work reveals a hidden privilege within academe and acknowledges that these questions have an impact on our research design without compromising the legitimacy of our work.

Chapters seven through eleven are the heart of what most methodology books attend to: research design, methods, and analysis. Each chapter is filled with invitations to reflect on a host of options that you might plan to consider *and* examples of how others have dealt with dilemmas that they may or may not have anticipated. As in other chapters, boxes illustrate the complications with examples to stimulate your thinking and offer additional reference sources to enable the reader to pursue given questions in greater depth. We refer the reader who focuses on Chapters seven through eleven back to Chapter three for its account of the research process, back to Chapter two for the way in which a research ethic can guide you out of certain dilemmas, and back to Chapters four, five and six to appreciate the ways in which earlier reflections may limit or inspire your methodological decisions during the execution of your research.

Chapter twelve offers some very concrete advice that applies to many research designs. In Chapter thirteen we take up writing and publication in the broad sense of sharing your findings with other researchers, your supervisor, peers or classmates, those affected by your research, those who have contributed to it, and the field (however you choose to define your field). We approach the writing process, publication, and sharing of findings as another step in the research process, not the conclusion of the research process. Writing and reading are methods in their own right that require collaboration. Feminism invites us to appreciate our work as incomplete without the work of others and always in dialogue with and often building on our own and other feminist work.

Finally, in Chapter fourteen, we reflect on how feminist research is evaluated. Through the life course of a project, it will be evaluated by supervisors, potential funders, ethical review committees and boards, as well as your peers. In this last chapter we show that a research project that defies some of the norms of social and political science research is held to higher and *more rigorous* research standards than those that do not interrogate the intellectual meaning and function of the standards by which they are evaluated. We discuss the way we might use a feminist research ethic not merely to guide our own research process and projects but also to critically evaluate other scholars' research process and research findings.

Is this Book for Me?

This book is written for both students and scholars from a range of fields. It will be especially relevant for readers who find themselves interested in research questions and subjects that are not yet on the mainstream agendas of disciplines. For instance, this might include students examining the practices and discourses of contemporary social movements. We also hope it will be helpful to readers who are interested in feminist methodological approaches and tools that they are not yet familiar with. For instance, the book will be useful to instructors teaching research design and methods that are not well versed in feminism but have students interested in feminist research questions and want a course text that can guide the whole class through the research process rather than one that favors one form of inquiry.

For a variety of reasons, you are exploring feminist terrain. You are reaching feminist audiences, seeking non-feminist audiences for feminist insights, retooling familiar methods for feminist questions, recontextualizing non-feminist questions, gathering data in feminist ways, and confronting ethical questions around publication and sharing of findings. You are criss-crossing the boundary between feminist and non-feminist, contributing to and remaking both feminism and your fields as you go.

1.7 INTERDISCIPLINARY, TRANSDISCIPLINARY, MULTIDISCIPLINARY

Feminist inquiry is known for working across disciplines. But what does that mean? Many terms are bantered about to describe this kind of work and the terms mean different things depending on whether we are talking about a space of scholarly engagement or a person's scholarship.

When we are talking about a space of scholarly engagement, *interdisciplinary*, *transdisciplinary*, and *multidisciplinary* are roughly synonymous. Academics from a range of disciplines come together to share their work and their disciplinary insights. This can happen in your classrooms, conferences, journals, peer workshops, and reading groups.

For an individual scholar, "interdisciplinary" means working between disciplines. Picture a scholar with a foot in two places, perhaps a PhD in two disciplines. Her work may import the insights of one discipline into another and may be read by one or both disciplines. A "transdisciplinary" or "cross-disciplinary" scholar works to cross disciplines; this scholar tries to create new spaces of inquiry. Her work may be read by a broad range of scholars who may or may not share her disciplinary expertise. A "multidisciplinary" scholar may work in interdisciplinary or transdisciplinary ways. The label does not tell us which, but it suggests that more than two disciplines may be involved, making us worry about how well-grounded the work can be in each discipline.

In this book, we use "multidisciplinary" to include both interdisciplinary and transdisciplinary work.

Many readers of this book will be transgressing boundaries for theoretically-driven reasons or because their question requires them to challenge disciplinary and knowledge-related, gender, or national/political boundaries. It is not unusual that feminist research projects transgress all three forms of boundaries by studying historically-excluded women or gender relations as research subjects in conventional disciplines, by engaging in interdisciplinary, collaborative research that also questions the boundary between the researcher and the researched, and by analyzing transnational phenomena that may fall outside traditional disciplinary boundaries (see Yuval-Davis 2006a; Peterson 1992). For example, Anna Sampaio's study of a transnational feminist network, Hermanas En La Lucha which connects Chicano/Latino women in Southwest USA and indigenous women in Chiapas, Mexico, illustrates this kind of research (2004). She uses a participant observation method and co-authors her text with the network. In so doing, Sampaio and Hermanas En La Lucha transgress the boundary between researcher and researched. They study and participate in *transna-*

tional feminism. They cross boundaries as they study a political phenomenon – in this case transnational feminism – that is itself a practice of negotiating national and ethnic boundaries, and the different political perspectives of women of, and in, the Global South.

In this book we seek to empower you to do feminist research that will be respected by both feminist and conventional scholars. We frequently refer to other feminist resources on feminist inquiry and methods in order to guide either the instructor in the classroom or the student who may be pursuing a feminist research project under the mentorship of a non-feminist scholar in her field. We intentionally use gender-specific male and female pronouns (for example, he and she, himself and herself) as a political strategy to make gender visible and to appeal to the men and women researchers that we hope will read this book. We also use first and second person pronouns to underscore that we understand ourselves in dialogue with the reader, herself likely cited in this text or otherwise influential in our feminist imaginations.

How to Use this Book

While we have organized the book loosely as a mirror of the conventional exposition of a research project, we expect that only some readers will use the text as their own introduction to feminist research. Others will use the book to help design research and anticipate challenges they are likely to face in the research process. Still others will use it to inspire reflection on work they have already done or are in the process of completing. The book is designed to be useful for all three kinds of researchers.

Among these researchers some may be new to feminism, some new to research, and some new to feminist research. The book is designed to be useful to all, but each will read it differently. The *researcher new to feminist theory* is encouraged *not* to dwell on theoretical puzzles that are unclear to her at first reading, but rather to focus on how feminism might be useful to her research (from the exposition in Chapter two). The *researcher new to research* may likewise go quickly over the theory that is familiar to her, but slow down to reflect about what these theoretical insights mean for empirical inquiry (again in Chapter two). She might spend more time in the chapters on picking a research question (Chapters three and four) and on research design and methods (Chapters seven through nine) rather than in the theory and conceptualization chapter (Chapter five). The *researcher new to feminist research* will likely take the most time with Chapters one and two and revisit it habitually as she moves through the later chapters of the book in order that she may be reminded what is distinctive about the *feminist* research project. Likewise, the researcher new to feminist research is expected to spend extra time with research design (Chapter seven). (It is possible to do original research using data created by others.) An undergraduate who is not expecting to do field work will focus on Chapters two, four, five, thirteen and fourteen.

The *researcher who reads cover to cover* may be just starting out on a feminist research project or career. She may be theoretically knowledgeable about feminism, but need some guide for assisting students with empirical projects. Or, she may be well-versed in feminist methodology but less familiar with the feminist theory behind it. Or, she may be practiced in innovating feminist methods, but less comfortable situating feminist methods within feminist theory and methodology.

The *researcher currently engaged in a project* may want to pick and choose her way around the book based on her point in the research process. As the research process is non-linear, so too may be the way in which a reader uses the book. Perhaps she is more or less curious about the feminist literature review or ethical dilemmas with data analysis for example. Perhaps she wants a "friend" to commiserate with about the unexpected challenges that life and family commitments can pose for research.

The *researcher who is finishing or has just finished a project* may wish to think about how to put her research in dialogue with other feminist research within and outside of her field. She may seek to be multidisciplinary by including perspectives on similar topics from across the disciplines, but may be challenged to see questions from perspectives not often articulated from others within her home discipline. The book is designed to help her see and work through those challenges.

There are as many ways of reading this book as there are paths on a research journey. We urge every reader to spend some time with chapter two as this is the chapter where we lay out the ethical space where feminist theory becomes feminist empirical research (see also Ackerly and True 2008b). However, while this book is a complete research guide from before beginning to after finishing, it is not a comprehensive guide. We can help you situate your work theoretically and methodologically, but feminist research is collaborative and needs to be contextualized by other research. So just as feminist research on the macropolitics of gender and globalization for instance may not tell us about the specificity of women's subjectivities and experience in particular locales (see True 2003), so too a feminist work on doing feminist research across the social sciences cannot guide you through the specific questions that your own research will face in its own places – political, geographic, disciplinary, and temporal.

Further, scholars will read the book differently in part because they are situated in disciplines in which the scholarly recognition of feminist work in the mainstream is unique to their discipline. Readers will use this book in different ways depending on their discipline and when and how feminist research emerged in that field. For example, there has been feminist political theory throughout the history of political thought; though Aristotle did not think much of Plato's proposal, Plato devoted a chapter of *the Republic* to utopian reflection on the possibility for genderlessness among the elites of a society. Contemporary Sociology and Political Science's engagement with feminism are closely connected with second wave feminism. Although feminist work on women and race was available, it did not become integrated into mainstream sociology and political science until the late 1970s. Inspired by the questions raised by feminist social movements in the 1970s, sociologists and political scientists began to study women, and to develop explanations of women's position in society based on gender analysis (Bourque and Grossholtz 1974; Okin 1991). Later, some feminist sociologists and political scientists interrogated the epistemological foundations of the category of woman (Sapiro 1981; Sylvester 1993) and examined the social construction of sociological knowledge in the discipline (Sapiro 1998).

By contrast, early feminist scholarship in international relations dates to the late 1980s and early 1990s when the insights of postmodernism invited feminists to take up political questions in ways that were attentive to the power of epistemology to condition and constrain even a feminist enterprise (Sylvester 1994; Tickner 1992). This meant revealing that the construction of the field of international relations itself reflected the biases of major powers and dominant western subjectivities in a cold war world (Ackerly and True 2008a). Revealing the ways in which political power structures conditioned the knowledge production of the discipline was important for revealing that the social construction of knowledge was also political – leaving women *and* gender issues outside of the most powerful political spaces. Feminists were not alone in challenging the power of epistemology in international relations (IR). Feminist challenges emerged as a part of broader epistemological challenges that included non-feminist critical theory, postmodern, post-colonial, and neoMarxist perspectives. Each discipline has its own history with feminism and multidisciplinarity.

This book is a product of these multidisciplinary feminist interventions and research agendas. We are able to write this book *because* there is vast feminist work across disciplines and *we* are able to write this book because our particular disciplines – Political Theory and International Relations – recognize feminism and methodology as important areas of scholarships.

In some forms of scholarship, the exposition of the work does not require the authors to situate themselves in the sociology of the field. For our purposes, it is important that this introductory chapter situate us in our fields. Though explicit self-situation is not always an essential element in the text of a given piece of feminist social science scholarship, *reflection* on one's

Box 1.5 About the authors

The sociology of our backgrounds in political theory, political science, and international relations (IR) certainly conditions our view of which struggles may be more difficult for a researcher. In political science and IR, the *science* of social science is highly respected and we seek to advise readers on how to be true to a feminist research ethic while being comprehensible to, and able to be judged "rigorous" by, a social science-oriented audience.

Our understanding of feminism and feminist questions are *global*. Because we think that it is empirically and normatively imperative to understand feminism in its global and local contexts, we read broadly about feminism around the world. Extensively referencing global feminism, we seek to share these references in order that we may all better understand our work in its global context.

We met and began collaborating in 2000. We each have two children and partners with full-time careers, one in academe, one not.

own location is. We situate ourselves in Box 1.5 because throughout the book we will further draw on our own locations and experiences. We do this not to portray ours as representative (in fact, ours are quite different from each other's), but as a friend, colleague or mentor would share her experience and from her experience and therefore our particulars are relevant to the readers' ability to interpret those parts of the text that draw on our particular experiences.

How *you* use this book will in part be conditioned by how feminism intersects with the mainstream of your discipline; whether you feel comfortable reflecting on the structures of power in knowledge production, and whether your home discipline acknowledges the implications for empirical research of such reflections. Consequently, feminist research will take different forms in different fields and in the hands of different researchers. There are not one or two replicable models of feminist research. We hope this book opens to you the possibility of learning from other fields even as you engage with the specificity of your own if that is your goal, or that it empowers you to cross disciplinary boundaries, confident in a compass that can guide you across and back.

However you read this book, whatever your research question, we hope that it inspires you to enjoy the intellectual fruits of a reflexive approach to research that encourages you to engage in the research process consciously and deliberately even while appreciating the distraction and inspiration of feminist inquiry.

Conclusion

Research is about listening, not expertise. Research is about being curious, skeptical, surprised, and sometimes helpless. Research is a process; even though in academe it is often assessed by an outcome or output, a final paper, talk, or publication. It is a process, one we muddle through, and one that challenges our ethical sensibilities if they are activated by the theoretical and personal commitments that bring us to scholarly endeavors.

While muddling through is expected, we must learn from our mistakes and averted mistakes, extracting from each quandary all of the theoretical, methodological, and practical insights to be gained so that each quandary is a maximally informative learning opportunity. This book contributes to the collaborative view of any inquiry – even individual scholarship – as contributing to shared knowledge by filling in, correcting, transgressing, challenging, rethinking, revisiting, reconceptualizing, and piecing together. The book should make it easier for us to notice and learn from the connections that can be made across research questions and disciplines. Ideally, we will be able to learn from our self-reflective questioning before the learning opportunities presented by a challenge or quandary in our research pass us by. In this way we show that curiosity, skepticism, persistence, and surprise can function as research tools, *rigorous research tools*, which are essential for doing feminist research.

Selected Sources for Further Reading

Cancian, Francesca M. 1992. "Feminist Science: Methodologies That Challenge Inequality." *Gender & Society* 6, 4: 623–43.

DeVault, Marjorie L. 1999. *Liberating Method: Feminism and Social Research.* Philadelphia: Temple University Press.

Fonow, Mary Margaret, and Judith A. Cook. 1991. *Beyond Methodology: Feminist Scholarship as Lived Research.* Bloomington, IN: Indiana University Press.

Harding, Sandra G., and Merrill B. Hintikka, eds. 1983. *Discovering Reality: Feminist Perspectives on Epistemology, Metaphysics, Methodology, and Philosophy of Science.* Dordrecht, Holland: D. Reidel.

Hesse-Biber, Sharlene Nagy, ed. 2007. *Handbook of Feminist Research: Theory and Praxis.* Thousand Oaks, CA: Sage.

Ramazanoğlu, Caroline, and Janet Holland. 2002. *Feminist Methodology: Challenges and Choices.* Thousand Oaks, CA: Sage.

Chapter 2

A Feminist Research Ethic Explained

Introduction

A fundamental concern of feminist researchers across a range of social science subjects is the study of power and its effects. The distribution of power within families, the struggle for power by social movements, and the use of power in the classroom are just a few examples. We are also directly or indirectly actors in the social dynamics we study, such as the political economy and the classroom. In addition, our primary tool, academic research, is also a particular form of power.

How can we study power and identify ways to mitigate its abuse in the real world when we, as researchers, also participate in the projection of power when we make knowledge claims based on our research? This is the question that feminist norms ask of research. Feminism also offers many answers. These answers inform feminists' epistemological perspective, theoretical choices, research design, data collection, data analysis, exposition of findings, and venues for sharing findings. Because it is relevant to *all* of these, a feminist research ethic is the most important tool for guiding feminist scholarship. This research ethic offers researchers feminist standards for assessing research despite feminism's multiplicity and its defiance of attempts to delimit its practice (Ackerly and Attanasi 2009). This chapter sets out a feminist research ethic, which is a set of questioning practices deployed throughout the research process. A feminist research ethic can be used to improve our scholarship regardless of whether it is feminist or not. Such a research practice can also help the researcher resolve ethical dilemmas in research in ways that enhance the quality of the research. While these questioning practices may seem quite heady, they have substantive import which we demonstrate throughout the remainder of the book.

2.1 FEMINIST-INFORMED RESEARCH

Research that is feminist-informed takes as its point of departure feminist normative concerns combined with knowledge of the diverse and complex theoretical interplays at work in any social science research project. Feminist-informed research, consequently, is self-reflective, critical, political, and versed in multiple theoretical frameworks in order to enable the researcher to "see" those people and processes lost in gaps, silences, margins, and peripheries.

We have chosen the term "feminist-informed" to refer to research that draws on theoretical, methodological, and empirical insights from a diverse body of feminist theories and feminist research.

This chapter is the most theoretical of the book and provides the intellectual architecture for the rest.

At any phase of research any researcher can reflect about her or his work using the research ethic we outline in this chapter. A series of research considerations that don't map narrowly onto questions of research design, a feminist research ethic is an essential heuristic device for non-feminist and feminist researchers. Heuristics are practical "intuitive" or "common sense" ways to facilitate our problem-solving but not in a mechanistic or prescribed fashion. They do not offer textbook solutions or model answers. They guide our thinking, but they don't determine it. As a heuristic, a feminist research ethic functions as a compass alerting researchers to possible intended and unintended consequences of research, and providing a range of tools for researchers to think through the dilemmas they face in doing research. These dilemmas are numerous. They include questions about knowing – such as why do we think about peace as the opposite of war or women as the opposite of men? Further, we might ask, why see the world in opposites at all? What could be the unintended consequences of studying social phenomena using this either/or way of thinking?

This chapter is our "theory and conceptualization" chapter. We review that feminist critical theory and research that we think can guide us in improving our research practice. We discuss four implications of feminist theory for research and argue that these provide a useful backbone for good political and social science research. Since the 1970s, feminist reflection on social science has generated a theory of knowing and studying that guides feminist research. A feminist research ethic is a commitment to inquiry about how we inquire. It requires developing your ability to be attentive to:

- the power of knowledge, and more profoundly, of epistemology;
- boundaries, marginalization, silences, and intersections;

KEY CONCEPT

2.2 SUBJECTIVITY

A wide-ranging term that signals the qualities (and questions) appropriate to a "subject" in a given moment. Attention to the subjectivity of the researcher is one way of paying attention to the political dimensions of social science research.

When discussing subjectivity in feminist theory, the term foregrounds the necessarily positioned status of a person within her context (her epistemological, political, and social position), her agency, her relationship to others, her capacities and potentialities, and even her normative responsibilities. Feminist theory tackles theories of subjectivity in order to understand how one becomes and knows oneself as a subject through questions of sexual difference, gender politics, social stratification, and political resistance. A feminist research ethic, in turn, demands that researchers attend to how the research process itself both instantiates and conditions relations of subjectivity that inevitably bear on the research.

- relationships and their power differentials; and
- your own sociopolitical location (or "situatedness").

After this brief introduction, the remainder of the chapter provides the theoretical background and application of each piece of a feminist research ethic.

Feminist theory has made empirical work particularly challenging because feminist theories reveal the politics in every aspect of the research process. Feminist scholars in the 1970s began by analyzing the everyday contexts in which knowledge was generated. On the basis of that detailed analysis they developed a methodological perspective that views the research process as central to any account of feminist research and as itself part of the research findings that should be subject to critical evaluation.

Being committed to self-reflection does not mean just reflecting on your own identity. This is a common misconception of feminist work.

Rather, feminist theories commit feminist researchers to exploring absence, silence, difference, oppression, and the power of epistemology. For example, criticisms of the sexism of science compel feminist empirical researchers to be attentive to, and indeed consciously to look and listen for silences and absences in the research process, and not only those relating to women's *subjectivity* (Benhabib 1986). These commitments have generated aspirations to do empirical work that, if fully practiced, would leave many scholars forever researching, always listening for new voices, always (respectfully) hearing cacophony, always suspicious of certain harmonies or recurring themes. Scholars with empirical questions have to wrestle with this irony, allowing it to affect their research without allowing it to derail their

2.3 IDENTITY

Much feminist scholarship has been about identity politics, generally focusing on political identity as a locus for politics (as in, people who share a particular identity share a paricular politics). On this view political recognition relies on people sharing a political identity. This is a problematic basis for politics, feminists researchers want to attend to the varieties of ways in which gender dynamics reflect race, class, sexuality, ability, immigration status, etc. and the ways in which difference is used to divide people politically.

research. This is important because not to do feminist-informed research would be to perpetuate the invisibility of gendered absences, silences, differences, and oppressions and the violations of human rights they conceal.

The potential for gendered absences, silences, differences, and oppressions to affect people is mirrored in the ability of these to affect the study of political and social phenomena. A researcher comes with particular race, class, and gender privileges which necessarily put her in political relations with the people and phenomena she studies. Such privileges may include having a stable income, being able to leave a conflict zone when research is complete, or to pick a life and research agenda that does not require being in a conflict zone. A researcher needs to be aware of how her own basket of privileges and experiences conditions her knowledge and research.

In these four ways – attentiveness to (1) the power of epistemology, (2) boundaries, (3) relationships, and (4) the situatedness of the researcher – a feminist research ethic is more than an ethical sensitivity. A feminist research ethic guides research reflection and practice. As we discuss these four, we give examples of the effects of each theoretical idea on substantive research. Throughout the book we will continue to illustrate the implications of these reflections for all stages of research from feminist researchers' actual dilemmas and methodological solutions. The dimensions of a feminist research ethic that seem theoretical in this chapter will be applied in the remainder of the book.

Attentiveness to the Power of Epistemology

Feminism is a critical research process that has the potential to transform the social science disciplines *and* the world that social scientists study. As Harding and Norberg, the former editors of the important feminist journal *SIGNS*, note in an introduction to a special issue on methodology, "research processes themselves [re]produce power differences" (2005: 2012), including power differences between different ways of knowing. An epistemology is the system of thought that we use to distinguish fact from belief. An epistemology is itself a belief system about what constitutes knowledge, evidence, and convincing argument. In some epistemologies scientific study is essential to knowledge. In others, personal experience is essential. A researcher's own epistemology has significant authority in her or his research.

The insight from feminist theoretical reflection on epistemology is that it is possible, and indeed essential, to reflect on the epistemologies that inform our own work. Disciplines, your course instructors, colleagues, researchers, subject-participants, co-authors, research assistants, and coders may be working from related or different epistemologies (See Box 9.4 for the impact of different people viewing the same data through different epistemologies). Feminists are known for having challenged scientific research and how scientific method is used, particularly in social science, as a way of masking the researcher's positionality (Bowles and Klein 1983). Recognizing that there are many epistemological perspectives each opening and foreclosing certain understandings of what it means to know and to contribute to shared knowledge enhances any scholarship. In the subsequent chapters of this book we show that such reflection can happen at all phases of the research process.

A feminist research ethic is above all a commitment to continually reviewing and challenging notions of what are appropriate and reliable ways of knowing and understanding the world – in particular by reflecting on the different ways they appear from the standpoint of different individuals and social groups. Further, and importantly, it is also a commitment to deciding when it is time to move on from one problem to another, that is, not to stay in one stage of research forever (Dever 2004). An *epistemology* should not prevent us from doing research; it should enable us to do it better (Ackerly 2008a). We have an ethical commitment to noticing the power of epistemology, particularly the power of privileged epistemologies. Privileged epistemologies are those that do not normally require a defense. For example, in an environment of quantitative social scientists, qualitative methods may require a more lengthy justification than quantitative methods. In a group of activists, illustrative examples may be more convincing than statistical data. We can recognize this dynamic in our own scholarship, in feminist-informed social science, and in political and social science disciplines as a whole (Ackerly and True 2008b). For example, we (the authors) are more confident in research that is explicit about how it attends to the power of knowledge (see Box 2.1).

By requiring the practice of this reflection, a feminist research ethic guides the asking of important questions about context, change, interrelatedness, relationships of power, boundaries, and embedded epistemology in ways that empower the researcher to break new ground.

Box 2.1 Revealing the power of epistemology: essentialism and queer theory

Much feminist-informed analysis can be seen as criticizing essentialism, that is, assumptions that naturalize identities, social categories and hierarchies and as such render invisible structures of oppression (Dietz 2003; Spelman 1988). Feminism is enabled and enlivened by the debate over of its key concepts: woman, gender, and feminism.

Queer theorists such as Judith Butler and Eva Kosofsky Sedgwick argue that epistemologies, including feminist epistemologies, mask power by creating false binaries such as that between sex and gender. "Gender ought not to be conceived merely as the cultural inscription of meaning on a pregiven sex (a juridical conception); gender must also designate the very apparatus of production whereby the sexes themselves are established" (Butler [1990] 1999: 7). The privileging of gender in an oppositional, binary relationship with sex constructs the epistemic frame that also privileges heterosexuality as a norm (Sedgwick 1990).

Gender analysis exemplifies the impact of a feminist research ethic. Power and privilege can hide behind certain approaches and methods of research that present themselves as "objective" or impartial (see Gluck and Patai 1991; Stacey 1999; Staeheli and Nagar 2002; D. Wolf 1996; M. Wolf 1992). Gender analysis is a conceptual toolkit for noticing the epistemological power that binary gender and heterosexuality constructs of man/woman, and sex/gender have on our understanding of a range of political and social phenomena including, for instance, freedom/vulnerability, war/peace, public/private, reason/emotion, mind/body, objective/subjective knowledge (Butler [1990]1999). In particular gender analysis reveals the power of epistemology to mask important differences, inequalities, and domination and to construct the language through which we understand our experience. For example, feminist political theorists critically analyze the framing of abortion politics using falsely gender-neutral language (in terms of the rights of "the parent" versus "the fetus" rather than in terms of the rights of women to make decisions about their own bodies and reproductive choices) (Okin 1992). Similarly, feminist scholars challenge the assertion that justice can be achieved through universalizing objectivity (Benhabib 1986) or that a gender neutral "anti-discrimination" law is fair (Crenshaw 1991; MacKinnon 1989). Further, they show us that mapping the world into dichotomies limits the possibilities we can consider (Confortini 2006). For example, is peace sustained by democratic self-governance, held together by external threat, maintained through a temporary detent, or so many other possibilities? Is war equivalent to military conflict, perpetual insecurity, and/or terror through mass rape . . . ? Moving away from the war/peace binary, we might

2.4 EPISTEMOLOGY

An epistemology refers to one's theory of knowledge; it is the system of rules, conditions, and beliefs that one uses to tell the difference between "knowledge" and "opinion," between fact and opinion. A feminist epistemology includes the belief that knowledge (truth) is produced, not simply found, and that the conditions of its production should be studied, critiqued if necessary, and certainly made explicit and exposed.

Different Kinds of Epistemologies

Positivism is a theory of knowledge based on the notion that there is a direct correspondence between empirical reality in the world and our ability to "see" and "know" it in an unmediated way.

Critical realism is a theory of knowledge following Roy Bhaskar and others (see Archer *et al.* 1998). It argues one can know reality without ever knowing it fully or exclusively. We can empirically deduce "causes" separate from their "effects" in an ontological sense. But "how" we know is both fallible and relative given our historically contingent, socially situated position in the world.

Standpoint epistemology is a theory of knowledge that argues that one can "know" the world more fully and more critically (with less of a material or ideological stake in maintaining the

status quo) from the subject position of the marginalized or oppressed, be it the worker marginalized by class structures or the female immigrant oppressed by gender/patriarchal structures and the political economy of global labor for instance.

Postcolonial epistemology is a theory of knowledge that calls into question western dualistic understandings of rationality, reason, and the mind set against irrationality, emotion, and the body. Postcolonial scholars argue that western cultural conceptions pervade our attempts to know, which posit an autonomous knowing subject counterposed to an "other" to be known, variously the "orient", "the third world woman", the "native" or "noble savage." The postcolonial epistemology rejects not only these associations, but also the dichotomous categories of analysis.

Destabilizing epistemology is a theory of knowledge that is "perpetually attentive to the power dynamics manifested in any account that is likely to be interpreted as in any way definitive" (Ackerly 2008a: 27). A destabilizing epistemology is useful for "non-ideal" theorizing about questions of injustice when the conditions of "justice" have never existed, may never exist, and if they do exist they may not be sustained without some vigilance (Ackerly 2008a: 60, 88–9, 313).

---

explore the personal backgrounds of those who joined armed opposition groups and learn that they are likely to have witnessed the humiliation of, or gender and sexually based violence against, close family members, or they have experienced violence and humiliation themselves, at the hands of those

Box 2.2 Stern on critical self-reflective epistemology

"In the course of conducting several pilot interviews with leaders of different organizations, I employed a qualitative interview method whereby I asked the people I was interviewing how they conceived of their security, as well as what they thought was threatening and dangerous. Their responses seemed to be particularly coded within an already established discourse. For example, in response to a question about her experience of threats, one person responded, 'No, I have not received any death threats this month.' I did not sense that I was 'getting at' the multiplicity or the depth of what security and insecurity meant for Mayan women in terms of the interrelated power relations and the different contexts that circumscribed their lives, fears, and hopes. It was also increasingly clear that their political identities as (self-defined) Mayan women informed how they expressed their insecurities; that is, their naming of particular dangers could not be separated from their representation of their (political) identities. However, since I was interested in understanding their security as integral to the multiple ways the narrators identified themselves, I found that my research question required a way of inquiring into the co-production of security (and identity). A 'feminist standpoint' epistemology, although tempting in its politics, fell short in reflecting the relationship between the discursive practice of security and the construction of identities" (Stern 2006, 180–1).

As Maria Stern's example illustrates, rethinking one's own epistemology may reveal biases that come from feminist theory itself.

in the opposing state forces (Mazurana 2006, 2004). With this commitment to noticing the power of epistemology, feminist-informed researchers make efforts to expose the power dynamics in language, knowing, and meaning that reach beyond gender, but gender analysis is always important to include in analyses of power.

However, the feminist researcher does not rely on gender analysis alone to rethink her epistemology. For example, experience in the field, conversing with subject-participants, led Maria Stern (2005) to rethink her feminist standpoint epistemology and to shift her theoretical perspective. Stern started out collecting life histories to consider how women define their security based on a politicized feminist standpoint that takes seriously women's experiences and the neglect of these experiences in mainstream international relations theories about security. During the research process she discovered that both her subject-participants' and her own epistemologies were shifting in part due to the research which involved the narration and mutual construction of identities. Should a scholar of international security pay attention to her subject-participants' *feelings* of security and political identity? What does that even mean? What would be silenced or marginalized by continuing with a methodology that treated security and political identity as fixed when the research revealed that these were fluid? Should the relative privileges of researcher and research subject-participant affect the epistemology from which research begins as well as the research question, design, or methods that follow from it? Rethinking one's epistemology may reveal other dynamics of power to which a researcher needs to attend – particularly boundaries and relations discussed below– and it lays bare the need for the researcher to notice her own situatedness.

Attentiveness to Boundaries

As we see above, attentiveness to the power of epistemology is a recurring feminist dilemma. Feminists can guide themselves through that dilemma by reflecting on all kinds of boundaries. Consider for example the social geography of the Bronx Slave Mart discussed in the preceding chapter (Box 1.3). The research puzzle and the landscape of its research exhibit a range of boundaries ripe for feminist reflection. They show us a class boundary that the employers' desire to cross (from being women who do housework to women who have household employees). They show us class solidarity, boundaries and boundary crossing among those selling their labor, those not willing to work for less than a family wage and those willing to work for any wage. The study shows that race and class are meaningful but not binary boundaries. Feminist reflection on boundaries may lead to exploring all of these questions. Next, consider the boundaries between Ella Baker (the social activist-researcher) and the women workers she studied. Consider further the method of selling her own labor, of crossing the boundary from researcher to working in order to do her own research (cf. Ehrenreich 2001). Further, consider the boundaries of scholarly study itself and how they might affect a contemporary scholar's choice of discipline in which to ask such questions (Sangari and Vaid 1989).

A feminist research ethic entails a commitment to a research process that requires being attentive to many kinds of boundaries – those related to our research questions and those related to our disciplines. Further, it prompts us to explore the significance of these boundaries for constraining our imaginations that is, to limit how we see problems. It may involve interrogating forms of inclusion and exclusion and breaking down boundaries. Likewise it may involve listening for silences and sometimes responsibly sustaining those silences, depending on the context. There are many boundaries that can inhere in the research process, for instance between disciplines, the researcher and the researched, among research subject-participants and researchers with different epistemologies or who use different theoretical

2.5 INTERSECTIONALITY

KEY CONCEPT

Intersectionality calls our attention to the fact that any situation, person, or research phenomena can be understood only in terms of intersecting and overlapping contexts and social forces such as race, age, gender, sexuality, income, nationality, historical moment, among many others. Consequently, attention to intersectionality provokes feminist inquiry to attend to the complexity of a problem that might serve to exclude or hide important dimensions that may be crucial to creating and/or sustaining a situation or problem.

perspective and methods. Not all boundaries are unjust or unnecessary, but we must be attentive to their power to exclude and marginalize both people and possible research phenomena. We should, therefore, examine the function of boundaries and consider their effects on what is important for us to study and how we can study it.

For example, historically scholars have thought that forces of oppression can be better understood when disentangled from each other as gender, race, class, ethnicity, sexuality and so on. But increasingly feminist scholars regard the conceptual boundaries between forms of oppression as perpetuating and creating new forms of oppression for individuals and groups who experience multiple, often overlapping oppressions. As Key Concept 2.5 elaborates, the concept of *intersectionality* has been developed by feminist and post-colonial scholars to analyze the complex, overlapping relationships among oppressions.

A feminist research ethic encourages us to consider research methods like those deployed by Baker. By breaking down the boundaries between researcher and subject-participant, Baker was able to learn about the mistreatment of workers that the workers themselves may not have revealed. Further, she was able to learn the norms among the workers selling their wages, from the workers themselves who sought to encourage their new co-worker (Baker) to adopt these norms.

A feminist research ethic alerts us to the implications of disciplinary boundaries as well as conceptual boundaries for accurate knowledge across a range of different fields. Research is often impoverished by accepting the conventional boundaries that separate disciplines. In particular, the study of women and women's lives has often been neglected precisely because of these disciplinary boundaries and the desire to maintain them even in the face of new and relevant data. For example, feminist attentiveness to disciplinary boundaries reveals how the political boundaries of the state system shape our

Box 2.3 Deconstructing disciplinary boundaries: Sangari and Vaid on "Women's History"

Kum Sangari and Sudesh Vaid argue that, women's studies "is a convenience for mainstream historians who can now consign the onus [of the gendered dimensions of history] on specialists in a 'separate' discipline" (1989: 3). "Gender difference is seldom seen as a structuring principle in economic processes . . . in concentrating . . . on issues of family, education, and economic participation, feminist research often implicitly accepts and locates itself within the division of public and private spheres constructed in the colonial period and neglects the materiality of the wider economic and legal processes by which these spheres came into being" (1989: 24). We must deconstruct the disciplinary boundaries of "women's history" because it is itself a product of dominating colonial categories.

Feminist historiography justifies the focus on women as historical actors not from a standpoint perspective of "herstory" but as a challenge to the grand history perspective that there is only one story to be told. Sangari and Vaid state that "[h]istoriography may be feminist without being, exclusively women's history. Such a historiography acknowledges that each aspect of reality is gendered, and is thus involved in questioning all that we think we know, in a sustained examination of analytical and epistemological apparatus, and in a dismantling of the ideological presuppositions of so called gender-neutral methodologies" (1989: 2–3).

knowledge about international relations and continue to render women invisible as international subjects and actors (True 2009a).

In setting up our inquiry, we reflect upon the disciplinary boundaries that might incline one researcher to be more attentive to a certain body of literature and another to other literature even though, in a multidisciplinary context, they would appreciate the insights of both disciplinary literatures. Guided by a feminist research ethic, attentiveness to disciplinary boundaries should encourage us to become more interdisciplinary in our search for knowledge and inspiration (see Box 2.3 on the development of feminist historiography in and against the field of women's history).

A feminist research ethic helps us to put into practice our awareness of the way humanly-constructed boundaries (or lack thereof) can lead to marginalization, exclusion and silencing in our research process involving subject-participants who are people living in the world. It reminds us that boundaries are an inevitable part of knowledge-creation but that, as feminist-informed scholars, we need to be conscious of and take responsibility for their intended and unintended effects.

2.6 RESEARCH SUBJECT-PARTICIPANT

Subject-participants of your research can be individuals, groups, or organizations. They may be interviewed by you or observed in a participant observation. They may be a "case" (see Chapters seven and eight) or a source for generating data (see Chapter nine).

In socio-political research, it is problematic to call them "research subjects" because that language treats them as immutable objects in a way that is logically inconsistent with the study of social and political phenomena. The phrase "research subject" disassociates people from the socio-politics which are the dynamic context of their lives and were so before they became the subject of social and political science. We trouble that language by referring to those who provide and generate data in our research as "subject-participants." By informing our work they are participants in the research process, helping us to define the question, to create the data, and to analyze that data.

A feminist research ethic's attention to relationships has implications for all dimensions of how we conceive of research, down to the language we use to characterize the stakeholders in our research.

Attentiveness to Relationships

The discussion of Baker's methodology in the preceding section raises the role of the relationship between the researcher and the subject-participant that is an important consideration for the feminist researcher. A feminist research ethic is concerned with the ways in which social, political, and economic actions are interrelated with the actions and lives of others, including those of our research subject-participants. Participants include subject-participants, research assistants, and instructors. Other potential participants include translators, facilitators, gatekeepers, drivers, and administrators (see Chapter twelve). Each has a different relationship to the research project. As you proceed with your own project, we suggest noting that every time you say "research subject" to yourself is an opportunity to reflect on the relationships of research. Such reflection entails thinking about the meaning of these relationships. This is a foundational reflection on our view of research.

Of course, being attentive to relationships and relationships of power in our research requires us to recognize those between the researcher and research subject-participants. This is the most common focus of attention to power dynamics and the vulnerability of feminists, other researchers, and ethical review boards. After discussing this, we will also discuss the ways in

Box 2.4 D'Costa on shifting the research question after listening to research subject-participants

When she began her dissertation research, Bina D'Costa's research subject was rape as a war crime. She was interested in bringing into the historical record the experiences of women in the wars of separation of south Asia: Pakistan from India at Partition (1947) and Bangladesh from Pakistan during their Independence War (1971) (D'Costa 2003).

However, D'Costa, in relationship with her research subject-participants as co-creators of the meaning of their experience, as resisters of the meaning of their experience that had been created by the state, saw a need to shift her research question given that speaking out about experiences of rape may have further harmed these women.

"I began my methodological journey by asking questions about a gendered silence – the rape of women during this war – and ended up exploring the story of nation-building. The subjects of my study were written out of that history but that history was drafted on and with their bodies and families. Placing their stories as the focal point of my study, I demonstrate that centering the marginalized yields otherwise inaccessible theoretical insights to the question of nation-building, a central theme in mainstream IR" (Bina D'Costa, personal communication)

which attention to other relationships of research – among research subject-participants (organizations or individuals), between researchers and others on the research team, and among researchers – should be part of a feminist research practice. These dynamics may have important consequences for our research process and findings, as well as reputational and resource implications for our research subject-participants.

Relationships with Subject-Participants

Many of the instances of attending to relationships entail rethinking the relationship between researcher and research subject and may come from *a priori* feminist commitments, or can emerge during the research. For Bina D'Costa, a commitment to developing ethical relationships with her research subjects meant listening to their concerns about being interviewed on the subject of rape during the partition of India and Bangladesh's war of independence. As Box 2.4 illustrates, she revisited and ultimately changed her research question as a result of this attentiveness to relationships. As you can see, and as Key Concept 2.6 explains, when we think about subject-participants in this way, it is a problematic misnomer to call them "research subjects."

Relationships of Research Subject-Participants

In order to appreciate our research subject-participants as subject-participants, we not only appreciate the impact of our research on them (either directly through knowing us, or indirectly through the impact of our work), but also and more importantly, we appreciate what it means to them to be in their own context, in relationship with other people, including other people who may be subject-participants, translators, facilitator, gatekeepers, research assistants and others related to the research (see Chapters six, nine, and twelve). Our research may disrupt their context and their relationships.

The examples from Baker's and D'Costa's empirical research may seem to focus on the first, that is, on the relationship between researcher and subject-participants. However, they are also examples of researchers being very attentive to the relationships of power in which their subject-participants are embedded. Feminists have approached this second dimension through competing lenses. For some feminist-informed scholars, the recognition of human embeddedness in relationships with others may lead us to adopt an ethic of care or moral responsibility that is not confined to women's experience (e.g., Robinson 2006; Tronto 2006). Theirs is an anti-essentialist interpretation of the importance of relationship. Its provides an important counter hypothesis to a gender identity politics of earlier feminisms that can be read as giving women's social and political positions the status of nature (Elshtain 1987; Ruddick 1989). For other feminist-informed scholars, recognition of human interconnections requires empirically mapping those interconnections in their research. For instance, as Box 2.5 illustrates, some feminist scholars critically analyze the linkages between women consumers and producers in the global market to forge a global political movement that could advance women's economic rights and well-being more universally.

These reflections have many practical implications for research design which we discuss primarily in Chapter twelve. As an indication of where such reflections might lead in selecting our research methods, consider the impact of being a subject-participant in an organization where others are also participant-subjects. How will you maintain the anonymity and confidentiality of each?

Relationships of Other Research Participants

Consider the relationships among members of a research team: research assistants who are aspiring researchers, paraprofessionals who may stay in the community or organization after the research is concluded but who may want to leave, translators who may be from the community and returning temporarily or permanently, facilitators who are insider-outsiders who may cross and maybe transgress the boundaries of community by participating in the research, researchers who have a particular standing within the research team and in rela-

> ## Box 2.5 A relational epistemology: feminist economics and gendered value chain analysis
>
> A gendered value chain analysis addresses power within production and exchange relationships. It highlights the different positions and contributions of men and women across the value chain and uncovers the economic, organizational, and asymmetric relationships among actors located along different points of the industry. This involves a segmentation analysis of the gender, race, ethnicity, and immigration status of individuals in labor markets at different points in the value chain. Gendered value chain analysis also considers entitlements and capabilities, including those factors and characteristics that mediate women and men's entitlements to productive resources and their capabilities to deploy those resources (see Barrientos 2001; Carr 2004).
>
> Without a feminist research ethic that requires us to be attentive to these relationships we may easily overlook the power dynamics within and across the subject organizations we research, among our research facilitators, and between translators and interviewed subject-participants. All good researchers want to attend to these things, but a feminist research ethic compels and guides our doing so. Other relations that inform feminist inquiry include relations of production and reproduction, signification and representation, power and subjection.

tionship to the participant-subjects which varies significantly depending on whether one is a first time young researcher or a seasoned degree-bearing researcher. Consider the status hierarchies among research assistants.

Relationships with Instructors

If you are doing research for a class or with a supervisor for a course or degree requirement, you have on the research team someone whose professional obligations and joy include mentoring through the research process (see also Chapter six). Even when an instructor has lots of experience, she has never guided *you* (a unique individual with particular strengths and experiences) through your project (a product of your intellectual imagination). While you have written papers before, now you are faced with a new challenge, hopefully one that is commensurate with your abilities and yet offers you the opportunity to expand these.

Relationships with Other Researchers

Finally, consider the relationships among researchers. We often find ourselves "running into" other researchers, particularly when we choose events or organizations as venues for research or when many members of a class take an interest in the same topic. Are you competitors? Co-travelers? Interlocutors? Peer-mentors? See also Chapter six. We encourage our students to see each other as co-travelers. We encourage scholars to see each other in this way as well (Ackerly and True under review).

To conclude, such considerations may also be affected by the perspective of the researcher. An undergraduate relying on another researcher's primary source research has a different relationship with the subject-participants than the researcher who originally gathered the data. Consider the ways in which the race, gender, and other identity markers may affect the relationships between the researcher and all other participants in the research project. These are all considerations of the situatedness of the researcher (discussed below) that intersect with considerations of the other dimensions of research relationships. In the next section, we consider other implications of a feminist research ethic's attention to the impact on the researcher of her particular social location as well as her particular epistemology, boundaries, and relationships.

Situating the Researcher

The final element of a feminist research ethic asks the researcher to situate herself within the three preceding power dynamics – of epistemology, boundaries, and human relations – and to attend to these as a matter of methodology. When we introduced this fourth dimension of a feminist research ethic we referred to "the researcher's own sociopolitical location," but now that we have explained the other dimensions of a feminist research ethic more fully, in this section we show that a feminist research ethic requires more reflection than merely reflection on socio-economic privilege.

Self-reflection is good practice for all researchers. But a feminist research ethic invites the researcher to be particularly reflective about her situatedness as a researcher. For example, all feminism is global, because of globalization (Ackerly and True under review). We define globalization as a set of fundamentally constitutive social, cultural, economic, and political processes (and not merely economic transactions across borders) that "promote competing models of gendered social relations on a global scale" (True 2003: 165). How does a researcher's particular situatedness in globalization affect her epistemology and her belief system about how to study social and political questions?

For a feminist-informed researcher interested in engaging in the academic study of the political projects of feminists and women's movements, the researcher's own identity as a scholar, policy analyst, or advocate may be multiple. The ethical challenges posed by this multiplicity may be less obvious for the scholar whose research question is not specifically connected

---

Box 2.6 Situatedness of the researcher

A fascinating article about women diplomats by Iver Neumann (2008) ("The Body of the Diplomat") includes methods of participant observation and ethnography over several years in Norway's Ministry of Foreign Affairs. The research involved personal interviews with a small number of former and current women diplomats. While we find the article's story compelling we are curious about Neumann's own insider-outsider position in the Ministry and what bearing this had on his relationship vis à vis his subject-participants. A feminist research ethic reminds us of the importance of reflecting on our situatedness as researchers and the import that this can have for our findings and as well as the impact it may have on our research subject-participants.

---

to feminist political action, but it is no less imperative. A feminist research ethic asks us to be attentive to situating ourselves and these connections in order to do *ethical* scholarship.

Committed to reflection on her research process, the researcher can attend to her own epistemological myopia and those of her discipline without rendering herself unable to research given the prospect of on-going self-reflection. That is, a feminist-informed research ethic entails a self-reflexive commitment to revisiting epistemological choices, boundaries, and relationships throughout the research process. Most importantly, committed to the politics of every stage of the research process, the feminist researcher guides her work with a research ethic. In the rest of this book we show how it is possible to concretely attend to each of the four aspects of the research ethic by working through each of the stages in the research process.

Throughout the research process, ethical questions are bound to emerge. Many of these relate to the revelation of previously masked forms of power and privilege. However, a feminist research ethic is attentive to the researchers' social, political, and economic relationships to research subjects, and not just their academic connections to their research subject-participants (Box 2.6). This means being attentive to the ways in which social, political, and economic processes make many people and social processes themselves invisible or silent. It also means being committed to self-reflection to guide researchers so they anticipate ethical issues that may occur throughout the research process – even if they cannot anticipate the exact form of them.

Guided by a feminist research ethic, we can build into our research design, from the beginning, deliberative moments where we consciously pause to consider the ethical questions of each aspect of the research process. For instance, when the researcher understands her project at the outset in relation to the advocacy agenda of her subject-participants or the lives of her subject-participants as connected to her own (Staeheli and Nagar 2002), she might be inclined to interpret her ethical obligation to require supporting their advocacy through her research question. Such an obligation may also be worked into the research design. A researcher might work in collaboration with her research subjects to design her project as service research. On this model, the research provides something the organization needs, like inputs for evaluation. These could include developing the skills of the researched community (Sampaio and Hermanas En La Lucha 2004), perhaps the skills of evaluating and documenting the work of an organization (Ackerly 1995; True 2008a). Such an obligation might also be realized by sharing findings in a certain format or with a certain audience (in addition to how they might be published for academic purposes) (Ackerly 2007). Attentive to the research ethic, the researcher can make choices that fulfill these ethical commitments and prepare her to deal with some of the unintended ethical challenges of research.

Conclusion

Feminist theory helps us identify a demanding research ethic for political and social science inquiry. A feminist research ethic includes attentiveness to power, especially the power of epistemology (including the ways in which exercises of power can conceal themselves). It expects on-going concern about boundaries, silencing, absences, and marginalization. A feminist research ethic supports our attentiveness to the relational context in which we research. Such a research ethic also requires that we situate ourselves in our research and cultivate a habit of self-reflection about the research process and the power of epistemology at work even in our ability to conceive of our research. With these expectations, a feminist research ethic can be used to explore a full range of political and social science questions informed by a full range of theoretical and empirical theories and puzzles. As you do your work, consider yourself to be contributing to a feminist research ethic, not just drawing on it. What is important for your research is not a *consistency* of research method from plan to published account, but rather *continuity in the thoughtfulness* that you exhibit about your project throughout.

A feminist-informed research ethic is appropriate for all social science inquiry because it makes visible the power of research epistemology to structure what we know. Feminist inquiry reveals that power can function to render some power dynamics invisible. Feminist inquiry criticizes the power of disciplines to define the field of knowledge inquiry. As a result, feminism is often directly engaged in reflecting on or pushing the boundaries of established disciplines.

Lastly, there is a feminist answer to the important question with which we began this chapter: How can we study power and identify ways to mitigate its abuse in the real world when we, as researchers, also participate in the powerful projection of knowledge in this world? The answer is that a feminist research ethic can give us limited confidence that our epistemological perspective, theoretical choices, research design, data collection, data analysis, exposition of findings, and venues for sharing findings are attentive to power. Yet, the tools of research informed by a feminist ethic can guide us in always developing and improving our commitment as researchers to keep this the most important question social science researchers share. It is our collective responsibility as ethical researchers to put our commitment to self-reflexivity, our attentiveness to the power of epistemology, of boundaries and relationships into the practice of our research.

Selected Sources for Further Reading

Benhabib, Seyla. 1986. "The Generalized and the Concrete Other: The Kohlberg-Gilligan Controversy and Feminist Theory." *Praxis International 5*, 4: 402–24.

Harding, Sandra, and Kathryn Norberg. 2005. "New Feminist Approaches to Social Science Methodologies: An Introduction." *Signs: Journal of Women in Culture and Society* 30, 4: 2009–15. See also the rest of the issue.

Hawkesworth, Mary E. 2006. *Feminist Inquiry: From Political Conviction to Methodological Innovation*. New Brunswick, NJ: Rutgers University Press.

Hesse-Biber, Sharlene Nagy, and Michelle L. Yaiser. 2004. *Feminist Perspectives on Social Research*. New York: Oxford University Press.

Sprague, Joey, and Mary Zimmerman. 1993. "Overcoming Dualisms: A Feminist Agenda for Sociological Methodology." In *Theory on Gender/Feminism on Theory*, ed. Paula England. New York: Aldine de Gruyter, 255–80.

Chapter 3

Feminist Roadmaps: Planning, Doing, and Presenting Your Research

Introduction

Chapter two set out the key elements of a feminist research ethic: (1) attentiveness to power; (2) attentiveness to boundaries of inclusion and exclusion; (3) attentiveness to relationships; and (4) commitment to self-reflection. In this chapter we turn to the research process itself and show how a feminist research ethic can serve as a heuristic device for thinking through and documenting the full range of decisions – planned and unplanned – that the researcher makes over the life of her project. This heuristic helps us attend not only to anticipated and unanticipated ethical dilemmas but also to the more conventional questions of research design, implementation, and analysis in a feminist way. We offer concrete suggestions for: (1) how to think through your research process; (2) how to keep track of your reflections and work throughout the project; and (3) how to show your work to others. We aim to make transparent what every researcher knows – that research is messy. These messy processes need to be conveyed in a non-messy way. Thus, we offer tools for thinking about exposition, too.

This chapter presents a way of conceiving of a feminist research process so that you can have a plan, attend to those factors that make research messy, and then offer your audience(s) a logical, transparent account of your research process. We invite you to think of your research project as a journey, and your responsibility includes the creation of maps for and of your journey. You will

40

create at least three roadmaps. Before you start your journey, you chart out your journey from question through publication, *a research plan*; that is your first roadmap and it gets you on your way. Throughout your journey, you will need to make choices that may alter the plan or make you think differently about that plan. Make these opportunities for reflection and the decisions you make transparent to yourself by keeping *a map of the process*. Having a sense of the overall research process will enable you to respond confidently to the many challenges that you will confront during each phase of the process and ultimately to give an account of your research to myriad audiences, *the account of research*. This last one is the one that appears in your research paper, your dissertation, your talk, and certain final publications.

What is the Research Process?

Familiar Models of Mapping a Research Process

Two ways of mapping a research process are familiar to those who have taught or read about research design: linear (Figure 3.1) and circular (Figure 3.2). The first includes the familiar stages of theory and conceptualization,

3.1 FEMINIST RESEARCH MAPS: THREE TYPES

KEY CONCEPT

Feminist roadmapping is a way of reflecting on both the research journey already taken, as well as how it might move forward by way of three different maps.

The Research Plan is a map of the entire trajectory of the project, from question to publication, prepared as you begin your research.

The Map of the Process is a map created during the research process that makes transparent (and able to be recollected) the difficulties and complexities of the research project by tracing the development of the question and the research through deliberative moments, methodological choices of research methods and data collection, as well as personal or institutional obstacles that you worked through. Thus, the map gives an account of your decisions and their context throughout the research process so that you can defend your choices later to an audience.

The third roadmap is your *Account of the Research*, which is a map with your honed and crafted narrative created after you have completed the substantial part of your project. It draws on your research – from question to conclusion – and will likely be in your published article or conference presentation. This final roadmap will not include everything in the first two maps, but it is certainly shaped by them.

Figure 3.1   *Linear research plan*

including development of hypotheses and operationalization of concepts as data, design and method of data collection, data analysis, and presenting findings. In the simplest version, the researcher plans to move through each stage and does so sequentially. In more complex versions, the research moves from stage to stage, but at each stage the researcher revisits and reconsiders his research question.

In the simplest version of the circular model, the elements of research are the same as in the linear model. When research findings lead to new questions, around we go again! In this regard, the circular model may better characterize a research agenda. In the more complex model, any stage of inquiry can send the researcher back to an earlier stage of inquiry. Unless the answer to the question is foretold, a typical research process will have many moments in which one "stage" of the research process makes the researcher reflect back on prior stages. The data collection process may require us to rethink our question as in the example from Bina D'Costa in Chapter two

Figure 3.2   *Dynamic research process (with feedback loop)*

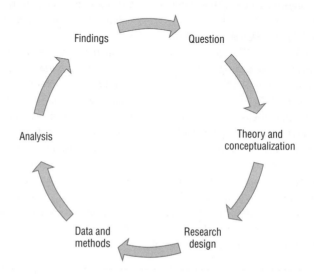

3.2 DELIBERATIVE MOMENTS

Deliberative moments are moments of decision-making in the research process. They are moments when the outcome of a decision has important consequences for the theoretical conceptualization, data collection, and analysis of the research. Deliberative moments are deliberative because they involve reflection and struggle where the interplay of the researcher's questions, theories, constraints, and challenges in the research process creates opportunities for learning. Their effect on the trajectory of the research may be significant and therefore these decisions may need to be revisited.

(and Box 2.4). Or fieldwork in a pilot study can make us rethink our theoretical conceptualization; for example, security needs to be differently defined, as Maria Stern finds in another example we discuss in Chapter two (Box 2.2).

Obviously, the research process is neither linear nor circular. Yet, these familiar models are helpful for exposition. Many of us think in linear ways and are better able to move a research agenda forward with a clear plan. Moreover, many of our potential audiences are also comfortable thinking in linear ways. So for ourselves and our audience, a plan is good. But as we will see, straightforward exposition of our research cannot make the process itself straightforward.

Why Multiple Plans? Political and Social Science Research is Dynamic

Even if you have never done research yourself, you know that the research process is dynamic if you have spoken with someone in the throes of research. Feminist research requires on-going self-conscious reflection about every aspect of the process. This reflection occurs at planned moments in the research process, but the researcher is also attentive to the possibility of unplanned moments emerging. We call both kinds *deliberative moments*, when we stop, reflect, reassess, and think anew. Feminist researchers make the most of both (and some entail a bit of both).

Planned deliberative moments occur at expected punctuating moments in research; research proposal, grant proposal, presentation of partial findings, final publication. They also occur at transitional moments in research: writing a proposal or literature review, beginning carrying out the research, switching to a next phase or method in the data collection, leaving the place of data collection for those whose research requires a change of venue (and friends), beginning to write, hearing feedback, preparing submissions. We planned deliberative moments in writing this book by workshopping key parts of the argument and each chapter with undergraduate, graduate students and colleagues from eight countries (South Africa, Canada, USA, UK, Australia, New Zealand, The Netherlands, and India).

Feminist researchers confront unplanned deliberative moments, like planned deliberative moments, not as failures or problems, but rather as puzzles and learning opportunities for themselves in the moment and an opportunity to contribute to the field. By engaging in our research in ways that are process focused, not outcome focused, feminist empirical researchers often contribute to normative theory, conceptual theory, methodological innovation, and enhance our knowledge of the world. By design, they notice and attend to these deliberative moments because of a feminist research ethic.

Every state of the process presents both kinds of deliberative moments. For example, Marsha Henry gives an account of her frustration with field research, not having anticipated that her ethnicity and gender could be factors in her ability to gain access and conduct her work work (Henry 2007). Reflecting upon the difficulties we encounter, we can notice much about the kinds of power affecting our ability to do research, our own subjectivity's complicity in the unanticipated moment, the conceptual boundaries we have constructed around ourselves as researchers and the ways in which those intersect with culturally constructed boundaries in the sites of our research.

Or, data analysis can provide deliberative moments that lead you to reassess your sampling method or your method of data collection. For example, if you cannot see much variation in your data, perhaps it is because you are looking at primary and secondary sources only in English. Perhaps primary and secondary sources in another language would enhance the range of data collected. Perhaps you need to explore methods for doing primary source research in a language in which you are not fluent. For certain kinds of research, especially single country case studies, we would expect the researcher to be fluent herself. But for other kinds of research, such as comparative institutional analysis requiring multiple cases and research in multiple languages, the researcher needs to be creative, perhaps employing local research assistants and translators of original sources.

Preliminary research about the incorporation of gender analysis into UN human rights instruments and decision-making bodies showed Ladan Radami that there might not be variability in the phenomena she was studying. Therefore, to study the extent to which the various United Nations instruments for promoting human rights had come to understand gender and use this understanding in their work, she needed multiple methods and multiple sites of inquiry (2005). Across these sites of inquiry there was little variation in certain variables. For example, there were few women on all but the Committee on the Status of Women (CSW) which hears country reports in compliance with the Convention on the Elimination of All Forms of Discrimination against Women (CEDAW). Sometimes the problem of variation can lead you to collect more data. Sometimes it makes you see different methods of analysis.

Why Should We Keep Track of a Non-Linear Process?

On one level, the feminist researcher can anticipate both planned and unplanned deliberative moments. We know that unplanned deliberative moments will come, we just don't know when or why. If in the end all that we need to do is be able to convey in a linear way what we did during our research process, why do we need to keep track of its nonlinearity? The rewards relate both to our research process and to the academic quality of our research.

The practical rewards of transparency in methodology are few, but meaningful. From the perspective of a feminist research ethic, if we share our methodology with our subject-participants they may become partners in our research, collaborators even. This partnership can make it easier for us to collect valuable data. It can also allow our subject-participants to benefit from and put into practice our analytical findings sooner rather than later when they have been peer-reviewed (this is particularly important for work that seeks to evaluate groups, networks or organizations and their effectiveness in achieving certain goals). Involving subject-participants as co-researchers enhances the impact of our findings and helps us to achieve the social change purposes of our research. Finally, feminist inquiry is collaborative. We do feminist research in a broader feminist community. We provide each other accountability and support at every stage in the process (Box 3.1).

The academic rewards of transparency in methodology are also meaningful. First, in the spirit of contributing to the field we should make our methods transparent. Transparency and accountability enable our students and colleagues to learn from us on many levels. Second, to the extent that our work raises the ethical standards of academe, we enhance the reputation of academics and thereby contribute to keeping open or to opening up research access for our colleagues. Third, there are individually instrumental reasons for being systematic in our tracking of our work. For example, when we seek the advice of our colleagues in writers groups or other forums, if we can be transparent about our non-linear process, we can get better advice. If

---

Box 3.1 Carpooling through the research process

Whether you are an undergraduate in a course, a thesis writer, or an academic in an established career, it is good to find a fellow traveler when you research. You are taking different trips, making different maps, but sometimes you get together to share progress against the plan. Your course instructor may ask you to meet interim deadlines. Even if she doesn't or if you don't have a course instructor anymore, find a partner with whom you can share your writing and research process. I (Brooke) call this carpooling in appreciation of the monthly conversations I had with Elisabeth Friedman in the carpool from Oakland to Palo Alto as we wrote our dissertations.

---

we are using a theoretical framework that calls for multi-vocality, but we are engaged in single-authored or single-researched work, this tool can enhance the multi-vocality of our project. Further, when we use a feminist research ethic, we have a guide to tell us when we need to press on with our critical reflection and when we are "done" with it and need to press on with the writing.

For these practical and academic reasons, we need to keep track of our non-linear process.

Feminist Roadmaps: Keeping Track of a Non-Linear Process

Just as with every other part of this book, we invite the reader to take and adopt what works for her, to reflect on those examples that stimulate her thinking, and to set aside those that don't for another day. Here we emphasize the importance of adopting this feminist research ethic and in the process *adapting* it as a method. We outline a way of guiding and documenting scholarly reflection; the important thing for the reader to take away from this discussion is the inspiration to map out her own technique for her research journey, and not a commitment to adopting ours.

Picture yourself planning a road trip. You chart your plan with a yellow highlighter. As you go, you mark the important stops and decision points. You might circle specific places that you want to go back to or recommend to a friend. Then, when you are home, you put together a scrap book to remind you of your trip. On the first page you put a map on which you have marked the main path you actually took. You may also highlight some of the places on or off that path that you circled during you journey, but not each

Box 3.2 Feminist road maps

Research plan	Map of the process	Account of research
To guide the researcher in the initial stages of the research	To enable the researcher to keep track of changes in the research plan	To convey the logic of the actual research plan
To help anticipate certain deliberative moments	To help the researcher document the important learning opportunities presented by a deliberative moment	To show the key insights – of theory, conceptualization, research design, method, analysis, findings – of the project
To serve as a reference point when unanticipated deliberative moments occur	To serve as a reference point when other unanticipated moments occur	To offer a bases for peer evaluation of the project's methodology

one is important. In the scrap book, you include photos or descriptions about the more important circled places. You distinguish between the places you went that were adventures you want to share and those you would recommend to others. For some friends who may take the same trip, you want to share the information you gained about wrong turns or unrewarding side trips. For others, you just want to share the highlights.

We devote subsequent chapters to each aspect of the research process. In this chapter we look at these in relationship to one another and to the research ethic. There are three parts to our research roadmap: the research plan (an organization plan written *before* research begins), the map of the process (an accounting of your actual process made *during* research), and the account of research (the exposition of your research constructed *after* your research) (Box 3.2). Your feminist roadmap is the sum of all three of these.

The Research Plan: Getting Started

To begin your research, you need to chart a course. Pick a model: one of those set out in Figures 3.1 or 3.2 or your own variation that speaks directly to your commitments and use it to lay out your *Research Plan*. What are the steps of your research project? We use: question, theory and conceptualization, research design, data and methods, analysis, and exposition of findings. What are yours? We find that the steps run together, but for expository purposes there are reasons to separate them as we have.

Use the research ethic and your knowledge of your preliminary research to *anticipate* the questions you will ask at each stage. Which questions can you answer now? If not now, at what stage should you revisit the question? (See Exercise 3.1 on the website http://www.palgrave.com/methodology/doingfeministresearch.)

Consider again the key elements of a feminist research ethic, attentiveness to: (1) power; (2) boundaries of inclusion and exclusion; (3) relationships; and (4) the situatedness of the researcher. As an exercise, let's apply them toward anticipating deliberative moments during data collection.

Attentiveness to power: you might anticipate that your own privilege or lack thereof will become an issue during research. Perhaps your status as a professor or a student will incline someone to work with you. Perhaps your race or gender will make you subject to harassment (see Box 6.6 about Johnson 2007). Johnson did not anticipate harassment but you might.

As Johnson found, you might anticipate that your own identity (ethnic, gender, age, sexuality) and positionality (non-national, location as an outsider in some sense, a scholar, an activist, or policy i.e. non-university context) diminishes your credibility in the eyes of facilitator-participants or subject-participants.

Attentive to boundaries: you might anticipate that *only* women can go to certain places and that no women can go to others (Carapico 2006; Henderson 2009; Ortbals and Rincker 2009a, 2009b; Schwedler 2006).

Attentive to relationships: when you start to collect data, you should expect that your research facilitator will ask "what does this research mean for me and my community" (Sapra 2009). What can your research facilitator reasonably expect of you as the researcher? If your research question is an identity-related one, the relationship you establish with subject-participants may be relevant in itself as a form of data. For example, one Political Scientist examining gender differences and dynamics among US state legislators experienced an interview with an older male legislator "that can only be described as harassment" (Bennion 2007: 22–3). Illustrating his point that men cannot focus on battle with women, the legislator imagined "that he and [the researcher] were in a foxhole together after dark: I wouldn't be thinking about fighting or my duties then, would I?" The subject-participant displayed sexually harassing and potentially threatening behavior during the interview. Yet the interview provided highly relevant data for the researcher's project. Honesty in relationships is considered in Box 3.3.

Attentive to your own situatedness: you might anticipate that a research participant will say things that you will find unethical. Which might affect

Box 3.3 Honesty in relationships

Reflecting on unanticipated deliberative moments can help us anticipate some of our own possible deliberative moments. For example, reflecting on Tami Jacoby's problem of realizing that her subject-participant felt threatened *after* the interview when she discovered that Jacoby was married to an Israeli man (2006), we might plan our field work to anticipate such concerns. On a related issue that resulted in a missed opportunity, Diane Wolf tells the story of not being able to talk about relationships with her subject-participants because she had not been honest with her hosts about her relationship with a fellow researcher (1996). Reflecting on either example, I may influence how I reveal my relationships with others and with subject-participants. I may decide that in establishing my relationships with my research participants, I need to anticipate that questions of my own marital status will come up during the process of building relationships with my subject-participants. Deciding how to respond to these questions in the moment is difficult. These are aspects of research design that can be worked through if the moment is anticipated. The author's degrees of freedom are more limited if they are not anticipated and have to be worked out in the field, or worse in the moment.

your research plan? Which not? For such dilemmas, you might look at Cohn (2006) and Fine *et al.* (2004).

At every stage, attentiveness to the research ethic can help us be prepared for the deliberative moments of our projects.

Map of the Process

Whether or not we anticipate deliberative moments, when they occur, plans may change. You need to keep a record of these changes as they occur. Of course, sharing these with colleagues in a research group, with a carpooler (Box 3.1), with select people in your professional network (Box 6.2), or in a field note diary enable you to make the most of the opportunities each presents. As importantly, you need to keep a map to keep track of all of them. It is more challenging to map the unanticipated moments. But it is possible to be systematic in our noticing, assessment of, and learning from these deliberative moments as well.

Before setting out the steps of this process, let's consider an unanticipated deliberative moment at the stage of writing up findings. Of course we expect to face such deliberative moments during field research; however, as we will see in Chapter twelve, some of our unanticipated deliberative moments occur as we share our findings. For example, Anne Marie Goetz and Rina Sen Gupta (1996) studied gender and microcredit programs in Bangladesh just as these programs were scaling up and increasing their reach. They needed to present findings that included gender analysis of these microcredit programs; their findings could have implications for the future funding of such programs were they taken as reasons for discrediting these organizations. As they presented their findings to an organization in the study, a woman from one of the organization asked, "do you think that we are ready for gender in development when we don't yet have women in development?" In her organization, a focus on "gender" was being interpreted as a justification for turning away from programmatic attention to the impact of microcredit on women's well-being. An obvious deliberative moment about the publication stage – Should Goetz and Sen Gupta shift from discussing their work in terms of "gender" as this language seems to legitimate decentering concerns for women's well being? This deliberative moment also prompted the authors to think about their conceptualization of gender, about their research design, and about how they did their field work. Whatever they decided to do in response to this deliberative moment, they needed to reflect on it and to document in their map of the research process.

In such deliberative moments, you need to revisit, even rethink, any and every step of your plan, including even changing your theoretical framework and conceptualization, to change the concepts, not just the language you use to talk about them. True, you might have anticipated some of these with cross-cultural communication while doing fieldwork. However, you can't know how your language, concepts, and prior assumptions will misinterpret and be misinterpreted with consequences for your data collection. Moreover, this kind of engagement enables ground-breaking work.

At each moment, be deliberative, think about what caused the moment, what brought you to this moment, and then, with most difficulty, how you should characterize the moment. What brought you to this moment? Review your research plan thus far. Situate this moment in your research. Perhaps you are having trouble because it is time to focus on an aspect of your research to which you haven't attended yet. Perhaps, it is time to model your hypotheses, time to theorize about which variables are appropriate control variables and which would be intervening variables, time to operationalize your variables, time to choose a case study, a comparative or large N research design. Some stages of the research process can be anticipated at the outset, but sometimes, some aspects of some projects can be explored only after other aspects.

Other moments make us go back and revisit earlier stages in the research process. What triggered this moment? Perhaps it is time to write the methodology section of your dissertation proposal, or perhaps you read a piece of research that specified its hypotheses in very clear but theoretically problematic ways, or perhaps your interview subject-participant asked you how your research would affect her life.

The most difficult aspect of assessing a deliberative moment is characterizing the moment. In our examples so far we have characterized the moment for you: D'Costa has a deliberative moment about her research question (Box 2.4); Stern has a deliberative moment about her conceptualization of security (Box 2.2); and Goetz and Sen Gupta (1996) reflect on the language and framing they use to present their findings. However, drawing on their own reflections, we have characterized these moments *in retrospect* after the authors (and we) have thought through the deliberative moments as we understand them. In the moment, that may not be so easy.

You have an opportunity to use the research ethic as a compass. What does it mean to (1) attend to power, (2) attend to boundaries of inclusion and exclusion, (3) attend to relationships and (4) self-reflect, if you understand your moment as a moment *about the research question*? What does it mean to (1) attend to power, (2) attend to boundaries of inclusion and exclusion, (3) attend to relationships and (4) self-reflect, if you understand your moment as a moment *about your conceptualization*?

Continue through each stage asking yourself what kind of moment you are having and what kinds of questions (and possible insights) that attending to power, boundaries, relationships, and your own previous thinking raises. Craft a set of questions and considerations to guide your thinking through each aspect of the research ethic for each stage of the project.

1. Power

- Consider the ways in which power makes apparent or conceals the following considerations.
- Consider the ways in which power enables or inhibits our ability to attend to these.
- Consider the power that your epistemology exerts over your project.

2. Boundaries, exclusion and inclusion

- Consider the boundaries, including the disciplinary boundaries you have put on your thinking about question, theory, and conceptualization, research design, scope of data and methods for collecting it, analysis or findings. Are they appropriate? Do they mask or inhibit any aspect of your research?
- For example, consider the boundaries that have made certain subject-participants available and others unavailable.
- What boundaries affect your work? Which do you notice as a result of this deliberative moment?

3. Relational subjectivities

- Consider the relationship between you and your subject-participants (differences in kinds of epistemological authority, resources, opportunity cost of time, life experience, familiarity with the topic, knowledge of the terrain, etc.).
- Consider the relationships among subject-participants, be they individuals or organizations (transnational organizations competing for funding, states differently located in the international system, etc.).
- Consider the intrasubjectivity within a subject (an identity as a performer, identity as interview subject, identity as one of many subject-participants, identity as important subject, identity as a leader).
- Consider the relationship between subject-participants and non-participants (non-participants include those who did not fit the selection criteria *and* those who fit the selection criteria, but were not selected as subject-participants; how does your interview affect these people and their relationships with each other?).
- Consider the relationship between yourself and other researchers: those doing research where you are, those asking similar questions, those who feel in competition with you (for resources or recognition), those who stand to learn from your research, those who have used similar concepts, those who have challenged your use of concepts.

4. Situatedness of the researcher

- Be self-reflective as you consider each of the above.
- Consider how others may *see* you.
- Revisit your epistemological perspective.
- Survey how other epistemological perspectives would view this decision moment.

Even going through this process, you may not be able to figure out what kind of moment you are facing or what it means for your research. It may be a while before you figure out how this moment should affect your research. Having gone through this process, you will have a landscape to refer to as you think it through. At later stages, you can go back to the research process map of this moment and revise it based on your subsequent research and reflections. With a research process map of your dilemma, when you find yourself with a classmate or colleague, you can share your dilemma and your reflections to date. You can raise a piece of the issue in a class or at a conference where you might get valuable insights. Even if you don't have a clear understanding of the best way to attend to your dilemma, having constructed a research process map, you have a good platform to continue deliberating about it – with yourself and others.

Account of Your Research

When it is time to present your research, you do not need to share every thoughtful moment in the map of your process. Rather, you review the map to identify those moments that in final reflection were most salient to your project. These are the basis of the account of your research that you share when you share your findings. The point is to use these to do better research and to share that research with audiences of other researchers, of subject-participants and of a general public interested in research-based knowledge.

We have offered a way of thinking through the planned and unplanned moments in the research process. Here, we suggest how to give an account of our research for different purposes. The account looks different at different stages of the research process – the pre-dissertation grant application, the dissertation proposal, the grant application for field research, the grant application for funds to write up the project, presentation of preliminary findings (which differs depending on audience – see Box 3.4), book proposal, and publication of findings in peer reviewed venues (which differs by venue).

The point of critically assessing the planned and unplanned moments of our scholarship is *not* to turn such reflection into the purpose of scholarship itself, nor is it to give ourselves a sense of "reflexivity as an epistemological achievement" (Lynch 2000: 46). A clear account of your research is an important piece of good scholarship.

In peer reviewed feminist scholarship, when we evaluate scholarship, we look at the methodology including the ethics of the process and not merely

Box 3.4 Kirsch and Mortensen on audience and account of research

Consider Kirsch and Mortensen's reflection on how they have portrayed their scholarship on literacy:

"Public accounts of how we have handled ethical dilemmas are perhaps most useful to graduate students who are planning their first major foray into the qualitative study of literacy. Because of this, it is important that such accounts be as constructively self-critical as possible. That is to say, they should not be forums for apology or justification, nor should they simply narrate triumph over adversity in the field. But whether writing for graduate students or a broader audience, we must remember – and communicate – that self-reflexivity is not an end itself; it does not change social conditions, improve people's lives, or distribute material resources more equitably. Self-reflexivity is only one step in the complex process of redefining what it means to do research in a postmodern world often lacking in social justice" (Kirsch and Mortensen 1999, in Kirsch 1999: 99–100).

Box 3.5 Feminist roadmapping (Brooke's approach)

I (Brooke) begin every project by trying to pack the whole project into a ten page exposition, a paragraph, and then a sentence. As I read more and think more, various parts of the plan get refined. I think through the anticipated deliberative moments and write up my research plan. At each anticipated deliberative moment, I go back to the plan and rewrite it as necessary. Sometimes these moments correspond to an occasion: the need to submit a grant application or the need to present a book proposal. Or, they correspond to a puzzle presented by the research process. Due to the questions I ask and my own thinking style, each such presentation of my project is generally a significant reworking of prior expositions.

the significance of the finding. When we follow a feminist research process, the ethics of the process is formative of our interpretations. Therefore, when we share our work, we need to make visible that part of the research process.

In order to describe this process and to reveal the opportunities for feminist reflection throughout the process, we have deployed the metaphor of a journey and maps. At the moment of publication, we look back over a path that has taken us from defining and refining the research question, past research design, through to publication and give an account of the whole journey and its key moments. Looking back at that journey, the researcher can reveal to her audience the process, at moments seemingly linear, at moments seemingly circular, that led to her findings and to their being presented in the venues of her choice.

Ultimately, she and her audience will need defendable answers to the six basic questions that Jennifer Mason sets out:

- Are my concepts meaningful?
- Are my methods appropriate?
- Have I designed and carried out the research carefully, accurately, well?
- Have I analyzed my data carefully, accurately, and well?
- Are my conclusions supported by my data analysis?
- Are they more widely applicable? (Mason 2002: 40)

The research plan is where you plan your answers to those questions, the map of the process is where you reflect on your plan and make changes, and the account of research is the account that in its final instantiation you use to justify and defend your research.

> ## Box 3.6 Feminist roadmapping (Jacqui's approach)
>
> I (Jacqui) begin my research projects similarly to Brooke, usually with a funding proposal that requires one catchy sentence, an abstract and a longer discussion of the theoretical literature, potential hypotheses, research design and specific methods for carrying out the research. I note the partially unresolved issues and questions surrounding my research and how I tentatively expect to address them but I push on. At regular intervals I assesses my research progress against my original outline, writing up my revisions and why they are necessary based on the dilemmas I have encountered so far in the research. Since my work is theoretically-informed but empirical in nature, often I do this revision "in the field," after a participant observation experience or a series of interviews. It is important for me to build in deliberative moments at times when my data are fresh and I can engage in some preliminary analysis. I tend to develop one or two parts of my overall research project fully through to presentation of research as a microcosm of the larger project that explores its feasibility. This "building blocks" approach helps me to construct and substantiate my argument from the ground-up, deductively, weaving piece by piece together.

Conclusion: What it All Looks Like

In what we have offered above, we suggested that the researchers have a *plan*, keep track of changes to the plan using the *process map*, and then give an *account of* our research at the end highlighting key moments in the research process. A research project generally offers a researcher a number of opportunities to write up her process (see Chapters ten and twelve). Moreover, for some, the discipline of expository writing about the research process enables her to realize the significance of certain deliberative moments for theory, methods, analysis, and findings.

How we present our research to outside audiences looks different at every stage and for every author (see Boxes 3.5 and 3.6). At the beginning of your project your research plan and the presentation of your research are the same thing. When and how you revise the presentation is quite dependent on the researcher and her project.

Sometimes in writing an exposition of your work you may feel an incentive or pressure to write as if you are at a different stage in the research project. You may be at the pre-dissertation proposal writing stage and be tempted to act as if you were in the book proposal writing stage. Perhaps you are in a course on research design, but you don't yet have a clear research question. If you have never done a research project of this kind from start to finish, you may not know the difference between the different kinds of exposition. Resist writing about your research as if you were at a different stage then you actually are. Such exercises take time away from the progress of research.

In this chapter we have offered a discipline for thinking about the ways in which the research process is punctuated by planned and unplanned deliberative moments. And we have offered a structure for mapping and then writing about research. Doing this research process work takes practice. The more you do it, the more confidence you will have in what you are doing and the less derailing a given dilemma might be. Stay the course and you will get the practice and gain confidence in your ability to anticipate moments, think through both planned and unplanned moments and to write up your work. Until you have that confidence, trust that you will gain it and in the mean time use the structuring devices we suggest.

Sometimes, for whatever reason, a research dilemma can set you adrift. No disciplined approach can help you think through your dilemma if what you are experiencing is a loss of orientation. If a feminist research ethic is the basic compass of a feminist researcher, her research question is her orientation. When she is lost or confused she needs to return to the research question. In the next chapter we discuss the feminist research question, what makes for good research questions in general, what distinguishes feminist questions in particular, and how to come up with a compelling one situated in both feminist and mainstream fields of knowledge.

Selected Sources for Further Reading

Burnham, Peter, Karin Gilland, Wyn Grant, and Zig Layton-Henry. 2004. *Research Methods in Politics*. New York: Palgrave Macmillan.

Mason, Jennifer. 2002. *Qualitative Researching*. London: Sage.

Ramazanoğlu, Caroline, and Janet Holland. 2002. *Feminist Methodology: Challenges and Choices*. Thousand Oaks, CA: Sage.

Sprague, Joey. 2005. *Feminist Methodologies for Critical Researchers: Bridging Differences*. Walnut Creek, CA: AltaMira Press.

Chapter 4

Question-Driven Research: Formulating a Good Question

Introduction

In Chapter three we argued that you should always return to your original research question when you encounter unexpected deliberative moments where the choice of how to proceed is a difficult one. Your research question is the first principle of your research project: it is what orients and sustains it, and it is what makes it both compelling to do research and to learn about others' research.

Having made clear the background theory and processes that affect empirical research in the first three chapters, in this chapter we begin our guide through the more visible stages of research, starting with the research question or puzzle and making explicit use of a feminist research ethic. This stage of the research process corresponds to the first part of the research presentation, dissertation/funding proposal, or publication. In its final form, the research question will be stated in one or two sentences, while the puzzle that it summarizes will be formulated in a paragraph – one compelling paragraph that draws the reader or audience into the world of your research.

The founding step in the research process is deciding on a research question. Even though the research question may change during the research process, the determining of the research question is an important (if recurring) starting point. In deciding her question, the feminist-informed researcher is guided by a feminist research ethic, and the attentiveness to power, to boundaries, to relationships and our situatedness as researchers that it demands. Putting this ethic into practice leads her to consider the importance of research questions whose answers have the potential to make visible the invisible, to give voice to the voiceless, to make central analyses that are marginalized or neglected by mainstream lines of inquiry, and to bring to our attention processes and institutions that have been absent in the mainstream of our disciplines. By its very definition, a feminist research question is often "cutting edge."

Part of learning to ask a good feminist-informed question is being well versed in our field(s) and taking account of the silences and neglected topics within it, relative to what we observe in the world around us. In this chapter we discuss and illustrate how feminist scholars craft their research questions dialogically with their subject-participants *or* by drawing on women's and men's experiences and their gender analysis of their subject or field *and* on existing feminist and non-feminist scholarship in related fields. We show that feminists make convincing arguments about the relevance and importance of their research questions to central questions and pervading problems in their political and social science fields by situating their scholarship in relation to other pursuits within their field, other pursuits of related questions in other fields (including other feminist pursuits), and the concerns of affected actors. The multidisciplinarity of feminist research does not exempt its author from building on research, including non-feminist research that has already been done. Rather feminist transdisciplinarity (see Key Concept 1.7) requires us to situate our work broadly in relation to our subfield, our field, other feminist inquiry, policy relevance, and activist concerns. In so doing we explore the boundaries and power dynamics of research. A feminist research ethic is a guiding tool in developing a research question that is puzzling and important.

What is a Great Question?

> Most importantly, I have learned that you have to ask important and interesting questions. That is the hardest thing to do and the hardest thing to teach. We can teach paradigms, analytical perspectives, and methods by taking them off the professional shelf and transporting them to the classroom. What we cannot teach so readily is how to ask important and interesting questions (Evans *et al.* 1996: 11).

Both feminist and non-feminist researchers struggle to ask good research questions – whether they are "what," "why," or "how" questions. Our research questions are at the heart of successful research enterprises; they animate our research, reminding us of what we are doing in our research and why, especially at those times when the way ahead seems less than straightforward, when we confront expected and unexpected challenges and dilemmas. Both of us have always found it assuring to know that "the river runs muddy before it runs clear" and to be able to return for clarification to the research question that got us started along our way. Thus, we believe it is crucial to spend quality time developing and honing your research question or problem and stating it in such a way that its meaning is clear to both you and others.

Peter Katzenstein suggests in the epigraph above that our research should be driven by important and interesting questions and puzzles rather than by particular methods or paradigmatic concerns specific to a particular theoretical perspective or discipline. Indeed, Katzenstein and Sil (2008) argue that paradigm-oriented research can blinker our vision and lead us to take for granted some of the most interesting and important questions that lie around us and that require illumination or explanation. In the field of international relations, for example, the dominant realist paradigm did not see or analyze the problems of dissent and the abrogation of human rights in Eastern Europe that gave rise to local civil society struggles for freedom as significant for understanding change and continuity in international relations. Focused instead on the superpower relationship between the Soviet Union and the United States they completely overlooked the decaying of power within the states and societies of the East Bloc that led to the toppling of communist regimes, the break-up of the Soviet Union itself and the end of that bipolar international system.

Likewise, many of the dominant paradigms in political and social science have assumed gender injustice and women's absence from their fields as background conditions or part of the way the world "is" and not something to be problematized or explained through research. In response, much feminist work in the political and social sciences has been devoted to unmasking concealed social and political phenomena and making compelling arguments based on research evidence for why these phenomena should be considered problems and questions to be addressed – and not only by researchers but by all of society at large.

Feminist research is both strongly question-oriented and problem focused. Political theorist Ian Shapiro advocates a question-driven approach to research which is potentially compatible with a feminist research ethic. Shapiro (2005) encourages us to address "the great questions of the day" rather than get mired down in narrow and exclusive disciplinary debates. But what are these great questions and do we agree on them? Our feminist attentiveness to power and to marginalization is provoked here. In the discipline of Political Science for example, we may, broadly speaking, know what the great topics or themes are about; they are about the nature and dynamics of democracy, citizenship, political community and power as well as justice, world order, and equality. However, there are many possible research questions and problems that could be posed within the porous boundaries of any of these topics. Who gets to decide and define the questions which are the truly great ones should be "up for grabs" and a matter of the force of the best argument (which may require contesting the norms of "best argument" as well).

More likely then, the questions that are considered great questions (with the emphasis on *great*) are determined by questions of politics and power themselves, as feminists and other critically-minded scholars have pointed out. "How people see the world and what they perceive as problems are determined to a great extent by their location in the social structure" (Karraker and Larner 1984: 497). In particular, the resources and accolades attributed to different research questions and research agendas are shaped by the structuring of gender, race, class, national and international privilege in and through knowledge production.

We need to be self-reflective about how and from what location we construct our research questions and it is important to consult with research subject-participants. The great question of the day for a Soweto widow caring for six grandchildren who have lost their mother to the HIV/AIDS pandemic may not be the same as the great question of the day for a Yale professor of politics. We may be able to persuade a professor of politics, other scholars, and other citizens that one of the great questions of our day is about how gender relations shape sexual practices and specifically, the spread of HIV/AIDS. This research question responds to the observation that many more women than men are infected by HIV/AIDs in Africa, and seeks to examine the social roots of the global disease. The question is not great until we make the argument for its greatness. And *that* is a political argument.

Contrary to some claims, feminism's normative commitments are not what distinguish it from mainstream research. Like critical theorist Robert Cox (Cox with Sinclair 1996), feminists argue, "theory is always for someone, and for some purpose", and thus, that all research on politics and society is inherently normative whether consciously or not (Haraway 1988). What distinguishes feminist research questions is that they are constructed from critical perspectives that seek to understand and transform existing social relations rather than to solve problems within the existing social and political order.

Conceptualizing research as question-driven gets us beyond research that is narrowly driven by adherence to a single technical method (where methods seek questions rather than the other way around) or theoretical paradigm (where the theory selects and *a priori* frames the acceptable questions). However, it does raise other problems about "who knows" and "where our research questions come from." The experience of feminist researchers in opening innovative areas of research by asking new questions and reframing old problems is illustrative. For example, feminist psychologists asked new questions about the effects of divorce on the health and wellbeing of single mothers when most research was questioning the loss of masculinity for fatherless boys. They also reframed old problems such as rape as an act of aggression rather than as an issue pertaining to sexuality (Worrell 2000: 188–9). As good scholars we need to argue, and not merely assert that our research problem or question is a vexing problem or question in the first place, and why it is important, interesting and puzzling. An essential starting point for research and for generating research questions is, therefore, that we must take nothing for granted; to paraphrase one of Marx's better aphorisms, a researcher should be "ruthlessly critical of all that exists."

Where Do Good Questions Come From?

Conventional scientific disciplines have had very little to say about where good, or even great, research questions come from. Although they may acknowledge that research questions are informed by the values and normative preferences of the researcher and community of researchers in a given field they treat this "context of discovery" apart from the "context of justification" where research is carried out through the testing of hypotheses. Indeed, the generation of questions and hypotheses is seen as outside of science itself. Consequently, there is no accountability for the process of deciding among them (which questions and hypotheses are included and excluded) within a research discipline, paradigm, program, or agenda (see Key Concept 4.1).

Karl Popper argued that science does not have an account of itself and that there is no sure method for arriving at valid new ideas (Popper 1959). Popper's view is that we generate ideas through a whole range of means and sources including observation, inspiration, tradition, dreams, and studies of previous attempts to solve similar problems, perception of flaws in old or new problems and solutions. But in his account, the various means by which we generate ideas are irrelevant since the main thing is to subject all our ideas to critical analysis and testing. Unfortunately, this position shared by many researchers has left the question of how we come up with research questions largely shrouded in darkness. It has also foreclosed the ethical and normative issues that are raised by our choices to pursue some research questions or address some problems over other research questions and problems. For feminist researchers this is a significant issue: Why, for instance, have more resources been poured into studying terrorism in terms of threats to state borders rather than the political and economic inequalities within Islamic countries vis à vis the West or the constructions of masculinity in western and non-western contexts that contribute to global insecurity? (e.g. Agathangelou and Ling 2004; Kaufman-Osborn 2006). This is one just example of the kind of trade-offs continually at work in the privileging of certain research questions and agendas in a world where power relations and political considerations almost always shape our research within it.

4.1 PHILOSOPHY OF SCIENCE: A QUICK REVIEW OF POPPER, KUHN, AND LAKATOS

For Popper: Researchers stumble onto empirical problems or questions by any means. They then propose theories containing specific hypothesis to explain these phenomena or answer these questions. These hypotheses can only be falsified by evidence, they can never be confirmed. Scientific change and revolution are thus continuous, but scientific progress is not ensured.

For Kuhn: Science and scientific research communities that pose problems are based on dominant paradigms characterized by shared research problems, as well as shared norms and values. Normal science conditions the dominant paradigm, determines which problems are solvable, and solves them with certain methods (unsolvable problems are excluded). Against this backdrop, the presence and persistence of anomalies (including anomalous questions) leads to a crisis within the paradigm and possibly an abrupt paradigm shift to a new dominant paradigm. The new paradigm has a different conceptual framework that suggests new problems and methods to solve them. Scientific revolution is thus discontinuous and scientific progress may occur within but not across paradigms.

For Lakatos: Rational progress in science is possible through research programs that contain a hard core of theories and answerable questions, a negative heuristic to guard the hard core theories and assumptions and a positive heuristic which augments the hard core and enables it to deal with new research questions and methodological innovations. Paradigm shifts in science can occur but only when the hard core can no longer address the new problems.

Feminists challenge the distinction in positivist science between the context of discovery and the context of justification. As Sandra Harding (2000) argues, the social and often gender-biased assumptions made in the questions mainstream disciplines ask and in the conceptual frameworks used to constitute a research program can completely escape the kind of critical examination to which more explicit elements of scientific projects are subjected during the context of justification. "The best methods used in the context of justification provide no resources for identifying social or cognitive assumptions and frameworks (such as androcentric or Eurocentric ones) that are shared by an entire research community" (Harding 1991, 2000). In the feminist view, the researcher's normative context affects the entire research process. This feminist perspective contrasts with that of conventional scientific research which is focused mostly on scrutinizing already-established hypotheses rather than the generation of hypotheses and thus is inattentive to the normative commitments sustained by established hypotheses.

A feminist research ethic guides us to be critical of our values and the impact of our personal experiences on our research, and indeed on the development of our research questions. We argue that how our social context shapes us and our research questions should be a part of our account of research in the political and social sciences, making visible the research process as an integral part of research (Bristow and Esper 1984: 492). We should consciously seek to make the assumptions behind our research question explicit. Standpoint theorists place the context of discovery under critical methodological scrutiny by self-consciously generating research questions and hypotheses from "the standpoint of the lives of women and other marginalized groups whose interests have been neglected in the constitution of scientific problematics" (Harding 2000 online; also 1991, 1998). But one need not advocate a standpoint position in order to situate and scrutinize the assumptions of our research questions.

Sometimes a research question becomes salient because of dominant framings by powerful institutional actors. We need to acknowledge this so that we do not uncritically accept the institutional actors' frame but rather frame the question in ways that are open to many possible interpretations and not one predestined answer. For example, there might be the way in which "sex trafficking" has recently come to be seen as a major problem of national interest and global scope as if it did not exist prior to its articulation on the policy agenda of dominant states. Trafficking, for instance, is often seen as a problem of illegal immigration, prostitution which is a criminal offence, money laundering, and racketeering rather than a violation of women's human rights, the right to decent work, violence against women and so on (Berman 2003; Sullivan 2003). Research projects are always constituted through economic, social, cultural, and political values, including gender values. The point is to make the acknowledgment of these values a productive site for probing and further clarifying our research questions.

Generating Questions through Gender Analysis

Gender analysis is a common analytical approach in feminist research – although researchers whose research is not explicitly feminist-informed increasingly use some aspects of gender analysis. It is typically seen as the quintessential and unique feminist approach to research. That is not the argument of this book, however. As we show here, it is the use of a feminist research ethic to guide it that makes gender analysis *feminist* rather than vice versa. But gender analysis opens up a whole landscape of new research questions as well as giving us tools to rethink old research questions. Given the pervasiveness of gender norms and structures across societies, gender as an analytic category can illuminate new areas of inquiry, frame research questions or puzzles in need of exploration and "provide

> ## Box 4.1　Neglected research questions: Goldstein on war and gender
>
> In *War and Gender* Joshua Goldstein (2001) starts with this puzzle: Why has war been primarily a male activity across history, culture, and countries despite the considerable variation in gender relations across cultures and history?
>
> Goldstein observes that: "The most warlike cultures are also the most sexist" (2001: 20). He then asks two further *questions*:
>
> 1. How do constructions of masculinity motivate soldiers (men and women) to fight (to protect)?
> 2. How does war-making shape masculinity? (2001: 9)
>
> As Barbara Ehrenreich (1999) argues, it is not only men that make wars but wars that make men.

concepts, definitions and hypothesis to guide research" (Hawkesworth 2005: 141). It can also help us to critically analyze data, observations, and interpretations.

For example, feminist-informed researchers are led to *gender analysis* and to ask gender-sensitive research questions by our observations that something is missing from existing accounts of social and political reality. In Mala Htun's words, we engage in "gender analysis because women are not there" (Htun 2005: 162). If you want to study women in politics and there is an absence of women politicians or leaders to study this you may lead you to shift to studying gender norms and structures and how they shape politics and constrain political representation.

Feminist scholars have exposed how gender values have conditioned research questions. Until recently in the international relations field these questions were largely to do with the "heroic and masculine domain of wars and politico-diplomatic struggles among the only actors judged significant – nation-states" (Bleiker 2003: 416). This feminist "uncovering" has in itself been a major contribution to knowledge; making possible a new set of research agendas and questions about how gender dynamics shape and are shaped by international relations. The masculine values informing the field have led to a glaring neglect of important problems and patterns in international relations. For instance, Katharine Moon (1997) asks: What role does the sex industry play in military relations between countries? In so doing she uncovers prostitution on foreign bases and shows how the international relations between the US and South Korea depend on its existence and management. Joshua Goldstein's research on war and gender illustrates this point as well (see Box 4.1).

When we decide on our particular research question, a feminist research ethic reminds us to consider what further research questions are potentially included and excluded, what is being remembered and what is being forgotten, who will be silenced and marginalized or remain silent, absent and marginalized if we ask this question in this way? For instance, when we highlight the gender dimension of a problem, such as the transmission of HIV/AIDs in Africa are we potentially neglecting analysis of sexuality, including positive accounts of diverse, desiring sexualities (see Reid and Walker 2005)?

How Can I Come Up With a Good Question?

Having established that we need to be conscious of the starting points for research, to explicitly argue for rather than merely state the research questions, we have some advice for developing and refining your research questions before discussing the development of feminist-inspired research questions. Clearly posed questions are an excellent way to begin a dissertation or funding proposal, a research presentation, or publication (Przeworski and Salomon 1995).

As Goldstein illustrates in Box 4.2, a good study has one clear puzzle or question that explores one limited concept or thesis. This puzzle may have one or two more related questions as does Goldstein's puzzle about why men and typically not women go to war across history and cultures. The puzzle may require paper/article-length treatment or thesis/book-length treatment. Regardless of the anticipated length of the final work product, you should be able to state your puzzle succinctly. By the time you are done, you should be able to state it succinctly in a way that your aunt or high school friend could understand. Kirshner (1996: 511) suggests that the author should be able to write down his question on a three by five index card and then tape it above his desk.

We have found it useful to keep a folder that contains various iterations of our research questions on any one project. In the proposal stage and as we work through the project, we refine our question as we go and add to the folder. This folder reminds us of where we started, helps us to be able to review our research journey, and prompts us to reflect further on the dynamic nature of the research process as we experience it and when it is time for exposition. For example, a dissertation proposal defense that includes the history of the development of your research question can be very effective.

Importantly, you should be able to communicate your research question to a non-specialist in the space of the time you are in an elevator together – "the elevator test." We typically recommend that you discuss your question with a friend or family member. How will you persuade them that your research question is an important one using both your own opinion and some preliminary evidence? Writing an email or letter to a friend telling them about your question and why it's a crucial one can be a good way to start. We have done this with each other during this project a lot and have found it an extremely fruitful way of crystallizing ideas without belaboring them. It is incumbent on feminist researchers to share their research with a broader audience beyond academic specializations, so it is good to start by making sure your research question resonates with other concerned citizens and groups.

For many feminist and non-feminist researchers, research questions do not come from the mainstream scholarly literature. That is not to say you should not familiarize yourself with the debates and contestations in your field and related fields. Doing this is important for inspiring research questions but also for thinking seriously about the debates to which you want to contribute – from the outset and for enabling your colleagues to consider your work in its intellectual context (see Chapter six).

Types of Research Questions

There are different types of research questions which entail different epistemologies, kinds of research design, methods of data collection and analysis and so on (also Knopf 2006). There are research questions that address new issues or phenomena that have not yet been researched in a particular field or that have been "forgotten". In addition, there are research questions that challenge existing mainstream knowledge on a particular topic or issue with new empirical research or theoretical interpretations. In generating the first ("new" research questions), a scholar cannot easily build on existing scholarship. For instance, Cynthia Enloe's research has self-consciously gone against the grain of disciplinary concerns. In the late 1980s she asked "where the women are in international relations" which animated a new subfield of feminist international relations and encouraged mainstream scholars to question their questions (Enloe [1989] 1990). Now that the field of feminist IR is developed, Enloe asks the second type of question, using "new" data to inform her questions and analysis. In *The Curious Feminist* (2004), she asks where are the women in occupied Afghanistan and Iraq? Enloe foregrounds the perspectives of those women on the margins of world politics, including prostitutes on US foreign military bases, servicewomen in the military, Afghani women organizing under military occupation, women in Asian multinational sneaker factors, privileged diplomatic wives and women leaders. In this way, she is able to show the connections between the so-called powerful and powerless and how international relations depend on particular configurations of gendered social relations.

New questions and questions that challenge familiar approaches are related. In Enloe's case and that of other feminist researchers, engagement, experience, and events in the world, both personal and vicarious, can reveal new research questions. We encourage researchers to share ideas with fellow travelers, to attend seminars, discussion fora, meetings and conferences, to read and be attentive to a wide range of scholarly and non-scholarly sources and media, including Internet blogs and publications, newspapers, newsletters, and journals, and to talk with classmates and friends outside of class. We want our imagination to be sparked, to be prompted to see new phenomena and in new ways, and often this happens in unexpected places and times. If we put ourselves in many different spaces, relevant to our general areas of interest, then we are more likely to be inspired with a question than if we sit isolated in a university library. James Scott, a political scientist with close affinities with anthropology and feminism, is even more categorical about reading beyond your discipline:

> If half of your reading is not *outside* the confines of [your discipline], you are risking extinction along with the rest of the subspecies. Most of the notable innovations in the discipline have come in the form of insights, perspectives, concepts, and paradigms originating elsewhere. Reading exclusively within the discipline is to risk reproducing orthodoxies or, at the very least, absorbing innovations far from the source. We would do well to emulate the hybrid vigor of the plant and animal breeding world (Evans *et al.* 1996: 36).

A broad literature review that includes scholarly and non-scholarly sources, as we will see in the next chapter, may also help to illuminate your research questions. Working through the Exercise on the book's website www.palgrave.com/methodology/doingfeministresearch is also intended to help you craft your questions.

Researchers often ask whether it is better to choose a research question on a current hot topic or on a less-studied issue or topic (see Chapter six for a discussion of real world constraints in determining your question). If it's a hot topic it is also likely to be a crowded field. "The competitors will be more numerous and the competition less interesting than in truly unfamiliar terrain. Unless you have something original to say about them, you may well be advised to avoid topics styled of central interest to the discipline ... someone else may have already made the decisive and exciting contribution" (Przeworski and Salomon 1995). For feminist researchers it is more often the case that few people have researched your topic and that you, whether working in a class or independently, will need to generate new hypotheses and uncover new sources of information to research it. Our advice in either case is to choose a "fresh" question – particularly if the topic has an emerging literature. If your instinct leads you to a problem far from the mainstream, follow it. Most breakthroughs in scholarly research and feminist knowledge broadly have come from this kind of trailblazing and such papers are more fun to research and write.

Good Questions have Surprising Answers

We also suggest choosing a question that is truly vexing to you, to which the answer is not obvious to you or others. You will be much more likely to sustain your research over a relatively long period of time if you really are curious about the possible answers to your question. If you are genuinely surprised by your provisional research findings as you are immersed in the research process you will be much more motivated to complete the research and share your findings with your audiences. Recounting his research on transnational/transversal practices of dissent by powerless citizens of authoritarian regimes Roland Bleiker (2003: 419–20) acknowledges his surprise that "seemingly mundane everyday forms of resistance" repeated over time were ultimately more powerful mechanisms of change than the often heroic, masculine street demonstrations projected around the world by the global media. Sasha Gear (2005) set out to explore how the rules, codes and meanings surrounding sexual practices in prisons in a South African province reproduce gendered identities. She found that male prisoners negotiate sex and gender, by both vehemently asserting oppressive power claims through "outside" and "inside" hegemonic masculinities, and also subverting them.

We have also encountered surprises in each of our own research projects. In my study of globalization and post-socialist transformations I (Jacqui) found feminist activism in strange and unexpected places, for instance, on the pages of localized versions of foreign multinational women's magazines such as Cosmopolitan and romantic novella such as Harlequin (True 2003). This "discovery" led me (Jacqui) to question some of my own assumptions about feminism, and this questioning had theoretical implications for my understanding of the gendered opportunities as well as constraints made possible by global markets. Ask yourself: do you expect to be surprised by your research or what are we going to learn as a result of your research that we do not know now? Identifying the key research questions of a project focuses and structures the project – making it manageable to get started with the research (see step five in the practical exercise on the website, http://www.palgrave.com/methodology/doingfeministresearch). It is a crucial preliminary step. Only once you have identified the parts of the argument you want to make can you think through theoretical approaches and methods that will help you develop and frame the research you will actually do. This advice on the ingredients and sources of inspiration for good research questions are summarized in the practical exercise on the website and in Box 4.2.

Box 4.2 Checklist for a good question

Our version of a checklist for a good question is inspired by Baglione (2006):

- My question is *vexing* to me.
- My question is (or should be) *interesting* to me, scholars, policymakers, and citizens, and interesting enough to sustain my interest throughout the life of the project.
- My question is (or should be) *important* to me, scholars, policymakers, and people.
- My question is *fresh* (whether new or addressing a familiar topic in a challenging way).
- My question relates to *one key concept* or theme. I can state my question clearly in one sentence, and very clearly in one paragraph.
- My question can be *plausibly answered* in my time-frame.
- The answer(s) to my question might be *surprising* to scholars, policymakers, people, and me.

What is Distinctive about Feminist Questions?

In the preceding section, to simplify a bit in order to focus on how to engage the challenge of coming up with a question that is worth arguing, we said that feminist-informed questions could be "new" or "challenging." Not all good questions are feminist questions of course, but in this section we consider some of the questions feminists have asked and ask: "What makes them distinctly feminist?" Feminist research is often distinguished by its feminist research questions and conceptualization (Ackerly and Attanasi 2009), but in this book we have been arguing that feminist research is most distinctively recognized by its research ethic, more explicitly, by the methodological implications that follow from a commitment to a research ethic. Many questions that are best researched guided by a feminist research ethic may not have a substantively feminist concern and may not be about gender relations or women, for instance. In Box 4.3, feminist scholar Ann Tickner engages in an exchange with Robert Keohane and discusses among other things the very different ways feminist and non-feminist international relations scholars go about constructing research questions.

How does attention to power, relationality, boundaries, and our situatedness as researchers lead to research questions? All of these are at play when feminist researchers confront the question of how to recognize themselves in fields founded on the exclusion of women and women's experiences. One way feminist scholars have addressed this dilemma has been by suggesting new questions that put the effects on women of power, relationality, bound-

Box 4.3 "You just don't understand": the Tickner-Keohane exchange in International Relations

Feminist scholars are often asked by non-feminist colleagues: "what is your research programme?" or "why does gender have anything to do with . . . ?" And "how can feminism solve real world problems such as . . . ?"

The topic of these oft-asked questions was the starting point for a dialogue between a feminist and an oft-cited neoliberal institutionalist scholar of international relations that took place in *International Studies Quarterly*, the flagship journal of the International Studies Association of North America.

Tickner: Feminist and IR research questions reflect different realities and ontologies: for IR the universe consists of unitary states in an asocial, anarchic international environment, whereas for feminists individual and groups are embedded in and changed by social relations. They also reflect different epistemologies: feminists construct knowledge from marginalized and previously not heard, unfamiliar voices and issues and use this knowledge to challenge the core assumptions of the IR discipline. (1997: 617)

Keohane: Why don't feminists specify their theoretical hypotheses in ways that are testable and falsifiable with evidence? (1998: 197). For instance, hypotheses about the affect of gender hierarchy on inter-state behavior? Or about whether domestic gendered inequalities extend to transnational relations, e.g. foreign military bases, multi-national corporations, aid programs, etc. Gender could provide a new explanatory variable.

Tickner: "You just don't understand." Because of the power inequalities between mainstream and feminist IR we are skeptical of your efforts to label some of our work more compatible than others. We need to take *each* other up on the other's terms rather than apply the standards of one group to the other (1997: 619).

Keohane: "Questions are not enough, feminist IR scholars will need to provide answers that will convince others – including those not ideologically predisposed to being convinced" (1998: 197).

Tickner: Conversations such as these will not be successful until their legitimacy is recognized as part of the discipline (1997: 630).

aries, and situatedness onto the research agenda of our fields. In the most simplistic formulation – the searching for "Her-story" – this sort of feminist scholarship puts new content, content about women, into our fields. It is hard to construct the experience of women from archival records that were not created by men who were interested in the experience of women. It is particularly hard because, women were not writing much of their own history, those men who were writing history were not writing about women, and those who later collected the artifacts of past civilizations were not interesting in the artifacts that women used (household objects), but rather were interested in the public buildings for politics, markets, and cultural displays.

Of course, some invisible women's experience is not historical but contemporary. As with doing archival and archaeological work to recover a lost past, uncovering women's experiences in the present can also require methodological innovation as much of the data necessary to understand women's contemporary lives are not visible or readily visible (Roth 2004).

As difficult as these kinds of work are, feminists have made great strides in recovering women's experiences, past and present. A related set of questions emerge from our observing this history and present: feminists seek to understand how and why women are devalued and disempowered across societies, cultures and history relative to men, and how this situation of inequality and injustice can be changed. Often gender is introduced as an analytic tool both to explain the absence or neglect of women, addressing a "why" question, i.e. "why are there so few women" possibly with an epistemology that assumes we can disaggregate causes from their effects and a statistical research design that explores common patterns of factors affecting women's political representation (see Tremblay 2007). Gender analysis may also be used to formulate "how" research questions that seek to gain a particular vantage point on the nature of social and political institutions and are often explored with a post-positivist epistemology (standpoint, postcolonial, postmodern) and ethnographic or in-depth single case study research designs. "How" questions that address how the political reality of male dominance is produced and reproduced may include asking *how* gender constructs are deployed in different contexts, *how* gender operates under specific historical conditions, and how therefore, to transform *how* gender works at all levels (see Garwood 2005).

Feminist research questions also ask "how" gender inequality and injustice affect a whole range of non-gender specific social and political issues, thus reframing them as feminist issues. For example, consider Brooke's research question: Is there a theory of human rights that can respect diversity and obligate us to action? (Ackerly 2008a). This question is inspired by reflexive feminist theory and its attentiveness to cultural diversity but also by the practical need emanating from global women's movements for a human rights framework that recognizes women's rights as integral to human rights.

It is posed to enable connections between different communities of scholars, activists and policymakers. Carol Gilligan's work on moral development and Ester Boserup's work on economic development illustrate how mainstream research questions and related policy practices can be reconceived through a feminist lens.

Further, understanding the ways in which social, political, economic, and cultural experiences of women are different relative to men, feminists ask, what does understanding these differences do for our understanding of important social, political, economic, and cultural phenomena such as globalization, democracy, governance, religion, etc. For example, consider Jacqui's research questions in light of the transformations from communism in Eastern Europe: First, "how" (i.e. through what processes) are changing gender relations shaping and being shaped by marketization and liberalization? And second, do these new forms of economic and cultural globalization open up spaces for women's empowerment and feminist politics? These questions are inspired by an understanding of gender as a social construction, which is constructed differently across place and time with different implications for women and men's lives.

Often plainly-stated, feminist research questions can be *telling* for the power relations they reveal. In their collaboratively written, *Undivided Rights*, Jael Silliman, Marlene Gerber Fried, Loretta Ross and Elena Gutiérrez begin with an account of their connection to their subject:

> We are not dispassionate observers of our subject – from the outset this book was conceived of as a political project. We set out to "lift up" the voices and the achievements of women of color who are transforming the struggle for sexual and reproductive health and rights into a movement for reproductive justice (Silliman *et al.* 2004: vii).

Their principle finding does not surprise them, but it has important political implications for human rights theory and women's health policy:

> Activists must be firm in their support for abortion rights, but at the same time not let abortion politics eclipse equally pressing issues such as access to health care or racial disparities in health care delivery … Only comprehensive, inclusive, and action-oriented agendas will redirect the reproductive and sexual rights movement in a way that is relevant and compelling to the diversity of women who constitute America today (Silliman *et al.* 2004: 304).

Not only do feminists pose "new" and "challenging," "how" and "why" questions for the mainstream of their fields, but also they pose important questions to each other. The preceding example from Silliman et al. is one such example, but these questions can be theoretical and methodological as well. Feminist questions may be concerned with theoretical debates within feminism and with the tools of feminist research, both of which are questions about empowering feminism as a field of knowledge.

How do we judge a good feminist-informed research question? Here a feminist research ethic is your guide. Whatever sort of problem you are pursuing a good question from a feminist perspective will have both normative and practical relevance and be attentive to all of the forms of hierarchy that determine "relevance." It should be attentive to possible marginalization and silencing and the broader context in which the question is posed. These contextual considerations are not only the politics surrounding the substance of the question, but also the politics of the disciplinary context in which it is studied. The researcher should consider her relationships with the question, those affected by topics related to the question, and with others who are studying aspects of the issue from within her home field and in cognate disciplines, particularly other feminists.

The question should be fresh, making strange what was previously familiar (e.g. Harding 1991; Kronsell 2006). The question should be openly but not naively asked such that the researcher can maintain a self-reflexive stance given the likelihood that the question will change its form as it is pursued through research. In addition, a research question informed by a feminist research ethic should allow the researcher to reach out beyond disciplinary debates to broader knowledge-based communities to address shared, everyday concerns and to make visible gendered power relations and the status of women in the process.

We should always ask ourselves the purpose of our research and who will benefit from our efforts to ask and address this research question. Ian Shapiro observes that "in discipline after discipline the flight from reality has been so complete that the academics have all but lost sight of what they claim is their object of study" (Shapiro 2005: 2). Feminist scholars are not immune to "losing touch" but one of our hallmarks is to keep our feet firmly on the ground with a sense of accountability to a larger constituency and social movement.

Answers to research questions informed by a feminist research ethic are not predetermined by the normative commitments of a feminist theorist to gender justice any more than a democratic peace scholar's normative commitment to peace influences her findings about democracy and conflict. Indeed, it is possible to start with a feminist question and complete your research with an answer that extends beyond feminist theory, synthesizing feminist and non-feminist traditions. For example, Lynn Savery probes why gender inequalities persist in the world despite the existence of an international convention on the elimination of all forms of discrimination against women (CEDAW) and why these CEDAW commitments fail to filter down to states and local communities (Savery 2006). Part of her answer to this question is a constructivist analysis of state identity and its gender-biased nature. Savery identifies the gendered identity of the state as the most significant barrier to CEDAW's diffusion based on a comparative institutional analysis and critical realist epistemology (see also Archer 1995).

Situating Feminist Questions

Feminist research departs from many of the norms of mainstream fields. This makes it vitally important to communicate and justify your research in the mainstream field as well as in a feminist context on the terms that you choose. As Tickner (1997: 629) points out (and Box 4.3 illustrates moreover), the power inequalities between feminist and conventional perspectives in a field generally mean that feminists cannot afford to be as ignorant of the mainstream as conventional perspectives are of feminism. In the practical exercise on the website http://www.palgrave.com/methodology/doingfeministresearch we share some advice on how to situate your research within a broader field. It is a matter of becoming very familiar with the scholarship in your field from a range of perspectives and actively choosing your entry points, guided by a feminist research ethic. Using the criteria suggested by a feminist research ethic – attentiveness to power, boundaries, relationships, and our situatedness as researchers – will help you to identify the perspectives and conversations which are conceptually and ethically most compelling.

While a feminist may wish to challenge the norms by which her discipline has engaged with a question or may wish to challenge the norms and disciplinary expectations of her course instructor, she must do so in a way that conforms to professional norms so that she does not alienate herself from her field while she tries to contribute to it and so that she can do well in the class. Therefore, your research paper or proposal will need a "situating the research" section in which you:

● review what is known about the puzzle in the field;
● assess the strengths and weaknesses of the literature that exists on the topic; in a class context, your course instructor may expect you to focus on the literature in the syllabus, or at least to *include* it in your broader survey; and
● identify the significance of gaps in your field's knowledge such that your research should be conducted (and funded).

In this section, the researcher displays her knowledge of the field *and* her ability to think critically about it and to improve it. Further, this section makes obvious to her supervisor or granting organization why this project is important. For a granting organization or job talk, the justification will be framed more broadly, for a more specialized audience, more narrowly (see Chapter thirteen on writing and presenting your research).

One strategy for situating your research question is to think of it on a continuum between problem-solving and critical theory approaches (Cox with Sinclair 1996). At one end of the continuum you identify a problem or puzzle in existing society and politics and aim to provide practical knowledge that can address that problem in the short to medium term. Much policy analysis takes this approach and one of the limitations of problem-solving questions is that they are relatively less attentive to deeper causal factors. At the other end of the continuum, taking a critical theory approach, you are critical of the existing society and politics, questioning the research questions of mainstream fields and the way problems and issues are framed by dominant actors. Such an approach is wide-ranging and often involves taking a historical or meta-theoretical perspective. As Keohane notes in the context of the scholarly exchange with Tickner discussed in Box 4.3, there are trade-offs made in the decision to locate your research question on this continuum: "the more critical and wide-ranging an author's [research question], the more difficult it is to do comparative, empirical analysis" (1998: 196). Many feminist questions are on the end of the continuum that worries Keohane. Not all are, however (e.g., Caprioli 2000, 2003, 2004; Caprioli and Boyer 2001; Joachim 2003; Kinsella 2005; True and Mintrom 2001). As we previously noted, some "why" questions that seek to explain social and political phenomena and informed by a feminist research ethic are particularly suited to comparative, small n or large n statistical research designs (see also Chapters seven and eleven).

Where is your feminist research question positioned on this continuum? What is the trade-off in pursuing the more critical approach, or a more problem-solving approach? Guided by a feminist research ethic, we can be self-reflexive about these ethical choices, and choose a research question that is more or less problem-solving, more or less critical by design.

Conclusion

In a feminist research project, the literature review does not reveal a gap ("*lacuna*" if you want a fancy Latin word) in the literature, but rather lays out the intellectual debts of the author, her principle interlocutors, and a landscape of opportunity for exploration. We should be looking not to fill niches in an existing mainstream field but to open up horizons, whole new landscapes for exploration and expose canyons of neglect in conventional research. Beyond each puzzle lie so many more.

Choosing and framing a research question is a crucial anticipated deliberative moment in research design. Asking the right question is at least as important as how we answer it. Applying a feminist research ethic, a scholar can make political and ethical dimensions explicit as she develops her question.

In the next chapter, we discuss how theory and conceptualization can illuminate our research questions and puzzles. The literature review in particular, is a way of illuminating a puzzle by establishing what is and what is not known about the puzzle. It opens up a greater range of research questions and agendas for exploration and different interpretations of them. Importantly, it can serve as yet another intended deliberative moment to rethink and reframe your research question.

Selected Sources for Further Reading

Enloe, Cynthia H. 2004. *The Curious Feminist: Searching for Women in a New Age of Empire*. Berkeley, CA: University of California Press.

Harding, Sandra. 1991. *Whose Science? Whose Knowledge? Thinking from Women's Lives*. Ithaca: Cornell University Press.

Mason, Jennifer. 2002. *Qualitative Researching*. London: Sage.

Knopf, Jeffrey W. 2006. "Doing a Literature Review." *PS: Political Science and Politics* 39, 1: 127–32.

Przeworski, Adam, and Frank Salomon. 1995. *The Art of Writing Proposals: Some Candid Suggestions for Applicants to Social Science Research Council Competitions*. New York: Social Science Research Council.

Chapter 5

Theory and Conceptualization, including the Literature Review

Introduction

This chapter outlines the process of conceptualizing your research question in a theoretical context; that is, in the context of debates and conversations that other scholars are having in your field(s) of study. The conceptualization of your research is *not* a process of trailing through the literature in your field(s) without a sense of direction or purpose. It is crucially important that researching your question contributes to broader knowledge, and that it be of interest to others, even those who are researching very different topics. Done well, your research will be considered; but it will be much more likely to gain attention if it is clear exactly to which piece in a bigger field or inter-disciplinary-wide puzzle it contributes. You need to be able to clearly answer the question, put rather crassly but aptly by one of our former course instructors, "why bother" with this research?

An illuminating literature review is particularly important if you are writing on a topic that can be approached from any number of disciplines or theo-retical angles. Your assignment in the "literature review" section of your project is to lay out the theoretical and conceptual bedrock of your project by situating it in the literatures of your field. What this means for your research may be best illustrated by thinking about the case of an *inductive research* project in which you expect the theoretical import of your research to be revealed through your analysis of the data. In such projects, the "literature review" section of will likely be different in the research plan before the research is done and in the final write up after the research is done (see Chapter three). For this researcher, the literature review changes because the researcher cannot (fully) know the theoretical import of her research until she has done it. Clearly, then, *many* topics can be approached from any number of perspectives and many literatures can be explicated through any number of lenses. You are in charge of those lenses. They don't come preset by a field.

Toward this end, we encourage you to engage in conceptualizing your question and your project by building on the most relevant theoretically-informed and empirical literature in your fields. We encourage you to see yourself in conversation with some of the major interlocutors in these fields and to understand your role as one of *explicating* the landscape of the field and the place of your project in it. In order to do so, you will construct a narrative of the field, which may follow that provided by others or may assert a new way of looking at the landscape of the field. For some this may be a contested account of the field; for others it will be generally recognizable to all.

Although theoretical conceptualization is by no means a linear process, to provide a useful guide in this chapter, we have broken the conceptualization process into three main steps: (1) Considering the relevant theories for your problem or question from disciplinary literatures and research subjects; (2) Developing concepts from these sources that help to make sense of your question or problem; and; (3) Synthesizing these concepts in a theoretical framework that is somewhat unique to your research.

We begin with a discussion of two types of research – theory-testing and theory-seeking – often characterized by distinctive research designs and methods i.e., quantitative versus qualitative methods. Both of these types of research involve conceptualizing your question or problem in a theoretical literature but they differ over the aim of that conceptualization; whether it is to test out and refine an existing theoretical framework or to generate a new theoretical framework in the course of the research process. We discuss the implications of the differences in these types of research; however, we recommend the same three steps in the conceptualization process for both theory-testing and theory-seeking research.

Getting Started

So now you have a vexing, interesting, important, fresh, focused, and answerable question that either breaks new ground or challenges ways of approaching familiar terrain. You are anticipating unanticipated moments. You are ready to think about these in an ethical way (attentive to power, attentive to boundaries, attentive to relationships, and self-reflectively). You have a sense of the theoretical and empirical work related to your question. Now you are ready to chart the scope and depth of the theoretical work that will enable you to contextualize your work in your field and show your audience what kind of contribution answering your question makes to your field.

This chapter is about making clear and informed theoretical and conceptual choices that enable you to formulate your question as a theoretical argument. This framework of contending hypothetical arguments sets out the relationships between the important concepts that are raised by your question. The standards for theorizing are high. You should aim to create an argument that does at least some of the following things:

- provides a contextual understanding of your question;
- reveals patterns and linkages between themes and concepts that are important to the question;
- has explanatory power;
- has consistency and internal coherence; and
- offers the scope for engagement with contending theories necessary to demonstrate the significance, and meaning of the project.

The list of what we might hope for from a theory is daunting if you take it as a check list. Don't take it as a checklist. Instead, use this list as an invitation to consider what *you* expect from a theory and what you hope a theory will *do*.

Many things can make your research practice *not* conform to your theoretical argument. In Chapter three we showed that the research *process* itself may make it hard for you to research following the theoretical argument you develop as part of a research plan. In Chapter six we discuss those politics, constraints, and opportunities for research that emerge from considerations that are not specifically related to your question. Even more elementary, in social science, no theoretical argument can be fully actualized in a research plan. As we discuss later in this chapter (and in Chapter eight), in social science we know up front that we cannot gather data that perfectly match our conceptualizations.

So we are not looking for – or striving to author – "the" theory for our question. Let's be more modest. We are looking for ways of understanding our question as it relates to other questions. Our theoretical research enables us to have informed reflection about *what kind of problem or puzzle* our question poses. Our theoretical reflection will yield *one* way of understanding our question as it relates to others in our social and political time. Theoretical reflection is a deliberative moment to which we continue to return as long as our question interests us.

Although theoretical reflection is not in practice able to be isolated from other stages of the research process, focused reflection on the theory of your question is valuable for you as a *researcher* in order to make conscious theoretical choices that are respectful of the range of approaches used by others in your chosen discipline (and cognate disciplines) and in your research site. In this chapter we focus on the challenges of theoretical reflection itself and on the related challenges of conceptualizing your own theoretical argument.

Theory-Testing versus Theory-Seeking Research

Theory and theorizing are themselves concepts and in many fields they are contested concepts. Thus, contestation can be *between competing accounts of the purpose of theory* as well as *between competing theories* that share a similar philosophy of inquiry. Therefore, we take a moment here to conceptualize theory and theoretical practice: what is theory, where does it come from, and what is its role in our research? What are we doing when we theorize? While there are many ways to define theory, we offer a classification that is useful for determining the relationship between your theory and your research design. In particular we discuss two conceptualizations of theory and its role in research that reflect and cover much actual research in the political and social sciences. We refer to these two approaches broadly as (1) *theory-testing research*, and (2) *theory-seeking research*, either of which can apply to feminist research questions. Whether we follow one or the other of these approaches to theorizing depends to a large extent on the nature of our research question.

Just as there are different theoretical lenses, there are also different approaches to theorizing. The theory-testing approach follows the view that the research process is *conceptually linear*, even though unanticipated moments throughout the research process send us back to theoretical reflection (or even to ask a different question) and render the *actual* research practice dynamic and non-linear. The theory-seeking approach aims to understand and interpret a given phenomenon using conceptual tools developed while reflecting *on the phenomenon* in question. This approach is an *explicitly non-linear* approach to theorizing.

The first concept of theory is more familiar to positivist researchers. According to this concept, researchers survey existing literature for theoretical approaches in their discipline (and related disciplines) that may offer insight about how to think about their question. They interrogate each theory for its understanding of key concepts related to their project, and restate their question as a theoretical argument consisting of different theoretical hypotheses that suggest different relationships among those concepts. This is the *theoretical argument of the question*. In theory-testing research, this model or set of hypotheses must be tested empirically to answer the research question and to contribute to a richer explanation or understanding of the subject. In order to be able to test your theoretical argument, however, its concepts, and the relationships between them, need to be approximated by real-world *proxies* that can be measured. We call this specification of the research question the *operationalization* of concepts, which we discuss in Chapter eight. Thus, theory-testing research requires developing a theoretical argument of your question *prior* to generating your research plan, as the centre axis of the wheel in Figure 5.1 shows. This argument may be refined

Figure 5.1 *Theory-testing research: spokes and wheels model*

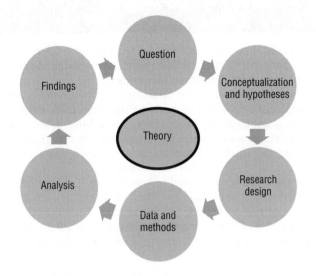

as you analyze your data and return to your theoretical argument to assess its validity in interpreting your findings.

Theory-testing research can use any range of research designs and methods, involving quantitative or qualitative data. But it is true that the frustrations with the boundaries of theory-testing quantitative research led to the "qualitative revolution" in which alternative ways of thinking about theory *and* methodology emerged and remain in productive tension (Denzin and Lincoln 2005). Box 5.1 gives an example of a feminist research question that is conceived as a set of hypothetical theories to be tested out in a statistical research design.

The second concept of theory refers to how researchers derive theory endogenously from within empirical research. In this practice, researchers *generate* rather than test theoretical hypotheses. Seeking to break away from existing theoretical accounts of the problem in question, feminists using this approach most often work within a broad theoretical paradigm that includes influences from postpositivist, constructivist-interpretive, critical, poststructuralist, queer, cultural studies, postcolonial, and/or race theories. Such a multiperspectival theoretical starting point does not generate a single hypothetical model of the problem in question (or a single family of hypotheses) but rather proposes culturally, historically, and analytically informed hypotheses about why the problem may be difficult to study and how one might go about studying it.

Ontologically, this second concept of theory assumes a multiply constructed world and comprehension of its social and political phenomena. Theory-seeking researchers conceive of the researcher as inseparable from the

Box 5.1 Feminist theory-testing research on gender equality

One example of theory-testing feminist research on gender equality examines patterns of global diffusion of gender equality mechanisms, such as state institutions for mainstreaming gender analysis and electoral gender quotas for representative candidates. From political science and international relations literatures this research considers a range of existing theoretical explanations for the patterns of diffusion of gender-attentive institutions across countries with different national gender structures and different relationships to international gender justice norms over time. It explicitly tests these different theories – coming from sociology, political science and international relations fields – against one another using a multivariate, event history model made plausible by qualitative illustration and process-tracing (True and Mintrom 2001). See Chapter ten for discussion of these common analytical techniques; also Box 8.2 on Operationalizing gender equality and Key Concept 10.2 on process-tracing.

social and political world she studies. This theoretical approach can be combined with many methodological tools. There are many approaches to this kind of theorizing and this form of theorizing is an area of feminist trailblazing (Benson and Nagar 2006; Hesse-Biber and Piatelli 2007). What they all share are research maps that will follow a less linear path than theory-testing research (from theoretical argument of their question to research design to data collection to analysis). In theory-seeking research each research map will be somewhat unique; marked by many anticipated and unanticipated moments for theoretical reflection and *reformulations* of the research question. In theory-seeking research we seek to understand a phenomenon using concepts developed while reflecting on the concrete phenomenon under study rather than being limited to the use of established concepts developed in the study of other questions and phenomena.

The feedback loop in figure 5.2 shows the circular but progressive nature of the theorizing process. It may be possible to publish at different stages of the project, not just after the project is over, and it is typical to consider any "last word" or "final" draft to be a temporal claim not a conceptual claim, provisionally, not universally true. We may finish *our* work, but *the work* on the subject is on-going. In theory-seeking research, a preliminary theoretical framework is intended to identify conceptual categories and processes that can then be used in considering how to collect and analyze data. Data collection and analysis may occur in several phases, continually building on theoretical insights gained at each stage of research. Box 5.2 below illustrates just one example of feminist research on gender equality that is theory-seeking

Figure 5.2   *Theory-seeking research: the feedback loop*

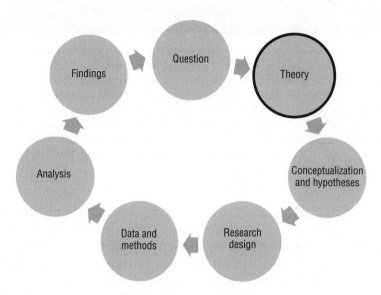

because its purpose was to explore changing concepts and meanings of gender equality in policy.

While it is common to view theory-testing and theory-seeking research as opposed because they have often drawn on different theoretical paradigms, these need not be seen as conflicting or oppositional approaches. Theoretical reflection occurs throughout the research process in both theory-testing and theory-seeking approaches as Figures 5.1 and 5.2 illustrate. Even if you choose a theory-seeking approach you will still need to have done the work of surveying the theoretical landscape through the secondary scholarly literature prior to your empirical research. Moreover, you will need to draw upon that work even as you generate new concepts and analyze your data in the field (and consider why and how existing theories cannot conceptualize adequately the phenomena you are studying, thus contesting and reformulating them). Certainly, you will also draw on your survey of the theoretical landscape when you write up your project – both at the project proposal stage and in your final publication of findings.

Theory-testing is familiar to many using quantitative methods and to those who have argued that qualitative work should proceed along the same models as most quantitative work – that is, using a literature-based approach to developing theory and testing hypotheses (King *et al.* 1994). The theory-seeking approach has many practitioners; a few key texts to guide researchers in this way of theorizing are listed at the end of this chapter. For feminists, the concepts and hypotheses generated in theory-seeking research can be used to contest established theories and concepts and their applica-

Box 5.2 Theory-seeking research: Verloo, Lombardo, and Meier on gender equality

One example of theory-seeking feminist research on gender equality considers how gender equality policies construct gendered representations and concepts of politics and challenge accepted social and political understandings of gender. It aims to understand better not the diffusion of gender equality (see Box 5.1) but the underlying concept and changing meanings of "gender equality" articulated in different European countries and in the European Union with varying gender structures, policies, laws, memberships, and cultural norms (Verloo 2005b; Lombardo and Meier 2006).

tions; and they can be later tested as explanatory theories in theory-driven research designs. However, unlike theory-testing scholars, theory-seeking scholars cannot generally announce that they are using a "feminist" or "queer" theory approach without providing an account of their philosophy of inquiry *and* methodology for theorizing because feminist and queer theories do not determine the appropriate methodology for inquiry into "their" questions.

Feminist scholars employ both approaches to theorizing as shown in Boxes 5.1 and 5.2 on research on gender equality. Both kinds of theorizing are enhanced by a feminist research ethic but there are at least three reasons why a theory-testing research model might leave a feminist researcher wanting additional theoretical models. First, though a question may have been previously researched from a non-feminist perspective, the theoretical perspectives deployed may not have included ways of conceptualizing multiple and dynamic relationships of power. Although there are many theories of democracy, some of these have been developed without attention to the ways in which gender or gendered racial hierarchies condition our understandings of democracy (see the discussion of feminist challenges to the concept of democracy and its import in empirical research in Box 5.3). Second, a question may be approachable from a range of theoretical perspectives, each with *a priori* conceptual assumptions (often reifying gender norms) that go unchallenged by the way that each theory understands key concepts. Third, the theoretical options may not cohere with research subject-participants' understandings, suggesting that the theoretical contribution may be to offer a new competing theoretical perspective rather than a modest reconstruction or verification of an existing theory or theories.

A feminist research ethic can help you conceptualize your research question because theorizing and conceptualizing are opportunities for power, exclusion, marginalization, relationships, and your own situatedness to influence the entire trajectory of your research. So, it is important that we

> ## Box 5.3 Feminist perspectives on the study of democracy
>
> In a review essay on gender and the study of democracy, Georgina Waylen (2010) identifies the implications of competing conceptualizations of "democracy" on the study of the history of democracy.
>
> Paxton (2000) observes the disconnect between conceptual definitions of democracy, which note the importance of including all adult citizens, men and women, and the operationalization of democracy in empirical research, where countries may be coded as democratic in datasets although that may not have extended the suffrage to women (at least 50 percent of the population). This gendered disconnect has implications for studies about democracy.
>
> Paxton demonstrates that if women's as well as men's suffrage was made a fundamental criterion, democracy datasets would look very different. Huntington's (1991) three waves of democratization, moreover, would have to be rethought. As Waylen (2010) argues, [w]omen are therefore often excluded from the measurement of democracies even if they are implicitly included in the ostensible criteria used to judge whether a country is democratic or not.

reflect on these foundations broadly. We theorize so we are sure that we have a complete understanding of our theoretical resources and so that we do not by omission practice a form of epistemological power or bias.

Using a feminist research ethic to identify and interrogate the range of relevant theoretical perspectives, you may find that *all* existing theories *and* efforts to theorize from the scholarly literature are incomplete or unsatisfactory. You may realize that *your question* requires an approach for discovering the theoretical insights of your subject-participants or for theorizing from the context of the phenomena you are studying. However, choosing to use a theory-testing or theory-seeking approach to research is not itself a feminist research choice. Rather, each approach raises a different set of questions.

First Steps: Theories for the Problem

Most political and social researchers are engaged in ongoing theoretical debates about their subjects of study – what we referred to in the last chapter as the "great questions of the day" or the big ideas. Whether you are researching for a class, your dissertation, or a publishable article or book, theoretical debates engage scholars and broader publics because they resonate outside of any one discipline or community (Evans *et al.* 1996: 5). Any given research question can be approached from a range of different perspectives involving different theoretical assumptions. Your question may have been approached by many in your field or by people in other fields, but not your field. Regardless of how your question is positioned vis à vis your field, your job is to find the theoretical tools for conceptualizing your question in ways amenable to research.

In theory-testing research our questions and puzzles typically come from engagement with disciplinary literatures whereas for theory-seeking research the influences extend broadly, even into the conceptual worlds of research subject-participants.

Reviewing Disciplinary Literatures

Disciplinary literatures provide theoretical resources for conceptualizing the research questions or puzzles that emerge from a literature and usually suggest one or more hypotheses to be tested. A feminist research ethic ensures we attend to and sometimes challenge power and epistemological privilege, theoretical boundaries of particular approaches, and our relationships to various theoretical approaches. It prompts us to ask what theoretical assumptions are implicit or explicit in the conceptualization of our question/puzzle. It expects us to acknowledge and investigate these assumptions rather than ignore or leave them unchallenged. For example, in my (Jacqui) article on transnational networks and policy diffusion with Michael Mintrom we make explicit the feminist inspiration for our research question about the rapid diffusion of gender mainstreaming institutions across more than 100 countries. This question had received scant attention outside of feminist circles. Our intention in this research project was to test out the theoretical assumption that transnational feminist networks have affected institutional and policy change. Box 5.4 summarizes this example of theory-testing feminist research.

A feminist research ethic also requires us to take seriously our commitment to reflexivity. Such reflection means reviewing the theoretical approaches of all related schools of thought in your field and in cognate disciplines as well, including those that are least familiar to you and to which you may not be initially sympathetic. Depending on your education and previous study, you may already be aware of all of the appropriate theoretical perspectives to consider. Cross-referencing by looking up the sources in the bibliographies of works in your bibliography, by asking for help in identifying texts and sharing what you have already read is one way to expand the theoretical perspectives that you consider.

Interestingly, disciplinary constraints on your theoretical work are not usually of the limiting sort. Rather, they obligate you to consider certain literatures in order to be able to connect your work to the field at large. By referencing discussions in the literature, you invite participants in *those* discussions into your project. The more narrowly you define your literature;

> ## Box 5.4 Transnational networks and policy diffusion: True and Mintrom make the case for gender mainstreaming
>
> "How can we account for the global diffusion of remarkably similar policy innovations across widely differing nation-states?" (2001: 27). In an era characterized by heightened globalization and increasingly radical state restructuring, this question has become especially acute. Scholars of international relations offer a number of theoretical explanations for the cross-national convergence of ideas, institutions, and interests. True and Mintrom examine the proliferation of state bureaucracies for *gender mainstreaming*. These institutions seek to integrate a gender-equality perspective across all areas of government policy. They are now in place in over 100 countries. As a policy innovation, the speed with which these institutional mechanisms have been adopted by the majority of national governments is unprecedented. They argue that transnational networks composed largely of non-state actors (notably women's international nongovernmental organizations and the United Nations) have been the primary forces driving the diffusion of gender mainstreaming.
>
> Analyzing 157 nation-states from 1975 to 1998, True and Mintrom assess the extent to which various national and transnational factors have affected the timing and the type of the institutional changes these states have made. Their findings on the diffusion of gender-mainstreaming mechanisms support theories that highlight the role played by transnational networks, in particular by the transnational feminist movement, in bringing about international and state-level policy change (True and Mintrom 2001).

the more narrowly you delimit your audience. By exploring the literatures that audiences familiar with your topic would expect you to engage, you will have a greater skill set for reaching a range of audiences (on this point, see also chapter thirteen). If you work in an intellectually parochial space, you will need to frame your research question so that it moves from expected theoretical starting places. In either case, disciplinary constraints on appropriate literatures are an opportunity for improving your scholarship.

Engaging with Conceptual Worlds of Research Subject-Participants

As we consider our research question from different theoretical perspectives, we may also engage politically with the conceptual worlds of our subject-participants. Not all theoretical insights will come from reviews of disciplinary literature. As Richa Nagar recounts, a subject-participant may specifically ask you to consider non-academic theoretical accounts or conceptualizations of your problem. A woman in one of the Bundeli grass-roots organizations she was studying said to her: "[Suppose] you tell my story in a way that makes no sense at the conceptual level to me or my community, why would we care about what you have to say about my life?" (2002: 184). If a research subject-participant does not speak to you, how might you find such insights? In some fields you may be able to find the theoretical insights of subject-participants from their own or others' published accounts of their ideas. For others, to include such insight might require its own research project. We aim to generate new theories and hypotheses from further engagement with subject-participants.

In my (Brooke's) project on human rights, the process of reviewing theories led me to seek theoretical insights not from further immersion in the scholarly literature where there was a fairly narrow view of rights and for which the boundaries of disagreement and dissent were consistent, but from women's human rights activists, who argued that their claims for human rights had local and universal moral legitimacy (Ackerly 2008a).

The process of trying on different theoretical hats compels you to engage in theoretical debate on terrain you might otherwise take as given. Through this engagement, you will identify multiple ways of approaching your question and choose the most fruitful from them. For example, in researching her question about how transnational feminist movement organizations manage intra-movement differences and build solidarities within their movement Lyndi Hewitt (2009) considered differing theoretical perspectives, including social movement resource mobilization theory, feminist theories of difference, and collective action frame theory that led her to focus on the deployment of "discursive frames" by movements.

Second Step: Conceptualization of the Problem

Once you have a list of related theories from your field and cognate fields, the next step is to consider how these theories conceptualize the building blocks of the question you are asking. We cannot avoid conceptualization so we must do it with attention to the necessity and the risks of abstraction (Dever 2004: 7).

Different theories often highlight different concepts and place them at the centre of study. As Box 5.5 describes, coming from a feminist political ecology perspective, Sonalini Sapra was initially interested in the concept of "gender essentialism" in her research, but later came to focus on the concept of participatory democracy for illuminating her observations of women's environmental activist organizations.

As you chart out theories and related concepts on your research question, you will begin to have your own insights – some about concepts that are

---

Box 5.5 Sapra changes her theoretical framing

When Sonalini Sapra began her dissertation, she thought that she would study women's environmental activist organizations and their strategies. Her dissertation proposal anticipated that analysis of these organizations and their frames would contribute to the Feminist Political Ecology literature by developing a more integrated analysis of gender, environment, and material conditions. The literature review of her proposal focused on the latent gender essentialism in this literature, an essentialism that she expected the organizations to challenge through their activism.

What she found was that the organizations often practiced their own form of strategic essentialism. She also found that the organizations were developing a notion of participatory democracy that guided their own work and yet in some areas was constrained by their strategic essentialism.

Her dissertation differed from her dissertation proposal in that the final project brought the lens of participatory democracy to bear on the Feminist Political Ecology perspective, giving it a more grassroots political agenda despite the more politically ambitious goals of structural transformation. This finding competed with what she expected her research to yield, but it also gave her a concrete way in which her research could contribute to the groups' own self-analysis (2009).

---

shared, some about conceptualizations that are mutually incompatible, some about the relationship of theory to conceptualization and research. You will likely notice that some theoretical approaches borrow from other approaches and concepts that they think are valuable, often importing without examining conceptual problems along with those conceptual resources (Johnson 2002). You may decide at this point in the theorizing process that your project requires theory-seeking rather than a theory-driven approach. For instance, True and Mintrom may have judged that existing theories of transnational advocacy networks did not adequately capture the nature of feminist networking across borders and that they needed to develop new and better theories of networking by closely examining particular feminist networks active in promoting gender mainstreaming. But even if you decide to generate your theoretical framework in the process of doing research, a careful attempt to conceptualize the key aspects of your question using the language and associations that others have used will be an invaluable resource in your future effort to articulate your theory.

In theory-seeking research we move back and forth between theory and data. For me (Brooke), the process of moving back and forward between "theories" (from scholarly literatures) and "data" surfaced a key paradox: While activists struggled for justice using the language of human rights, academics argued about whether or not there were universal human rights. As I engaged in some preliminary research analyzing online discussion groups, I was further struck by the juxtaposition between the activists who asserted a theoretical grounding for human rights as universal and local and the scholarly theorists who found such assertions untenable.

In the example in Box 5.6 of research on political resistance to capitalist globalization we can see how very different theoretical conceptualizations of

---

Box 5.6 Theoretical perspectives on a key concept: resistance politics

Note that some of these are explicitly normative perspectives whereas others are explicitly, positive theoretical approaches.

NeoMarxist political economy maps material and discursive patterns of global power to understand the possible conditions for anti-capitalist resistance globally rather than the actual details of resistance or its local existence (e.g. Gills 2000).

NeoGramscian perspectives locate diverse counter-hegemonic forces within "[global] civil society" that unite to oppose class forms of oppression against the hegemony of the capitalist state and transnational business interests (e.g., Chin and Mittelman 1997; Cox with Sinclair 1996).

Poststructuralism focuses on the transitory and contingent nature of activist politics and their diverse expressions as "dissent," transversal politics, "resistances," or a "politics of alterity" that oppose all strategies that are based on a totalizing analysis of oppression, including those of "movements" (e.g., Bleiker 2000).

Constructivism theorizes new forms of political agency motivated by principled interests rather than instrumental agendas and realized through NGOs and Transnational Advocacy Networks to change and create new norms by lobbying, pressuring, and shaming international organizations and states (Keck and Sikkink 1998; Wapner 2000).

Social Movement theories conceive of individuals and groups as having a collective identity , characterized by their capacity to mobilize resources, and engaged in strategic collective action to bring about change depending on the available political and cultural opportunity structures in a given institutional context (Joachim 2003; Tarrow 2005).

Feminism focuses on the *subject* of the politics of resistance and on how resistance is enacted and expressed in multiple ways and locations; turns to the conceptual work done by subject-participants about their own condition to reveal diverse strategies and results across global-local struggles against exclusion and discrimination (Vargas 2005); conceptualizes power within movements as well as global power relations making women's and feminist movements central objects of study and subjects of knowledge with their own theories of resistance (Eschle and Maiguashca 2007: 285–6, 296; Hewitt 2009; Maiguashca 2006).

the same question are possible. As we discuss in the chapters seven through twelve, these different conceptualizations have implications for our epistemology, research design and ultimately the specific research methods we use to generate, collect, and analyze our data.

For many feminists, the shortcomings revealed by the conventional review of the disciplinary theory is that those conceptualizations that are taken as given often come from theories based on historically elite or exclusively male human subjects. Because these conceptualizations are not the terrain of debate, the impact of their conceptual assumptions on the question that *is* in question go unexamined. For instance, Box 5.3 discusses the example of democracy being conceptualized as requiring universal suffrage, but being operationalized as meaning universal *male* suffrage (see also Paxton 2000). It is crucial to acknowledge and investigate such assumptions about gender or about race, nationality, sexuality and so on, that are embedded in social science theoretical perspectives.

In theory-testing research, the meaning of concepts needs to be limited to allow for their measurement. Of course, the problems associated with biases imported from certain conceptualizations into the understanding of related concepts can lead feminist researchers to turn to theory-seeking research. However, the challenge for you as a feminist theory-testing researcher is to get clear on how each concept should be understood in the context of your project. This will allow you, at the next stage, to specify the theoretical relationship among concepts in a way that they can be tested or refined – with qualitative or quantitative data and analysis.

The challenge for theory-seeking researchers is to treat concepts as dynamic – both *synchronically* across myriad contexts at a given point in time and *diachronically* in the same context across historical time. Chapter seven discusses particular research designs that support this dynamic conceptualization.

Third Step: The Theoretical Framework for the Problem

Now that you have reviewed the theories related to your question and analyzed them for their conceptualizations of the key concepts related to your question, how would you restate your question as a question about theory – for example about democracy, global diffusion, social movements, resistance, or identity? As you attempt to do this, you will face a range of difficulties. The first is usually "where do I start?" and that depends on whether your question has a large or small secondary literature.

If you are working in an area that has been fairly well-studied, you may start by assessing how each theory might restate your question as a theoretical puzzle. Now you need to return to the empirical dimensions of your growing bibliography. Do the contending theories take into account the range of empirical work on the subject? Following the True and Mintrom example in Box 5.4, do the contending theories of international relations and policy diffusion take into account the empirical work on global women's movements and transnational feminist networks?

If you are working on a question that has been explored only minimally, which is often the case for feminist questions, the theories you are drawing upon will have a different relationship to the theoretical framework you are developing. You will need to self-consciously build from these theories. Have the theories used conceptualizations that are meaningful to your question? How could those conceptualizations be adapted to address your puzzle?

Conceptual Relationships

It is possible, but difficult, to contribute to the big questions of the day through theoretical and conceptual clarity. So many big questions are "big" precisely because they wrestle with what have come to be called *essentially contested concepts*, which we discuss further in Key Concept 5.1 (Gallie 1962). One way to contribute to theoretical clarity is to reveal conceptual over-inclusion or under-inclusion and to specify your theoretical argument in a way that doesn't replicate the conceptual confusion of others. For example, feminist political scientists ask whether women politicians represent women's interests once in political office. In so doing, they interrogate our over-inclusive and under-inclusive theoretical understandings of "representation." Moreover, this research on women's descriptive and substantive representation has suggested new hypotheses about representative models of democracy that apply to all groups and not just to women (Childs 2002, 2004; Ross 2000; Sanbonmatsu 2004).

5.1 ESSENTIALLY CONTESTED CONCEPTS

Essentially contested concepts are concepts that are *by their very nature* unstable and difficult to define or delimit (whether politically or epistemologically) such that they are, in fact, *defined* by their contested status.

By extension, they are concepts that are dynamic and always contingent. That dynamism is part of the concept's meaning and efficacy rather than a limitation as a subject of study.

Yet another approach is to extrapolate from theoretical insights developed in one context by applying the theory to your question which is articulated in a different context. Specifically, feminist scholars developed their critiques of international relations by extending two decades of feminist interdisciplinary theorizing about the state (the "capitalist" state, the "welfare" state, the "bureaucratic" state, the "security" state, and the "masculinist" state) to the global political economy. Still another approach, and one that is often a good, practical choice for a first research project, is not to come up with your own theoretical argument at all but to *use your supervisor's* (or another's) theory. In this case your innovation is to test it out with different methods or different examples. Of course, you may start there and as your project develops you make your own theoretical innovations as well (e.g., Attanasi 2008; Confortini 2009).

In all of these approaches, the strategy we suggest is to look for major "hooks" in the existing literature that you can "hang" your project on. You might choose multiple theoretical hooks, empirical hooks, or one theoretical hook. Contextualizing your research in conversation with significant theories and findings of other scholars will enrich it and ensure that you attract an audience. The more you do this, the more interesting your project will be to others, and the more likely that you will engage others, and that you will be on the frontlines rather than the sidelines of scholarly debate.

Causal Relationships

Theory-testing research not only sets out the precise conceptual relationships to be studied but specifies the *causal relationships* between the phenomena you want to study (the dependent variable) and the factors that you think influence the dependent variable (independent variables). The anticipated causal relationships between dependent and independent variables are articulated as theoretical hypotheses about your puzzle to be tested. Such a *theoretical model* is necessary for empirical research that measures the key variables and relationships as a way of testing their theoretical purchase (see chapter eight on operationalization). Returning to the True and Mintrom example in Box 5.4, we were relatively open to different explanatory theories about causal processes but had some strong hunches about transnational feminist networks as key drivers of the diffusion of gender mainstreaming. We needed to test these hunches vis-à-vis other plausible explanations suggested by political science, international relations and sociological theories.

In theory-seeking research, the process of developing theoretical understanding often involves several waves of data collection and inventing new methods to generate new data. For example, for my (Brooke) book on universal human rights through a series of interviews and instances of participation observation, I (Brooke) used theoretical reflection to develop specific methods for identifying "silent voices" not expressed in the public venues and finding "dissenting voices." Methods included *anti-snowball sampling* (discussed in chapter eight) for interviewees.

Theory and conceptualization continue through data analysis and sharing or presentation of findings, which offer further opportunities to generate theoretical meaning from data and in conversation with audiences of your work. For example, again for the human rights book, I (Brooke) sent a letter with a summary of findings along with the full manuscript and highlighted passages in which an interviewee was cited or her ideas were influential in my analysis and invited feedback on all of these.

A Feminist Research Ethic

In seeking to connect a research question to a broad range of theoretical frameworks, a feminist research ethic asks us to be attentive to the boundaries and power dynamics of disciplinary knowledge. In the contemporary academic environment, some social science research attempts to mimic natural and physical scientific research. As a result, the mainstream of many conventional disciplines demand and reward generalizable claims, encouraging scholars to leave behind the specificity of their research subjects and the contingency of their research question. By contrast, a feminist research ethic encourages scholars to conceptualize their research question from the perspective of concrete and located experiences, including the experiences of the powerless. Such reflection, does not, however, lead away from research that can be generalized across a population. Such analysis may be exactly what the powerless need!

It does, however, require some humility. Applying a feminist research ethic to guide our theoretical reflection, we should be prepared to reconceptualize our research question in light of our commitment to self-reflexivity about power, boundaries, and epistemology, and our political commitments to ending exploitation and injustice. Ara Wilson, in Box 5.7, conceives her research question differently as a result of her theorizing about the nature of sex work in the Thai emerging market economy. She considers the potential impact of her conceptualizations of sex work on her subject-participants and changes these conceptualizations as a result.

Wilson gives us one example. But there are many such examples and even more possibilities. How can you think through the implications of a feminist research ethic *for your project*?

Recall the research roadmap from chapter three. Researchers lay out their research plan that guides them in the initial stages of research, they map their process in order them to keep track of changes in the research plan as they research, and they share their findings and convey the logic of the actual research to a broader audience in their research account. How can a feminist

---

Box 5.7 Wilson reconceptualizes her research question using a feminist research ethic

Putting your research question in a theoretical context allows you to assess its effects in the real world; for instance, whether or not it creates or reinforces marginalization and othering.

Ara Wilson began her research with a question about the position of sex workers in Thailand. As she engaged in theoretical analysis she observed that Thai sex workers were "hyper-represented" in government, media, and international organizations' policy discourse. Focusing her research on sex workers alone would only serve to further stigmatize these workers in the Thai context.

Wilson recognized the discursive field in which both her research object and subject of study was embedded. As Harding and Norberg (2005) stress, "the research design should take into account the discursive field it enters; otherwise feminists risk re-inscribing dominant power relations." She reflected on her research question as she theorized its meaning and broader context, and decided the best way to study sex work in Thailand was to study it differently; alongside other local labor markets that are also feminized, including direct selling and telecommunications. In reconceptualizing her question, Ara Wilson opened up new possibilities for theorizing the relationships among gender, work, and globalization, thus making an original contribution to feminist knowledge (2004).

---

research ethic help you work through the process of theorizing? Set out the deliberative moments you anticipate. For each deliberative moment, assess the moment and the learning opportunity it presents. As you reflect on a particular issue, you may discover other questions you should ask yourself that would enable you to approach this and other deliberative moments more systematically and thoughtfully. Throughout the research process, we invite you to return to the practical exercises on the website associated with this book (http://www.palgrave.com/methodology/doingfeministresearch) to guide your thinking when you face unanticipated deliberative moments.

In our exposition of theorizing we have oversimplified the linear schematic. In practice, researchers using this approach *conceive* of their project in a linear way, and may even successfully describe their project(s) showing how the elements in the theorizing process logically follow each other. They do not actually *work* in a linear way. All theorizing whether it begins with a well-specified theoretical model or not, is dynamic, moving back and forward from theory to puzzle, to hypothesis formation, to research-design, to operationalization, to data collection, analysis, interpretation, and results, as Figures 5.1 and 5.2 illustrate.

For example, at the data analysis stage, you may ask whether your theories can explain the relationships your analysis shows. If these relationships are not the ones you hypothesized, you may have to look beyond the theories you started with (as in the case of "democracy" in Box 5.3). Moreover, in quantitative analysis, if your results are not statistically significant you may ask whether there is a missing variable, or whether there is an interaction between your variables that is not specified in your theoretical model? In another scenario, it is possible that introduction to new theoretical concepts or debates even after the research design and data collection phases may cause researchers to reinterpret their data and reconceptualize their theoretical framework albeit within the limits of an already executed research design.

Theorizing is an ongoing process and plays a role at every stage of research, and a feminist research ethic can help researchers to be more fully aware of this process. Theory not only frames and drives the search for causal knowledge, it "allows us to interpret the *larger meaning* of our findings for ourselves and others" (Hoover and Donovan 2008: 33). But however comfortable you are with linear thinking and exposition, a feminist research ethic will prompt you to be less so. It asks you to go back and rethink the power/boundaries/relationships/ manifested in your earlier reflections, in light of your more recent reflections. There is more than one way to theorize rigorously in the political and social sciences, and the type of theoretical process you engage in is largely dependent on your research question or puzzle.

Conclusion

The activity of theory is literally, about seeing. *Theorein*, the Greek word from which our own derives, means "to watch or to look at" (Elshtain 1981: 301). Of course, we see, watch or look at the world in ways that reflect our own particular biases and vantage-points. This is precisely why it is incumbent upon us as good researchers to be self-reflexive about the position from which we theorize about the political and social world, and to locate our own subjectivities in our research. Further, in order for our research to be thorough and rigorous, we need to think through a broad range of different theoretical standpoints and ways of conceptualizing social and political phenomena related to our question. Theory-seeking researchers view the *transparency* of this theorizing process as crucial to the account of the researcher's methodological rigor.

Regardless of whether you use a theory-testing or seeking approach to your research, at certain moments in the project it makes sense to pause and reflect again on your overall project, reviewing your plan and your process to date. These are important deliberative moments. One such moment is when you go on to design your research, the concern of the next two chapters.

Selected Sources for Further Reading

Ackerly, Brooke A., Maria Stern, and Jacqui True, eds. 2006. *Feminist Methodologies for International Relations*. Cambridge: Cambridge University Press.

Charmaz, Kathy. 2006. *Constructing Grounded Theory: A Practical Guide through Qualitative Analysis*. London; Thousand Oaks, CA: Sage.

Denzin, Norman K., and Yvonna S. Lincoln, eds. 2005. *The Sage Handbook of Qualitative Research*. Thousand Oaks, CA: Sage.

Hoover, Kenneth, and Todd Donovan. 2008. *The Elements of Social Scientific Thinking*. Belmont, CA: Thomson Wadsworth.

Chapter 6

The Personal and the Political: Constraints and Opportunities of Research Design

Introduction

When a friend gives you advice, she tries to personalize it to *you*. In this chapter we discuss the personal dimensions of methodological reflection. Before you can move on from asking and conceptualizing your research question to designing your research plan and methodology, it makes sense to figure out what kind of research suits you, your life, the particulars of your professional ambitions in institutional and disciplinary context, and your political, social, and economic context. Casually, many researchers talk with fellow researchers about the ways in which these factors weigh in on their research aspirations and plans. We think these factors are significant. In this chapter, we make explicit the range of constraints, politics, and opportunities that play a part in designing research. These issues should not be neglected merely because they may not figure in the final exposition of the research.

Personally, people are suited to different kinds of research; some are willing to work to develop the skills of a good interviewer; some *assume* they have them and, therefore, might be better suited to participant observation while developing their skills of observation and interviewing. Some are willing to develop their quantitative skills; others are taxed by mathematical conceptualization. We have a colleague who is afraid of flying, another who needs access to medical facilities, another with a bad back. Personality and personal traits such as these and many others can and should affect research design. We should not plan to do work that we cannot do well.

For some, this may be the first time you have thought of yourself as a "researcher." For others, this may be a new way of working.

For students, post-graduate researchers, non-academic researchers, and course instructors, the challenge of balance is different, but all researchers must fit their research into the rest of their lives. Students may be away from family support for the first time, working an internship, trying to juggle other classes, or job hunting for after graduation. For the authors, our life style requires that we support others financially and with our time (as children, parents, partners, siblings, neighbors). These have varied with our age and stage of life, as with the age and stage of life of our dependants. We may have partners willing to support us, but that support is always subject to negotiation (and reciprocation if we want the relationship to last). Your ability to do research may depend on your spending time also teaching, mentoring, being a teaching assistant, or being a research assistant each of which can take time away from our own research. We may live in a political context that makes some kinds of research not possible because it cannot get funded or because it cannot be done. On the other hand some opportunities can come our way that make our research able to be conceived in new ways. For example, through my work on gender equity and regional trade, I (Jacqui) became involved in auditing a trade organization which gave me an opportunity to conduct a survey of member states and gain access to organizational documents that advanced my own research project simultaneously and that would not have been possible without the organization requesting it. Unexpected funding and a commission to go to the World Social Forum changed my (Brooke's) access to a range of well-networked women and transformed my methodology for theorizing about human rights.

These are some of the politics, constraints, and opportunities that are not typically considered part of the research process, but that are part of the researchers' lived reality. It is explicitly feminist to make the reflections these require visible in the research *plan* and *process map* though not in every exposition of the research project. For example, they don't belong in your grant application or your thesis proposal. Although not every account of our research includes a discussion of personal constraints and opportunities, it is important for the transparency and accountability of our work to note these and their effect on our research because they can and do affect our methodological choice. Very often, these constraints and opportunities make our research questions or methodology manageable so we may need to reflect on them when we interpret our research and findings. As authors, we have generally made these invisible aspects of our work visible in our acknowledgements.

We discuss how these constraints and their political dimensions might influence your research plan. We also consider each stage of the research plan and offer examples of how personal, familial, professional, and geographical considerations might be dealt with at each stage. We offer these two methods of exposition in order to share the greatest variety of examples, but these by no means exhaust the landscape of the politics, constraints, and opportunities of research design. We conclude with reflections on the feminist import of giving methodological attention to the typical constraints that are generally invisible to our academic audiences.

Should these personal and political constraints affect our research? They do, so whether they should is a spurious question. *How* do they affect our research? That is up to each researcher and it is an important methodological question.

The Personal and the Political

In the first part of this chapter we discuss examples of the range of ways in which many constraints on research can emerge from the *contexts* of our lives and work. Some of these can be anticipated. Perhaps the most obvious is the number of weeks left before the paper is due! Some of these cannot. These are general considerations that, big or small, can have an overarching impact on our work.

Personal and Individual: Being Your Own Person

Not all personal constraints on research design are political, but each can serve as a window, inspiring us to be attentive to a range of issues that can be politicized. Start with the simple. A colleague has a fear of flying. This personal trait affects his research agenda; he studies questions that can be asked with quantitative data gathered by other survey researchers. Another colleague has a physical disability that makes research in places where medical facilities are not available unimaginable. For both colleagues, the location of their work and therefore their methodologies will be affected if not determined by considerations outside of their research questions.

Personally, we should each acknowledge our weaknesses as researchers. I (Brooke) enjoy taking interviews, but find that I do much better with semi-structured interviews rather than open structure interviews (see Chapter nine). In the latter, I get so interested in what the subject is saying, I follow them, sometimes forgetting to make sure all of the areas of inquiry are covered. This is a matter of style, one that I can overcome when I am doing interviews regularly, but often I conduct interviews after having been out of practice.

Our personal politics can also influence our research design. We might believe in building local capacity and therefore train local paraprofessionals to gather our data. We might prioritize mentoring of graduate students which may mean structuring the timing of our research to intersect at key moments with a particular student's needs.

Our politics may lead us to a particular methodology. Yet, the politics of our research participants' context may not demand that methodology. For example, what do we do if a community-based research question is best researched using methodology that is not participatory? Or if our institution's Ethics Review Board (IRB) requires each community research partner to go through IRB training? Or, what would happen if our political commitments could lead us to abandon or significantly rework a question altogether? A researcher who is committed to the rights of trafficked people writes a proposal to do a comparative study of state policies on sex trafficking but becomes aware that exposing some of the impacts of these policies on migrant trafficked women and sex workers may result in the research having a negative impact on them, especially those who are illegal immigrants.

For a novice, these are particularly difficult questions to answer. You may discover with experience that you have very keen interview or observer skills. You may discover you have a way with numbers. Research skills are skills developed with practice. We are not born with these skills. Still, personal preference can affect our choices of *which* skills to develop. Personal constraints can be overcome with training. Personality traits relating to preference have to be faced differently.

Most of the examples that we have discussed thus far, and frankly most of the examples we will offer are of the sort that can be anticipated, but some cannot. You cannot anticipate the impact that the field work experience or the traumas of your subject-participants will have on you personally. You might find yourself unable to reread transcripts. You may find yourself compelled to write political material or become an activist. You know you will be changed by the experience of doing research, but you cannot imagine how. This may be the one context in which failure of imagination is good – perhaps it will leave you open to surprise and engagement of a kind you could not anticipate.

Relationships: Composing Your Own Life

When feminists say the personal is political, many picture the politics of the family first. For a student, this means that you may have a job, internship, sports, performance, or other campus responsibilities. You take many classes some in new areas for you. Many academics have families and partners who don't understand academe. They don't understand our scholarship, our work hours, what we do in the summers, etc. These academics struggle with and against such expectations and use these as opportunities to improve our communication skills. They try to be mindful of others' lack of understanding of academic research by deciding on and communicating clear boundaries around the time and space devoted to this work. Others have academic partners or family members who can be helpful interlocutors about how to

---

Box 6.1 Partnerships and childcare (examples from the authors)

We are both are in mutually supportive relationships with partners who are active parents and professionals. Jacqui's partner is an academic. Brooke's is a corporate professional. We have not inverted traditional gender hierarchies, but neither have we fully refashioned these, as our social contexts have a lot to do with our ability to do so.

Furthermore, "sharing" childcare responsibilities doesn't mean we don't have any, it means we share them. Our partners travel regularly. Our (male) partners have flexibility around how they spend their time when they are home and no flexibility when they are away. We schedule our research and speaking engagements well in advance where possible so that our partners can plan to be home to take care of children.

The value of these elements of our work context is that *we think it is doable*. We pursue our research not with the illusion that it is easy, but with the confidence that it is doable. Lacking any one of these elements, we might wonder if it were possible.

---

compose a research life, comprehending more profoundly the constraints that we discuss in the next section (see Box 6.1).

Confidence in the possible comes from knowing that others have done it. Confidence in your ability to make it possible might come from knowing *how* others have done it. The challenge for a researcher is to compose a life that lets you do the research you want to do and to do research that is compatible with the life that you are trying to compose. For inspiration, see Mary Catherine Bateson's *Composing a Life* (1989). Lots of good examples exist:

- A student lives an hour and a half from her university campus so that her mother can take care of her 2 children.
- A student schedules all of her classes to end by 12:30 so that she can keep a 5 day a week afternoon shift.
- A colleague went back to university after her children were grown.
- Another and her partner shifted their research agendas for about five years so that they did field work in the same country at the same time . . . and they brought their children along.
- Another colleague's partner is a school teacher; through her child's formative years, when school was out for the summer, the entire family re-located to the site of her anthropology fieldwork. When her child reached middle school, her family was less interested in this annual migration.
- Another has two preschool children. He chose a research design that allowed him to do his field work in a short amount of time and his

analysis at home around children's sleep schedules. He broke his project into tiny increments so that he could complete them in a small amount of time and not be interrupted (or not forget his thought process if he did get interrupted).

Not all research life challenges center around children. A lesbian colleague has an academic appointment in a town that is not a place where her partner could get a job and where they could live comfortably. She arranges her research to take her to places where her partner can spend long periods of time or can commute to easily.

For academics, like us, our family relationships are not the only relevant ones. Our relationships with our students and our teaching obligations (noted in the next section) require that we not be out of town for extended periods. In the 1990s we each used research designs that required extensive fieldwork (in Bangladesh and the Czech Republic respectively). Now, we use research designs that allow us to be flexible as to how, where and when we acquire the necessary data. Our current projects have involved gathering data during trips of no more than two weeks, scheduled to minimize time away from children, to meet teaching obligations, and to avoid conflicting with our partners' work travel schedules.

Political Geography: Knowing Your Place

Because of the large size of North American academe and the concomitant degree of academic specialization, North Americans often consider the world as our potential research context. There are resources available to study in a particular country anywhere in the world (Fulbright, Peacecorps, Macarthur, Social Science Research Foundation), a particular trade network or global institution, or a range of these, and recognition for doing so. From the United States, a comparative project does not have to have the United States as an example. By contrast, from New Zealand or Australia, a comparative project does need to have relevance to New Zealand or Australia.

For my (Jacqui's) PhD in Canada, I studied gender and, globalization in the Czech Republic. Now, located in New Zealand, a small, geopolitically marginal country, the range of questions I ask has shifted, and the way I write about them has shifted. At the same time however, I have access to intergovernmental meetings through my small country government that would be afforded few researchers in the US due to security concerns.

The influence of political context on research design fuels feminist considerations consistent with the feminist research ethic. To whom is my research puzzle relevant (Cancian 1996)? What kind of power do I exercise by doing research that is relevant to academics, but not to my political context? How can I use the power of research for social change (Snarr 2009)? What will make my findings relevant? How do geopolitical boundaries influence how I understand my research? How *should* they influence my understanding? How important to my research design is my relationship as a fellow citizen with my subject-participants and audiences? When should changes in the geopolitical context of my research spark the need for self-reflection?

Being the Captain of Your Ship

When an academic thinks of institutional constraints, a student thinks of his course instructor, a graduate student thinks of her supervisor, and a junior academic thinks of her department. Additional pieces of an academic's institutional context include her discursive communities (perhaps an assigned working group, a chosen reading group, or colleagues she sees at conferences), the structure of her position and the responsibilities associated with it, and her disciplinary context. These vary and include professional associations, networks, friends, and *their* institutionalization. For example, do colleagues work across subspecialties? Does transdisciplinary work have an audience? These affect our research designs very differently.

To some extent we choose our institutional environments. You chose your college or university. You chose this class. You chose to write a thesis directed by your present supervisor. In other cases and in another sense, we do not. Once you are planning a research project, your institutional environment is probably already set.

A supervisor is central to a thesis-writer's experience. Get two or more thesis-writers together and you will hear stories, not all of them heartening. But a student's primary supervisor is just one of her mentors. Be the captain of your ship, recruit your own crew; your supervisor is just one in the crew. Each person needs a range of mentoring. Some mentoring roles are inconsistent with others. You can undermine one mentoring relationship by asking too many different roles of that mentor. To be well mentored, you need to develop your own mentee relationships. The perfect mentor is a myth. What we all need is a network of developmental relationships (Hill and Kamprath 1991, 1998) (see Box 6.2). Relationships take time to develop and they shift through the dynamics of the relationship and the people in the relationship.

Be imaginative in your development of your network. Think outside of your subfield, your field, your department, your university, your time zone, your country. Think outside of academe. Academe is an enterprise of networks. It is a good idea to have a cheerleader and a confidante outside of academe; also retired academics in a different field make good cheerleaders and confidants. You need people you can tell your tough stuff too and you don't want to put constraints on your institutional networks inadvertently. (When my friend in another subfield calls me and says "we are interested in hiring a student in your department, do you know so and so?," it is so nice

Box 6.2 Networks for professional development

Instead of relying on individual mentors, everyone needs to develop professional and personal networks. While we enter into relationships for non-instrumental reasons, you might recognize that different relationships fill your needs in different ways. A secure personal and professional network includes:

- a **friend** who knows you and whose interest in being with you is unrelated to work.
- a **cheerleader** to whom you can complain and who will remind you how great you are without trying to solve your problems for you.
- an **advisor or "supervisor,"** according to the ethics of academe, this person is professionally obligated to read your work carefully.
- a **challenger**, is someone who reliably stretches your thinking, invites you to work and think harder in different ways.
- a **professional** role model who demonstrates what it means to be a professional in your field.
- a well-positioned **fan,** someone who sings your praises to others, gives you exposure and visibility, and writes letters of reference for you.
- an **insider** or institution specialist who knows the ropes at your institution and department and is willing to reveal the less visible aspects of these.
- a **confidant** to whom you can confide in your mistakes and annoyances.
- a **protector**, someone who can look out for your workload, the unreasonable expectations of your advisor, etc.
- an **advocate**, someone who can open doors, give you support, help you secure resources.
- a **counselor**, someone to tell you the truth you don't want to hear (a secondary advisor, perhaps official, perhaps unofficial); someone with good advice.
- a **carpool buddy**, someone with some expertise in what you are doing, who is in a similar place in her work process with whom you can talk through your challenges. This person is often a classmate for an undergraduate, a graduate student for a graduate student, a colleague in a cognate discipline within your university or a colleague in the same discipline at another university for an academic.
- a **host**, someone who can introduce you to an intellectual community or potential social and intellectual partners.
- a **group**, people with like or overlapping interests, questions, methodologies, or approaches who give you a sense of community.

A list like this for professionals inspires this one (Hill and Kamprath 1991, 1998). For each of these roles above, you need at least one mentor! Some issues are appropriate for one counselor and not another. As your research agenda broadens (and personal life becomes more complicated), you will need more.

when I can say, "oh, I haven't worked with her directly, but she always has a smart question at our talks . . . " or "my own student has found her to be a good dialogue partner . . .". If all I know about the student is her complaint, however justified, I don't have the opportunity to share information that would be helpful to the student securing the job interview.)

We all have opportunities to mentor and to be mentored. Cultivate these relationships and support others as you have been supported as soon as the opportunities present themselves, which will be sooner than you think. Take these people for granted at your peril. An intellectual life, especially a feminist intellectual life is not lived alone!

Despite this range of mentors, an undergraduate student doing research for a course, likely has one clear mentor, the course instructor. However, others who have taken the course before, others who have done a significant research paper before, and your classmates are all part of your network. Find a car pooler, someone willing to discuss your ideas and read drafts in exchange for your doing the same.

In some departments, in some colleges and universities, it is easier for undergraduates to identify and connect with course instructors than with other faculty. If your program has graduate students, you might talk with them. Talk with other students in order find out how they have made such connections. Many students expect office hours to be time to "get help," but most faculty are open to talking about anything during office hours. Explore common interests. Try out your ideas. Academics love talking about ideas, not just our own! Show up with ideas, a pad and a pen, ready to think.

Despite this range of mentors, a thesis or dissertation research design will be significantly affected by the supervisor. In writing your thesis, you have the unique opportunity to have one person care about your project almost as much as you do and to be professionally obligated to read it attentively. Never again will someone have that kind of ethical obligation to read your work. After this you will need to be more compelling. So as supervisors we offer some advice for how to manipulate a thesis supervisor. Be easy to mentor (arrive to meetings prepared, on time, knowing what you need to talk about – "I'm lost" is a reasonable topic, but it is best set as an agenda item rather than a discovery). On the flip side, if you know where you are going, don't ask for approval or agreement; rather, make the argument for going there; don't sound lost when you are found. If you know what kind of advice you need, ask for it. Be pleasant to mentor by being thoughtful of your mentor's needs and interests; if you drop in without an appointment, ask if it is a good time. Get the best advice you can from each person in your network (for example, don't ask the person who gives you conceptual guidance to read material that is not edited or to read multiple consecutive drafts – make strategic use of conversation and well-edited drafts.) As appropriate, appreciate those in your network and let them know it.

Know that supervisors are human. You are entitled to good mentoring, but humans have limitations. You and your supervisor may not be personally or intellectually compatible. She may remind you of your mother or father. She may not "get" you. Do not let personal and personality traits interfere with your sense of entitlement. Whether or not you are friends with your mentor, you are entitled to her professional respect, including attention. And she is entitled to the same. For so many reasons, it may be difficult to have a healthy relationship.

Whatever your relationship with your course instructor or supervisor, it will be your own. It will be different from other supervisor-advisee relationships you have and it will be different than another advisee's relationship with the same supervisor. You two will compose that relationship together. Remember you are one of the authors of that composition. See Box 6.3 about making the most of your supervisor or course instructor.

An untenured professor has mentoring needs that are similar to the graduate student, but without the supervisor. As helpful as your supervisor has been, you need to work on your own now, in a way that makes the difference between your work and your supervisor's work visible. For you, the import of professional mentors outside of your institution cannot be underestimated. By getting integrated into the life of the profession outside of your

Box 6.3 Making the most of your supervisor or course instructor

For a meeting with your course instructor, send an agenda prior to the meeting. Writing an agenda will help you. Receiving an agenda will help your supervisor or course instructor offer the kind of advice you need at that moment.

When you need to think through big picture or conceptual issues ask your supervisor if the best way would be to *talk* through a puzzle. When we are unsure, our written prose is uneven and this may make a supervisor focus on editing and not on thinking through your big issues.

Be mindful of your course instructor's "fresh" eyes. Limit the number of drafts of a document you show her. (This is doubly true for the secondary advisors you may have. Circulate drafts at key moments; choose these thoughtfully.)

Make long documents easy to read. Have a table of contents, have clear topic sentences, and sound organization.

Your course instructor knows more about writing than you. If you are doing your job, you know more about your topic than her.

Your course instructor's approach to research and writing is just one approach. Appreciate her offering it; if it doesn't fit with your work style, don't try to force it.

home institution, you gain a source of affirmation that is independent of your home institution's personality, including the particulars of the constellation of colleagues, expert and not, in your field (see Box 6.4).

One thing that can influence how we design our research is the dialogue partners we keep. Besides each other, we each have lots of dialogue partners: a global feminisms collaboration focused on research *for* social justice, other feminists who keep a strong sex-gender distinction, ecologists, analytic philosophers, human rights scholars, women's human rights activists, gender and institutions scholars and policy makers, gender and global governance activists, scholars, and policy makers. These can be important for all aspects of the research roadmap (and we turn to these in the discussion of working though constraints).

We don't always get to pick our discursive communities but they can have a formative influence on any stage of our work. For example, our work might take a resistant form if we are in a discursive community that works within epistemological assumptions we find problematic. Or, our work might shift from working within one intellectual tradition to working within two or more as we become educated in our discursive partners' intellectual traditions.

At the moment the authors are very privileged with thoughtful feminist research communities. The book has been co-authored in a collaborative fashion, outlining together, taking turns writing the first drafts of chapters, and reviewing these with engaging, and thoughtful graduate, and undergraduate students from a range of disciplines. From May through August of 2007, and 2009, these students met nearly weekly, providing us with a live audience of the pre-blog variety. From August through December of 2007, a group of students who knew neither one of us, from six social science disciplines, at different stages of their research experiences, read the first half of the book, and offered critical feedback that enhanced the readability, and the usefulness of the book.

Over our careers we have valued both the discursive communities we have found and those we have made. Both sorts have the ability to influence our

Box 6.4 Advice outside your institution

When I (Brooke) began my career, I found my department colleagues' helpful advice and constraining warnings loud and distracting. Going outside my US department, I asked Jacqui's partner (a tenured academic) about how to navigate what I perceived to be a changing context. He gave me the straightforward advice: "You are trying to get *tenure* [a professional status of US academics that enables a permanent position] in the field. If you achieve that, tenure at your home institution will follow."

research with the power of suggestion, or by tempting us in one direction or another with resources. Our discursive communities can be both constraining and stimulating influences on our research designs.

The particulars of our position exert their own influences on our research. Everybody experiences time management and balance challenges in their research. Over time you will continue to improve skills for dealing with these. Everything is a learning opportunity. You are not expected to be "perfect"; we are all learning and improving in these areas. And as you enter new stages of life you will have more skills with which to deal with yet new challenges.

At an institution that trains graduate students, a research design that can incorporate students as research assistants is possible and potentially rewarding for the students. At an institution that does not have graduate students (or if the researcher is a graduate student herself), the possibility of using paraprofessionals for certain kinds of research or for designing the data collection so that undergraduates can be involved stimulate other kinds of research design considerations.

One of the important aspects of context is whether your research is at the center or periphery of what is considered important in the many contexts in which you circulate. In feminist sociology and in feminist international relations, methodological reflections are seen as central. For some political theorists, methodological reflection is important, for others not. In some departments, feminist inquiry is one of the anchors of the field. In others, it is peripheral. At some institutions, transdisciplinary work is considered cutting edge; at others it is not. If your research design might be interdisciplinary, the acceptance of such a design in your specific professional context should be a consideration.

Where you are in your career affects your research design in temporal ways as well. If you have two years left of funding you may choose a different design than if you have one year left. If you need to finish a project before tenure you may choose a different design than if you do not have a deadline. If you can secure a research leave you may have one research design, another if no leave.

Your other responsibilities also affect the time you have to work. Teaching assistant work, research assistant work, dissertations advising, teaching load, service responsibilities, and time in reading groups can limit the time you have for research. In different academic systems these look different. Be careful in comparing your experience with those of colleagues in other departments, other institutions, other countries. Others may be able to advise you on how to navigate them, but your institutional constraints are your own.

You have some agency in choosing your institutional context, but for most academics, the landscape of graduate school options is not infinite, the landscape of job options is not infinite. As a student you may choose an institution because of your desire to work with a particular supervisor and then discover the teaching requirements are quite heavy or the environment between graduate students competitive. You may want a college teaching environment and end up at a research institution. You may want a research position and get a state university position with teaching obligations that make it very difficult to publish research at a rate comparable with colleagues with lesser teaching obligations.

Finally, shifting institutional locations can impact your work. When Jane Mansbridge was a young graduate student she felt she was perceived differently by her subject-participants than when she was a full professor at Harvard. Depending on research design, when we move from graduate school to an academic post, our research can be significantly affected. A colleague engaged in participatory action research at a site very close to her graduate program was delighted when she secured a faculty position at an institution likewise proximate to that site, enabling her to stay active in the community and commute to her academic job. Another colleague doing ethnographic work in a location near his graduate institution ended that project and began an entirely different research agenda when he took an academic position in another part of the country.

In many ways the institutional context of the researcher affects the research design, scale, and time frame of his project. The researcher has agency within these constraints. He can choose how to communicate with his supervisor. He can decide if his department or members of the professional associations of his field are his audience.

Partnerships and Collaboration

As we saw in the exposition of the feminist research ethic in Chapter two, collaboration is important in building feminist-informed knowledge and projects. As we saw in Chapters four and five, that means we understand our questions and concepts to be engaged with those of others. How we define the boundaries of our project, where our work ends and another's begins is itself an ethical dimension of research. When you work in explicit collaboration, those boundaries and the ways in which those relationships affect your work need to be attended to.

Research collaboration can be an effective and meaningful way of getting beyond your discomfort with the isolation of writing and research. Co-authorship is also a great way to do feminist research that is attentive to relationships and that aims to bring the social world and the world into relation. Working and publishing in an international research project alongside other researchers can empower researchers. Belonging to a research team helps you to know the field to which you are contributing and the audience for your research. That is not to say that co-authoring does not bring dilemmas of its own, which a feminist research ethic highlights.

Single authorship is privileged in most social and political science disciplines. Because of this there is a tendency to interpret co-authorship as a hierarchical relationship depending on the institutional location, ethnicity, race, seniority and so on of the authors. Such interpretations undermine the collaborative model of feminist scholarship since under this model it should not be obvious whose work is whose. Yet co-authors will likely have to confront this issue directly and together. In reality, sometimes one collaborator will have more time, resources, job security, seniority, race or nationality privilege etcetera that may have implications for the division of labor, the feedback authors get on the work, and the credit or rewards that accrue to each. We suggest co-authors work through these issues as openly and respectfully as possible. We recommend you share an account of the rationale for your collaboration; for example, authors' expertise might be complementary contributing different strengths including different questions, theoretical or empirical research experience, methods, and/or disciplinary literatures.

A Non-Hierarchical Collaborative Team: Students and Academic Peers

Teams of peers include students assigned to work together in a class and academic peers who decide to collaborate by choice.

Sometimes students are assigned to work collaboratively. I (Jacqui) get my International Political Economy students to co-research group presentations addressing one research question; they then write individuals papers drawing on the group research and process. I (Brooke) ask my Global Feminisms students to share their background research which they present in coordinated class presentations. The students then write individual papers on their own topics.

Some student teams work well. Others struggle with issues of division of labor, accountability, and recognition. These are important issues with which to struggle. You may try to establish your own systems for dealing with these without relying on the course instructor. Relying on the course instructor's grading or peer assessment scheme alone to provide the incentives for you and your peers to behave collaboratively may not work because different people respond to incentives differently. Before trouble begins, set yourselves up for success. Talk about what you would like the team to be. How might you best achieve your desired teamwork? Is everyone willing to do that? These three questions discussed *before* you begin your research will enable you to attend to the feminist research ethic in your work process and provide an infrastructure for dealing with difficulties that may emerge.

Even when we work in a non-hierarchical relationship, we work across differences. Our skills are different; the literatures and theoretical languages with which we are familiar may be different. These differences can be complementary opportunities but we still need to attend to them. We may not know the extent of our collaborator's tools or what it took to develop them or what it takes to carry them out.

We may be perfectly complementary and yet have different schedules. In different hemispheres, New Zealand and the United States do not have similar academic calendars resulting in very few months when our co-authorship could work at the same pace. But working in different timezones does allow for a 24 hour round the clock collaboration! You may be on a team with someone who plays sports and so your meetings have to be at night.

Many differences can become hierarchies. We attend to these in the next section.

A Collaborative Team of Academics: Peer to Peer?

Some of the differences discussed above, and others, can create hierarchies. We need to be attentive to these in our collaborative relationships, even if we understand these as a collaboration of peers.

Bina D'Costa and I (Brooke) have been thinking about a project on transnational collaboration and the ways in which differences can affect collaborative relationships for many years. Our preliminary research on this topic has led us to consider that differences can be a function of hierarchies – differences to which *others* attribute status – and a function of differences that are not in the abstract hierarchical. Because both these have the potential to become a dimension of your relationships, they need to be attended to. For example, you may both be colleagues, but on different career paths. You may be at institutions with different resources. You may be of different academic rank or experience. If you are of different ranks within the same institution, your collaborator may vote on your tenure. If you are graduate student and professor, you may also be student and supervisor on a dissertation. Geographic differences that affect who can get to research sites or professional venues more easily may become opportunities for hierarchies, or even just emerging anxieties around such potential hierarchies. We have already addressed hemispheric differences in collaboration, which often involve inequalities in resources and status; differences in other aspects of schedules can affect the ways we work in ways that affect our relationships. Differences in resources and the possibility for research assistance can also influence otherwise non-hierarchical relationships. For all of these reasons, we need to attend to the *potential* for hierarchies to emerge, even if we do not want to have a hierarchical relationship.

We can attend to this potential through initial and on-going communication. Collaborators need to communicate about their expectations and their changing expectations. Are you collaborating on this project or on all research that may come from the data you collect together? Conversations should include – shall we and how shall we share resources? Can we align each person's contributions to the project with the ways in which their institutional environment rewards them? As you work together you developed shared intellectual capital. How will you acknowledge your shared intellectual capital in your respective individual projects that are not explicitly part of the collaboration? If your collaborator is junior to you, can such acknowledgement be a mentoring opportunity?

Appropriate questions along these lines will probably occur to you once you start thinking in this way. Just as with student collaborators, academic collaborators would do well to spend a little upfront time thinking about the different meanings and expectations you each may be bringing to the relationship. However, time can change relationships and what each collaborator needs out of a relationship.

Having clear plans for your collaboration does not prevent those plans from changing, but clear communication provides the avenue for discussing changes should they be needed. In two of my (Brooke's) collaborations, we conducted our research together, co-authored one piece and separately authored very different work using the same data. In another of my (Brooke's) collaborations, a research assistant developed the argument of the paper in a direction entirely differently from what I had intended. Discussing this shift we decided that she should write the paper alone and be a single sole author even though the idea grew out of an intersection between our research interests. In another similar example, a research assistant did such a good job writing up the work that we felt we had contributed equally to the project intellectually, and her more of the sweat equity, so she is first author on a co-authored piece.

Working as a Collaborative Team from a Variety of Contexts

Just as you compose your own life and just as you take responsibility for your research relationships, so too, when you work in collaboration with non-academics, you need to develop those relationships with intentionality. The variety of considerations here is too vast to cover briefly. We invite you to return to many of the relationship considerations discussed in Chapter two and to think about the ways in which external hierarchies and differences that you do not intend to create hierarchical relationships may in fact create such hierarchies in your collaborations with non-academics (see Box 6.5).

The field of participatory action research has explored lots of models of collaboration. Feminists with other methodologies are also exploring a range of partnerships (Ackerly and Attanasi 2009).

> ### Box 6.5 Larner and colleagues' community–academic partnership
>
> A collaboration of the central government, two city councils, community leaders, advocates, and researchers from the sociology department at the University of Auckland studied governance in state and local partnerships.. The project goals and desired outcomes were established by the community participants and government funders. Each researcher contributed a different understanding of local partnerships drawing on their different expertise and the different groups/community dynamics they knew best, for example, sexuality, ethnicity, gender, family, environment, socioeconomic class, and governance. The academics went on to publish theoretically-informed articles as well as policy-friendly reports and presentations based on data generated by the project; while the results were also usefully used in the design of policies in a local urban government context (Larner and Butler 2005; Larner and Craig 2005).

Working through Constraints on and Opportunities for the Research Plan

In this section, we move through the ways in which we might consider and plan through a variety of context-based influences on the research plan. We show that these are constraining *opportunities*. Whether anticipated or unanticipated, these may be frustrating constraining opportunities, but they should not prevent you from doing your work. You are the author of your research, including your strategies for dealing with all of the constraining opportunities you face.

Politics and Constraints on the Question

Context can constrain our question in many ways. If personal relationships and circumstances make it impossible for you to travel to study the effects of globalization around the world, you might frame your question around globalization as it is transforming local sites such as through immigration or foreign investment flows. If in your disciplinary context there is a particular norm around certain discussions – for example if you study cultural difference, you have to talk about cultural relativism and the particular example of female genital cutting – even if you reject discussing that example, your disciplinary context requires you to explain why not.

Your geopolitical context can influence your question. For example, in smaller or less well resourced countries, you cannot be hyper-specialized. You need to choose a research question that reaches the academics around you as well as an international audience. In the United States, it is possible to be successful with a national, but not necessarily international reputation. For academics inspired by this constraint, we choose comparisons with an eye toward reaching multiple audiences. Any research on ethnicity, race, or culture in New Zealand will have to discuss indigenous Maori issues, biculturalism, and the Treaty of Waitangi even if only to give reasons why they are not going to further explore those topics.

Finally, the geopolitical context of *your subject* can influence your question. For example, we must study AIDS in a geopolitical context in which Africa is paramount. This does not mean that we have to design a research question about AIDS that must be studied in Africa, but we must contextualize our project with reference to Africa.

Politics and Constraints on Your Theory

Personal constraints may limit your theoretical formulation of your project. Of course, you need to attend to the range of literatures that have a bearing on your project, but you are not obligated to *contribute* to these literatures. Your project should be informed by these literatures, but you are not obligated by your question to write for the audiences who have already considered your question. Personal preference certainly has its connection to intellectual interest and rigor. We want to emphasize the latter without ignoring the former. It would be dishonest to ignore the role of our own preferences for certain ways of framing arguments in our research.

Politics and Constraints on the Research Design

As we have seen in this chapter, a whole range of contextual constraints: individual, relationship, professional responsibilities, limited funding, geopolitical context, may create the conditions where even to research a global phenomenon, you cannot leave your home base. You may respond to these constraints by modifying your research question. However, it is also possible in some cases to modify the research design.

Some archival work can be done at home with the help of a photocopy machine and a post office. Increasingly too archival work can be done on the Internet and through the purchase of microfiche, which although expensive may be significantly cheaper than international travel to an archive or similar institution. Some interviews can be done on the Internet. These are not substitutes for other methods, but researchers have thought imaginatively about how to gather the data they need based on the information available.

Politics and Constraints on Data Sets and Case Selection

Political and other constraints can influence our data sets or case selection in interesting ways. For example, we might choose cases that keep us closer to our funding, scholarly, or other discursive communities. We might choose cases that our scholarly community thinks are significant, or data sets that our scholarly community has already treated as legitimate. Additionally, constraints on our time might prompt us to use other peoples' data sets. Sharing of data is consistent with a collaborative view of scholarship and is encouraged by many funding sources as is generating collective data sets for others to use and build on. See, for example, Mazur and McBride (2006) and their dataset on state feminism and women's movements in North American and European cases and Caprioli *et al.*'s (2008) WomanStat project with data on social and political conditions for women around the world.

The feminist research ethic asks us to be particularly attentive to the role that data collection and case selection can play in mediating power and strengthening feminist relationships. For example, if we are studying activist organizations, particularly when studying well-studied organizations, can we use existing data rather than burden organizations with yet "another" researcher or should we reanalyze existing data using different theoretical lenses? Can we gather as much information as possible from other researchers and the Internet before selecting cases and collecting data? Traditional research plans ask us to lay out all of our methods in advance, but attentive to power dynamics and differentials in resources, this may not be the most ethical approach to our research.

Politics and Constraints on Research Methods

Many considerations can affect your methods for gathering data. It may be politically untenable for a non-indigenous person to do research in Maori communities (see Smith [1998] 1999). It may be traumatic for subject-participants to offer first-hand accounts of their experiences (D'Costa 2006). In such cases, you might use a wider range of secondary sources, paraprofessionals to gather data, or rely more heavily on archival materials. You might also use multiple case studies rather than an ethnographic method. Research in settings known to be dangerous, difficult, or violent can be a major constraint on ethnographic and case study research. Janet Johnson in Box 6.6 describes how she shifted her research question when she realized her initial choice of question and research site was not a safe place for her to conduct participant observation.

Sexual Harassment

Often the interview method can threaten personal safety, including through sexual harassment, which is often a particular issue for young women researchers. Based on her experiences interviewing a US state legislator who

---

Box 6.6 Johnson's unplanned deliberative moment: researching gender violence in Russia

Janet Johnson confronted an unplanned deliberative moment in her research on gender violence in Russia and treated her experience of researching as a crucial insight into the research topic itself. As part of her data collection, she attended a police training seminar on rape and sexual harassment. The police trainees made her presence as a young American woman researcher at the seminar an experience of harassment. In her unplanned deliberative moment Johnson reflected on the nature of the situation and what it foretold for her research question. She decided to reframe her research question and focus on "women's organizing rather than the police response to gender violence," preferring to "hang out with women activists" than to put herself in potentially dangerous contexts with aggressive male police (2007).

---

sexualized all his responses to her interview questions, Elizabeth Bennion (2007) now recommends that dealing with sexual harassment should be part of every researcher's toolkit. We should anticipate what our response would to a situation where an interviewee, subject-participant, or facilitator sexually harassed us:

> Under what circumstances would you speak out? Under what circumstances would you leave the room? How might you change the subject or cut an interview short? How will you ensure your safety in the event that advances move beyond talk? These are issues I never considered before going into the field. However, some fieldwork brings researchers into peoples' homes or isolated offices. Some locations are more remote than state capital buildings. Unfortunately, plans for dealing with verbal and/or physical harassment should be part of researchers' toolkits – something we consider before going into the field (Bennion 2007: 23).

Language

Your own language and time constraints might prevent you from gathering data using certain methods. For example, for my (Brooke's) data collection on the views of women and feminist activists, I wanted to interview people from all over the world unconstrained by my own language skills. I designed a structured interview of open-ended questions. These were translated into French, Spanish, Portuguese, Chinese, and Hindi. Interview subject-participants read the questions, and answers were then recorded, transcribed, and translated. Additionally, one respondent read the questions in English and answered in Russian. This was also recorded, transcribed, and translated. Like every other choice of method for data collection, this was a compromise. It enabled a range of participants to inform the work; it enabled us to hear the views of language-outsiders, people for whom these meetings were often experienced in a foreign language.

Resources, including personal financial resources, can be a significant constraint on research design. Early in our careers, economic constraints had one kind of influence on our research designs. We chose single country cases due in part to limited PhD research grants. Now, with permanent academic positions and the financial responsibilities of families, our constraints are different. For each of us, shifts in economic means, change in family status, and developments in career status have each opened up opportunities and added other constraints. Our research designs continue to have to respond to these.

Politics and Constraints on Findings

In other parts of this book, we discuss ethical considerations around sharing our findings. How can we enhance the impact of our findings given our personal, relational, institutional, and geopolitical constraints? One way is by working in feminist collaboration. Taken alone, singular pieces of scholarship can have only a modest impact. One feminist way to think about our research is how we can leverage it in dialogue with others. Some projects exist to share data sets, oral history data, and archival data. Other projects gather feminist scholarship and make it accessible to those outside of Western academic institutional networks.

Conclusion: The Meaning of Political Constraints and Opportunities for Feminist Research

Many of the considerations of this chapter might be understood by positivist or non-feminist researchers to be *outside of the research design*; however, the feminist research ethic, directs us to attend to these.

In the feminist context, we are attentive to the political and context constraints that affect individual researchers and research teams because the first consideration of the feminist research ethic is power. However, the feminist research ethic can also help us think through the implications for our research of this range of considerations that a positivist researcher might understand as unrelated to the quality of the research. In addition to attention to power, the feminist research ethic entails attentiveness to boundaries of inclusion and exclusion, attentiveness to relationships, and commitment to self-reflection. These are essential in reflecting on the constraining contexts.

In many of the examples that we have shared in this chapter, being attentive to our political constraints and self-reflective about these has been a good thing. It has led us to conceive of our work in a broader theoretical and political context. It has directed us to be more locally relevant or to study a local case. In some cases it has made our work more concrete, opened it up to more audiences, and made us more attentive to real world issues. It has freed us up so that the reception of our work is conceivably broad with no one audience determining the fate of the academic or those affected by the issue she studies.

We have been prompted to work in more collaborative ways, working with others and developing the skills of others. It has prompted us to share our work in collaborative ways as well, always conceiving of ourselves as part of research teams or at least of feminist research networks. It has prompted us to reflect on what it means to be mentored and what it means to be a mentor. We can understand our work as distinct and yet in relationship with all of those in our networks.

Some of our considerations make our work feel more political. The political distance that is possible when working in distant geopolitical space is not as readily available to the researcher now working with a local immigrant community, for example. Her relationship to her subject-participants and the impact of globalization on their lives, though theoretically no less personal by virtue of its proximity, can be experienced much more intimately when the research site is close to home.

Adapting to geopolitical contexts can make our work more political, more sensitive, subject to greater likelihood of abuse. Our work can be more scrutinized in the political realm. It may be harder for us to criticize a context in which we are also social and political actors, making it more difficult to share our findings if our research site is also our "home." It may be harder to share frank findings when we know our audience (because they are all around us). We introduced some of these considerations in Chapter two's discussions of power and ethics in research and we elaborate more fully in Chapter thirteen's discussion of sharing our research findings.

Accommodating our research to our circumstances is common. Reflecting on the politics that render those circumstances constraints is feminist. Revealing the intellectual work that makes those constraints into opportunities is feminist. And making the impact of these on our work visible *is feminist*.

Selected Sources for Further Reading

Bateson, Mary Catherine. 1989. *Composing a Life*. New York: Plume.
Lamott, Anne. 1994. *Bird by Bird: Some Instructions on Writing and Life*. New York: Pantheon Books.
Rothman, Barbara Katz. 2005. "Pushing Them Through." *The Chronicle of Higher Education* 52, 4: C2.
Tripp, Aili Mari. 2002. "Combining Intercontinental Parenting and Research: Dilemmas and Strategies for Women." *Signs: Journal of Women in Culture & Society* 27, 3: 793–811.
Zerubavel, Eviatar. 1999. *The Clockwork Muse: A Practical Guide to Writing Theses, Dissertations, and Books*. Cambridge, MA: Harvard University Press.

Chapter 7

Designing and Timing a Research Project

Introduction

So here you are, seven chapters into *Doing Feminist Research*. We have given you a lot to think about – ethics, mapping, question, theory, constraints! It is amazing anyone ever gets *started* let alone *finishes* a feminist research project. But we do. We start, we finish, and we hand in or even publish our analysis. And you are wondering when you can begin to conduct actual research. The answer is, "not yet." Before you can start gathering data, you need a research design that will enable you to gather and analyze those data necessary to answer *your question*. Your research design needs to be clear to you, so that you know what to do when. Your research design needs to be clear to others so that they can find your conclusions credible and, if they are inspired by your work, so that they can be inspired to further your research agenda, not only by exploring related questions with similar methods, but also by exploring similar questions using different methodologies.

Scholarship gains its *credibility* from its research design and execution. Appropriate choices in research methods and analytical tools enable findings to be convincing to other researchers (and plausible to non-academic audiences, including those who informed your project perhaps by being close to the problem of study, but who did not have access to all of your data). You choose methods for generating and analyzing data that enable others to access how transferable these claims are to related contexts or whether they can be generalized all like contexts. You keep careful track of your methods for generating and analyzing data such that others given the opportunity to acquire the same data would acquire sufficiently similar data (interviewees would have said approximately the same things; coders would have coded variables the same way). Likewise, given access to your data, others could replicate your findings (even if they might analyze or interpret those findings differently). Finally, your analysis must be substantiated, perhaps through multiple forms of data perhaps through multiple tools of analysis, such that the findings are substantially the result of your *research* and not your opinion perhaps formed prior to research on the topic. This last point may be *particularly* important to feminists who often take up questions of normative import to them personally, but opinion bias is not the purview of feminists. All academics risk importing such bias; the risk is perhaps greater for those who are unaware of their own biases (Sullivan and Tuana 2007). The research design choices you make can mitigate that potential (Erlandson *et al.* 1993).

Recall from chapter three that there are three parts to a feminist research roadmap – the plan before you research, the process map during your research, and the account you provide after your research. In this chapter, we focus on the first of these, that is, the general design of your plan before your experience of doing the research prompts you to change your plan. In order to set out your plan, you will likely go back and forth between this and Chapter eight on selecting cases and data sources, Chapter nine on generating and collecting data, Chapter ten on analyzing data, and Chapter eleven on structured forms of inquiry.

There are a few different ways to categorize research design which we appreciate but do *not* use for *Doing Feminist Research* as the bases for structuring our exposition of research design because these categorizations potentially constrain our imagination just when we need it most: to figure out the *best* research design for exploring our question. Some categorize research by the kind of data it relies upon (quantitative or qualitative), by the kind of analytical tool it anticipates (descriptive, interpretive, relational, statistical), or by the kind of method for data collection and analysis that structures the inquiry (statistical, participatory action research, grounded theory, ethnography). We do discuss these aspects of methodology in the following, but we think that the question of research design is more general than these and that focusing on kinds of data or analysis as a way of characterizing research might give the impression that it was method not question that guided choices in research design. The research question guides research design.

Our approach is intended to inspire research designs that may follow and build on what has been done or that set out new approaches or new combinations of approaches. Unlike those methodology books that guide the researcher through one kind of research design or another, we want to show you what a *feminist approach* to research design entails. In our view it entails:

● being aware of the landscape of methodological options and the ability to utilize them to study a question like yours, which means being aware of ways of using different kinds of data (Chapter nine), tools for its analysis (Chapter ten), and methodologies for structured inquiry (Chapter eleven);

- designing your research, which includes selecting cases, deciding how to measure or assess the concepts you are studying, and choosing methods for data collection and methods for analysis, that is making choices about the best way to study social phenomena that have to be approximated;

- mapping out a research plan (see Chapter three) that is doable given the constraints you attended to in Chapter six; and

- setting that plan to a reliable schedule (see the practical exercise on the website, http://www.palgrave.com/methodology/doingfeministresearch).

You need to plan a research design that you are able to do in both senses: it is *do*able and *you* can do it. This has been the focus of the book so far. The second half of this book is about developing a plan that will yield *credible* research regardless of your choice of methods.

Our purpose in this chapter is not to prescribe or proscribe "the" feminist research design. There is no such thing. Rather feminism can guide each researcher in her own effort to design her own research. Use a feminist research ethic for developing a research design as if you were Super Researcher and then adapt an "idealized" research design to your context, allowing the reflection on the "ideal" design to inspire your reflections as you move from an ideal design to a concrete plan with a time table.

As we have argued throughout this book, for many feminists, feminism is a contested terrain in which we engage with caution about the adequacy of feminism itself as a theoretical and methodological guide. Many feminists, whose questions work from multiple theoretical frameworks, challenge epistemological norms. These feminists draw on competing and critical theoretical perspectives and associated epistemologies. For these feminists, research design is one of the more creative moments in the research process, one that requires charting one's own course. Here, we invite you to be one of these feminists.

Common Confusion: Unit of Analysis

Even though we organize our discussion of research design around one and multi-case research projects, maybe *because* we have done so, we need to put up front a caution. Think carefully about the design that is appropriate to your project and make sure you can explain it to someone else.

Let's do a little exercise before we think about whether our question is best pursued with a research design that is based on one case versus many cases. In the following three examples the researchers are interested in similar subjects – women's activism. Hopefully, because of this similarity, the differences in their questions and their research design, including their *units of analysis* or cases, will help us think carefully about what *particular* choices a given research question requires.

Consider Catherine Eschle and Bice Maiguashca's (2007) study of women's activism in the anti-globalization movement. They approach this topic by studying women's activism around the World Social Forums and European Social Forums supplementing those data with interviews with local activists in the venues of those Forums (we return to this example in Chapter eight). What is their question? What is their "population"? What is/are their case(s) or units of analysis? What are their data? Here's a brief answer: Their question is what forms of agency are manifest in women's resistance. Their population is all women's resistance activism across time and nation, whether transnational or local. All cases of that social phenomenon would be impossible to identify. There is good reason to think that we can learn a lot about women's resistance by studying one case where the obstacles seem particularly numerous and challenging. Their case or unit of analysis is women's activism in the anti-globalization movement, and even more specifically, women's anti-globalization activism in the World Social Forums. There are so many kinds of data that they might choose to try to observe women's resistance. They choose participant observation and interview methods that enable them to glean from subject-participants how they conceive of their own resistance. They treat (correctly so) the World Social Forums and European Social Forums as one case (a site that exists in more than one place and more than one time) of women's resistance. The actual meetings are not cases but rather places for gathering or co-producing the data (we discuss the distinction in Chapter nine) with women in those movements. Their data come from participant observation techniques, gathered activist documentation and conducted in-depth, semi-structured interviews with women and some men we identified as feminist (Eschle and Maiguashca 2007: 288). They, however, do not refer to their project as one in which they have selected women's anti-globalization activism in the World Social Forums as a case of women's resistance, but rather as an "entry point" for mapping "the history, structure, ideologies, identities and practices of what we are calling feminist 'anti-globalization' activism" (Eschle and Maiguashca 2007: 287) with feminist "anti-globalization" activism understood as the site of resistance.

As an entry point, data collection at those venues in 2004 and 2005 is supplemented with interviews in Europe, Brazil, and India. These additional interviews yield data that is not about the "case" if we understood the "case" to be women's anti-globalization activism in the World Social Forums, but rather are part of their mapping of women's anti-globalization activism. Their case is a phenomenon. The phenomenon they hope to study is so vast, that they can only incrementally build an understanding. Their findings are not representative of the movement as a whole, but rather a piece of the picture, a picture that they and others will fill in over time.

Consider Sonalini Sapra's doctoral dissertation, *The Politics of Women's Environmental Action in India*, in which she studies women activists' strategies around environmental justice in India (2009). She studies three organizations in three different locations working on three different understandings of environmental justice. She uses a range of methods for co-producing data with her subject-participants: participant observation, interviews, and organizational documents. Her question is what theory of justice is put into practice in the work of women's organized environmental activism. Her population is all environmental activist organizations across time and nation, whether transnational or local, in which women are activists. Her cases are three women's organizations in India. She choose one national context, three different local contexts, and three different organizations in order that her study enables her to focus on strategic differences in dealing with some dimensions that are similar (globalization, national economic policy) and with some dimensions that are different (agriculture related environmental activism and mining related environmental activism). Her data are the content of the interviews, the notes of the participant observation, and the texts of the documents.

Now consider a third example. Lyndi Hewitt studies the kinds of arguments that transnational feminist networks (TFNs) are making, the organizational factors that contribute to their making one kind of argument or another, and how TFNs use these arguments as discursive tools "in their efforts to manage intra-movement differences and build solidarities" (Hewitt 2009: 2). Her goal is to "extend existing research on transnational social movements and framing, much of which relies on case studies, by providing a theoretically grounded, systematic analysis that employs a comparative design" to allow her to generalize her findings (Hewitt 2009: 2). Because her question is about how activists' arguments are used across organizations, hers needs to be a study of the population of transnational women's networks. Therefore, it needs to be a multi-case study. She drew a random sample from the population of all transnational feminist networks across time and nation, whether transnational or local. She gathered mission statements from that sample. Those were her data. She could have gathered all documents or a selection of documents; she could have interviewed the leadership of the organization about the arguments they made. She chose mission statements and defends that choice in her dissertation.

However, she was interested in how organizations use these arguments *with* one another. Mission statements at the organizational (or case) level are not interactions with other TFNs. So she supplemented her study with participant observation of transnational women's networks as they made their arguments at three sites where TFNs were active. Was the site-based study of transnational women's organizations' arguments another way of collecting data on the organizations and part of the same study or was it a different study? Had Hewitt made observations of only her sample of TFNs, she could have had two kinds of argument data on these organizations: mission statements and oral arguments. Were it possible, it would have made her random sample of transnational women's organizations suspicious, because the odds that of a population of X organizations Y get selected at random and all *also* go to the WSF are quite low. Unless all or most TFNs go to these meetings, such coincidence would raise suspicion about the credibility of her sampling method. Her sites were key sites for TFN activism, but the research at these meetings was not a way of getting more data on her sample TFNs (or cases) for her statistical study. It was a separate, related study.

Hewitt sought arguments made by TFNs in the context of overcoming movement differences and building a global women's social movement. For this study her population was all those arguments women's organizations make when they are trying to build consensus and overcome difference. Her sample was a "convenience sample" of arguments heard in three sites where TFNs are expected to confront difference and attempt to build solidarity. For this part of the study, she was not trying to learn about the sites or the organizations, so the "cases" she needed to study were arguments, each argument. (Although the questions of her dissertation required this use of these data, in another project she might use the same data to understand something about those sites (Hewitt 2008).)

Hewitt's was a "mixed methodology" research project. It had two parts, two methodologies, each with different populations, different sampling methods, and using different kinds of data.

We introduce our discussion of research design with these three different examples to underscore that a non-linear research design process enables a researcher to trip over her own process. In single methodology social and political science research, you are studying some subset (a "*sample*") of a larger set of phenomena (the "*population*"). For example, three women's environmental organizations in India are three in a larger population. Which population? The population of women's organizations; of environmental organizations, of organizations in India; or of women's environmental organizations in India? The population is determined by the research question. For Sapra's *question* about the theory of justice revealed through women's strategies for environmental justice, the population is all environmental activist organizations across time and nation, whether transnational or local in which women are activists. For a different question about women's activism or environmental justice, the population would be different.

The jargon of "population" and "sample" comes from the field of probability study which underlies the mathematical programs we use to do statisti-

7.1   TWO MEANINGS OF "SAMPLE"

In statistical research designs, a sample is a "portion drawn from a population, the study of which is intended to lead to statistical estimates of the attributes of the whole population" (second meaning *Oxford English Dictionary* (OED) online accessed June 14, 2008). In order to make generalizations about the larger population, in political and social science research we try to get a "representative" sample whose characteristics closely parallel those of the population we are interested in studying. The social science meaning of "sample" is often intended to be an approximation of the scientific statistical sample, that is, to get a "representative" sample. However, in studies that use one or few cases, the meaning of sample is better captured in the *OED*'s first meaning, "A fact, incident, story, or suppositious case, which serves to illustrate, confirm, or render credible some proposition or statement" (accessed June 14, 2008). These general meanings of "sample" are quite different. From the statistical sample we expect to learn about the *other cases* in the population. From the illustrative sample we expect to learn about a *phenomenon*.

Both meanings can be found in feminist research.

---

cal analysis. If we want to be critical of the epistemological imports of mathematical concepts into the study of social phenomena, this would be a good place to start. However, another view is that such jargon helps remind us that our research is driven by a *question* not a phenomenon or a case or an issue.

As you develop your research design you are choosing two different things that are related – the kind of data you will collect and how you will analyze it. You could collect lots of data using ethnographic methods – such as interviews, focus groups, and participant observation – and analyze that data using the triangulation of statistical methods with which you treat each interviewee as a data "case" and interpretive methods with which you treat the entire setting of your data (say a country or an organization) as a "case."

While a mixed approach can be skills and resource intensive for an individual, we think it is *very* important for feminists at least to consider their individual research as fitting into such a portfolio of a range of feminist research designs that people have used to study related questions. As we noted in Chapter four, we do not look for "gaps" in the literatures. Rather, we look to make connections across literatures. Functionally, such a perspective may lead to our scholarship doing the same thing as the gap-oriented scholar. But if the purpose of feminist research is to change the world, not just study it, we think that the approach of building connections (in order to take us to new insights) is a more appropriate metaphor for our work, than that of filling gaps (in a leaky dyke).

Obviously, it is very important to let your question determine your population. What is less obvious is that, when you ask yourself "which is the more interesting question . . . ? Or . . . ?", the answer may have a profound influence on your research design. One may require an in depth case study of one or a few cases as in both the Eschle and Maiguashca and the Sapra examples. Another may require a large sample of cases, as in the first part of Hewitt's project.

The question guides your methodology. Change your question and you may change your methodology, your population, your method of selecting cases to study, the data you decide to rely on, and the way you decide to analyze that data. In order to know what your options are, you need to be familiar with the range of options. In order to do some methods well, it is highly desirable to take a course on those methods. When you take a course on methods, you will likely face the challenge of coming up with a research question that can be researched using the methods of instruction. This is a necessarily awkward moment in methods instruction. Be clear that this is about methods instruction and *not* about research design. *Research design is question driven.*

Research Design in Question-Driven Research

In order to stimulate your feminist imagination, we offer a brief schema of two kinds of studies: single case studies and multi-case studies. Your own project may take the general form of one or the other, or may require a two (or more) part design, perhaps a large case statistical study and a case study of one or two examples from the multi-case study. Each study will have its own questions, methods, tools of analysis, ways of adapting its methods with a feminist research ethic, and findings. While you may casually refer to these projects together in the singular as "my project," keep them distinct. Develop a Research Plan for each and put them together in order to follow the project as a whole.

Our introduction to these two general approaches is designed in part to facilitate your reflection on the relative merits of each approach for your question (or part of your question) and to illustrate the use of a feminist research ethic to prompt deliberative moments in research design. We describe each common research design or methodology. We define the methodology and suggest which sort of question it is well-suited to answer. We enumerate the methods of data collection and creation often associated with a research design of each sort. Finally, guided by a feminist research ethic, we identify the kind of deliberative moments that a feminist who uses this research design can anticipate and may be surprised by.

We choose to introduce these reflections with regards to these two general project designs. As you work through the potential research designs that you may find appropriate to your question, you will ask yourself:

- What are the questions for which this approach is generally deployed and is it appropriate to my question?
- What methods of data collection or co-creation will I need?
- What deliberative moments will I encounter?

This chapter, then, guides the researcher through her reflections on research design. You will put flesh on this design, by choosing methods of data generation from Chapter nine and methods of data analysis from Chapter ten, or by structuring your research following one of the meta-methodologies discussed in Chapter eleven. We expect the researcher involved in the design process to move back and forth among these chapters as she thinks about the best methods for her question.

For each general research design, we identify the kinds of questions for which it is appropriate, the sorts of methods of data collection with which it is commonly associated, and how we might apply a feminist research ethic to provoke deliberative moments that enable us to be adaptors, not just adopters of a given research design.

Single Case

Research Questions for Single Case

The single-case methodology is generally appropriate when the research question requires exploring a question about which there has been very little related research, particularly when the subject is an experience or concept previously invisible or comprehended in only a superficial or anecdotal way. The single case may study a country, an organization, a city, a firm, a social movement, etc. Single case research design may also study an event – often from multiple perspectives so that we can understand its significance (for example, see the special issue of *Development* 2005 on the "World Social Forum"). Most single case projects are trying to do some version of "learning from samples of one or fewer" (March *et al.* 1991). They study phenomena that do not happen often by studying very closely the occasions when they do, or in the case of averted accidents, nearly do.

A single case study is a methodology that can be used to develop our theoretical and empirical knowledge about an understudied subject and generate new hypotheses that might be tested with other studies in the future. Examples include Frey and Crivelli's study of Women's Participation in Argentina's Picketing Movement (2007), Garwood's study of the Global

Garment Industry (2005), Han and Ling's study of Korea as a hypermasculinized state (1998), or Kanuha, Erwin and Pence's study of a collaboration between feminist advocates and the US Marines (2004).

Or, a single case can be the locus of the study of a more general phenomenon when an argument can be made that the case is a particularly good case for observing the phenomenon of interest, for example my (Jacqui's) case study of the transformations in gender relations brought about by globalization in the Czech Republic after socialism (True 2003). In Box 7.1 Sarah VanHooser discusses her single case study design that involved using ethnographic methods and a feminist research ethic throughout the research process especially with respect to developing relationships and knowledge relevant to women in the recovery community studied.

A single case study can also lay out terrain for further theoretical explo-

---

Box 7.1 VanHooser's multiple methods of producing and analyzing data in a single case study

"Women who have been involved in sex work and have suffered from addiction are a particularly marginalized group of people, even (or perhaps especially) as they leave the streets and enter into recovery. In order to explore the lives of women living in a two-year recovery community, I conducted a single case study with ethnographic methods, guided by theoretical questions of self and freedom.

Before beginning my formal research, I spent about 18 months volunteering in the community by coordinating their student interns, and assisting with general office work. During that time, I was able to form relationships and experience life and work in the community in a way that allowed me to develop research questions and epistemological approaches that were relevant to the women in the community, their interests, and their ways of constructing knowledge. Specifically, I learned that the process of sharing and developing knowledge within the community was one that was based in experience, grounded in relationship, and reliant on story-telling.

My formal research process included 25 individual interviews, 2 group interviews (each with approximately 10 participants), and 3 months of participant observation at the collective work place run by the women in the recovery community. Once I had collected my data, I developed analysis codes based on an iterative process that worked to draw relationships between my guiding theories and the concepts, themes, and ideas presented by the women I interviewed. I then coded my data using qualitative analysis software, and presented my preliminary findings to the women in the community. I invited them to correct, add to, or otherwise comment upon my findings. Their comments were included in my data and used to guide my final analysis" (VanHooser 2009: pers. comm.) See also VanHooser (2009).

ration. For example, Elisabeth Jay Friedman explores the Venezuelan women's movement during the process of democratization. This study reveals key variables – women in party leadership, the roles of women in party membership, the state bureaucracy, international opportunities, and political discourse (Friedman 2000) – to which one would want to attend in studies of women's national social movements around the world whether using a single case or a multi-case research design.

As the cited examples illustrate, the single case is common among feminists in political science, anthropology, sociology, and international relations. It is also used in history and geography. However, as we discussed in Chapter six, in some political science and sociology communities, a single case study may be an inadequate research design for meeting disciplinary expectations. While the feminist researcher may seek to destabilize the epistemological foundations of her field that make a case study design implausible, the way to do that may be to combine a case study methodology with a methodological approach that is more acceptable to her anticipated audience in a multi-method or mixed-model design.

Regardless of the comfort level of your discipline with single case research designs, your claims will be evaluated. The legitimacy of your claims stem from the credibility of the design and execution of your project.

Methods of Single Case Research Design

Methods of single case methodologies can be broad reaching. The data for a single case study could include participant observation, text, media, and organizational, community or network maps (which are sometimes necessary before doing interviews, but certainly necessary to capture the relationships among informants). The methods for gathering data could include oral histories (which you might take yourself or find archived), interviews, surveys (including time use surveys or photo surveys, again done by yourself or by others), and statistics from secondary sources (like governments). We discuss these methods in Chapter nine.

Often the single case methodology has much in common with ethnography and may use ethnographic methods as VanHooser describes in Box 7.1, although as a methodology, ethnography generally requires a long period of immersion in a field (see Chapter eleven). However, a single case methodology can differ from an ethnography, depending on the research question, in that for a case study, a case (an organization, a country, etc.) can be the *setting* of a study, but not itself the subject of study (for example, gender mainstreaming or the relationship between women's movements and the state, respectively) (Box 7.2). Additionally, single case methodologies can involve nested designs that explore cases within the case study (such as many organizations in one country) (Lieberman 2005).

Box 7.2 Studying emergent social phenomena: gender mainstreaming in international organizations

Although there has been at least ten years of experimentation with gender mainstreaming in international organizations, it is still an emergent and contested social and political process and more amenable therefore to case study analysis. Gender mainstreaming is simply-defined as initiatives and methodological tools to integrate analysis of gender equalities and differences into routine organizational procedures and policies (see Key Concept 1.6). Some researchers have been eager to conclude that gender mainstreaming is a failure since it has not had any demonstrable impact according to indicators of gender equality or women's empowerment. Other researchers have argued that despite the promises of gender mainstreaming, it is, in effect, a problem-solving device for liberal institutions that legitimizes rather than transforms the existing gender order.

True studies such an emerging phenomenon. She argues that there has not been sufficient time to evaluate fully gender mainstreaming's impact and outcomes and that there are few cases where gender mainstreaming has been institutionalized to the point where we can actually study it – even as a contested process. It is also difficult for scholars to get meaningful data on gender mainstreaming from outside international institutions since analyzing the mainstreaming process involves at least some direct observation of bureaucratic and organizational politics. True set out to study gender mainstreaming in trade organizations with a comparative research design that disaggregates the different factors shaping variation in its impact and outcomes. She discovered in the research process that such a comparative analysis could only be conducted once an in-depth organizational case study of one experiment with gender mainstreaming had been completed. She chose the Asia Pacific Economic Forum (APEC), an intergovernmental trade and economic policy organization, for this case study for two reasons: (1) it had adopted a fairly comprehensive gender mainstreaming framework in a policy area where gender issues have conventionally not been addressed; and (2) she could gain access to the organization as a participant observer.

One organization, APEC, is used to test some of the general claims made by scholars and policymakers about gender mainstreaming, to generate more specific hypotheses to study in other cases, and to develop a methodology for studying the impacts of gender mainstreaming in other international organizations (see True 2008b; 2009b).

Using a Feminist Research Ethic to Anticipate Deliberative Moments in Single Case Research Design

The key anticipated deliberative moment of the case study methodology is the selection of the case (see Chapter eight). Justification of the selection of the case is an important part of the write-up of the research design so it is important to consider from the outset. Why does *this* case enable you to research your question? To understand the role of feminist ideology in women's social movements, should we study negative as well as positive cases, that is, cases of women's collective action that do not explicitly use feminist discourse (Bayard De Volo 2003; Frey and Crivelli 2007; Katzenstein 1998)? Does your choice of this case follow a norm of your discipline that needs interrogating (for example, comparative politics in the US is defined as studying a foreign country whereas in other Anglophone countries the expectation is one studies one's own country in cross-national comparison)? Will choosing this case study destabilize power relations i.e., by making an organization more visible, or will it exacerbate them by making a dominant organization even more visible? For instance, will it affect power relations within an organization or a country, for instance by contributing useful knowledge and publicity for women's empowerment? Finally, how will the situatedness of the researcher affect the study? Can a woman researcher move freely in order to gather the data she needs in this country or organization (Schwedler 2006)? Will her unchangeable personal characteristics affect her ability to engage openly and respectfully with her subject-participants? Will the presence of the researcher within an organization change the organization, perhaps by enabling or prompting greater reflection within the organization and potentially improving practices within the organization? What are the implications of our impact on the organization we are studying for the ethics of the research relationship (see Chapter twelve)? What are the implications for your research (for example, if your research is to be credible and useful to a subject-organization, you need to present findings that do not rely on assumptions or interpretations that are unfounded either in their support or criticism of the organization)? To summarize, which case you choose to study will have implications for social reality and the world we live in, for good and for bad, so it is critical that you make this choice with as much foresight and reflection as possible.

In addition to these anticipated deliberative moments in single case research design, there are countless others that you will confront during the research process. Most of these have to do with specific methods for collection and analysis and so will be discussed in the following chapters.

Additionally, as the example of Maria Stern from Chapter two shows, the researcher may discover that her methodology is not enabling her to "get at" her question and she may need to switch, add or adapt methods (Stern 2006). The single case study researcher needs to be open to the unanticipated deliberative moment in which she needs to consider complementing her research methodology with other methodologies or shifting her research methods to enrich the data she can gather. For Stern it was a matter of reconceiving the interview process (and her epistemology) as one of co-constructing a narrative with her subject-participant. Solutions to such problems are again as varied as feminist research questions.

In another example, the researcher discovers through her research that she really should compare her subject of study with another, thus adding the need to gather additional data. For example, near her conclusion, Elisabeth Jay Friedman adds a brief comparison of the women's movement in Venezuela with the neighborhood movement in Venezuela (Friedman 2000: 266–71). This was not a central research question of her project, but the brief comparison shed light on the central question of her project, offering evidence of the credibility, transferability, and dependability of her claims.

Comparative Case

Research Questions for Comparative Case

The range of research designs that fall under the rubric of *"comparative case"* is likewise broad. A comparative case research design may seek to expand the scope of inquiry of a single case methodology – for example as Box 7.2 describes, expanding the APEC study of the impacts of gender mainstreaming to a comparison with other international organizations. Or the comparative case methodology can enable the researcher to focus on a particular hypothesis about *why* something happens by choosing cases that are very similar except with regard to a particular aspect (or variable) and study these across a large number of cases using statistical methods.

Such choices need to be justified conceptually as we will discuss in Chapter eight on case selection. For example, in *Fields of Protest* Raka Ray (1999) compares the women's movements in Bombay and Calcutta. Through a comparison of multiple groups, some autonomous, some politically affiliated in each city she offers an assessment of the *political field* of women's activism and the role of such a field in the kinds of activism and successes of movement actors. The political fields were different in these two places, different in more than one dimension. The two places differ on more than one variable, but she makes a sound theoretical and conceptual argument that the comparison of women's movements in these two places gives us a transferable argument about women's movements and their responsiveness to the political field of their activism and the factors – party politics, political affiliation of women's groups, caste, and so on, that affect women's movements' issues and strategies. Ray studies women's movements in Bombay and Calcutta as two distinct cases.

By contrast, Benita Roth studies African American, white, and Chicana feminist movements in the US as a "linked set of cases," and she used a comparative historical method to look at their similarities and, especially, at their differences (2004: 17). She argues that they are organizationally distinct "but situated in a social movement milieu that created awareness and connections among them." She argues that the three feminist movements that emerged out of grassroots and student activism in the 1960s and 1970s "can only be understood in relation to one another" (2004: 17).

Certain comparative methodologies – those that require a certain number of cases and variability among them on key variables – are designed for research projects of already established phenomena, phenomena so established that we can observe variability in the variables because the phenomena have occurred in many places, many times, under the leadership of different people, under different economic conditions, in different cultural contexts, and so on. Feminists are often studying emergent or non-emergent social phenomena. Sometimes we can go back and add more cases if we discover that there is not enough variability in our variables. However, in emergent social phenomena there may not be more successful cases (see Box 7.2 for a discussion of the methodological implications of studying gender mainstreaming as an emergent phenomena in organizations).

The flexibility of comparative case research design makes it at home in all social sciences – though your own field or subfield may privilege a particular methodology as we say in Chapter six. However, because it enables one to do in-depth analytical description as well as test hypotheses, comparative case research can be a valuable methodology for bridging positivist and non-positivist epistemologies (see Key Concept 2.4). More than the single case study, it may appeal to positivist-oriented researchers. As with single case study research designs, comparative research designs turn on the selection criteria and selection of the cases (see also Chapter eight). Many potential biases threaten your ability to generalize from your findings. If your cases draw from a particular region or country, then you may introduce some findings that are not able to be generalized, or some findings that may be able to be generalized and others that invite further inquiry across more contexts. Some of the most interesting projects are constrained in this way and yet open up new research agendas for just this reason (see Sapra discussed above).

Methods of Comparative Case Research Design

As with the single case, the methods of comparative case research designs are many. The data could include participant observation, text, media, and organizational, community or network maps (which is sometimes necessary before doing interviews, but certainly necessary to capture the relationships among research participants). The methods for gathering data could include oral histories (which you might take yourself or find archived), interviews, surveys (including time use surveys or photo surveys, again done by yourself

Box 7.3 Talley's Face Work: an example of a comparative case dissertation

"This sociological and cultural analysis of facial disfigurement employs multi-sited ethnographic methods, participant-observation, content analysis, interviews, and autoethnography to examine four sites in which faces defined as disfigured are repaired. Characterizing work aimed at repairing the face as face work, I demonstrate that face work is a multi-faceted, complex, and contradictory process wherein the face is technically repaired and what disfigurement means is negotiated. I examine an emerging and contested biomedical technology, face transplantation; facial feminization surgery aimed at and used by male-to-female transsexuals; reality television show Extreme Makeover; and international not-for-profit Operation Smile. I argue that face work is not simply a conglomeration of reconstructive techniques aimed at the human face but rather the work of making the disfigured human" (Talley 2008: Abstract).

or by others), and statistics from secondary sources (like governments) (see Chapter nine).

The analysis of comparative cases may also be done by a range of methods including comparison or discourse analysis. And a comparative case research design can be the context of a structured inquiry such as some grounded theory and all statistical inference projects. Box 7.3 describes a particularly innovative comparative case design that involved using a range of methods to collect and analyze data on different cases of the same phenomenon.

In addition, if your cases are related, as in the example of Benita Roth's work, then you will need an element of your research design that enables you to map the landscape of your inquiry. What landmarks are important in this landscape will vary by discipline and research question, but they might include noting who has more visible and overt forms of power and who has more subtle forms of power. It might mean mapping formal organizational structures and informal organizational structures. For example, a very dynamic personality maybe the leader of an organization, but someone else may be the person that members go to get decisions made. Or an organization may have a formally egalitarian structure, but function with deference to hierarchies, like caste, age, gender or other marker of status, that come from the social context or that may be particular to that organization. Description (Chapter ten) and Participatory Action Research (Chapter eleven) are tools of analysis and structured inquiry respectively that may provide important tools for mapping the landscape of your project.

Using a Feminist Research Ethic to Anticipate Deliberative Moments in Comparative Case Research Design

As with the single case, selection of the cases is the most central anticipated deliberative moment of the comparative case methodology. For comparative case work, there must be clear hypotheses about what variable or variables might matter in one context versus another. The cases are selected in order to get variation on those variables (see Chapter eight on case selection). If you have one variable that is important to your theoretical argument then you need at least two cases with two different values with regard to that variable. So for example, perhaps you think that "electoral system" (plurality or proportional) matters in the election of women to the legislature. As you reflect about the cases, you may realize (in the case of this example *you certainly will realize*) that there is more variation among them than just the variable in question. One solution is to switch methodologies to a more quantitative approach. The more dimensions in which your cases differ or the more variables you are interested in identifying as *the* key variable, the greater the number of cases you will need relative to the number of variables you are studying.

Here again, a feminist research ethic invites us to consider epistemology, boundaries, relationships, and our situatedness. As shown above, Benita Roth reflects on the relationships among three movements and argues that African American, white, and Chicana feminist movements are organizationally distinct even while existing in relationship to one another and while working in a shared political field and social movement context that they experience differently.

Generally, we consider *intersectionality* an analytical device for deconstructing systems of power that make interrelated exercises of power seem disconnected (see also Crenshaw 1989, 1991). However, in order to do such analysis, we need to collect the data that makes such analysis possible. Therefore, intersectionality can be used to provoke deliberative moments in research design to make sure that you are gathering the data necessary to evaluate the intersectional dimensions of power at work in and around your research question. Of course we are reminded by history and feminist and other critical research that we need to pay particular attention to inequality and exclusion based on gender, sex, sexuality, ethnicity, class, caste, religion, country of origin, national identity, aboriginal status, immigration status, regional geography, language, cultural practices, forms of dress, beliefs, ability, health status, family history, age, and education. See the discussion in Box 7.4 of a research design for a study of urban social inequality. However, as we argue in an article analyzing data on women in the field of international relations, depending on your question, intersectional analysis may require you to get data on a range of dimensions not normally (defined rela-

> ### Box 7.4 McCall's use of intersectionality in urban survey
>
> Leslie McCall analyzed large scale urban survey data to explain the increasing economic inequality in the US in the 1990s (2005). She analyzed data on gender, class (using education as a proxy), and race in many US cities explicitly looking at the context-based interaction of these structures of wage inequality. Despite commonplace narratives associating "the new economy" with the decline of men's wages and job opportunities, McCall found different configurations of inequality in different cities/local contexts, between and among different groups: "No single dimension of overall inequality . . . adequately describe[d] the full structure of multiple, intersecting, and conflicting dimensions of inequality" (2005: 1791). For instance, among the higher-educated group, gender was the most salient factor explaining earnings inequality by contrast with the lowest-educated group. Similarly, in postindustrial, immigrant rich regions class inequality was more of a driver of wage inequality than gender or race. This intersectional analysis has important implications for the design of policy and action. McCall suggests in contexts where class is more salient making minimum and living wage campaign will be more relevant whereas affirmative action programs will likely be more effective in settings where class and gender and race inequalities are more pronounced (often due to the different economic structure).

tive to your question) understood as a dimension of power or privilege (Ackerly and True 2008a).

Conclusion: Committing to a Doable Plan

The next five chapters help you consider many more concrete dimensions of research design. Every research design is not just a conceptual design, it is a practical design. What do you need to do where and when? What plausible schedule will yield completion by your desired date?

Consider your project as a whole. What are its parts (e.g., one case study and one statistical comparative study)? What is the research question for each part? You may use the practical exercise on the book's website http://www.palgrave.com/methodology/doingfeministresearch to identify the key elements of each part of your project and develop a viable work plan. Aggregate these and use that master plan to enable you to keep track of the logistical connections between the parts.

The process of planning your research can drag out as you go back and forth between your research question and your ideal design, what is doable and back to whether that doable design will answer your question. Allocate some time to this process, but sooner rather than later, based on your assessment of how long each aspect of your data collection and analysis will take (informed by the discussions in the following chapters). Allocate a realistic estimate of time required to complete each stage of your research plan . . . and get going!

Selected Sources for Further Reading

Charmaz, Kathy. 2006. *Constructing Grounded Theory: A Practical Guide through Qualitative Analysis*. London; Thousand Oaks, CA: Sage.

Mason, Jennifer. 2002. *Qualitative Researching*. London: Sage.

Ragin, Charles C., and Howard Saul Becker. 1992. *What Is a Case?: Exploring the Foundations of Social Inquiry*. Cambridge/New York: Cambridge University Press.

Ramazanoğlu, Caroline, and Janet Holland. 2002. *Feminist Methodology: Challenges and Choices*. Thousand Oaks, CA: Sage.

Sprague, Joey. 2005. *Feminist Methodologies for Critical Researchers: Bridging Differences*. Walnut Creek, CA: AltaMira Press.

Visweswaran, Kamala. 1994. *Fictions of Feminist Ethnography*. Minneapolis: University of Minnesota Press.

Chapter 8

Sampling Cases, Operationalizing Concepts and Variables, and Selecting Data Requirements

Introduction

We began Chapter seven on research design with a caution about making sure that you have a research design that can answer your question. *After* you are done with your research you should be able to provide an account of your research such that your analysis and conclusions are credible to your audience. Because social scientists study complex social phenomena that do not fit within tidy boundaries, we either have to treat them as if they do or figure out creative ways to attend to the non-uniform dimensions of social science research while enhancing the credibility of our claims. Ways to do this include stating your question clearly (Chapter four), defining your concepts carefully (Chapter five), describing your research accurately (Chapter three – "Account of Your Research"), and defending your choices of cases to study and data to collect using justifications that enhance the transparency of your thinking (this chapter).

In this chapter we discuss ways of thinking about *and describing* your choices of cases, of how to operationalize your concepts and variables, and of which data to create in order to measure your concepts and variables so that they are clear to yourself and to other researchers. Your course instructor and your audience may have reasons for preferring one or another term to describe what is at stake in each of these decisions.

We use the ideas of "population" and "sample," introduced in the preceding chapter, to select the cases we study. We use the idea of "operationalization" to guide our thinking about how to assess the concepts we are interested in understanding using variables that a social scientist can observe and measure. We use the idea of data "selection" to discuss how we decide to observe, measure, and even create the data that measure our "variables." Finally, we offer a list of ways of thinking about and describing processes of selection. They may be the ways we identify our cases or identify data sources. The point of introducing these terms is to enable you to think through your range of choices and to describe those choices. Of course, other researchers may not take such care with their use of these terms or with their descriptions of their methodological choices more generally, but part of doing feminist research that is destined to be read and valued by feminist and non-feminist audiences alike is to give your exposition the clarity necessary to build the field.

Though the exposition above may suggest otherwise, most of this process is non-linear. There are four decisions to be made and more than one of these can be unsettled at a same time: determining your question, population, cases of study, and data. For the same topic there are multiple possible questions each with correspondingly appropriate populations, cases, and data. The process of determining your population, cases, and data may also further clarify your research question. In this chapter we discuss the theoretically informed work of using your question to guide your determination of your population, your case selection, operationalization, and choice of data and sources. Perhaps because of uneven adoption and adaptation of scientific ideas for the study of social scientific questions, researchers refer to different sampling techniques to describe how they identified interviewees or texts without actually thinking about how they would define the "population" from which that "sample" is drawn. This problem is not unique to qualitative work. Quantitative researchers may also mistakenly follow a methodological approach used by others studying a related subject without thinking about how *each question is distinct* and requires the researcher to justify the choices of cases, operationalization, and data. The following clarifies what is at stake in each of these decisions, identifying potential pitfalls and focusing your attention on what is the key driver in each methodological decision: your research question.

Why Is This So Hard?

So here is an awkward truism about research: almost every question worth thinking about is difficult to think through at first. However, that truism has a corollary that is equally true, for almost any question you have about your research you can get a little more clarity if you restate your research question. Countless times instructors and supervisors rub the salt of this truism in the wound of a student who thought he was coming for some methodological advice and ended up confronted with this question: what is your research question?

The reason instructors and supervisors keep asking that question of everyone with a research project – whether it is going well or has stalled over a methodological puzzle – is because we cannot help someone else define a population, figure out which subset of that population to study, evaluate existing data sets, or figure out which data to gather or produce unless we clearly understand the research question. If supervisor and author don't see the same question guiding a given research project, they will disagree about whether the research design is the best plan for answering that question. We cannot tell even what kind of methodology problem you are having if we don't know your question.

Recognizing the interdependence of question, population, case selection, and data selection makes us refer to the feminist research process (indeed all research processes) as "messy"; but to be honest, the process feels "messy" because it is hard and dynamic, not because your final decisions or your exposition of your choices will appear messy to others. Once you make sense of these choices and their interdependence, you will justify the choices you make. Many of those justifications will not require a retelling of your earlier confusion, though occasionally, you might need to revisit something that was particularly difficult to work through in order to explain the choices you considered but did not take. You will be clear because you will know what you are doing . . . guided by your research question.

To illustrate this dynamism, we discuss briefly an article by Mary Caprioli and Kimberly Douglass (2008), "Nation Building and Women: The Effect of Intervention on Women's Agency." By assessing their methodology we assess their question, population, sample, and data. The contingency of each on the others, the mutual dependence of these, is transparent in their project and thus we hope a discussion of this contingency can help provide a clarifying caution to the researcher as she thinks through the interdependence of question, population, case, and data in her own project.

In Caprioli and Douglass's article there are three statements of the research question. The first two are explicit:

- In the abstract, they offer the general theoretical statement: "does military intervention lead to democracy if what we mean by democracy includes women's participation in democracy?"
- And in the first line of the paper: "When states intervene [militarily] to aid in nation building is women's equality increased?" (Caprioli and Douglass 2008: 45)

These are not restatements of the same question. But the authors are not "confused" about their question. The first is used to situate the more specific question in the field of foreign policy. The article is published in a foreign policy journal. The literature review discusses the appropriate literature and situates their project in the context of on-going work in the field. *Their* research question is the question above in the first line of the abstract. However, as they go on, they further clarify that their question is actually whether *military* intervention increases the equality of women *after* the intervention.

What population are Caprioli and Douglass studying? The question as stated suggests that the population is those states where there has been a military intervention for the purposes of nation-building. That list could be quite large; moreover, it is hard to know what its bounds are. It could include all conflicts with military intervention by an external power for the purposes of state-building. Caprioli and Douglass follow Dobbins *et al.* in their definition of military intervention:

> Military intervention shall be understood as the use of armed force by one party, such as the UN, in a target state. Thus far in the post-Cold War period, only the UN and the U.S. have led nation building efforts. Nation building is understood as "the use of armed force in the aftermath of a crisis to promote a transition to democracy" (Dobbins *et al.* 2005:xv) (Caprioli and Douglass 2008: 46).

Yet, whereas Dobbins *et al.* study all such conflicts since the Cold War, Caprioli and Douglass include in their only those states which were states prior to the conflict and where the intervention has ceased:

> We do, however, limit our analysis to those involving recognized sovereign states and to those cases in which the intervention has ended. This restriction of cases is necessary for our analysis because most data is only collected for sovereign states and an on-going intervention would preclude a post-intervention assessment. Operations in Bosnia, Sierra Leone, Afghanistan, and Iraq were ongoing as of 2005, thus post conflict data is unavailable for assessment (Dobbins *et al.* 2005). We focus on the six remaining instances of military intervention aimed at nation building: Cambodia (1991–1993), El Salvador (1991–1996), Haiti (1994–1996), Mozambique (1992–1994), Namibia (1989–1990), and Somalia (1992–1994). Of these cases, only the military intervention in Haiti was U.S. led (Caprioli and Douglass 2008: 52).

In their specification of the cases examined, only one is a military intervention led by a state. So, we must redefine their question as follows:

When a military power intervenes to aid in nation building is women's equality increased? (cf. Caprioli and Douglass 2008: 45)

How did they make these choices? Clearly the "population" for studying the original question is all such interventions. There are lots of differences among such interventions (e.g., pre- and post-Cold War, whether the post-conflict state was a state before the conflict, duration of conflict before the intervention, the duration of the intervention, the size of the military presence during the height of the intervention, whether the military intervention took place after UN Security Council Resolution 1325 which in 2000 pledged UN peacekeepers to attend to gender in all operations).

Conceptually, there are two ways of thinking about their choices. Either they delimited the population or they selected cases among that population to study. Given their question, on our read, the "population" is all such interventions throughout history. They studied a subset of that population which they selected for a variety of reasons – availability of data and ability to follow a legitimated methodology (Meernik 1996) primary among them. Each of these choices is defended in the text.

Having discussed their operationalization of the concept of "military intervention" in the context of clarifying the research question, population and sample, we still need to discuss how they operationalize the concept of "status of women." They use three variables: measures of fertility rates, women's labor force participation rates, and the literacy ratios of women to men. These measures follow qualitative and quantitative research that which enhances the legitimacy of that way of operationalizing women's equality Caprioli (2009). (See Box 8.2.)

One might argue that the choice to study only those states that were states prior to the conflict left out a number of nation building conflicts in which gender-based violence is known to be virulent was a problematic choice given the research question (on gender and nation-building see D'Costa 2010). However, social scientists study social phenomena; sometimes we cannot study all aspects of the subject that interests us. Sometimes we have to scale back our question to a "doable" question. As long as we revisit our research question and make sure that we can answer our question using the research design we have planned, then there is nothing *a priori* wrong with scaling back a question.

Population

Your population is every case to which your question applies. For "when a military power intervenes to aid in nation building is women's equality increased?," the population is "all such interventions." For "what forms of agency are manifest in women's resistance?,'' the population is all women's resistance activism across time, nation, whether transnational or local. For "what theory of justice is put into practice in the work of women's organized environmental activism?,'' the population is all environmental activist organizations across time and nation, whether transnational or local in which women are activists. For scientific study using statistical tools, the "cases" in the population need to be "identical" so that the mathematics of probability which underlie statistical analysis are appropriate. Social scientists, therefore, sometimes delimit a population to those cases that are more "alike" as we saw in the study by Caprioli and Douglass above.

The challenge for the social scientist is to make sure that her *question* is guided by her *theory* and not by the methodology of statistical analysis. The population is all those "cases" to which, according the researcher's theoretical conception of the question, the research question applies.

What are Cases?

Not all social and political scientists view even "the case" in the same way. Charles Ragin identifies four different conceptualizations of "case" that reflect the philosophy of social science of the researcher. Each conceptualization is epistemological at its root. The labels are Ragin's (Ragin and Becker 1992: 8–11); the descriptions are ours.

- *Cases are objects.* They are empirically real and bounded, and conventional so there is no need to defend the unit, as in a sociologist studying families or an international relations scholar studying nation-states.
- *Cases are found.* They are empirically real and bounded and we can assess the boundaries of the case as an anthropologist defends the boundaries of a community of study and as a political scientists needs to justify what is a "nation" in a study of nationalism.
- *Cases are conventions.* They are theoretical constructs imposed on the world as in the "developed countries" or people in "poverty" with such shared scholarly reflection that they become conventions. These units are constructed from the interaction of ideas (people in poverty cannot live sustainably) and evidence (in most of the world a dollar a day is too little to live on sustainably).
- *Cases are made.* They are theoretical constructs imposed on the researcher's study through her research. Grounded theorists create their categories of data through their study of their data (Charmaz 2006: 47). For instance, imagine a study of "ecofeminism" or "indigenous rights" through a study of the claims of those who advocate "ecofeminism" or of those who identify as "indigenous" (Sturgeon 1997).

When you think about what you are looking for in a case, you might ask yourself, what kind of thing do you think a case is? Is a case determined by conventional understandings that existed prior to your study (and will possibly persist afterward) or that will be developed through your research? Is it a generally studied unit (like an organization or a state), or is it one chosen for *this specific study* (as in states that went through post-conflict intervention)? And you might follow-up your answers to these questions by asking, how would my project be different if I understood a case differently (all conflicts about nation-building)? You may not be able to tell which epistemological view of "case" someone else is intending, but you should know your view. Careful exposition of your choices, not either conformity or nonconformity with existing literatures, gives credibility to your definition of the case.

Operationalization of Concepts

Return to your question. What are the important concepts in your question? Which of the concepts in your question are ones that everyone would agree upon and which are contested and perhaps the subject of your study?

Start with the uncontested concepts and define these with reference to the literatures on these concepts. Then consider the contested concepts and all of your concepts in relation to each other. In what context did the use of each concept develop? What are the dominant and less visible accounts of the concept? When the meaning of the concept became visibly less contested, what were the interests and questions that "lost" the contestation and what is the status of those concepts now? When we study a concept we need to take an interest in the contestations within the theoretical and political history of the use of the concept. How will you use the concept for your purposes? Where does this use fit in its theoretical and political history?

These same questions can be extended to the use of the concept in constellation with other concepts. Concepts often function in relation to each other. For example Aristotle uses the concepts of democracy, equality, and freedom in relation to each other. His uses are different from Rousseau's uses of the constellation of the same concepts. Most would argue that these authors mean three different things by these concepts. Further, the political leaders of two democracies in the present may use these concepts differently. Moreover, two candidates for office in the same country may use these concepts in constellation with each other differently. What constellation of concepts is at work in your project? You should look at their theoretical and political history in relation to each other.

Revisit contested concepts. What is the contestation? How does your project related to that contestation? How does the contestation relate to your research question? Is it core to your research question or is it not relevant to your question? Does the concept travel across questions? How does the meaning of the concept change across questions? Can you study *your question* with a measure that measures only one notion of the concept, or do you need a way of assessing its multiple meanings?

We use the idea of *operationalization* to guide our thinking about how to assess the concepts we are interested in understanding using variables that a social scientist can observe and measure. In Chapter five we focused on how you conceptualize your research question. As you do that work, you are likely thinking about how to measure or evaluate the concepts related to that question. First, start by considering the research design that Super Researcher – the Super Hero of research who has no practical obstacles and no personal constraints – might plan. Super Researcher can get all data all the time from anywhere. What do you need to do in order to answer your question? Then, consider the constraints of the real, political world many of which have to do with the fact that you are studying social not physical phenomena. What *can* you do? What data *can* you gather? You cannot read minds, so if you are researching values, you are going to need measures of values. If you want to know the human rights conditions in many countries over many years, you will need to draw on *others'* data about these conditions. What do you think of the ways that others have gathered the data you need? Can you use their data or do you need to modify what they have done? You need to evaluate existing data and the data you might be able to gather from the perspective of: (1) how well does it measure the concept you are studying; (2) how well was the research done; and (3) how credible will research based on these data be to your audience. This second stage of research design is about how to operationalize your variables.

Every empirical researcher, whether using qualitative or quantitative data, in fact *before* figuring out which methods to use, needs to operationalize her variables. Operationalization is an intermediate step between research design and data collection or production. (From a perspective of the critical use of power in social science, this is the step when our theoretical assumptions get masked such that we can refer to our "data" as "*variables*" or with adjectives like "*independent.*")

When we do empirical work whether qualitative or quantitative, *operationalization* is the step in which we decide what "data" best captures the concept we are trying to study. Operationalization is particularly difficult for feminists because we often seek to research essentially contested concepts like the family, empowerment, power, gender, sexuality, and gender equality and we often contest widely accepted concepts like equality, freedom, rights, democracy, and the state as well. Moreover, we are frequently very interested precisely in their contestation or in the ways in which they are unstable (Barker 2005; Lombardo, Meier and Verloo 2009). To operationalize such variables with certain measures therefore would be to limit the range of find-ings our research could generate. For example see Box 8.1 on the challenges of operationalizing a contested concept that also has political import because at stake is the funding to organizations who can prove that they do "women's empowerment."

Sometimes a feminist wants to measure gender (an aspect of social, polit-ical and economic life and identities). Sometimes she wants to measure women (how many women are affected by an issue). Often we use women

---

Box 8.1   Operationalizing empowerment

In the 1990s feminists wanted to study the empowerment of women through burgeoning credit programs. Credit gave women and their fami-lies a surge of capital. Researchers struggled to find ways of measuring the impact of this surge in dept on women's empowerment, a word that was difficult to define in English and lacked adequate translation in most languages.

Other changes in the family that cause such an increase in money included having a son go work in capital city or abroad, or having a son get married and receiving a dowry. Studies that operationalized "empow-erment" by assessing "decision-making" by women that did not include other sources of money were not able to tell if the increase in "decision-making" by women was a result of the opportunity to make any deci-sion (created by having money to spend) or because the *woman* of the family had received credit.

A study by Hashemi *et al.* (1996) has a version of this problem. They use eight measures: "mobility, economic security, ability to make small purchases, ability to make larger purchases, involvement in major house-hold decisions, relative freedom from domination within the family, political and legal awareness, and involvement in political campaigning and protests". Of these, four – economic security, ability to make small purchases, ability to make larger purchases, and involvement in major household decisions – are highly correlated with having money to spend and thus the study seems bias toward finding that credit is empowering, by virtue of the particular operationalization of empowerment.

In a study at about the same time Ackerly measured empowerment as having knowledge of the accounting – the cost of inputs, the income, and the profit – of the enterprise funded by the loan. With this measure a woman would be considered empowered if she knew about the econom-ics of the enterprise funded by her loan. If her husband labored using the credit and she knew about the profitability of the enterprise, she would be considered empowered. She would not be considered empowered if she did the labor of the enterprise but did not know of its profitability. Changes in family dynamics were not measured (Ackerly 1995).

as the dependent variable to tell us something about gender. For example, Neumayer and Plümper (2007) tell us something important about gender by measuring the numbers of women and men killed in natural disasters. Women are up to 14 times more likely than men to die in a natural disaster but where gender equality is relatively greater, that number goes down; under conditions of poverty, that number goes up (for a further reference to this research see Chapter nine).

The feminist operationalizes her concepts in ways that are theoretically and empirically informed by the contestations around the concept in question. We often hear, "why do I have to be a feminist in order to use gender as a variable?" The answer is that feminism informs us about the full range of contestations around the concept of gender. Therefore, well-immersed in contemporary feminist theory and practice, we can better operationalize the concept. (see Box 8.2).

When we use the concept of gender as an independent variable, we treat as static and uncontested a political reality that is the terrain of contestation. This basic insight has been used by Lisa Cosgrove (2003) in psychology and Drucilla Barker (2005) in economics to point out that such framing imports an essentialist view of women and gender differences into an empirical inquiry, such that conclusions from such research cannot help but reify essentialisms, i.e. the idea that women are inherently different from men. For example, a study designed to explain the gender pay gap using a large n statistical method may end up justifying this gap without feminist theories of gender that question gender divisions of labor. The finding that women's greater family responsibilities are correlated with their lower pay compared to men may be sufficiently explanatory from the perspective of non-feminist researchers and policymaking communities, but not to feminists (Nielsen *et al.* 2005; see also Sax *et al.* 2002; Steinberg 1991).

Feminism can help us better operationalize concepts that are not obviously gendered as well. Consider measures of poverty. Most measures assess

Box 8.2 Operationalizing gender equality

Feminists have shown that gender is an aspect of social, political, and economic life. When trying to choose what to measure as a proxy for gender equality, we necessarily have to make difficult choices that reflect the relevant aspects of gender and gender equality, but that don't inadvertently misrepresent others. We might measure the ratio of female to male literacy, percentage of national elected offices held by women, maternal mortality rate, sex ratios, women's salaries as a percentage of men's or even the percentage of men who have had a vasectomy cross-nationally. See Boxes 5.1 and 5.2 on theorizing gender equality.

Box 8.3 "Human security": a feminist research ethic's reflection on the construction of a concept

The concept of human security has been defined by some researchers as referring only to cases where at least 1,000 civilian deaths have occurred (see www.humansecuritygateway.info). These cases then are able to be labeled "human security" crises. The "population" constructed by the concept of human security is deliberately narrow and exclusionary.

This operationalization excludes many cases of the kinds of insecurity, for example insecurity due to environmental, economic, and gender-based threats, that the concept of *human* security as opposed to national security was developed to take account of in the first place. The "human" part of the concept was intended to challenge and redress not only the traditional concept of security in which the state and its borders rather than the individual was the object to be "secured," but also the *ways* in which human insecurity is experienced such as in violence against women or by immigrants and minority groups. Violence such as rape or loss of property which may not result in death, may nonetheless leads to profound insecurity and vulnerability to further violence, particularly for those functioning at the cusp of survival. While considered path-breaking in its earliest formulation, over time, the concept of human security has become more limited as policymakers and researchers have sought to "measure it," i.e. make it amenable to quantification, and "apply it" by targeting international policies to certain "populations."

Many researchers have challenged the narrow concept and operationalization of the human security concept for its implicit privileging of physical security and military threats over other threats and forms of insecurity (food, housing, environmental, domestic, psychological etc.). Feminist researchers have argued that like the concept of national security it renders threats to women's insecurity invisible since they often occur in the private or domestic sphere (even when they are politically motivated), are less able to be counted due to gender ideologies that keep women silent, and may not result in death or certainly "mass death" in any calculable way (Truong *et al.* 2007).

poverty at the household level. There is significant evidence that resources are unevenly distributed within households (Borooah and McKee 1994; Cantillon and Nolan 2001; Davies and Joshi 1994; Dwyer and Bruce 1988; Phipps and Burton 1995). A feminist research ethic makes the researcher attend to the literature that reflects on the power of epistemology to make the poverty of women invisible. Therefore, a feminist researcher might deploy economic data that uses nonmonetary indicators as Cantillon (2001) does in her study of household poverty or measures of "cost" that take into account human capital (DeRiviere 2006). Further, familiarity with the feminist literature related to your project can let you know what other "vital variables" feminism tells us have bearing on our question, as Nielson *et al.* (2005) do in their study of gender equity in a university context.

A feminist research ethic helps you operationalize your variables by reminding you to attend to the power of epistemology that is potentially concealed in this step of your research process (see Box 8.3). It reminds you of the disciplinary and conceptual boundaries that may constrain your imagination about how best to operationalize the concepts in question, and commits you to noting those aspects of your world view (ontology) and assumptions (epistemology) that will play a role in your research design. This research ethic reminds you not to let that role be clandestine.

Selection Jargon and Challenges

Social scientists have developed language for the different methods we use to describe *how* we choose cases and how we identify which data to collect or which sources to draw on to generate that data. Using this language can help you be precise in your account of your choices. To improve the quality of your work, you might reflect on these choices in light of the potential challenges of the respective methods.

As mentioned in Chapter seven, the idea of "sampling" comes from mathematical probability theory. If a sample from a population is selected at random then the patterns of correlation found based on studying the sample can be generalized across the population. Social scientists often use the word "sample" to refer not only to case selection from a population, but also to the products of other kinds of selection – people to interview, documents to analyze, etc. In this section we discuss methods of selecting cases and data. We choose methods of selection, guided by our research question and the choices we have already made about theoretical and practical plausible operationalization of the key concepts at stake in our question.

When you make choices, be sure to be clear: (1) what you are selecting; (2) why; (3) how; and (4) at what cost? That may seem obvious, but return to the study by Caprioli and Douglass (2008) with which we opened the chapter. Look at the article yourself. They are very clear about the logistical reasons that they make the choices they do. Do they reflect on the potential limitations of the choices they had to make? No, in part because they mischaracterize their delimiting as a limiting of the "population" of cases to a certain subset, rather than a *selection* of the population made for logistical reasons. Just be clear. As you make those choices, you may be choosing not from the entire population but from a large subset of that population. Maybe you are selecting from a pool of not all countries, but countries in Latin America. Maybe you don't speak Portuguese and so you decide to select your case or cases only from a pool of countries where Spanish is the dominant language. Maybe there are unstable governments in your population and so you decide to narrow your pool to exclude those. In social science, there are social and political reasons to remove cases from your population; these reasons cannot be justified using scientific methods and/or discourse, although you will often see scholars doing so. However, you can and should explain why, given the theoretical, historical understanding of your question and concepts, these choices are not theoretically (or politically) problematic.

Selecting a Case for a One-Case Study

To select your case for a single case study, you need to pick a case that will enable you "to illustrate an idea, to explain the process of development over time, to show the limits of generalizations, to explore uncharted issues by starting with a limited case, and to pose provocative questions" (Reinharz 1992: 167). Reflect on both the reasons why observations and analysis based on your case may be extended to other cases and reasons why these are unique to your case. Often in qualitative research, the case "chooses you" in the sense that some other research or puzzle has led you to stumble on *this* case and not another (Stake 2005: 450). Bourdieu carries out an ethnography of Kabyle society because it is "a particularly well-preserved androcentric society" (Bourdieu 2001: vii). Elisabeth Friedman chooses Venezuela in which to study women's mobilization during democratic transitions because:

> Its two transitions to democracy and corresponding waves of women's mobilization allow for a broad range of comparisons. Political opportunity structure analysis can be used to compare the effects of regime phase – authoritarian, transition, or consolidation – on women's organizing within and across two democratization periods (Friedman 2000: 8).

Mary Beth Mills studies women's resistance to the oppressions of newly industrializing economies by studying factory-level activists in Thailand because these workers' struggles "have much in common with other workers' struggles in similar settings of new industrialization" (2005: 119). Features that she identifies as salient include rapid economic growth, cash-strapped agricultural regions, strikes and other organized forms of labor protest (2005: 117). (See also Bennett and Elman (2006) and Hesse-Biber (2007) for criteria for picking a single case.)

In a book-length treatment it is easier to give a full account of your reason for choosing a case than it may be in an article. Every case-based researcher must justify her selection if only briefly. Feminists must also consider these choices in light of a feminist research ethic. Depending on audience, these reflections may not be included in the methodological sections of published scholarship. Thus, in seeking insights from other scholars' case selection you may need to read between the lines.

Selecting Multiple Cases for a Comparative Study

If we cannot study *all* cases, how should we select which ones to study? Whether we are planning on a large sample or a small sample, we have a variety of tools available to us.

In *Qualitative Research Methods for the Social Sciences*, Bruce Berg (2004) summarizes the different kinds of sampling techniques. In general, forms of *probability sampling* techniques are used when we cannot study an entire population and we want to identify cases or subject-participants that can represent the whole population. We expect to see variation among the subject-participants in the sample and that variation is expected to be like the variation in the population as a whole in the relevant respects.

Often we associate random or probability sampling with quantitative, statistical methods. However, they are appropriate for many research designs that plan on using qualitative, interpretive methods as well. Perhaps you know your population, but you do not have a theoretical reason for studying one or another case within the population. So you pick a *random sample* or a convenience sample (see Box 8.4).

However, random sampling by virtue of its association with scientific and

---

Box 8.4 Random sample and convenience sample: example from Feliciano, Robnett, and Kolmaie

Feliciano *et al.* (2009) reveal the gendered nature of racial preferences in their study of dating preferences among a random sample of white men and women on the most popular US Internet dating website. They find that the racial hierarchies of white men and women are significantly different. Overall, white men were more willing to date non-whites although white men were more likely to exclude blacks as possible dates, while white women were more likely to exclude Asians. The intersectional analysis made possible by these data uncovers not merely racial stereotypes but also racialized images of masculinity and femininity and the way these racialized gender stereotypes shape prejudices with material consequences for marriage and social integration outcomes.

Their data come from a random sample of the white men and women on the dating site. However, for their research question, their population is actually all white men and women who date. The use of a particular dating site is a way of obtaining a convenience sample of that population.

statistical techniques may conceal some of the problems associated with studying social phenomena: there may be selection bias introduced in your definition of the population. For example, Carrie Lui Currier notes that because in China the municipal roles are incomplete and faulty with addresses for buildings that are not there, etc. the "population" cannot be identified so one cannot take a random sample of it. Instead surveyors in China use other means to assemble a sample that is approximately capable of representing the population as a whole (Currier 2007a: 108–9; 2007b 76–7). Other problems with random sampling may be encountered in the social context of research and addressed with an alternative, purposive sampling approach. For instance, imagine that you are studying microfinance in Afghanistan. You see that there is Y number of microfinance programs operating there and you randomly select a subset of those for study. Claiming a random sample of programs masks how the entire population came into existence, that is through competitive proposals reviewed by Women for Women International (2008). Organizations applied to set up programs in certain places, with certain populations, drawing on their relative strengths and their assessments of where the opportunities lay. To study the role of microfinance programs in Afghanistan today based on a random sample misses a system level dimension that might suggest that all microfinance programs established in Afghanistan after 2001 were in fact one case.

This would be an occasion for *purposive (or theoretical) sampling*, that is, selecting to study *particular* cases because together these promise to give you diversity on the variables you have chosen to assess your key concepts. However, you might be fully aware of the structures constraining the possibility of a representative random sample (hopefully you would be if this were your area of interest), but not know *which* organizations to select in order to get a purposive sample. In this case, it may make sense to use a random sample, but you would expect to defend your choice of random sampling not because it is statistically reliable but because your preferred method of sampling – theoretical – would not be available without doing the study you are proposing to do on *all* of the microfinance programs in Afghanistan.

Lack of variability in your cases and sources may be evidence that you are selecting on the dependent variable – that is, examining only those cases or sources for which your major hypothesis or argument holds (see Box 8.5 on selection bias). Identifying this problem is an opportunity for a deliberative moment. What in your theory, conceptualization, or selection method made you do that? Such an approach to research design not only compromises the credibility of your research and your ability to generalize from your findings or to generate new questions based on your findings, but it can cause you to miss much of the picture of the phenomena you are seeking to study. For example, in studies of gender and nationalism the dominant hypothesis theorizes a single, common relationship between hierarchical gender relations

> ## Box 8.5 Caprioli and Douglass on non-probablistic selection bias: women and post-conflict nation-building
>
> Caprioli and Douglass (2008) explore the impact of post-conflict, internationally-administered nation-building initiatives on women in the population. They select a sample of six comparable, contemporary cases of countries that were sovereign territories prior to the conflict and military intervention and where that intervention is officially terminated. However, their theoretically informed selection of cases requiring the cases to have been fully sovereign countries prior to international intervention imports a substantial bias into the analysis of the relationship between women and nation-building. The case selection excludes two of the most well-known, recent cases of nation-building – Timor Leste and Kosovo – where the very raison d'être for the conflict and post-conflict nation-building was foreign occupation and the violent squashing these nation's claims to state sovereignty. Both these nation-building cases involved significant commitments by the international administration to gender equality and women's empowerment in the post-conflict rebuilding. Thus their exclusion from the six cases selected is likely to have implications for the study of the connection between military intervention, women's status, and nation-building. Further, reflecting on the exclusion of those two sites where attention to gender was a part of the peace-building operation makes us think about the theoretical implications of such exclusion; that is, a key variable – the intentionality of the intervention – is left out.

and typically violent nationalist movements. Yet women's involvement across the full range of national projects is quite diverse across time and place. Thus, selecting only those country cases where nationalist movements have led to civil war, secession, or state failure biases research findings about the relationship between gender and nationalism. It also fails to explain the causes and effects of women's involvement in national projects, on domestic and international conflicts for instance (cf. Vickers 2006).

Testing several contending theoretical hypotheses in a comparative research design of a range of cases prevents the "selecting on the dependent variable" scenario just described. In the gender and nationalism research project, deliberately selecting cases that do not correspond to the dominant argument is a good starting point; you would choose country cases where there is no significant nationalist movement and cases where there are non-violent nationalisms. If you find yourself with only cases that confirm your hypothesis, you are not actually testing it. Either you may need to introduce a greater range of independent variables and cases or you may need to go back and rework your feminist theory of the relationship between gender and nationalism.

What makes a sampling mechanism "rigorous" is not how closely it approximates statistical methods (cf. King *et al.* 1994), but rather how reasoned a defense of your choice you can offer. As we said in Chapter seven, the credibility of your research conclusions depends on how you describe and justify your research design. Your choices of cases, and the methods you use to identify your sources and data, are of principle importance in that justification.

Selecting Sources

To identify sources to inform you about your cases, you will consider a range of selection techniques and you need to justify these in your account of your research.

For identifying sources, *non-probabilistic selection* techniques are chosen for theoretical and instrumental reasons. However, for each non-probabilistic technique, you need to reflect on what possible biases may become buried in your data due to your technique.

A *convenience selection* is chosen because gathering information from these cases is possible logistically. When studying an entire population over a period of time, how should we select when that period of time should begin and when it should end? Sometimes there are landmark events that are theoretically appropriate beginning and end points. But often, as in the case of Caprioli and Douglass (2008) or Neumayer and Plümper (2007), or Eschle and Maiguashca (2007), we study *these* cases, we interview *these* people because they are here now, accessible, willing, and we have had the proper introductions. For example, Neumayer and Plümper studied 141 natural disasters from 1981 to 2002 because there were data available on these (Neumayer and Plümper 2007). They did not study all natural disasters but rather all those during a period for which there are existing data. A convenience sample may be combined with other methods. You might randomly select ten organizations to study and then rely on a "convenience" sample of their documents, workers to interview, or clients to interview. The sampling of your "cases" is random. You have a convenience selection of data on those cases. Note that the sampling method you use to select your cases is NOT the same as the method you use to identify the data sources.

A researcher with existing theoretical or empirical knowledge of the issue of study may use purposive, judgment, or *theoretical* selection to identify those sources that are most likely to be able to inform her about her question. For example, when asking communities about their water, it is often best to ask those whose job it is to get the water.

The researcher who wants to get the views of people from a range of categories of people (because you theoretically expect certain variables to be important and therefore need variability on those dimensions) may use *quotas*. For example one might want to interview subject-participants who work at different levels of an organizational hierarchy, some men and some women, some of each age group, some with different levels of education. If these attributes are not widely distributed across an organization (there may be only one woman with a masters degree), then a probabilistic or convenience selection technique may not give you the range or representativeness your project requires. For quota selection techniques, identify the categories (variables) that are theoretically important to you. Then use some other method of selection to get a certain number of interview subject-participants with characteristics of the relevant categories. In this example, you might purposively select to interview the one woman with a master's degree, but select at random a subset of the larger number of men and women with at least secondary schooling. As always, reflect on what additional information is revealed or masked by your selection technique.

How do you know who to interview about a phenomena when you don't know enough about the phenomena or the people involved to be able to identify interview subject-participants? Because feminists are often studying hidden phenomena, our interview subject-participants may also be hidden or hard to find, known to each other, but not publicly known. *Snowball* is a method of identifying interview subject-participants by which you ask each subject-participant to recommend other interview subject-participants (Atkinson and Flint 2001; Clark 2006: 419). This is the tool used by Eschle and Maiguashca (2007) to identify women activists in the anti-globalization movement. *Note, this is a selection tool for sources, not a "sampling" tool for cases; yet researchers often refer to "snowball sampling" when referring to identifying sources.*

Snowball identification yields a biased selection of sources and thus requires you to explore qualities and the import of the bias. A feminist research ethic reminds you to worry about what sociological or epistemological boundaries influence your roster of sources if you use a snowball method for identifying them. The snowball method should not leave you at the whim of research facilitators. Rather, the point is to identify interview subject-participants "with certain attributes or characteristics necessary in a study of a particular population" (Clark 2006: 419; also Berg 2004: 36). Snowball referrals should be used when you *cannot* identify these subject-participants by other means or when those other means might have a different and politically problematic particular bias. Snowball should not be the chosen technique because it is an easier way of identifying subject-participants. Just because it is *an* acceptable method for some research designs doesn't mean it is appropriate for your research design.

Sometimes, it is difficult to get introductions. Snowball selection should not be used to get introductions. If you can identify your research subject-participants through another more theoretically appropriate selection mechanism, you should. In Chapter twelve we discuss the roles of research facilitators, gatekeepers, introductions, and social networks. Snowball is a method of identifying those potential sources that you may not be able to identify yourself through other means. Using social networks to gain introductions to those sources does not mean your selection mechanism was "snowball." Do not confuse your method for deciding *who to interview* with your method for *getting the interview*.

By contrast the *anti-snowball* method is a form of identifying a purposive sample. If your theory says to seek information from non-elites as a feminist research ethic would likely encourage you to do, then you need a method of identifying sources that does not track a particular system of power. In fact, you need a system for identifying sources that explicitly works against the systems of power that your background research indicates are at work. These include formal institutional power, but they also include the power embedded in social networks and social capital. A snowball selection process may not attend to the epistemological power embedded in those networks.

Let's say you are studying the views of those marginalized within women's movements. How do you identify them? They are, by definition, marginalized. A random sample of all people in women's movements is not possible and, in fact, the population as defined by a third party (a donor, an association, or a previous study) might actually exclude those marginalized by movement organizations. A snowball method would yield people in a network and so, by definition, would not include the sources you are interested in identifying. An anti-snowball sample works in tandem with another methodology to enable you to identify those at the margins.

For example, if looking for activists at the margins of their social movements, the researcher uses methods such as focus groups, participant observation, review of newspapers and movement documents, observation at public venues in order to identify those at the margins of the subject of inquiry. She might identify the person who says nothing in a meeting or the person who asks a question that no one answers. In listening for anti-snowball sources, the researcher looks for people who are self-advocates rather than those who are advocating on behalf of others. She looks for people who do their activism politically not professionally (for their livelihood). She looks for people with intersectional concerns such that they might find it hard to get their issues heard as the "big" issues of a movement (see for example Ackerly 2008a).

Anti-snowball is purposive in that it is theoretically informed (for example, select those who are marginalized). However, the anti-snowball technique does not tell you which sources to select exactly, but rather guides you in your effort to identify them. It is a method that challenges the power of social networks and yet often is loosely dependent on them though in ways that risk mimicking a snowball method. Attentive to this potential and to the benefits of both snowball and anti-snowball methods of identifying sources, researchers can practice a feminist research ethic using either tool.

Conclusion

No matter what your research question and the research design most appropriate for exploring it, you will be confronted by choices over which cases to select and which sources and data to use. You will need to decide what kind of cases and sources to examine, how many to select, and how to select them. Your main concern throughout will be to make choices that best enable you to address your research question in a defensible, thoughtful, and, therefore, rigorous way. We need to be aware of the potential pitfalls, advantages and biases involved in making any selection choices and to make these explicit in the presentation of our research. In the next chapters we discuss the various methods and tools for generating and collecting data. The same attentiveness of a feminist research ethic to potentially concealed bias that applies to this aspect of the research process applies to case or source selection.

Selected Sources for Further Reading

Goertz, Gary. 2006. *Social Science Concepts: A User's Guide*. Princeton, NJ: Princeton University Press.
Narayan-Parker, Deepa. 2005. *Measuring Empowerment: Cross-Disciplinary Perspectives*. Washington, DC: World Bank.
Ragin, Charles C., and Howard Saul Becker. 1992. *What Is a Case? Exploring the Foundations of Social Inquiry*. Cambridge: Cambridge University Press.

Chapter 9

Generating and Collecting Data

Introduction

In Chapter seven we offered you a theoretically informed approach to research design and in Chapter eight we unpacked the issues associated with selecting populations, cases, and samples for empirical research. In this chapter on methods for data collection we offer you a theoretically informed approach to using research methods and to making them feminist methods. Whereas in Chapters seven and eight we discussed the kinds of reflection that inform your choices about the architecture of your research design, in this chapter we discuss the method choices that you make and the ways you make them.

In order to make choices about the appropriate tools for creating and gathering data for your project, we preface our discussion of various methods with feminist-informed reflections on two key questions: First, to what extent do we gather, discover or produce data? We consider the import of the range of ontological, epistemological, and methodological reflections about data that feminists and other interpretive methodologists have encouraged. Second, are there distinctly "feminist" methods? Here we propose the view that "methods" are not "feminist"; rather scholarship is. When a scholar adopts and adapts a method in ways guided by a feminist research ethic, she is doing feminist scholarship. Finally, the body of the chapter explores a range of methods, identifying for what questions they are commonly valued, showing how they are used, and describing how feminists may adopt and adapt them in their research.

What are Data?

Sandra Harding argues there are three methods of social inquiry: "listening to (or interrogating) informants, observing behavior, or examining historical traces and records" (Harding 1987: 2). The first produces "talk data," the second, "participant, visual, or numerical data," and the third, mainly "textual data." Although social scientists tend to treat "observed" data as "gathered" data, in fact all three kinds are co-created through the power of epistemology, attending to boundaries and intersectionality, relationships, and the situatedness of the researcher and research subject-participant. In this chapter, we discuss ways of attending to these commitments across all kinds of data. Through the lens of a feminist research ethic, the differences across kinds of data are *not* differences in how objective or *subjective* we view the data, but rather in how consistently we apply a feminist research ethic in collecting and analyzing this data. What kind of concrete data do you need to research your question? And how will you collect or generate it?

Whether a researcher gathers, discovers, produces or co-creates data (with her subject-participants) depends on the researcher's epistemological perspective. For instance, Dvora Yanow (2006) has argued that it is inappropriate to refer to the material of qualitative, interpretive research as "data." One way to deal with the limited language of the scientific method is, following Ramazanoğlu and Holland, to be clear that the social scientist is engaged in *data production*, not *data collection*. Ramazanoğlu and Holland go on to show that the understanding of what it means to produce data differs by theoretical perspective. Consider social constructivists and poststructuralists whose ontological perspectives both view knowledge as produced through research and yet who disagree as to *how* that knowledge is produced (see Box 5.6 on theoretical perspectives on resistance politics).

We mean this book to guide the researcher regardless of her theoretical perspective. Therefore, we switch among references to data "production,"

9.1 DATA PRODUCTION AND DATA COLLECTION

KEY CONCEPT

"The term 'data production' implies that information gathered by the researcher is produced in a social process of given meaning to the social world. This is distinct from 'data collection', which, at its simplest, can imply that 'facts' are lying about waiting for the researcher to spot them" (Ramazanoğlu and Holland 2002: 154).

In social science, it is most common to refer to "data collection," "gathering data," or "creating a data set." This view is consistent with an epistemological view that is not reflective of a feminist research ethic. Guided by a feminist research ethic, we reflect on the production of our data. We may then decide to refer to the process as "data collection," but that "collection" will be more rigorous because we will have reflected on the potential for the politics of knowledge to influence the form and content of our data.

"collection," and "generation" in an attempt to destabilize a reader's commitment to one view or another of data. Recall your reflections guided in Chapter five about the theoretical perspectives that could be brought to bear on your research question and your reflections in Chapter eight about case selection. Throughout this book we have been guiding you to think about how meaning is created through research. Even though you may have chosen to work within one or two theoretical perspectives, consider what the others might say about your choice of method and use a range of theoretical perspectives to reflect upon your methods. We focus on the role of a feminist research ethic in guiding your reflections on method, but these are not a substitute for considering the particular insights of certain theoretical perspectives. While we offer some examples of these, our examples can be only illustrative. You will need to find your own habits and heuristics for theoretical reflection because one unavoidable feminist insight is that research is always constructed through the researcher's own particular engagement in her research (Gilgun and McLeod 1999; Presser 2005). A feminist research ethic can be a guide to developing these habits, but the habits must be your own.

Although this book works within the tradition of social science, it is our belief that a feminist research ethic can transform this tradition in incremental ways. In this chapter, that means developing ways of talking about and doing our methods that are recognizable to traditionally trained scholars. However, if after ontological and epistemological reflection on how and what it means to know, I view the purpose of research as to change the world, what methods best enable me to change the world through my research?

What are Feminist Methods?

In this book we uphold the distinction between methodology and method because we consider this distinction to be useful both conceptually and practically: first we set out our research design and then we proceed to do it. Those should be two different steps in the process. Yes, they are distinct in conception. But in feminist practice, when we do the work of defining and refining the methods that we will use to gather evidence, we are also doing methodological work that requires us to think epistemologically and theoretically about the meaning of what we are trying to study.

For some, there are no particularly feminist methods, only feminists deploying them. For others, there are indeed feminist methods (Ramazanoğlu and Holland 2002). In our view, feminism is itself a contested concept so to assert that there are "feminist methods" is theoretically problematic (Ackerly 2008b). If by "feminist methods" one means that there are methods that all feminists use or that there are methods that feminists use and others do not use, then the claim is not descriptively accurate. Likewise, to suggest that "feminist" methods are used by all researchers who were feminist is so vague as to be meaningless as the claim doesn't tell us at all what to do and how to do it.

However, we might say that there are "feminist methods" in the sense that when a feminist adopts and adapts a research method to her project, she does so by reflecting on the method through the lens of feminist theory or through what we have been calling a feminist research ethic. On this view, we make a method into a feminist method by thinking through our use of the method in light of a feminist research ethic. Now many feminists have done this before us and don't call that reflection "practicing their feminist research ethic." However, the steps they take exhibit a feminist research ethic such as we set out in Chapter two and have been deploying throughout the book. Thus we offer it to you as a tool for turning any method into a feminist method *and* as a theoretical basis for the intuitions that lead to those modifications.

For example, when doing participatory rural appraisal, Lorena Aguilar and Itzá Castañeda (2001) use a gendered lens to design a process by which men and women contribute to the assessment of the community's resourcees and needs. Knowing that men and women have socially determined roles and relationships, they include some gender segregated and some mixed activities. However, there is a problem in calling this adaptation of the participatory method "feminist" because it really is about making the research better by any standard, so what is feminist about that? Anyone who notices that different people in a community have different perspectives on its resources and needs can attend to gender difference among these. If "everyone" notices gender, then there is nothing *uniquely* feminist about attending to gender in participatory rural appraisal. This common retort of scholars who do not consider themselves feminists is often articulated as a criticism of feminism; it may be used to suggest that feminism doesn't contribute anything in particular to scholarship. Actually, such a claim, even when delivered as a criticism, is in fact evidence of feminists' successes at influencing their field. I might respond, "I agree. Isn't it great to see mainstream social scientists' recognizing the importance of feminist considerations – whatever they call them – to their own work?" In this sense, the feminist contribution is the *developed practice of theoretically informed and experientially informed research that attends to power dynamics, boundaries, and the situatedness of the researcher*. A given feminist researcher may be no better than a researcher who does not recognize the importance of feminism on her or his research. However, continued resistance to considering the importance of attending to *power dynamics, boundaries, and the situatedness of the researcher* provides evidence of the need for continued feminist scholarship.

Method Selection, Adoption, and Adaptation

Here we set out common methods for data production and how they might be adopted and adapted in feminist scholarship. As you make your own choices, we invite you to ask yourself, how can reflecting on epistemology, boundaries, and the situatedness of the researcher improve upon my use of this tool in my project? Consider yourself to be *contributing to a feminist research ethic* as you do your work, not just drawing on it.

Methods are specific tools not only for producing data (the subject of this chapter), but also for translating, interpreting, and analyzing that data (see Chapters ten and eleven). Methods not only specify ways of identifying whose insights and experiences we should draw upon, but also give an account of the steps we take to mitigate the potential for reading our epistemological perspective into our observations. A method may also specify how power dynamics in the relationship between the researcher and her interlocutors are to be navigated. With a clear account of your methods, others can assess and contribute to your research agenda, thereby enabling your work to be collaborative in the feminist sense, even if you work on a discreet project.

Students, particularly graduate students heading off to the field to collect qualitative data and having had limited course work and mentoring in qualitative methods, are often disappointed that so much of the discussion of qualitative methods focuses on theoretical concerns when what they feel they need are concrete usable suggestions. However, all methods are skills developed with practice so concrete suggestions need to be treated as ways of developing your skill. Whatever your methods, you cannot develop your skills by being well read in methods. It takes *practice* and critical reflection on that practice.

Qualitative methods need to be adapted to each project. Each researcher becomes a methodologist when she takes ownership of the intellectual work involved in making methodological choices. Having developed your sense of a feminist research ethic throughout this book, we invite you in this chapter to use your attention to epistemology, boundaries, and the situatedness of the researcher to guide your choice and adaptation of the methods you will need for your particular research question. Students who are engaged in secondary source research and not gathering their own data should use these tools for assessing the secondary research available to them.

Selecting an appropriate method for generating or collecting data entails: (1) being aware of the various methods available; (2) adopting each method you use in a way you can defend as appropriate to your question and research design; and (3) adapting the method to your purpose in ways that you can defend to experts in your field. As we discussed in Chapters three and seven for other stages in the research process, as you choose your methods you should also map out a research plan that is doable given the constraints you attended to in Chapter six, and prepare yourself to document changes in your method that become necessary during the research process. This chapter is organized so as to facilitate your awareness of the landscape of options and to empower you to adopt and adapt methods that enable you to gather the kind of data you determine are necessary for the analysis you want to bring to your research question.

Depending on your field of study, accounts of various methods and how one adapts them to inquiry may or may not be generous. In Education, there is much more written on the methods of case study than there is in Political Science for instance. We hope that in fields where methodological divisions themselves characterize the subject of scholarly engagement that cross disciplinary engagements will lead to more publications in which scholars share and defend their method choices. Concrete accounts of how we do our work, for example Raka Ray's account of how she chose her cases for studying women's activism in India (1999) (see discussion of Ray in Chapter seven) and Alker's reflections on *inter-coder reliability* in quantitative Peace Science (1996) (see Box 9.4 on inter-coder reliability) are needed.

Between us, we have used or supervised research that has used all of the methods discussed below, so we are personally familiar with many of the dilemmas that researchers using these methods face. Yet, each researcher, in each discipline, for each question, using each method, must adopt and adapt for herself and be able to defend those choices in the moment and over time. Consequently, as we set out in Chapter three, reflections on research methods take place in (at least) three stages of the research process: when you plan your research process, as you are carrying out your research, and when you offer an account of your research methods in your publication. Each stage requires its own justification; these may be very similar, or as the research yields unforeseen insights, these may be quite different. What is important for your research is not a *consistency* of research method from plan to published account, but rather *continuity in the thoughtfulness* that you exhibit about your project throughout.

In this chapter we share with you a broad range of methods for you to consider adopting and some insights from experience to help you adapt them to your project. Whether that alchemy changes *you* or the *method* into a "feminist" is really labeling. If these ways of *reflecting* on methodological choice become more broadly practiced in social science, feminism will have played a key role in transforming our social science disciplines. Pockets of transformation can be seen, but there is significant variability within institutions and across countries (Ackerly and True 2008a).

As we saw in Chapter seven, your research design will indicate which methods you need to adopt. In a second level of methodological reflection, the focus of this chapter, you adapt a given method to your purpose: designing the questions for a survey or interview, deciding whether to gather data yourself or with research assistance, etc. Feminist and non-feminist adaptations of methods can seem very similar in a proposal description. Many proposals do not require the level of detail that would be required to exhibit the degree to which feminist reflection informs your project. Therefore, it can sometimes seem to an audience, that there is a mismatch between your theoretical work (Chapter five) and your methods. However, in your research practice, you adapt your methods to your project and in the process your methods may be different in their *conceptualization* and *execution* than those who do not adapt their methods using a feminist research ethic.

If you lay out the plan-roadmap-account picture of the research process to yourself, you may be able to be explicit to others about when and how feminism informs your data production/collection techniques. If you cannot do this at the proposal stage, by keeping a good account of your research process, you should be able to do this when you write up your project.

Tools for Generating, Producing, Discovering, and Collecting Data

Each choice you make about which methods to use and how to deploy these has an effect on the data you gather and the knowledge claims you will be able to defend. As you make these choices, defend them to yourself with reasoned reflection and argument and be prepared to defend them to others. In a dissertation or other research proposal, you are required to do this explicitly. When you get to the field, you will be forced to rethink some of your choices. As we discussed in Chapter three, you need to keep track of these choices in your process map. A choice you make in the field may have ramifications on your final project. You may discover during your analysis that you *wish* you had treated a dilemma differently than you did at the time. If you keep good records of your research process, you will be able to defend these choices in the field, and, if they later turn out to be choices you regret, be clear about the impact these choices had on what data you produced and how it can be interpreted.

Of course, most of the choices you make are not ones you will later regret. Rather, most of your choices will be based on your reasoned reflection and will enable you to carry out a research project that will enable you to answer your research question.

Most of these techniques for collecting social data have been themselves the topic of methodological scholarship. In this section we don't try to synthesize that work, but rather to complement it by suggesting how a feminist research ethic can guide your use of each method. Our exposition differs in one other way from common expositions in that we think that it is not useful to think about the gathering of qualitative data as different from the gathering of quantitative data. True, a positivist might approach data collection or production differently from a postpositivist and a positivist is often using statistical tools for analysis, but this latter fact is not important. All data can be better collected if the researcher reflects using a feminist research ethic. For each method we identify research questions for which it has been appropriate, how to deploy the method, and how to reflect upon it using a feminist research ethic.

Oral History and Autobiographical Narrative

For certain subjects, our theoretical work indicates that our data need to include subjective reflections over time. Questions related to identity are of this nature. Therefore, Lisa Diamond (2006) studies sexual identity redevelopment using *longitudinal data* constructed from interviews over ten years. Oral histories similarly rely on multiple interviews, using lengthy open conversations that are semi-structured or hardly structured at all (Benson and Nagar 2006; Gluck and Patai 1991; Green-Powell 1997).

These narratives are generally recorded, transcribed, reviewed with their respondent, and analyzed using a range of analytical tools and approaches including discourse analysis, content analysis, and grounded theory (see Chapters ten and eleven). If appropriate and possible, there are multiple interviews. It may also be desirable for the researcher to revisit the narrative or the researcher's findings with the subject-participant. During the interview process, the interviewer may take notes to remind her of dropped threads that may need to be revisited either in the current interview or in a subsequent interview.

Feminists have experimented with different ways of gathering data about lives in a way that minimizes the role of the researcher in constructing such narratives and maximizes the subject-participants' authorship of her own narrative (see Behar 1994 [2003]; Behar and Gordon 1996). Techniques can also prove a tool for empowerment of subject-participants as in Rita Benmayor's (1991) use of a literacy program to do oral history or for increased self-awareness on the part of the subject-participants whether or not this was an intended aspect of the research (Diamond 2006: 479).

Feminists have likewise explored different ontological relationships to their data, often in ways that highlight the changeable and constructed nature of one's own narrative (Diamond 2006), but also in ways that enable the researcher to convert a dynamic narrative of shifting understandings and self-understandings into a comparatively static resource for analysis (Gilmore 2005; Maynard and Purvis 1994).

The dilemmas of narrative are not resolved if the subject-participant and the researcher are the same, as in an autobiography or autoethnography. Here too the subject-participant cannot control how the reader will engage with her narrative (Herndl 2006: 223). Moreover, the researcher selects the experiences or "data" that are salient in her memory at a particular moment from which to construct a narrative

Interviews

Interviews can be ways of producing oral history, as in the preceding discussion, or survey data (discussed below), and all manner of information that only those with certain experiences can know. Consequently, interviewing is a method or tool often suited to a whole host of research questions.

A single interview cannot capture the constructed narrative of a subject-participant the way that multiple interviews with the same research subject-participant can. Yet, for many projects, a single interview is appropriate. Interviews can be more or less structured or have portions that are quite structured and other portions that are more open-ended. Generally, we structure the most open-ended questions to occur at the moment during the interview when the subject-participant is most reflective (and verbose). This can be at the end of a relatively short interview, or after a few warm up questions. You may have an interview format that builds logically and therefore requires you proceed in order. Or you may have a format that allows you to be flexible, moving to the questions of the interview that enable the interview to feel more like a conversation for both researcher and subject-participant. Semi-structured, in-depth interviews allow guided focus, but also the ability of the subject-participant to give answers that do not conform to the researchers' (known or unknown) expectations.

Whatever form of interviewing you use, it is very important that you do not code your data during the interview. This may seem a silly caution. Of course, you would not code your data during the interview; you are too busy interviewing. Well, actually, a good curious feminist will likely be engaged with her interviewee. There are lots of ways to be engaged. Instead of asking yourself "what does this mean?" as you interview, try to have your background question in your mind be "what is she trying to tell me?" This will help you avoid prematurely analyzing as you interview, which may have the effect of limiting the insights and data generated from the interview. On the other hand, as we discuss in chapter ten, sometimes a respondent suggests an analysis (see Chapter ten), either directly or indirectly, during the interview. In this case, respecting the respondent means gathering – during the interview in progress (and later with other data) – as much information as is necessary and possible in order to confirm the analysis later.

Having reflected on the risks and rewards before you begin interviewing, when the unanticipated moment of analytical import occurs during an interview, you will have an intuition about whether to pursue that possible analysis with further questions, or to set it aside for later consideration. Doing so is a way of "co-producing" your data with your respondents, or using more positivist language, of respecting your respondents by gathering the data necessary to pursue the import of her insights. Both are consistent with a feminist research ethic.

Semi-structured and open-ended interviews can take more or less time depending on how forthcoming your subject-participant is. Timing in an interview is important. If you need to build trust, begin with short, less pointed questions or sometimes even sharing a personal connection or shared interest to establish rapport. (Chapter twelve explores the importance of making a first impression). You might have early questions inviting the subject-participant to describe something concrete with which they are familiar and later ask them to reflect on the meaning of the example. You may begin with trust-building apolitical questions and move toward more emotionally or politically charged questions. Be aware that when adrenaline rushes, people tend to offer answers that they have given before. A calm interview setting is necessary for imaginative responses. Be aware of interview fatigue – yours and your subject-participants'.

Box 9.1 Ethics and interviewing: Cohn on facing the ethics of the interviewee

"Putting genuine intellectual curiosity – the desire to understand – at the center of who I am when doing research is not difficult. But some of the situations in which I have practiced that centering have made me feel that my head would explode. I will never forget sitting and having lunch with former Secretary of Defense Robert McNamara. For the preceding twenty-five years, he had been to me an icon of arrogant immorality, a man with the blood of hundreds of thousands of innocent people on his hands. It is hard for me adequately to describe the intensity of my feelings about him, especially during the height of the Vietnam War. And now here I was, sitting next to him – we placed our cloth napkins in our laps, were served by uniformed waiters, sipped our wine, and chatted, all as in any other upscale luncheon – except that I have always thought of him as a war criminal. I put that thought aside, and re-centered myself in my interest in how he thinks about nuclear weapons now, and why. (This was when he was still holding his long public silence on Vietnam – I knew that it could not be a subject of my questions.) I asked what were for me genuine questions about what he had said, why he believed it, and why he did not take some other position. I was impressed by his thoughtfulness and his intelligence. I remembered the blood. I returned to the connection and respect I felt for him in the moment. It happened several more times before the meal was over. I have never been able to sort out the morality of that particular interaction to my own satisfaction" (Cohn 2006: 106).

As the narrative in Box 9.1 reveals, while conducting an interview Carol Cohn found her ethics challenged by her interview subject-participant. Cohn reflects on *how* to collect interview data, focusing on her own desire to understand, and facing each interview as an opportunity to understand more (Cohn 2006; see also Jacoby 2006).

From the perspective of a feminist research ethic there are certainly merits both to disclosing your own political or ethical views when they are challenged by an interviewee and to maintaining your distance as a researcher. Your own judgment as a researcher and context are crucially important. Sometimes the strategy of maintaining professional distance or "acting dumb" in the face of an interviewee's controversial comments can protect you and also generate highly-useful data.

Janet Johnson considers that "playing traditionally feminine can actually be helpful" in interview settings: "Sometimes, men are more likely to talk to women whom they see as harmless, and women can be more open to other women, especially if there are kids as an entrée" (2007: 22). But being treated as dumb is a different story. Kathy Hochstetler describes her interviews with a congressman in Venezuela: "He insisted on treating me like I was an idiot – 'Venezuela has three branches of government'" (2007: 22). Box 9.2 discusses how you need to think about how you will "get at" the information you need in an interview.

Guided by a feminist research ethic, you can use these experiences with gender, age, race, status and all forms of difference and discomfort in your interview research process in your writing and publishing. They may be

---

Box 9.2 "Honing in" on your question

Say you want to know if women consider the domestic work they do to be "work." You cannot read their minds as Super Researcher can. This question calls for a mixed method research design. Preliminary research suggests that if you ask women who spend approximately 15 hours per day in non-monetized labor directly if they "work" they will respond in a survey that they do "work." However, in preliminary research using small group discussions, interviews and informal conversations, you find that women don't value domestic work even though they work hard at it and it is necessary for their family sustenance. You suspect that they value market-related work over reproductive labor and you want a research tool that will assess this across the society, expecting that variability on this concept will be illustrative of variability in gender norms. A common way researchers "hone in" on such attitudes is by reframing the question slightly: you ask "what does your neighbor do?" This is a good proxy for how women see their own work. (See Barton 1958; Stern 2006.)

Box 9.3 Intersectionality in survey research

Intersectional analysis tells us that the categories of race and gender are not distinct. "Race is already gendered and gender is already raced" (Steinbugler *et al.* 2006: 822). Therefore, race and gender should be analyzed together if important data and certain social groups and the forces that affect them are not to be omitted from our analysis. To address this intersectionality in survey research, Steinbugler *et al.* call on scholars to develop "a battery of survey items that measure how race is gendered across a number of gender/racial categories, that is, Asian masculinity, White femininity, Chicana femininity, and so forth" (2006: 822). These new categories could then improve our operationalization of intersecting identities and prejudices in new survey questions and analysis in order to understand the complicated and often mutually-reinforcing relationship between intersecting disadvantages, prejudices and public policy.

extremely relevant in reflecting on the problem or research question you are studying. Certainly, a record of them needs to be part of your documentation of your research process.

Surveys

Surveys demand many of the same considerations as interviews because surveys are a way of producing data using the direct input of subject-participants in response to questions the researcher poses. We can conduct surveys by paper or online questionnaire, and directly through an interview. When an interview seeks both statistical and qualitative information, you can ask the respondent to fill out the survey themselves then go over their responses as a way of transitioning into the qualitative part of the interview. Like an interview, a survey questionnaire can be either structured or semi-structured, involve closed (e.g., "yes or no," or a "strongly disagree" to "strongly agree" scale), factual questions that allow responses to be quantified, and open-ended questions. See Box 9.3 for a discussion of intersectionality in survey research.

Online surveys offer many new possibilities for generating good data as they can provide hypertext, multimedia and other information links that can inform and improve survey respondents' knowledge and deliberation before or while taking the survey. For example, Polimetrix and Harris Interactive are two social and political survey research organizations companies using both representative and purposive sampling of populations. Polimetrix's online surveys use samples that are more informed than the US population, on average, but allow for "embedded" questions involving technology, such as TV, video and sound clips, and other information.

Focus Groups

A focus group can serve not only as a method of trust building (to complement other methods), as mentioned above, but also as a method of data collection (see also Chapter eleven for a discussion of Austen *et al.* (2003) which is an example of the use of a focus group in grounded theory). At its most straightforward, the focus group takes to social research the idea that "two heads are better than one". Often multiple people who have shared the same experience can come to a different understanding of the experience if they arrive at that understanding through shared conversation than they might if they arrived at it through individual reflection. Focus groups enable deliberative data and dialogical reflection. They also may enable shared reflection of a number of people at an organization without taking up too much of an organization's time. Like participant observation, this can be a tool that is respectful of the needs of an organization.

The politics of such groups can be complicated. In designing the focus group, consider the conditions under which respondents will be most forthcoming. Would it be better if they knew each other or not (you may not have a choice)? Is there a dimension of status that it is appropriate for you to consider? Rank at an organization? Time on the job? Gender? Race? Religion? Should you have diversity or similarity within focus groups? Should participants be representative of a larger population? There is no *a priori* right answer to any such question; rather you need to decide the right answer for your research question and for the measurement of the concepts at stake in your question. Consider your question and context in light of the four dimensions of a feminist research ethic carefully. Sometimes in a focus group – particularly if the participants are not known to each other – the group format can be a way of mitigating power hierarchies while enabling people to think together about your questions. Where they are known to each other, it may be a way of reifying those hierarchies. A focus group method needs to be used judiciously which can be a challenge as, in many contexts, focus groups are places where relational subjectivities among subject-participants can be only partially known to the researcher.

Unconventional or Unique Ways of Collecting Data

In this chapter we have reviewed the range of common ways of gathering, producing and co-creating data. This section is intended to stimulate your creativity by offering examples of researchers who found ways of studying something seemingly inaccessible to the researcher, either because of the nature of the issue (intimacy) or because of the politics of the access to certain resources (racism). In Chapter six we discuss myriad ways in which the particularities of context and research generate obstacles to inquiry. Profound obstacles such as the data do not exist (for example, because the people whose stories we wish to recover are dead) or the data are not accessible to someone like me (because I am African American) have been overcome by researchers' creative methodologies. When Elizabeth Waylan Barber wanted to learn how women did their weaving 20,000 years ago, she tried to copy a recovered piece of fabric (1994: 18). When W.E.B. Du Bois, an African American, was denied access to southern archives in the United States for his study of reconstruction, he used newspaper sources which at the time were unconventional sources for a social historian (1956). These authors study social phenomena using techniques that do not generate "typical" data. They did not change their question in order to have a research question that was researchable using their skill set and their discipline's conventional norms, but rather used their imaginations to generate unconventional research tools. When doing research with unconventional tools we still need to ask the questions that Jennifer Mason (2002: 40) puts to all quantitative and qualitative research:

- Are my methods appropriate?
- Have I designed and carried out the research carefully, accurately, well?
- [Can I analyze] my data carefully, accurately, and well?

Creating, Acquiring and Developing Statistical Datasets

All statistical data was qualitative data once. In chapter eight we discuss assessing the appropriateness of given variables for measuring your concepts. This discussion is about assessing the quality of the underlying data. (See also discussion of inferential statistical design in Chapter eleven.)

For example, many countries have systems for tracking infant and maternal mortality. In some countries where many births and deaths are unattended, countries track maternal and infant mortality by asking women who do make it to the hospitals if they have a sister or sister in law who died in childbirth at home. How reliable are these data or the algorithms used to generate their estimates of maternal mortality? Can data collected by both systems be considered to measure the same thing? When you construct a data set of data from multiple sources, for example, from second hand reports in one country and hospital reports in another, or from household surveys in one context and individual level surveys in another, you need ways of maintaining consistency in meaning across methods and sources for your variables, or of reminding yourself of the underlying difference should it later be necessary for interpreting your findings.

It is possible to convert textual data – from newspaper articles or interviews for example – into statistical data through coding (McCammon *et al.* 2008). It is possible to convert a range of sociological, legal, or political data into a scaled statistical variable (Caprioli *et al.* 2008). These are social research processes that gain legitimacy through the tools of clearly defining your concepts (Chapter five), carefully operationalizing them as variables (Chapter eight), and testing for inter-coder reliability (see Box 9.4), that is, the likelihood that other coders will turn the same qualitative data into the same quantitative data.

We have already discussed using survey research to collect data for statistical datasets. It may seem that collecting the data is the same thing as creating the dataset. It is not. The creation of the dataset highlights the social, *productive* dimension of research.

While you conceptualize and operationalize your variables during the process of research design, you need to make sure that your system for measuring the variable in fact operationalizes the concept you mean to study. This is obviously an issue when you are producing your own data, but it is just as important when you are drawing on existing data sets. When we acquire data from other sources, it needs to be evaluated on many criteria: concep-

---

Box 9.4 Inter-coder reliability

The coding of qualitative data into quantitative data is done by creating a code book that specifies how particular qualitative data should be translated into quantitative data. The coding scheme is a set of rules designed for these particular data; the rules are refined through the process of applying them, modified when coders find them ambiguous or silent on how to code certain kinds of data. Multiple coders code the same data. The coding scheme has high credibility if different people code the same data in the same way. When coders differ in their coding, feminists are interested in the patterns to determine if these differences are potentially significant. This book is dedicated to Hayward Alker, who told the following story about inter-coder reliability.

"In the pioneering article by Lincoln Moses, Richard Brody *et al.* (1967) on the quantification of levels of cooperation and conflict in international events data, one graduate student coder (one out of about five) was a non-American, a citizen of a Third World Country, a woman. Her codings did not 'reliably' agree with those of the others and were discarded for most purposes. She then went on to co-found a new paradigm of international conflict research, lateral pressure theorizing, which redefined the meaning and significance of imperialism as it had been experienced by domestic populations within the Great Powers, their unequal allies, and Third World Countries". The graduate student was Nazli Choucri (Alker 1996: 339).

tualization of variable, coding scheme used, inter-coder reliability, and methods for cleaning data. Under what norms and definitions of concepts were these data produced? Look carefully at the coding guidelines for any data you acquire. How did they determine inter-coder reliability? This may even be a subject of scholarship – for example, Poe, Carey, and Vazquez compare the US State Department and Amnesty International Human Rights Reports to discover a difference in their coding of countries with implications for substantive international research on human rights questions (Poe *et al.* 2001).

When you come across missing data, will you delete the observation? If so, what biases may be introduced? Can you "fill in" missing data with an approximation (Caprioli 2000), or can you use random effects to estimate without the data (Apodaca 2009; True and Mintrom 2001).

Conclusion

The thoroughness of your data production or collection processes will greatly affect your research findings. Whether you go on to treat your data using interpretive or statistical analytical techniques, whether you process your data with a positivist or postpositivist methodology, your analysis is only as good as your underlying data.

It is often said that qualitative data enables description and quantitative data enables generalization. It is with some irony that we note that some feminist methodologists and positive methodologists agree on this distinction (Ramazanoğlu and Holland 2002: 155; King *et al.* 1994). Bennett and Elman (2006) follow Brady (2003) and Mahoney (1999) in distinguishing between the kinds of analysis enabled by qualitative and quantitative analysis. They argue that qualitative analysis enables the researcher to study the complexities of the world, pursuing the multiple and intersecting causes of effects whereas quantitative analysis enables the researcher to identify the effects of causes.

We differ. In our view, methods are just methods. The kind of analysis we are able to do with our data depends on the data we gather, produce, or co-construct with our methods and on how we conceptualize and interpret the data we use from others. Now, there may also be ontological differences between specific qualitative and quantitatively oriented researchers:

- "[W]hat kind of inference can you make from just a handful of cases?" the quantitative researcher may ask of the qualitative researcher.
- "How can you understand the complexity of the forces at work?" the qualitative researcher may ask the quantitative scholar.

These questions – which come from ontological differences – belie the complementary possibilities of qualitative and quantitative research. Evidence of this potential synergy can be found in our scholarship, for example, when a large n empiricist tests a proposition developed using qualitative work, as in Jacqui's quantitative study of gender mainstreaming institutions (True and Mintrom 2001).

Neither qualitative nor quantitative methods of analysis follow *naturally* from epistemological assumptions or from positivist methodologies. We choose our research design, methods for generating data, and methods for analyzing data. Of course, as we noted in Chapter six, sometimes those are very constrained choices. As Clark (2006) notes, sometimes we are not given the training necessary to make skilled choices, but in the beginning, middle and end, the feminist researcher is in charge of her research practice. The next chapter offers some further tools inspired by a feminist research ethic to guide our use and adaptation of the great range of methods for feminist analysis.

Selected Sources for Further Reading

Bennett, Andrew, and Colin Elman. 2006. "Qualitative Research: Recent Developments in Case Study Methods." *Annual Review of Political Science* 9: 455–76.

Harding, Sandra G. 1987. *Feminism and Methodology: Social Science Issues.* Bloomington: Indiana University Press.

Yanow, Dvora, and Peregrine Schwartz-Shea, eds. 2006. *Interpretation and Method: Empirical Research Methods and the Interpretive Turn.* Armonk, NY: M. E. Sharpe.

Chapter 10

Common Techniques for Analysis

Introduction

We began Chapter seven by noting that the common expositions of research methodologies may confine our imaginations. We don't want to follow a road well-traveled *just because* it is well traveled. We want to find the right road for our project. This leads us to analyze our appropriate data with appropriate tools. In this chapter we ask: How does a feminist research ethic affect how we analyze? How does it guide our analysis and make us carry out our analysis in a feminist way?

In Chapter nine, we argued that there are no feminist methods but rather a range of methods available that can be adapted for feminist purposes. Likewise, in this chapter we present ten common techniques for analyzing data that feminist researchers can use in a self-reflexive way consistent with a feminist research ethic. These techniques are generic analytical tools that you may find described in many books on methodology regardless of their theoretical or epistemological perspective. Everybody uses them. However, here we discuss what is involved in applying each of these techniques as tools of analysis in feminist-informed research projects. In so doing, we recognize both the commonalities across methodologies and the need to make the implications of our feminist reflections explicit so that we can execute them better and more self-consciously, being attentive to dynamics of power, relationships and marginalization in the analysis process.

Now you have collected or produced your data, how do you go about analyzing it? You probably have a vast quantity of information and in many different forms so how will you organize and manage it all? Analyzing your data involves converting all of your data, regardless of type, into findings. In general, theory guides analysis as we discussed in Chapter five. But the kinds of analysis that we use to manage and make sense of our data are wide-ranging. You will use many analytical tools, not just the tools employed by those who are expert methodologists in a given research design. Although an ethnographic research design employs description as its major analytical technique, an ethnographer may also draw upon techniques of comparison, contextualization, and box (see Chapter eleven). For most research designs, the analysis stage is not at all pre-determined and you may not know which analytical techniques or formal approaches are best to use until you have collected your data and reflected on how relevant and complete it is in light of your research question and theoretical framework (see Chapter three on keeping a process map).

How can you be confident that the analytical techniques that you use will produce meaningful findings and be defensible in your research community at the same time? How does a feminist research ethic help us to adapt the available analytical techniques to make good on our ethical commitments to noticing the power of epistemology and of boundaries to exclude, marginalize and/or silence, to addressing the context of relationships (not least between the researcher and the researched), and to noticing the effects of our location as researchers in the same social and political world that we are studying? This chapter shows how feminist-informed researchers think through these questions as they analyze their data. The examples highlighted are intended to guide you in thinking through your own process of analysis.

What is Analysis?

Before we look at specific analytical techniques, let's consider what we mean by, and expect of, analysis. Analysis allows you to interpret the results of the research you have undertaken in terms of your central question or puzzle and your theoretical framework. It is, in short, the mechanics of creating an argument. Typically, analysis involves an iterative process of reading data, constructing an interpretation or argument, rereading data, and reconstructing an interpretation or argument. The process of analysis is dynamic and ongoing, although it is often described in standard methodology textbooks and in this book for heuristic purposes as occurring *after* the stage of data collection.

To be frank, we have already begun our analysis we when decide on our question or puzzle to explore since making this choice is usually informed by our "lay" analysis of available data that suggest ours' are interesting problems or questions. But even as we collect different types of relevant data that will allow us to answer our research question, we are or should be tentatively converting this data into a form that we can analyze and ultimately into findings.

For example, in a semi-structured interview setting we are usually engaged in implicit analysis and not merely data collection as we converse with our research subject-participants, probing their understandings, comparing the research participant's analysis to existing theories and not merely requesting more information. When an EU official in a semi-structured interview with me (Jacqui) argued that increasing the number of women among the senior ranks of trade negotiators – rather than establishing a specialist gender analysis unit – would best promote a gender perspective on trade policy, I (even *during* the interview) analyzed the official's comment in terms of my project's theoretical framework connecting the descriptive (presence of women) and the substantive (policy outcomes in women's interests) representation of women. In Chapter nine we caution against analyzing *while* you collect data; yet, we also note that doing so enables you to "co-produce" the data with your research subject-participant or to "gather" as much data as you can from one interview. Moreover, if your theory and conceptualization creates clear hypotheses, you will likely notice evidence for and against these as you research, noting of course that you cannot know the sum total of those findings until you stop collecting data. Further, certain forms of structured inquiry – ethnography, grounded theory, some discourse analysis, and participatory action research – structure the process of analyzing while producing data.

Why are your tools the best ones to use with the kind of data you have collected? In this chapter the analytical techniques we discuss are employed to make an argument that makes sense of all our data, regardless of its type. We show how these techniques have been used in feminist-informed research.

Making an Argument: Common Analytical Techniques

Regardless of the methods we use to collect our data, most of us use a selection of analytical techniques to make an argument and not just those techniques prescribed by a particular research design. Here we strip them down to their bare bones, discussing each technique in its most basic form, how it contributes to analysis of different kinds of data in different research designs, and how it may be adapted by a feminist research ethic.

A feminist research ethic prompts us to notice *how* we analyze. For instance, it demands that we apply the same criteria to the analysis of documents from institutional or elite sources as from lower-status organizations, groups or individuals (e.g., the government department of labor or trade union association compared with the unemployed persons collective or the prostitutes collective).

A feminist research ethic can guide you to recognize the unintended epistemological bias that may inhere in the ways you privilege certain kinds of information or data in your analysis. We need to approach analysis with meaningful, theoretically-informed questions in mind, and a feminist research ethic requires us to make these questions or criteria transparent in order to address problems of inter-coder reliability, positioning, selectivity, and significant gaps or silences in the record (Trachtenberg 2006). We need to ask what information or data is not there as well as analyze that which has been transcribed or collected.

Description

The first technique we detail is description. It is often used in an ethnographic research design but it is almost always part of any research design including a quantitative research. Description as a form of analysis involves telling a story with words and numbers (read: descriptive statistics) that makes sense of all the data you have collected. The narrative or table of numbers reveals a pattern, a logic that is the scaffolding of your argument. Description is often trivialized by social scientists as "unscientific" and as the very opposite of "analysis." It is true, description is highly underrated in some disciplines or subfields of disciplines, but that is because the procedures of description have not been systematically or widely discussed in those fields. By contrast, in some fields such as anthropology and history, description is highly developed as an analytical technique. It is sometimes referred to as grounded theory and is discussed in Chapter eleven.

Memoing or "notetaking" are techniques of data collection that facilitate description as a mode of analysis. They involve literally writing up titled and dated memos or notes. For example, anthropologists engaged in ethnographic studies "in the field," which these days may range from a highland Papua New Guinean tribe to a large bureaucracy such as the Commission of the European Community produce memos to assist with comprehensive description of the social, cultural and semiotic contexts they are studying. These memos are later thoroughly read and coded to identify key themes in the data as it was experienced, and written up. Coding also involves identifying criteria for selecting and weaving together fieldnote excerpts allowing the initial codes to be applied to the whole body of data that included notes and memos. It is a reflexive process for the researcher that involves a back and forth interaction between the emergent codes and considering their fit with each recorded observation (Emerson *et al.* 1995).

A feminist research ethic alerts us to the interactive and interpretive processes in which your own disciplinary or normative commitments and relationships with research subject-participants in the field inevitably shape the character and content of these memos or fieldnotes. Such an ethic encourages you to reflect in the memos on your situatedness in the ethnographic field and in disciplinary fields and how that may affect your interpretation and coding of the data.

Good description entails converting narrative, observed or textual data into evidence in an argument, a potential piece of the puzzle. Emerson *et al.* (1995) show how transforming direct observations into vivid descriptions with the systematic use of memos or reflective notes results not simply from good memory but more crucially from learning to envision scenes as written. Note-taking is fast in danger of being lost, but it is crucially important for good analysis. Most of us now use computers, which often categorize our notes for us. Moreover, as students we are less likely to learn the practice of note-taking from university lectures since Power Point presentations and other visual and online aids have supplemented or replaced solely verbal delivery. This shift away from listening and transcribing what we hear and understand into note form affects our ability to use description as a technique for analyzing our data.

Whether or not your research question is explicitly feminist, descriptive analysis benefits from a feminist research ethic's attention to: (1) power, (2) boundaries, (3) relationships, and (4) situatedness of the researcher in both doing it and accounting for what it offers social and political science.

A feminist research ethic encourages us to use the accounts of our research subject-participants differently (see Box 10.1). In her sociological analysis Majorie Devault treats her subject-participants words "not as straightfor-ward accounts of 'what happens' but as hints toward concerns and activities that are generally unacknowledged" (DeVault 1990: 103). Listening is a part of the research process; and learning to listen in ways that are personal, disciplined and sensitive to differences should shape the collection and analy-sis of interview/life history data in particular. Devault suggests that feminist-informed researchers analyze not merely the talk that can be easily converted to textual data, but the whole context of our subject-participants' talk including body language. She argues: "Hesitant, halting, tentative talk tells you something . . . [that] language is wanted" but not forthcoming. Applying a feminist research ethic means being attentive to the "unsaid" and to notic-ing ambiguity in the analysis of interviews (DeVault 1990: 104). What gener-ates the analysis is the recognition that something is unsaid and that we must try to produce the missing part.

If you use memoing techniques to analyze your data – coding and catego-rizing themes – a feminist research ethic requires you to pay attention to the often unintentional ways we can inscribe boundaries, marginalizing some forms of data. For instance, how do you know when you have analyzed all the relevant data? Have you analyzed data that is not in textual form? Have you analyzed life stories, personal narratives, and non-scholarly publications such as Internet discussion, letters and so on using similar techniques? Is some data privileged in your analysis – for instance, scholarly literature or the so-called "authentic voices" of your research subject-participants?

Being guided by a feminist research ethic, we attend to power relationships as we describe, in particular the relationship with our research subject-participants. Considering the relationship with your research subject-participants gives rise to a number of vexing issues. How do you preserve the richness, contextuality, and authenticity of data from research subject-participants when you analyze it? (In Chapter fourteen we will attend to the security of data and identifying information.) Data need to be edited as you analyze in order to render it comprehensible and to preserve confidentiality. But the ethical and legal problems are considerable, for instance. When the data are transformed into hard text copy, then it is relatively easy to make it anonymous. And when research subject-participants are selectively quoted, then anonymity and confidentiality can be assured. But is this authentic data, true to the voice of our subject-participants? Have you described their perspectives using their own words – letting them represent themselves or by explicitly engaging them with your own analysis? Has a translator introduced some analysis without your knowing? How have you sought to authenticate data collected from your research subject-participants? Have you placed yourself and your own analysis in the story that you tell from your data? Box 10.1 summarizes these concerns about the authenticity and authority of our data from subject-participants. Guided by a feminist research ethic we can acknowledge and experiment with different epistemologies in our analysis to avoid co-opting our subject-participants into a dominant narrative or way of knowing.

Box 10.1 Authenticity: representing the other in our analysis

Mascia-Lees *et al.* (1989) draw attention to a concern among feminist anthropologists for modes of understanding – including analysis and writing – that do not reduce women to the position of voiceless *objects*, but treat them as subjects in their own right, entitled to their own voices. This echoes the very foundations of the feminist research process – the concern with voice and authority, accounts and experience (Smith 1987).

Lister addressed the tension between attempting to let her subject-participants' voices speak for themselves and incorporating them into her sociological analysis by combining her scholarly account with the raw journal writing of her subject-participants:

> In analyzing women's use of writing to explore memory, I outline the interpretive tensions I faced at a range of levels of analysis. I demonstrate how I tried to ensure that women survivors' voices were privileged, while I also engaged in the theoretical and political debates in the field. I conclude that feminist researchers need to develop epistemologies that can meet the complexity of the world as experienced and understood by our research subjects (Lister 2003: 45).

Such analytical work influences the production of data in important ways and leads some people to refer to descriptive analysis as more "art" than "science." To some audiences this metaphor betrays a value judgment, to others a misunderstanding of art. It is hard analytical work to think through a range of material offering different pieces of a puzzle without the box top image as a guide. It is a practiced skill to be able to create the scaffolding of your project with description without allowing that scaffolding to be over determined by the biases of your sources (say they are all activists in the same social movement). Likewise, use of description can be over-determined by your situatedness in a particular discipline in a particular place. For example, in the US, disciplines like sociology and political science devalue descriptive analysis because it provides only scaffolding and apparently does not generate findings that can be generalized. By contrast, disciplines such as anthropology and history are often biased against findings that are generalized, preferring the richness of descriptive scaffolding.

For an example of feminist-informed descriptive analysis, consider Arlie Hochschild's qualitative study of a Fortune 500 firm based on participant observation, surveys, and in-depth interviewing with employees at all levels as methods of data collection published in her book (Hochschild 1997). The three-year study began with a puzzle, why don't more employees take up the flexible work policies available to them to help balance their work and family lives? Hochschild analyzes her different sources of data to describe how things work behind the scenes at the Fortune 500 firm despite the official company rhetoric about total quality management and work/life balance. The story she tells makes two arguments from the data: (1) despite flexible work options the informal culture of the company conveys that "face time" and number of hours worked in the office are what earns job security, promotion and other benefits; and (2) due partly to management efforts to make the workplace into a safe and comforting environment for many employees, work is more rewarding than home life and people tend to want to do more rather than less work. Thus work/life balance policies have little impact. This finding is especially the case for parents and particularly mothers, for whom home and children typically involve intensive work (and less apparent rewards).

The description of work-life issues in the Hochschild study is compelling and contrary to conventional narratives. But even though her analysis was based on in-depth research over a lengthy period of time using several methods of data collection, the study reveals important methodological issues that a feminist research ethic teaches us are important. For instance, the analysis is limited to one single company and although the narrative resonates with experiences in other companies, the description technique only implicitly suggests the generalizability of the case study (for more on case selection see Chapter eight). The study is not sufficient to make causality claims; that is, while description produces a compelling narrative and set of findings, it does not tell us what has led to these outcomes or who is responsible – management, individual employees and/or families and in what ways (see below and Chapter eleven). Further, Hochschild does not situate herself in relation to the study and her subject-participants. Like all researchers, there are no doubt reasons why she decided to conduct this study and there are indications in the text of normative assumptions that influenced how she analyzed her subject-participants' responses to the survey and interview questions. Yet, Hochschild does not openly acknowledge or consider the effects of her relationship to the study and its findings (see Chapter four).

Although Hochschild's book, *The Time Bind*, is a very good example of the use of description as an analytical technique in the service of a research question that would be interesting to scholars of gender relations, it also reveals how description alone is limited from the perspective of a feminist research ethic. That Hochschild does not reflect (at least not in writing) on the power of her epistemology, on the boundaries of her study (why non-working women were not included as a control group, for instance), the relationships involved especially among her research subject-participants, and her own situatedness in the research process is problematic.

Illustration

Illustration is a tool that helps us to analyze our data and is a valuable partner with other methods of analysis. It is commonly used in qualitative single case designs that intend to generate new theory from intensive study but can be useful for all research designs, including quantitative large n longitudinal and cross-sectional studies. We think of examples, mini-cases, and vignettes (i.e., a narrative that is not a fully-developed case study) that either fit or do not fit the story we are tentatively making with our data in order to test out our description. Here we often highlight well-known cases, or existing typologies and check the degree to which they conform to the theoretical narrative or statistical model we are constructing as we consider all our data. This is often a useful technique combined with statistical analysis allowing macro findings to be made more meaningful (Lieberman 2005).

True and Mintrom (2001), for example, use the longitudinal data they collected on (1) NGO participation in UN women's conference official state delegations and (2) local membership of international women's NGOs in each country as a proxy variable for transnational feminist networks (TFN). They find this variable is a statistically significant factor in explaining the likelihood of a state adopting a gender mainstreaming institution. To make the analysis plausible and to explore the causal mechanism implied by the statistical association, they use description to show concretely how a particular TFN had a major impact on the adoption of gender mainstreaming institutions in specific states. For instance, a European TFN as well as peer effects of neighboring states, and less so the ratification of CEDAW, the membership of international organizations, and domestic social and economic factors, had an important affect on the adoption of gender mainstreaming institutions in the Baltic states after 1995.

In this way description as an analytical technique helps to convert the data generated by the statistical model into meaningful research findings. Description thus facilitates analysis, although it is not definitive, as a feminist research ethic reminds us that all findings are provisional only. In combination with large n statistical analysis it suggests the results of the statistical model are plausible findings. Quantitative analysis alone is typically insufficient for explaining the *meaning* of the findings, particularly when one has hypotheses about the causality of relationships among variables. By drawing on examples or mini-cases scholars can validate the implied causal mechanism in statistical analysis.

By contrast, illustration can also reveal stories and patterns concealed within macro or large n data. It can also lead us to further interrogate the boundaries inscribed in our analysis by the type of method we use. For example, Jill Vickers (2006) uses illustration as part of a comparative research design. She explores selected country cases that patently do not fit with feminist theoretical assumptions about the relationship between gender and nation. She uses these "misfit" cases to scrutinize this relationship being attentive to the power of dominant disciplinary theories and her own situatedness in the Canadian province of Quebec where nationalism has been known to advance some feminist causes. Vickers' analysis reveals the diversity of women's experiences within nations and nationalist movements. This insight leads her to provide further illustrations of positive cases where national(ist) projects open spaces for women and gender equality struggles. Vickers deploys illustrations of these cases to challenge dominant feminist theories but also to seek out new theories to research and test on her larger dataset and quantitative study of 30 country cases.

Triangulation

Triangulation is used with two meanings. Triangulation has been defined by several metaphors, including the metaphor of two or more information-gathering satellites used to locate a ship lost at sea. In mixed-model research designs, triangulation refers to analyzing data based on two or more methods of generating similar data (Lieberman 2005). Triangulation can also mean using different sources of evidence within a single research design and theoretical framework to corroborate your findings. Can your data from three or more different sources, for example, from primary archival data, interview data and/or some secondary empirical literature be interpreted as saying the same thing? If so, you can be more confident that your argument is plausible. Does the triangulated data confirm one of your hypotheses or theories in your framework? Or does it suggest a different pattern or relationship at work and therefore the need for a new investigation or revised theory?

Single case study designs in particular rest on the analytical scrutiny and triangulation of a heterogeneous dataset, including documents, interviews, and participant observations at different points in time. This reflects the conventional social science prescription to make many observations if your units of analysis are few (King *et al.* 1994). To the extent that they can be triangulated, each type of data consulted is an incremental step to increasing the plausibility of an argument by increasing the number of distinct observations. But the process of triangulation may also reveal a "smoking gun"; that is, some critical data such as an event or actor may stand out as *not* fitting the general pattern of the rest of the data. A feminist research ethic encourages us to explore this non-conforming data further and not to disregard it as an outlier or error. This outcome of analysis can be as important a finding as the corroboration of data. It may suggest a specific direction for further research to take (Ragin 1987: 69–84).

Guided by a feminist research ethic a number of questions arise including, which data do we triangulate? Does our data from different kinds of research subject-participants add up? If so how? We co-construct data and analysis in interviews with our subject-participants (Stern 2006). But triangulating this data and analysis involves a conscious effort to put them in conversation with one another and with your theoretical framework, which only you as a researcher can do. Box 10.2 describes how I (Brooke) attempted to triangulate data from subject-participants in a transparent and self-conscious way.

In her analysis of British Labour Members of Parliament (MPs) Sarah Childs triangulates three types of data to determine whether or not an increase in the number of women MPs – the descriptive representation of women – makes a difference to the substantive representation of women's interests in policymaking (Childs 2006; see also Childs and Withey 2004, 2006). She analyzes interviews with Labour women MPs first elected in 1997 (the first "Blair government"), male and female voting behavior and signing of early day motions in the 1997 parliament, as well as the substance of MPs participation in the parliamentary debates on the Sex Discrimination Act. Childs' analysis of data from each of the three different sources addresses different dimensions of her research question and the complex relationship between women's descriptive and substantive representation. In interviews,

Box 10.2 Whose analysis counts? Relationship to subject-participants

How are we to make sense of the range of views, characteristic of many, but representative of none, yet individually and collectively full of insights? Should all insights be taken at face value, or could we contextualize our readings of them, just as the interviewees contextualized their own arguments? Can we say that some arguments are wrong or that some activists are wrong and others right? Does employing a feminist methodology mean that we can only repeat what our sources say or can we develop and clarify an understanding of human rights based on what we have learned from them? What does it mean to be true to the activists? (Ackerly 2008a: 159, 168–70, 174, 196).

In my practice, the theorist does not merely reflect or represent the views of singular or plural others, but rather joins their effort by offering her *theoretical* analysis of the activists' analysis, using the argument of one to clarify, develop or triangulate the argument of another. In order to engage with the insights of these critical voices, we need to employ a feminist research ethic as we analyze just as we did in gathering our data. A feminist research ethic works in a dynamic way to challenge static notions within any given interlocutor or the researcher herself.

women Labour MPs are found to be attitudinally feminist; that is, they recognize the need to respond to women's differences (from men). This finding is potentially limited by the women's MPs party identification as a contending explanation. However, voting analysis, shows women behave differently from men MPs in the same party (party identification is therefore *not* paramount) although it does not tell us whether they act for women. Thus, a third form of analysis, the analysis of EDMs and the sex discrimination debate reveals "hard" data that women MPs are acting for women. So despite limitations, which Childs acknowledges, her triangulation across three different types of data "on balance supports the claim that women representatives will seek to act for women" (Childs 2006). In order to address a feminist-informed research question, Childs has thought carefully about how to collect and analyze data that comprehends all aspects of her question, while addressing past critiques of research on women's representation.

In a quasi-experimental, mixed-method single case study design, feminist researchers Nielsen *et al.* (2005) triangulate among multiple sources of data to explain patterns of academic gender inequity. Their data collection methods include demographic data, a survey of institutional climate, and ethnographies of individual career paths before and after a set of institutional interventions. However, they were unable to triangulate across their data. First, they experienced difficulty in operationalizing theoretical concepts into measurable variables for statistical analysis. Moreover, the authors self-reflected that the logic of regression is to explain away the variance, i.e. the gender inequity, inadvertently justifying it. Second, their survey questions on feminist consciousness (theorized to be a positive factor in an equitable university climate) were categorically rejected by many respondents to the survey. Considered to be a "vital variable," when translated into two-dimensional survey questions amenable to statistical measurement, feminist consciousness could not be contextualized or qualified enough to generate meaningful responses. Thus the survey analysis could not be triangulated with the demographic data in the statistical analysis.

In this example of feminist-informed research, the failure to measure "feminist consciousness" reveals the difficulty in triangulating different kinds of data on the same question, i.e. what factors shape gender equity in academe. Consistent with a feminist research ethic attentive to the power of epistemologies, Nielsen *et al.* learned from their survey analysis that quantitative data is always *contextual* despite claims to the contrary (2005: 15). As they state, it is "impossible to capture conceptual complexities and refinements in a few or even a series of survey questions" (Nielsen *et al.* 2005: 22). Yet while Nielsen and her co-authors recognized the value of open-ended survey questions in addressing the concerns and meanings of research subject-participants, they needed quantitative data to triangulate with their qualitative findings in order to produce the evidence-based analysis required by their university funders. This conundrum aside, Nielsen *et al.*'s research findings suggest that feminist consciousness itself needs to be a topic of study. Although a feminist research ethic would not prescribe any particular method of analysis, it requires that a given method be able to uncover and generalize dynamic meanings.

Comparison

Another extremely useful analytical technique is comparison. Comparison is typically associated with a qualitative comparative case study design but it is frequently used as a form of analysis "within cases" in any number of designs. We ask of our data "what's different here?" compared with what the existing literature says, compared with our other data or with other cases, most similar with different outcomes or most different with similar outcomes. Applying a feminist research ethic, we might also compare our analysis with the analysis of our subject-participants, being attentive to the power differentials between us and among our subject-participants.

Comparison can help us discover what is distinctive about our study and/or it can help us to explore the causal mechanisms in our study. You might simply engage in a thought experiment distilling what we know already about other similar cases or about different cases that have a similar outcome. You are trying to isolate the mechanisms that might help you to understand your question or explain our puzzle. Comparison may enable you to establish conceptual distinctions between your data and the stock of existing knowledge.

Comparison is also an empirical basis for assessing counter-factual claims, that is, an event would have happened in a different way had a key factor in our story been different or missing. For example, we know that the Solomon Islands and East Timor (or "Timor-Leste") have many similarities as post-conflict countries in the same region that have experienced a peacekeeping mission and are democratizing. Yet only Timor has made gender equality a central value and goal in the design of its democratic institutions. Without engaging in a formal comparative case method, thinking through the contrast and the factors contributing to different outcomes in Timor and the Solomons for women can help us to isolate important factors in our data such as, the mobilization of a unified women's movement in Timor and the presence of individual gender activists – neither of which have been present in the Solomons for reasons that are worth exploring in themselves (Hall and True 2009).

The point of comparison is that exploring and explaining the differences (or "variance") between relevant cases can help us analyze the critical factors or path that has produced the outcome we seek to explain or understand. Such an approach to analysis may lead us to further our research on a given topic exploring new or additional research questions with a formal comparative case study design.

Contextualization

Contextualization is frequently used in grounded theory research designs as well as ethnographic and case study designs to understand our data and its implications. It is a feature of most feminist-informed analysis since a feminist research ethic recognizes the socially-constructed nature of our world and the need to interpret and analyze our data in its particular contexts. We explain by making sense of the background information to our data. That is, we consider the historical, political, institutional, and socio-cultural contexts in which our data are embedded. (Recall the discussion of a feminist research ethic and the relationships of subject-participants and see Box 10.3 on how to be attentive to the linguistic contexts of interview data.) For instance, we may be interested in mapping the discourse of racism but the subtleties of discrimination and of racist or sexist language are usually specific to cultural/linguistic traditions, historical and local contexts (Weatherall and Potter 1992). A feminist research ethic is attentive to the context of relationships and epistemologies among subject-participants because they affect both how we conceptualize "racism" and analyze its presence in everyday talk between members of different groups or in institutionalized forms.

Box 10.3 Transcribing and contextualizing talk following DeVault

Majorie Devault discusses four ways of analyzing interview data that are attentive to language use: (1) constructing topics; (2) listening to respondents; (3) transcribing and editing interview material; and (4) writing about respondents lives. Transcribing talk, in particular, requires attention to context and that we use contextual analysis.

Transcription, as Devault describes it, should not be mechanical: "editing though usually relatively unnoticed is an essential and consequential part of the routine practice of producing a particular kind of analytical text".

She recommends:

1. Preserving the messiness of everyday talk (1990: 109) in the text, which is another way of saying preserving the context of the speech in your analysis.
2. Explaining the form of the interview as well as the content in the transcript. The halting, and the hesitancy is as important as the actual words. Moreover, the transcript should situate stories in longer stretches of discourse. Do not extract profusely as this may sacrifice important background context, necessary for analysis and explanation.
3. Looking for distinctive features of talk that reveal "the scaffolding of social structure" in a given context (DeVault 1990: 110).

Contextualizing is an analytical strategy usually employed in conjunction with data generated from qualitative research designs such as small n case studies rather than large n statistical studies, and in discourse analysis rather than *content analysis* (see Key Concept 10.1 and the discussion of discourse analysis in Chapter eleven). There is a tradeoff though, as Nielsen *et al.* (2005: 15) write, "contextuality makes data richer but less generalizable." At the same time, as we saw in the example of Nielsen *et al.*'s research on academic gender inequity, quantitative data also needs to be contextualized to make the generalization plausible. One option is to combine quantitative and qualitative methods to increase the validity of analysis. For example, feminist methodologist, Shulamith Reinharz (1992: 155) discusses using quantitative analysis, such as word counts or key word analysis, "to identify patterns" with qualitative data to place those patterns within an interpretive context that explores large scale themes (see also Lieberman 2005).

In her feminist theory of freedom, Nancy Hirschmann (2003) explores the debates over veiling as a prism through which to analyze women's agency and choice within oppressive patriarchal structures. Her argument employs contextualization effectively while analyzing many perspectives and cases. In

10.1 CONTENT ANALYSIS

In traditional content analysis, a researcher first identifies a body of material to analyze and then creates a system for recording specific aspects of it. The system often involves interpreting and coding in order to count how often certain words or themes occur. He or she often operationalizes information in the content as variables in an explanatory research design. Sometimes frequencies may be statistically analyzed. With the development of software for quantitative analysis of qualitative data, keyword, concept, discourse, and frame analysis is an increasingly common form of analysis that can reveal patterns even if it cannot adequately explain them.

Content analysis is increasingly used for exploratory and explanatory research but has historically been used in descriptive research (see Neuman 1997: 31). For example, feminist scholars have used content analysis to study representations of women in print media (Reinharz and Kulick 2007). See also (Leavy 2000).

See also and compare the Grounded Theory approach to content analysis and Discourse analysis discussed in separate sections of Chapter eleven.

---

particular, Hirschmann develops Arlene MacLeod's contextual analysis of veiling practices in Egypt in *Accommodating Protest* arguing that veiling is essentially ambiguous in its present cultural contexts: "If the veil enables women in Cairo to work for wages, it facilitates their choices and freedom, even as it signals how such choices operate within larger systems of gender inequality" (MacLeod 1991: 204). She explores this paradox in a detailed analysis of two contexts – Bedouin and Cairo – in which women talk about the veil and how they have used it "to establish identity and agency but to resist patriarchy as well" (MacLeod 1991: 184). Among women in contemporary Bedouin society segregation is seen as a source of pride, and as such, the veil is indicative of social deference and modesty but also of autonomy since it establishes a degree of emotional and psychological separateness and independence (MacLeod 1991: 185).

Hirschmann's theory of freedom is not only concretely applied to various sites but it is self-consciously advanced through contextual analysis, in this instance, of the veil and the debates surrounding it. From the perspective of a feminist research ethic attentive to both the power of epistemology and of relationships, the quest for generalization about the politics of veiling would only serve to mask these very historically and culturally specific dynamics that are critical in explaining the veil's contemporary significance.

As well as needing contextualization, large *n* quantitative studies can themselves produce findings that contextualize broad generalizations by

Box 10.4 Seguino's example of revealing patterns while putting them in context

Given the assumption that increases in women's labor force participation are markers of gender equality, we might judge the large increases in women's labor in East Asian countries such as South Korea at the same time as these countries replaced import substitution with export-oriented economic development as an indication of progress in gender equality. Stephanie Seguino's longitudinal, quantitative analysis contextualizes these descriptive statistics and challenges their generalization by revealing the gender wage inequality that accompanied these increases in women's labor participation and in export growth. At the same time, Seguino's qualitative research contextualizes her quantitative data by providing narrative data of prevailing patriarchal gender norms and family structures in South Korea that encouraged women to accept employment with low pay and status (Seguino 2002).

aggregating statistics about social and political phenomena. For example, the increase in women's labor force participation is often used by governments, international organizations and feminist researchers as a proxy for gender equality and women's empowerment (see Box 10.4). A feminist research ethic leads us to interrogate the marginalization and exclusion at work in this particular conceptualization.

Counterfactual Logic

If contextualization deepens the analysis of the data we have, then using counterfactual logic, increases the breadth and potential of our data to be generalized. Imagine the story you are developing from your data without a particular factor – could the outcome or end result still have been possible? Statistics can achieve this by holding constant all proxy variables posited to have an affect on the outcome except that factor hypothesized to be the key cause. But the logic of a carefully-constructed narrative distilled from our qualitative data can also persuade us that it is reasonable to assume that the factor(s) we have stressed in our analysis are the causal ones since it would have been difficult to imagine the outcome without them. Counterfactual logic is an important technique for making an argument and for helping us to see a pattern out of our often voluminous collection of data.

Returning to the example about gender equality norms in Timor-Leste's democratization, we might reflect on the data (Hall and True 2009). Without these actors and their specific efforts (the Timorese women's movements, gender entrepreneurs) would UNTAET in Timor have established a central gender equality office in its peacekeeping mission and later in its Prime

Minister's Office, given that other previous and concurrent UN missions did not have one? If the answer is no, then the authors know they have identified a tentative pattern and argument in their data and that they need to further build the rigor of the analysis by marshalling and scrutinizing the data collected from the perspective of this argument. With this example you can see that it is possible and helpful to use counterfactual logic in any given research design or argument. Of course all data may not line up behind the same argument and a feminist research ethic encourages you to continue interrogating your existing data or to collect new data. It urges you to be mindful of the potential pitfalls of forcing your data to conform to any one argument or pattern and therein marginalizing valid contrary interpretations.

Eliminating Possible Counter-Arguments

Closely related to counter-factual logic as an analytical strategy is the technique of considering and eliminating possible contrary interpretations or counter-arguments to the story you are constructing with your data. This technique resembles Popper's falsification theory; where the researcher attempts to find a case or example that their theory cannot explain or that is not consistent with theoretical expectations (Popper 1959: 78–92). Here the researcher follows a similar plan by considering all the possible arguments contrary to the one she or he is constructing and then analyzing the data in light of these arguments.

Statistical testing of hypotheses using bivariate or multivariate regressions is one way of doing this. However, from the perspective of a feminist research ethic attentive to boundaries, marginalization, and silencing, this analytical technique is flawed because it suggests there is only *one* model for explaining complex social phenomena. It also implies that a theory or finding is only plausible if it can discount every alternative interpretation of the data (Risman 2004: 434). But parsimony is not always desirable. A feminist research ethic reminds us that the world is not well described by elegant, mono-causal accounts that pay little attention to the power of epistemology, to boundaries, and to relationships of power. Feminist-informed analysis is integrative and synthetic (see Box 10.5). It builds on the complexity of others' ideas not merely to have greater purchase on social reality but to be able to transform that reality.

Qualification

Qualification is another analytical technique like contextualization that can help us make sense of our data and persuade others of its robustness. Qualifying our data and our analysis by placing clear boundaries around our findings, indicating what they say and what they do not say, and in relation

Box 10.5 Ackerly and True's intersectional analysis of gender and nation

While writing this book we were asked to comment on the category of women in a US-wide survey of International Relations scholars. On first glance at the data the survey authors felt there were some interesting patterns of difference between women and men scholars to explore. However, as we analyzed the data by gender on theory, methodology, and epistemology preferences we hypothesized that gender differences may be connected with differences in epistemology (that is, more women adopt post-positivist methodologies and the situation that both these methodologies and women have an overall lower status in the discipline has mutually-reinforcing effects on both – and on persistent gender inequalities). We were able to return to the survey data to further analyze this relationship with statistical tools.

Our analysis found strong correlations of these two categories, gender and epistemology across several survey questions. The implication of this analysis was that gender, the fact of being a man or a woman alone, could not explain field-wide differences in status, theory, method, and so on. Yet the differences in the International Relations field around theory, method, and epistemology could not be understood without gender – and gender analysis either. The dominance of certain theories and methodologies in the International Relations field mobilizes an implicit gender bias that has a particularly negative impact on women's status in the field despite their increasing numbers in the US in tenure-track positions. However, without intersectional analysis that is informed by a feminist research ethic attentive to all the ways data and meaning may be hidden within conventional categories and methods, the significance of gender in the survey of the International Relations discipline was unexamined and reduced to an essentialist, biological account of being a disadvantaged female or advantaged male rather than a sociological account of the field and its gendered development (Ackerly and True 2008a).

to which context and which theory increases their plausibility within the wider political and social science research community. See Box 10.6 for a good example of *qualification* as a strategy for analyzing research findings. We need to be self-conscious about whether we are testing existing hypotheses and theories or developing/building new hypotheses and theories as we analyze our data.

Qualification in statistical analysis often points out the limits of existing data and theory and supports arguments for additional data collection or studies designed to help with the conceptualization of key factors. For instance, Tremblay notes the difficulty in operationalizing "women's mobilization around electoral campaigns" as an explanatory factor for women's

---

> **Box 10.6 What are your findings about? Su on using qualification to analyze gender and political representation**
>
> Fubing Su's analysis of the factors shaping gender inequality in political representation in China looks at decision-makers at the provincial level where there is a lower presence of women officials (10 percent) compared with delegates at the official National Party Congress (20 percent).
>
> Her study is consistent with findings that there are differences in women's political representation among the three types of provincial level administrations. But importantly her analysis qualifies its findings about gender and political representation. Su explores only one dimension of representation – power and prestige in an official ranking system – essentially a form of *descriptive* representation. The substantive representation of women in terms of policies and policy outcomes reflecting women's interests is not explored. The author acknowledges that this institutional dimension deserves to be studied too, in order to interpret the meaning and significance of women's political participation in China and to empower Chinese feminist scholars and activists (Su 2006: 161–2).

---

representation suggested in the secondary literature (Tremblay 2007). An in-depth case study of women's mobilization around electoral campaigns might be able to explore possible proxy variables for meaningfully measuring the influence of this factor. Developing your own variable through exploratory qualitative research can address the "off the shelf" data problem common in quantitative analysis where variables are selected from existing datasets to study new questions even though they may not accurately measure what the theoretical framework describes or convey the richness of conceptualization in theoretical debates in the field.

Causal Inference

Causal inference is a common analytical technique, especially in political and social science research employing quantitative longitudinal, cross-sectional, or experimental research designs. It requires you to define and measure counterfactual conditions that make up each expected causal effect. For our purposes, causal analysis can take at least two different forms. The first involves using statistical techniques, usually bivariate or multivariate regression, to assess the degree of numerical correlation between key variables in the data that are theoretically expected to be in a cause-effect relationship. We term this analytical approach *thin* causal inference. In addition, there are various tests for assessing the validity and reliability of the statistical analysis, for example probability theory. But analysis with statistical tools requires careful delineation of cause and effect – and therefore dichotomous models and variables. A feminist research ethic requires statistical analysis using causal inference to be attentive to selection bias at the *analysis* as well as the research design stage. For instance, negative cases or correlations as well as positive cases or correlations need to be analyzed. It is difficult to address constitutive theories that see causes and effects are intertwined and mutually-constituted using this kind of causal analysis in particular. Applying a feminist research ethic may mean acknowledging this point explicitly and/or adopting an analytical method more appropriate for studying co-constitution of structures and agents.

Manon Tremblay's (2007) study of women's political representation in democracies illustrates causal inference in a feminist-informed statistical analysis. It draws inferences between the proportion of women in parliament and a range of factors theoretically assumed to have a causal effect on this proportion. Based on multiple regression analyses that test the causal affect of each factor controlling for the affects of the contending factors (or counterarguments – see above), Tremblay infers the causes of women's political representation in established democracies and in new democracies. In countries where democracy has only recently been established, she argues, the electoral system is the most statistically-significant cause of the proportion of women parliamentarians whereas egalitarian attitudes toward gender roles are the most powerful explanation in well-established democracies. This research analysis is very valuable for revealing this general pattern but a feminist research ethic would lead us to interrogate the boundaries within the categorization of established and emerging democracies further, possibly with the use of a small n design or qualitative method of analysis.

A second way of making causal inferences involves using qualitative process-tracing to reveal a chain of causal linkages in the data collected. In this way a causal mechanism that explains how an outcome was arrived at is identified. A compelling narrative drawing together a range of evidence reveals some data to be prior, that is, the cause, and other data to be its effect. We term this analytical approach *thick* causal inference. It is used very often in qualitative case study and historical research designs.

To make her causal argument that the gender equality transnational advocacy network's (TAN) groundwork over 20 years led to the adoption of a European Union law on sexual harassment, Katherine Zippel infers a causal mechanism using *process tracing* (see Key Concept 10.2). Specifically, she analyses a three-phase process of policy change she coins the "ping pong effect" involving multi-level interactions between the gender equality TAN, European Union Commission officials, and member states.

10.2 PROCESS-TRACING

Process-tracing incorporates historical narratives and documentation in a causal explanation and theory-testing framework. It is a method within case analysis of identifying causal processes and causal chains as well as the mechanisms that link them, helping to explain a given outcome. In Political Science process-tracing has been applied to the study of public decision-making and policymaking outcomes (see George and Bennett 2005).

Because of the legal institutionalization of the European Union (and the myriad documents it has produced) the ping-pong effect is easier to trace than in other supra-state organizations. Consequently, Zippel was able to infer the causal policy impact of TAN activities such as "introducing an alternative discourse on sexual harassment, sharing professional and legal knowledge about developments in EU member states and sponsoring empirical studies documenting sexual harassment as a compelling social problem" (Zippel 2004: 78–9). As well as causal inference however, Zippel used several other analytical techniques, including description, comparison, and contextualization to make her argument about the significance of the TAN.

Writing

Writing is addressed in depth in Chapter thirteen as we discuss how to present and publish our research findings. But writing is considered by many scholars to be a form of analysis itself (Richardson 2000), that is, not simply a "write-up" of already known findings. The writing process is often a thinking process that suggests new categories and ways of structuring your analysis. It may reveal to the author new theoretical insights. Indeed, converting your initial analysis to written text is a dynamic act mediated by the power and limits of language that may lead you to see new themes in your data.

Writing is always part of the research process. In Chapter three, we discuss the writing process in terms of drafting a research plan, mapping our research process, and organizing a research presentation. In Chapter five, we explore how learning to make a hypothetical argument involves writing in order to synthesize a range of theoretically-informed literature. Through memoing and notetaking, writing is a form of analysis that occurs throughout the research process. Finally, a feminist research ethic expects that analysis happens every time you write.

If you are writing a descriptive analysis as in the case of historical analysis or ethnography, the writing process most certainly constitutes an advance stage of coding or analysis as even your written notes must be converted to a more succinct and synthetic text which involves choices of what to foreground and what to leave out and how to develop your core argument or narrative in a way that is likely to be compelling to your readers. Given this, some scholars even see reading as part of analysis and a further interpretative process beyond that determined by the researcher (see Yanow and Schwartz-Shea 2006).

Even if before you begin writing your argument or narrative, you have fully and clearly described your method and engaged in theoretical reflection, historical or other contextual analysis, the final writing process will likely evolve in ways you do not expect with some benefits and setbacks for the argument you think you are making.

Conclusion

The quality of your analysis will greatly depend on both your skill in deploying at least some of the analytical techniques discussed above in building an argument, the kind of data you have collected, and how well they can be used to support, test, and refine your theoretical argument. Analysis occurs throughout the research process but there is a deliberative moment in the process where you need to consider all of your data and how you can analyze it with techniques to make a plausible argument. A feminist research ethic can help you to analyze your data in a way that anticipates and attends to potential biases in the process, and questions about the validity and trustworthiness of your approach overall. Above all, it reminds you that you must be accountable to your research subject-participants, your research community, and your broader potential audience, as you weave together the story you tell from your data.

The next chapter explores structured inquiry research designs where data collection and analysis are often inextricable and part of the same methodological process. It shows how such approaches have been adapted with a feminist research ethic to improve all research, feminist and non-feminist.

Selected Sources for Further Reading

Emerson, Robert, Rachel Fretz, and Linda Shaw. 1995. "Processing Fieldnotes: Coding and Memoing." In *Writing Ethnographic Fieldnotes*. Chicago, IL: University of Chicago Press, 142–68.

Reinharz, Shulamit. 1992. *Feminist Methods in Social Research*. New York: Oxford University Press.

Ryan, Gery W., and H. Russell Bernard. 2000. "Data Management and Analysis Methods." In *Handbook of Qualitative Research*, 2nd edn, ed. Norman K. Denzin and Yvonna S. Lincoln, New York: Sage: 769–802.

Trachtenberg, Marc. 2006. *The Craft of International History: A Guide to Method*. Princeton, NJ: Princeton University Press.

Yanow, Dvora, and Peregrine Schwartz-Shea. 2006. *Interpretation and Method: Empirical Research Methods and the Interpretive Turn*. Armonk, NY: M. E. Sharpe.

Chapter 11

Structured Inquiry Research Designs

Introduction

In this chapter we discuss five forms of what we have been calling "structured inquiry." These are methodologies for research design in which the methods of data collection and the methods of analysis are inextricably linked. In these research designs, the kind of analysis you want to do is predicated on a certain kind of data collected through a certain kind of data collection method; reciprocally, the kind of data you produce can be given meaning only through certain kinds of analysis. These methods of data collection and analysis may echo those described in the preceding two chapters; but, by contrast, the material discussed in this chapter could not be disaggregated into those because data production and data analysis are integrated in these structured inquiry approaches. In ethnography, grounded theory, and inferential statistical design the data and analysis are co-constructed. In discourse and frame analysis the question and analysis are co-constructed. And in participatory action the question, data, and analysis are co-constructed. For each of these inquiries, the nonlinearity of research is itself *structured,* and an explicit part, therefore, of research design.

Ethnography: A Special Single Case

Ethnography is a close and full study of human experience, usually in a community. Ethnographers aim to offer rich and nuanced description of human life in context.

Research Questions for Ethnography

In some corners of social science, ethnography is not scientific enough. It is story-telling. Ethnographers occupy one such corner themselves. In *Fictions of Feminist Ethnography*, Kamala Visweswaran sets out the differences between fiction and ethnography. Ethnography "sets out to build a believable world, but [unlike fiction] one the reader will accept as factual" (1994: 1). Historically, ethnography has referred to a methodology for researching a particular place in order to know the economy, politics, sociology, culture, values, fears, and history as lived memory of the people of the place. While its subject covers every social science discipline, it is a methodology most at home in anthropology, where it has been considered virtually the sole methodology of social and cultural anthropologists.

Ethnography can be used to describe, but as Visweswaran provokes by comparing ethnography with fiction, the author of ethnography builds a believable world with purpose. A feminist ethnographer would ideally be transparent about her theoretical purpose, as for example Saba Mahmood (2005: 5) when she describes her intent: "My goal, however, is not just to provide an ethnographic account of the Islamic Revival. It is also to make this material speak back to the normative liberal assumptions about human nature." Ethnographic description is guided by a normative thesis and substantiated with evidence produced through a range of methods.

Methods of Ethnography

Ethnographic methods include participation in the everyday life and routines of the community, organization, movement, (etc.) of study. Ethnographers accumulate data of many forms including conversations, texts, and *participant observation* in all aspects of life. The modes of data collection are in part determined through the research process itself. If an organization has weekly meetings, then participant observation in weekly meetings will be important. If testimony and personal narrative are an important part of the culture of the community or organization of study, then these will be important sources of information. If there is a strong public culture, then individual testimony through oral histories or interviews, secured with great respect for privacy will be important. Ethnographers are the masters of the "field note," a method of noting for further analysis pieces of data accumulated through sharing the lives and processes of the subject-participants (Emerson *et al.* 1995; see chapter ten on "memoing" and also Chapter twelve on documenting your thought process).

In ethnography, the processes of data production and analysis are inextricably linked. Consider the challenge of creating organizational, community, or network maps so that you can document and comprehend the social and political geography of your context of study. You might map formal and

11.1   PARTICIPANT OBSERVATION

Participant observation refers to the researcher being engaged in the life and activities of the context of study. For some studies everyday engagement means participating in all aspects of the context of study. For others, participation may be limited to certain activities.

For some participant observation, it is possible to take notes during participation. In some contexts, post-observation notes are more feasible. (See Tools for Practicing a Feminist Research Ethic "in the Field" in Chapter twelve.)

informal lines of authority. You might map formal and informal lines of communication. What is important to map to understand your context? You answer that question by analyzing data about the context and that analysis conditions what data you gather and how you map it.

A Feminist Research Ethic and Analysis in Ethnography

The feminist ethnographer includes in her research design and practice attention to the power of epistemology, boundaries, relationships, and her own situatedness. For example, if testimony is an important part of the community of study, the feminist ethnography may pay attention not only to those who testify, but also to those who do not testify and to seek their views through other means (many approaches for doing so are discussed in Chapter nine).

However, it may also be that an ethnographer does not anticipate what her work may require. For example, Susan Friend Harding discovers in doing an ethnography of the cultural movement led by Jerry Fallwell and his co-pastors that an ethnography of a faith movement committed to conversion requires the researcher to be open to conversion herself (2000). Jeanne Favret-Saada (1980: 22) makes the same argument about studying witchcraft, "there is no solution but to practice it oneself, to become one's informant." What position should a feminist ethnographer take when "there is no such thing as a neutral position, no place for an ethnographer who seeks 'information'" (Harding, S.F., 2000: 39). Feminist scholarship validates "experience" as a form of knowledge to be interrogated and that includes the experiences of the both researched and the researcher (Scott 1992).

For Harding, the deliberative moment around whether exploring her own faith commitment would enhance or undermine her ability to do an ethnography was unanticipated. However, as feminist researchers, we learn from each other's reflections that we must anticipate a deliberative moment

---

> ## Box 11.1 The insider-outsider in ethnography
>
> The challenge of the relationship of researcher to community is a core concern of ethnographers. It affects their work in matters of all dimensions of research in terms of their own security in the field (Guevarra 2006), the power dynamics between researcher and subject-participants (Miraftab 2004), and the relevance of their research (Nagar 2002).
>
> Some feminist researchers have negotiated these complicated dynamics by drawing methodological insights from participatory action research (Maguire 1987; Benson and Nagar 2006).

regarding whether our subject of inquiry precludes the possibility of a neutral space from which to study.

An ethnographer may gather many stories that don't seem directly relevant to her topic and yet offer insight into the context of study, or through the process of analysis she may determine are *not* part of the argument she is making. For example, Kate Gardner publishes material from her field notes in *Songs at the River's Edge: Stories from a Bangladeshi Village* (Gardner 1991). The connection between those stories and her work in *Global Migrants, Local Lives: Travel and Transformation in Rural Bangladesh* on global migration and its impact of rural villages may seem loose (Gardner 1995). Yet, taken together both books give us insight into the thought processes of an ethnographer.

More generally, recalling Visweswaran's argument, such deliberative moments point out that despite our feminist best intentions and self-reflection, we bring to the field embedded epistemological assumptions and that it is often beyond the ability of our cognition to interrogate them (1994: 98). For this reason, it is very important to take good notes about your deliberative moments. Within these notes will likely be buried insights about epistemology that may ultimately prove to be some of the most important insights from your research. Box 11.1 considers the relationship between the ethnographer and the community under study.

Grounded Theory

Grounded theory is another form of research design in which the relationship of data production and analysis are inextricably linked. Grounded theory is a method of understanding the empirical dimensions of a complex problem. That is, the "theory" in grounded theory is a positive or empirical theory. It is not a normative or ethical theory, the researcher's selection of a grounded approach may be guided by certain normative or epistemological commitments, such as understanding people as sources of knowledge not objects of study.

The basic structure of grounded theory is that the researcher analyzes data which may have been collected through a broad range of methods. This initial analysis may reveal the categories that should be of primary concern. Then the researcher studies the data again, guided by those categories. This may involve collecting more data or reviewing existing data.

Research Questions for Grounded Theory

Grounded theory is a form of structured inquiry that is useful for studying questions that themselves have been concealed by dominant discourses, conceptualization, and notions of what questions are important. By design, then, grounded theory is a research design that enacts a feminist research ethic.

Methods of Grounded Theory

Grounded theory research design develops analytical categories and theories from our data. That is, rather than fixing the meaning of a concept based on *a priori* theoretical and empirically informed reflection, in grounded theory, we develop the meaning of the concepts through reflection on the data. Then return to the data with those concepts and study the data guided by those immanently developed concepts. The theory is *grounded* in the data. For this grounded analysis our data include not only our subject-participants' views, intentions, and actions but also the contexts and structures of their lives (Charmaz 2006). As Corbin and Strauss state, "One does not begin with a theory, [and] then prove it. Rather, one begins with an area of study and what is relevant to that area is allowed to emerge" (1990: 23). Grounded theory analysis requires constant reflection, evaluation, and reconceptualization of our research questions and theoretical frameworks to align them with the data we have collected and to ensure our research findings are "grounded" in these data. With this method, the development of your theoretical framework is directly influenced by the process of collecting and analyzing your data.

> Grounded theory involves taking comparisons from data and reaching up to construct abstractions and simultaneously reaching down to tie these abstractions to data (Charmaz 2006: 184).

The aim of grounded theory analysis is to see beyond the obvious or dominant readings of a problem or situation and to generate new and innovative interpretations of these.

A Feminist Research Ethic and Analysis in Grounded Theory

Grounded theory analysis is highly compatible with a feminist research ethic. Both feminist and grounded theory accounts of research acknowledge that researchers "stand within the research process rather than above, before or outside it" (Charmaz 2006: 180) and view the research process as an integral part of the research product.

While grounded theory is a theory that puts into practice the theoretical commitments of a feminist research ethic, a feminist research ethic can guide you to do this work better. What happens when you use a feminist research ethic? Such a research ethic helps you reconceptualize the abstractions of theory to notice what they conceal, to notice gaps in the data, and to reflect on the theoretical frameworks that may be implicit in your question, design, and data as you analyze the data. A feminist research ethic prompts you to become more aware of the power relations in research (between researched and researcher) that may obscure the connections between concepts and data or make the fit between them too good. It may allow you to see how research subject-participants, facilitators, or research assistants may be led by, and uncritical of, concepts that are implicit in your language as a researcher. Guided by a research ethic you should be attentive to the possibility that your subject-participants are relatively marginalized or privileged and reacting against the conceptual worlds of the researcher's, for example, western, white, subject positions.

The grounded approach to analyzing data involves developing emergent theories grounded in the engagement and self-conscious interpretation of the raw data (although data is never entirely "raw" from a feminist perspective). Following such an approach, we should not look for the frequency of key words "gender" or "women" within official documents of government or international organizations to generate data on whether or not they have mainstreamed gender issues in their policymaking (a common, form of self-evaluation of gender mainstreaming in institutions). Rather, in grounded analysis that is guided by a feminist research ethic we should use a range of methods, including participant observation, document analysis, statistical analysis and interviews for instance, to collect and analyze data allowing us to examine the practical implementation of gender mainstreaming commitments. From analysis of these data we may determine the best measures of gender mainstreaming and either reanalyze our existing data with that in mind, or gather new data.

There are some benefits from developing the categories of the coding scheme before beginning the coding. For instance, the data generated is more likely to be comparable with other content analyses across time and subject area if you use the same or similar categories as previous studies have used. But the purpose of a grounded approach is not supported by predetermining the categories of the coding scheme. By developing the coding scheme during research using grounded analysis, your codes and themes are more likely to reflect and tap the specific meanings and the language of subject-participants.

Analysis is an iterative process in grounded theory and when approached with a feminist research ethic you may need to adopt multiple methods of data inquiry and to pursue inquiry in several sites as you go back and forth between your data and your emergent theories (Charmaz 2006: 178). For heuristic purposes, there are four basic stages to grounded analysis, each of which can be improved by attending to the power of epistemology, boundaries, relationships, and the situatedness of the researcher.

In the first stage you reanalyze your data with the theoretical categories and ideas generated from the initial coding process. As a researcher you continually ask "of which theoretical category are these data an instance?" (Charmaz 2006: 179). Here secondary data from scholarly literatures, official documents, and reports are not treated as unproblematic sources of evidence speaking for themselves but are analyzed with the same theoretical codes and categories as participant and interview data (see Charmaz 2006: 39–40). You may find that you need to collect more data based on your theoretical categories or to rethink these categories and the variation and gaps within them where they cannot sufficiently account for the data you have. Alison Wylie (2002) proposes ways to be empirical but not narrowly empiricist: "The fragmentary materials of the archaeological record are an asset because they force researchers to look beyond data to background knowledge and auxiliary assumptions in order to establish evidence that is believable. The data or material become laden with theory that enriches the analysis" (Wylie 2002 cited in Fonow and Cook 2005: 2297). A feminist research ethic will focus your attention on searching for silences, gaps and missing data in the grounded, iterative process of analysis. The example below of a research project analyzing women's empowerment illustrates how the commitment to noticing silences with a feminist research ethic can improve a grounded approach to analysis.

Employing a grounded theory approach, Siobhan Austen, Therese Jefferson and Vicki Thein sought to generate a set of gendered social indicators that would be based on concrete experiences of progress in women's empowerment in the provincial state of Western Australia. Austen *et al* analyzed a series of focus group discussions about what would constitute indicators of progress in women's empowerment. They used *Nvivo*, a qualitative analysis software package, to identify common themes – that is, where there was consensus and diversity of opinion across groups – and to note the linkages across these themes. "Relevant sections of each transcript, focusing on different themes, were assigned a code, which was applied to subsequent transcripts where the same theme arose" (Austen *et al.* 2003: 8). Having completed this first analysis, they then considered what themes were missing. To the surprise of researchers, a number of seemingly important issues relating to women's social and economic status did not arise during the early discussions. These issues included the availability of health and educational services and environmental issues. The researchers went back to the participants in the focus groups to explicitly ask about these aspects of women's empowerment. It was decided that the facilitator would introduce these issues to determine whether they generated significant debate or were in fact of little interest to the participants in these groups. The result of this iterative grounded process was also surprising:

> While these more specific questions initiated some conversation among participants the identified issues did not emerge as central concerns and we decided not to proceed with further specific questioning of other groups (Austen *et al.* 2003: 8).

At this point the women's empowerment researchers decided they had reached theoretical "saturation" or "sufficiency," the second stage of grounded analysis for our purposes. Here fresh data no longer sparks new theoretical insights. The method of grounded analysis encourages us to keep theoretical sampling until categories are saturated – the theoretical logic here is what is important and not the sample size. The attentiveness of a feminist research ethic to silences, missing data, and gaps in the data gives us limited confidence that this point of saturation has been achieved.

The third stage of grounded analysis involves sorting and integrating your theoretical categories in order to decide which ones are most important and to understand the relationships among them. At this point it can be helpful to draw diagrams or conceptual maps to tease out the relationships among the concepts in the emergent theory that you are drafting (see Clarke 2005).

Finally, the writing process is a crucial fourth stage of grounded analysis as your data analysis is refined and the iterative learning process of the research is shared. Chapter thirteen gives further guidance on how a feminist research ethic can help us to be attentive to multiple audiences for our research in the writing process, to the moments to share our research throughout the research and writing process, and to the potential uses and abuses of our research.

Grounded analysis with its emphasis on research as a lived, interactive process and on situating theories in their social, historical, and local contexts can be enhanced by a feminist research ethic and its commitments to noticing power, marginalization, relationships, and the situatedness of the researcher. Ironically, contextualization improves our ability as researchers to make generalizations based on "scrutinizing numerous particulars" and analyzing the results of multiple studies to construct theory (see also chapter ten). By requiring us to reflect continually on our theorizing process a grounded approach avoids forcing data into categories. It makes it less likely that we will marginalize and exclude certain data or "import preconceived gendered and other biased assumptions such as those about human intentions, actions and meanings" into our research (Charmaz 2006: 181).

A feminist research ethic requires us to take seriously the perspectives and meanings of research participants in constructing grounded theory. The process of achieving theoretical saturation or sufficiency in grounded analysis is enhanced by the feminist research ethic's attentiveness to our relationships with subject-participants in particular. Mindful of not wasting the time of our subject-participants, this attentiveness leads researchers to consider whether less rather than more interviews may be adequate for the purposes of building our grounded theory analysis. We should not keep interviewing or collecting data through other methods when what matters is the theoretical logic and triangulation of our research and not our count of the number of observations.

By making the situatedness of the researcher an explicit part of our methodological account of grounded analysis, a feminist research ethic also helps address the potential for personal bias. For example, Green-Powell explicitly situates herself as a black woman researcher within her research noting the ways in which her own experience led her to question why there are so few women black school principals and to study this question using grounded theory (Green-Powell 1997: 198; see also Lather 1986).

A feminist research ethic improves intercoder reliability in grounded analysis as well. Despite the individual researcher's close engagement in the entire research process – interacting with data, making abstract interpretations, and analytical writing, it is crucial to see if others, looking at the same data, or different data, would come to the same conclusion. If one's analysis is unique this may suggest serious limitations in analyzing the data. Grounded theory and analysis should be grounded in the data, not the single perspective of the academic. For this reason, a feminist research ethic encourages collaboration and attentiveness to all relationships involved in the research process. With this attentiveness we can draw on our research participants and/or research assistants or collaborators to give us their (multiple) perspectives on the data. If we do this as we collect data and begin analyzing it, we should expect some common themes to emerge that can guide further data collection and analysis. For instance, if you are using the interview method, these multiple perspectives on the data can suggest follow-up questions or new participants to interview.

Grounded theory is a research design for producing and analyzing data in a way that reflects the dynamic and changing nature of meaning.

Discourse and Frame Analysis

Research Questions for Discourse and Frame Analysis

Discourse analysis seeks to analyze the meanings embedded in texts that reflect other discourses and indeed the broader discursive environment in which language constructs both meaning and power relations. Frame analysis also explores how meanings are produced through the use of language and categorization. Discourse and framing can be the "subject" of analysis in questions about how social movements or policymakers frame their arguments for example. However, discourse analysis is also a way of looking closely at text (whether that text originates in oral or written form) in order to understand the meaning of the words. In fact, the two – subject and analysis – are inextricably linked.

Methods of Discourse and Frame Analysis

Discourse and frame analysis can be used in single or a small number of comparative case studies because extensive knowledge is needed to uncover meanings. Deployed in this endeavor, discourse inquiry is "case study plus" because the case is not intended to be representative in any sense but rather illustrative of "constitutive theoretical propositions." The case selected for discourse analysis is "used as a medium for continued theoretical and methodological discussions" (Hansen 2006: 11).

However, aided by qualitative software for managing one's interpretation of various texts, discourse analysis can also be used to interpret patterns of discourse and meaning across large amounts of textual data within a case study and even across numerous cases.

A Feminist Research Ethic in Discourse and Frame Analysis

Discourse analysis begins with (and regularly returns to) identifying the discourses to be studied and their boundaries; that is, what is to be included and excluded from the study. A feminist research ethic requires us to reflect on the possible marginalization and silencing that may result from our choice of discourse(s), even though the approach aims to uncover and deconstruct meanings including those that are obscured by the power of epistemology. For instance, objectivist, neoliberal discourses about economic growth and aggregate wealth typically obscure questions of human development, suffering, and wellbeing. They especially neglect women's suffering and wellbeing since women are so often the majority of the poorest and disadvantaged in their societies. Analysis of neoliberal economic discourses would need to include comparative analysis of historical and contemporary, elite and popular, dominant and marginal texts that reflect these different, gendered worldviews.

We can identify discourses and interpret them in texts that are "objects" of analysis rather than a window into an external social reality or "truth." For example, feminist researchers analyze the production of gender and race through talk – everyday talk and war talk – rather than through what people say about (their beliefs on) the construction of race and gender in society

(Cooke and Woollacott 1993; Spender 1983; Weatherall and Potter 1992). The concept of *intertextuality* in discourse analysis captures the way texts draw upon other texts to establish legitimacy and authority for their constructions of identity (Hansen 2006: 12; Weldes 2006: 180). Intertextuality is a poststructural concept: texts often unconsciously, implicitly invoke other texts due to the dominance of certain discourses, texts, and language norms that may be pervasive, if subtly so. It is the researcher's job to make explicit this intertextuality – the way the meaning of one text is dependent on that of another. Intertextuality can be observed in any combination of discourses including official institutional and political discourses, discourses of the media and business, and broader discourses from popular culture and marginal political groups from a variety of non-fiction and fiction genres (see Weldes 2006). But how can discourse analysis help us to generalize and uncover meanings in "texts"?

In her feminist-informed book on security as discourse, Lene Hansen (2006) suggests a "methodology of reading" (to identify identities and differences within texts) and a "methodology of textual selection" (to decide which forms of text should be chosen and how many). Hansen's methodology of reading identifies the discourse of security as produced through the construction of threats to a socially-constructed nation-state "self." Only certain security threats are given the status of a "national" security threat depending on the gendered, raced, ethnic, etc construction of the national self/identity.

Hansen details four analytical steps for systematically examining identity construction in a discourse, each of which can be enhanced by a feminist research ethic. First, we should look for identities that assume "degrees of otherness" or terms that clearly construct "the other" such as evil or good, civilized or barbarian, rational or irrational, victim or agent. Here, paying attention to gendered constructions can help us to notice and not take for granted constructions of identity and otherness. Second, we should look for possible instabilities and slippages between the linking of these constructions. How do competing discourses construct them with different effects revealing the location of identity in particular texts? Third, we should analyze the differences between these discourses of identity and how they change over time. Fourth, we should consider the "field" of political debate, including the gender dynamics of that field, which contains these discourses. This will enable us to identify the smaller number of basic discourses that structure the debate. In frame analysis, we look for these discourses called "master frames" because they function like hegemonic structures to shape the meanings of specific policy dilemmas.

Frame analysis is at once a research question and a way of analyzing the deeper structure of discourse. A researcher might identify the idea that men are dominant, aggressive sexual beings, for example, as a "master frame" enabling and constraining our ways of thinking about sexuality, reproductive rights or HIV/AIDs at local and global levels. Frames can be altered but only within certain boundaries since the master frames "delimit understanding of issues and steer people's frames in directions that express particular forms of gendering, racializing and/or sexualizing for instance" (Lombardo *et al.* 2009: 13). Moreover, aligning a particular frame or meaning with a "master frame" makes it more likely that it will be noticed and taken seriously.

The commitments of a feminist research ethic can strengthen analysis of historically and culturally-specific discourses or frames by foregrounding participants' experiential knowledge, agency and creativity and attending to experiences of "difference" in reading text and interviewing subject-participants that do not fit easily within any fixed theoretical framework or causal account (see Rice 2009). In feminist-informed research there is often a tension between wanting our subject-participants to voice their perspectives in their own terms and analyzing what we take to be their significance in terms of our theoretical framework (Lister 2003; Thompson and Barrett 1997). Bice Maiguashca (2006), for example, finds that although the Indian feminists participating in the World Social Forum use the language of liberal rights, their practices are actually socialist-feminist in her analysis, since their struggles include setting up micro-credit associations, and empowering women economically through education, training and organizing them into unions and trade co-operatives. Attentive to our relationships with subject-participants and our own situatedness, a feminist research ethic prompts discourse analysis in light of subject-participants' social and political "practices" and not merely what they say or write. We take seriously our subject-participants' speech and texts *and* we also probe their intertextuality in order to reveal their contested and constructed nature.

Guided by a feminist research ethic discourse analysis takes us beyond identifying constructions of identity and difference in the text and extends our analysis to interpreting the textual meanings of identity in terms of actual practices. Noël Sturgeon's research on ecofeminist activism shows just how important analyzing practices as well as texts can be in discourse analysis. Sturgeon (1997) critiques ecofeminist discourses that assume an essential (read: biological) relationship between women and nature but her analysis goes further. As well as uncovering the epistemological power embedded in the ecofeminist discourses, Sturgeon analyzes these discourses in light of activist practices. She finds that ecofeminist *essentialism* enabled different kinds of women to organize for the purposes of political action. And this political action in turn served to destabilize that essentialism by creating "radically democratic social movement structures – alliances, coalitions, networks, affinity groups, and consensus process decision-making" (Sturgeon 1997: 13).

Like Maiguascha (2006), Sturgeon (1997) looks at the narratives in ecofeminist texts *and* their practices. The commitments of a feminist research ethic improve discourse analysis by requiring us to both deconstruct and reconstruct textual practices. Discourse analysis guided by such an ethic also demands that we be explicit and transparent about the implications and audiences for our research.

Frame analysis interrogates data looking for the strategic and often explicitly political use of multiple meanings or "frames" to construct different realities (Lombardo *et al.* 2009; Keck and Sikkink 1998; Snow and Benford 1988). Frames link concepts together in a set of relationships that are underpinned by the power relationships that support the institutionalization of these ideas in texts or avowedly political discourses. Analyzing frames in discourse entails searching for the set of meanings that structure discussion of a particular social problem or policy for instance.

We may ask, for instance, what are the frames shaping the relationship between women and men in particular contexts and what are their effects?

Political or policy frames rest on deeper normative assumptions contained in or represented by master frames. But those who frame ideas and policies in certain ways may be unaware of these assumptions and their implications. Frame analysis involves interpreting text to ascertain how "fragmentary or incidental information [is transformed] into a structured and meaningful policy problem in which a solution is implicitly or explicitly included" (Verloo 2005b: 20; also Lombardo *et al.* 2009: 11). This is what scholars do in order to reveal the "an interactive process by which actors with agendas encounter specific discursive opportunities in the form of institutionalized texts." The active notion of "frame-work" conveys this process (Ferree 2009). Frame analysis allows us to uncover the "frame-work" of people and organizations.

Further, the feminist-informed researcher draws implications from the use of these frames for practice (see Winter 2008). For example, from the perspective of activists, the impact of deploying a "business" argument for promoting gender equality in a developing country on the marginalization of international aid funding for women's advocacy (and the human rights "frame") may be unintentional (True 2009c). When we as scholars analyze the frames in any given discourse our analysis is guided by a feminist research ethic that makes clear the trade-offs for political action of adopting particular arguments and meanings.

A feminist research ethic also uses frame analysis as a method to analyze and make visible the interactions between institutional and civil society (or non-institutional) actors as part of the social relations of framing within organizational structures and interests. Critical frame analysis developed by feminist scholars exemplifies the use of a feminist research ethic. It requires us to interpret texts noting whose voices are empowered by the way particular problems and solutions are represented (Lombardo *et al.* 2009; Verloo 2006). For example, critical frame analysts look at official texts relating to the question or issue they are studying to determine whose voice is present and whose is silent, which actors are included and excluded in the discussion of an issue and how power works in terms of what can be said and cannot be said about that issue.

> ### Box 11.2 Using qualitative software for discourse or frame analysis
>
> Statistical Software like Atlast.TI, MAXqda, NVivo, and Aquad provide researchers with a note-taking system that enables elaborate cross-referencing. Like bibliographic management software and statistical inference software, it does not do the reading and thinking for you. However, it does offer a way of storing, sorting, and aggregating your insights from textual data.

Qualitative software can facilitate frame and discourse analysis by allowing a researcher to identify key "frames" or "discourses" through patterns of language and/or concepts in multiple texts and to compare across different types of texts and different types of speaking subjects (see Bazeley 2007). But the use of software is a way of organizing and coding data for analysis rather than the analysis of the data itself (Box 11.2; for the same point, see Yanow and Schwartz-Shea 2006: 212). Recently there has been a lot of airplay given to these software packages perhaps because they seem to make qualitative analysis appear more procedural and systematic. Such software can be extremely helpful in managing a larger number of texts than would normally be doable for qualitative researchers. But it does not diminish or replace interpretation and fine-grained analysis – whether through the selected methods discussed in this or the previous chapter. As others have said long before us:

> Analytic procedures which appear rooted in standardized, often mechanistic procedures are no substitute for genuinely "grounded" engagement with the data throughout the whole of the research process. It is worth noting that the "usefulness" of such computer programs implies that you have collected and input all of your data, and this suggests that data collection and data analysis are discrete and linear when they typically are not. How we get our data and what kinds of data we collect greatly affect how we analyze this data and the findings we derive from it (Coffey *et al.* 1996).

Participatory Action Research

Participatory research, participatory rural appraisal, and participatory action research are approaches to research that structure not only the methods used for data production and analysis but also for the very questions to be researched. Research facilitators and subject-participants can be "co-researchers" in question formation, data collection, data analysis, and dissemination and ownership of the research findings since the research is intended to affect their situation or community. The extent to which there is co-research along these dimensions varies considerably across projects (Brisolara and Seigart 2007; Gatenby and Humphries 2000). A feminist research ethic asks us to reflect on the extent to which research facilitators and subject-participants should have "ownership" of the project – determining its questions, methods, analysis, and dissemination (Smith [1998] 1999). While the intellectual history of these fields suggests that even without a feminist research ethic, self-reflective attention to power, boundaries, and relationships has been important for participatory action research, a feminist research ethic can remind and guide a researcher in this area.

(Note there are other forms of action research. As we discuss in Chapters two, three, and particularly four, the source of the research question can be political and constitute a form of action research. This section discusses *participatory action research*.)

Research Questions for Participatory Action Research

Most questions can be approached with a participatory lens. In fact we qualify this with "most" only because we cannot think of a question that cannot and want to have some humility about the possibility that there is such a question. Sometimes the researcher develops a participatory research agenda in order to improve the lives of subject-participants. A scholar of urban neighborhoods, Susan Saegert (2006) has worked for decades on scholarship that supports the political actions of the residents of abandoned buildings.

Methods of Participatory Action Research

This is not to say that for every question participatory methods are the best *a priori*. Rather participatory methods can be brought to bear on most questions. While the normative commitments to participatory action research lead to integrated understanding of the relationship of question, data, analysis, and research design generally, this approach does not dictate a specific combination of these. So whereas ethnographers use "ethnographic methods" which predictably include participant observation, mapping, and interviews, participatory action research can deploy a broader range of methods that includes ethnographic, grounded, and statistical structured inquiries as well as the forms of data collection and analysis discussed in the preceding two chapters.

A Feminist Research Ethic and Analysis in Participatory Action Research

There are a few normative commitments embedded in the research that go by these labels and not everyone who does this work is devoted to all of these commitments. *Participation* can mean community involvement in question formation, data collection, data analysis, and dissemination and ownership of the research findings (Ackerly *et al.* 2009; True 2008d). Rural *appraisal* can mean that the community is involved in assessing its own resources, strengths, weaknesses, opportunities, and threats (Chambers 1994, 1997). Due to gender norms within communities it may be difficult to get full and equal community participation in such appraisal (Cornwall 2003; Guijt and Shah [1998] 1999). *Action* research can mean that the research should generate a social action (Brisolara and Seigart 2007; Clark *et al.* 2006; Cooke and Kothari 2001; Cornwall 2003; Crawley 1998; Currie 1999; Kesby 2005; Lennie *et al.* 2003; Lykes and Coquillon 2007; Maguire 1987).

Even with tools for attentiveness to power, participation does not make the research attentive to gendered power (Mosse 1994; Parpart 2000). Moreover, participatory research is not to be confused with feminist activism and engagement (Aggarwal 2000; Man Ling Lee 2007). Feminist academics can be activists, feminist academics can study activism, but these interests in activism are not themselves tools of participatory action research.

We might use participatory methods for questions when the relevant information is known only to the subject-participants. This reason for participatory work takes two asymmetries of power – asymmetry in academic audience and asymmetry in local knowledge – an attempts to use one to mitigate the other. In these circumstances researchers and participants work hard not to be exploitative or exploited by the new arrangement, as either could be.

Inferential Statistical Design: A Special Comparative Case

A fourth form of structured inquiry is statistical research. This approach requires data that can be converted to statistical form, a large number of cases or *observations* relative to the number of variables under study, and software sophisticated enough to process the data.

Research Questions for Large n Comparative Case Studies

When we are interested in patterns that can be generalized, and there are many variables to be considered, a comparison of many cases is necessary. In social science research the number of cases being compared is referred to as "n" as in "n = 3" to describe a project with 3 cases or "n = 189" to describe a project with 189 cases. These latter are called large n studies. In order to process large numbers of cases or observations, social scientists use statistical packages (SPSS, STATA, etc.). Large n statistical research designs are a special case of comparative case research design in which the cases are deemed sufficiently similar, such that the principles of probability that underlie statistical software can be reasonably expected to apply to the data.

These software packages applied to datasets of a large number of cases with multiple variables of interest, let us use mathematical equations to assess the probability that two variables are related to each other in a way that is more likely (or less likely) than would be generated by a random association. Theory and analysis can then be used to explain the correlations among variables: perhaps one variable causes the other or perhaps two variables are affected by a third factor and therefore are often correlated with each other, but not because one causes the other. Other methods and analysis are necessary for interpreting the meaning of the relationships among variables. Statistical models let us know how confident we should be that we have found an interesting pattern or relationship.

Feminist researchers have been using such designs to study questions of gender division of household labor (Brines 1994), disparities in public health (LeClere *et al.* 1998), gender and speech patterns (Carli 1990), gender and influence in groups (Ridgeway 1982), comparable worth and wage discrimination (Steinberg 1990), women's empowerment (Ackerly 1995; Hashemi *et al.* 1996) (see Box 7.4), gender policy diffusion (True and Mintrom 2001), women's human rights (Apodaca 1998, 2000), gender disparities in natural disasters (Neumayer and Plümper 2007) and so on. The first four examples are discussed in Sprague (Sprague 2005: chapter four). Where the researcher is interested in patterns that can be generalized in social, economic or political life, quantitative analysis of a large number of cases is an appropriate research design. Large scale statistical designs can often be very persuasive with politicians and government audiences.

Such work has yielded scholarship that is invaluable for policy influence. Feminist activists have sometimes expressed frustration with qualitative feminist researchers because these quantitative methods of analysis are not given the same political respect that they receive in policy circles (Hartmann and Spalter-Roth 1996). Such respect is due not just to a socially constructed predilection among policy makers for quantitative work, but also to the nature of such projects; they lend themselves to evidence-based claims which are instrumental in informing policy and defending politically difficult policy choices.

Methods of Large n Comparative Cases

The methods that we use to acquire data for statistical analysis, like those of comparative analysis, could include most forms of data collection. If data can be coded, that is, converted from qualitative into quantitative form it can be used for statistical inference. For example, in discourse analysis scholars code "speech acts" which can be drawn from interviews, texts, and participant observation. Because it is a lot of work to construct and assemble a data set, we may also acquire a dataset created by others. Acquired data needs to be evaluated just as critically as we would evaluate a dataset that we develop ourselves. Moreover, allow enough time to "clean" your data, that is, to prepare it for software analysis by making sure that all of the variables for each observation are filled in properly.

Often a software package is considered to be the analytical method in a statistical project. However, this is a misconception perpetuated by the frequent reference to "quantitative analysis." In fact, software packages generate statistical "results." The researcher then treats these as data and needs to use the analytical tools of Chapter ten and this chapter to comprehend those results and determine what "findings" they yield.

A Feminist Research Ethic and Analysis in Statistical Inference

The key deliberative moments in research design of a statistical project are generally around operationalization of variables (see Chapter eight) and deciding which variables to include as "control" variables which might explain some variation in the dependent variable (the phenomena you are studying), but that are not the subject of study.

When we rely on others' data collection, we also need to pay particular attention to how those data were collected and coded (see Box 9.4 on coding). As we have already seen, some coders have treated "universal male suffrage" as a measure of democracy whereas a feminist might expect "universal adult suffrage" as a better measure of democracy (Paxton 2000). Look at your borrowed datasets closely.

For statistical work, you need to be able to make an argument that the cases are similar units in the relevant respects. For *feminist* statistical work, you need to reflect carefully on the epistemological (even ontological) assumptions embedded in that argument. For instance, some data are not available or not collected on a gender disaggregated basis. Some are data "defined" by the state, or defined differently by different states, and therefore may not be comparable across states. States vary as to which labor counts as "labor" – formal, informal, basic needs provision such as fuel and water collection. Some data are collected at the "household" level making them of questionable use for deconstructing power imbalances and distributional inequalities within the household.

When we construct data for statistical work, we not only construct the unit of analysis (What constitutes a democracy or a human security crisis?), we also construct the variables we study and assert (or assume) that they are applicable to these units. For example, when we consider the deaths associated with a disaster, we might count the deaths during the event, or include those due to epidemics and to increased stress on the social networks after the event. There is some evidence that the number of people killed can be estimated with greater accuracy than the number of people affected by a disaster; see Guha-Sapir and Below (2002) in Neumayer and Plümper (2007). Do we choose to work with data that are less theoretically appropriate measures of the phenomena we wish to study because they are relatively more reliable, or do we work with less reliable data that are more theoretically appropriate measures of that phenomenon? This dilemma is the sort of puzzle that leads some to mixed method and triangulation analytical techniques (see Chapter ten).

Much feminist reflection in statistical work is around the lack of data (Apodaca 2009; Caprioli 2009; Parisi 2009), or the challenges of constructing data sets (Jayaratne and Stewart 1991; Stanley 1995).

Conclusion

Structured inquiries use many of the tools discussed in the earlier part of this book. They are patterns of research design that scholars return to for various sorts of questions both because they are appropriate methods for such questions and because their disciplines have given legitimacy to such approaches. There is increasing interest in mixed method methodologies in social science research. As scholars work with these method combinations, we may find new patterns of structured inquiry emerging. The reason to consider a structured inquiry design is not because it has been done before but rather because these approaches give a structure to the non-linear relationship among the various pieces of research design. While it is helpful to see how these might be useful for your question, you may also use them as a general guide as you develop your own structured inquiry, trying to design your own systematic way of doing dynamic social and political science.

Selected Sources for Further Reading

Charmaz, Kathy. 2006. *Constructing Grounded Theory: A Practical Guide through Qualitative Analysis*. London; Thousand Oaks, CA: Sage.

Hesse-Biber, Sharlene Nagy, ed. 2007. *Handbook of Feminist Research: Theory and Praxis*. Thousand Oaks, CA: Sage.

Lombardo, Emanuela, Petra Meier, and Mieke Verloo eds. 2009. *The Discursive Politics of Gender Equality: Stretching, Bending and Policy-Making*. New York: Routledge (EU Series).

Smith, Linda Tuhiwai. [1998] 1999. *Decolonizing Methodologies: Research and Indigenous Peoples*. London: Zed Books.

Visweswaran, Kamala. 1994. *Fictions of Feminist Ethnography*. Minneapolis: University of Minnesota Press.

Wolf, Diane L., ed. 1996. *Feminist Dilemmas in Fieldwork*. Boulder, CO: Westview Press.

Chapter 12

Methods for Data Management and Field Research

Introduction

There is a broad range of methodological considerations as we generate and collect data that are not normally method-specific. These considerations often occur to us just as we are generating our data. In this chapter we review the practical issues surrounding data collection while we document our work, work away from home (or in the "field"), and collaborate on research teams. We offer tools for addressing these practical issues. Crucially, we offer the tools of a feminist research ethic for adapting your methods of data collection and generation so that they can respond to the dimensions of epistemological power, boundaries, and our relationships with subject-participants, research team members, and others.

Tools for Keeping Track of Data While in the Field

Regardless of whether you are generating or collecting data by oral history, interviewing, survey, focus group, from secondary sources, or from the methods of structured inquiry, there are some tools that are generally useful for managing your data. Not all of these are generally thought of as research tools and they don't all require long discussions, but they each bear mentioning. All good researchers use these tools but with a feminist research ethic we can better ensure that they adequately attentive to issues of power, boundaries, relationships and so on.

Systems for Keeping Track of Your Data

Whatever data you are collecting, you need systems for keeping track of it. Find occasions to design and field test these mechanisms before you need to rely on them. Keep as much information as the ethics of your research design allows. Create a system for backing up your data – whether that means photocopying handwritten notes and putting them in different locations or typing them up and saving them to multiple hard drives. You will want originals and backups, both of which need to be secure.

Data from each organization, interview, text, statistical dataset or participant observation needs to be uniquely identifiable so that you can easily retrieve it. Try using date and time markers for meetings, with a prefix for the researcher gathering the data if you have more than one researcher in your team. This method creates a unique code for each piece of data (B 5-23-09-13:30 – for a piece of data collected by Brooke on May 23, 2009 at 1:30 local time). Then in a separate log the researcher can note the particulars of the data (B 5-23-09-13:30 – interview with Jacqui True). This is particularly appropriate if you have multiple kinds of data an individual researcher is collecting or if you need to protect the anonymity of sources. To protect anonymity, the log would have identifying information and the notes would not.

In one study, a colleague did not keep any identifying information about his sources. Consequently, he was not able to notice patterns in responses. All of the information about networks, resources, everything was lost and all he had were the sources' opinions and analysis. As the research proceeded, he developed hypotheses and was unable to explore them with his own data. With the note-taking and log system, qualitative and quantitative data can be linked and confidentiality protected. However, when gathering data in a chaotic setting, it may be difficult to keep to the system. This is why it is important to *field test* your system of documentation in advance just as you would field test your instrument for data collection.

Documentation

For ethnographic and interpretive work, you will need a constellation of methods of documentation. This may include photographs, audio recording, video recording, notetaking, and post-interview reflection notes. Not all of these methods will be appropriate for each interaction or interview, but all can be important for reminding you of aspects of the meeting that you may later discover are very important. Also, voice recorders fail, notes get wet, research materials get lost in shipping. The more redundancy you have, the more confident you are that you can do justice to the time your interview subject-participants gave to your project.

Documenting Your Thought Process: Journaling, Memoing, and Field Notes

There are many ways to document your thoughts. Some of these may become data, but they serve a range of purposes. Brooke always keeps a research journal, not only when gathering data, but also when reflecting on it. Field notes are a standard tool of interpretive researchers when collecting data. Statistical researchers may find that if they keep field notes on the operationalization of their variables, their coding process (sometimes called a "codebook"), and the various models they test and why, they will be better able to recall and defend their choices when it comes to the write-up and review process.

If you are studying an organization or a network, consider organizational mapping from multiple perspectives by drawing visual diagrams. You might map how a credit program is experienced by a borrower; map separately how an organization is experienced by a field worker, and separately again how it is perceived by a donor in your field notes. In her memos from the field Rachel Silvey (2007) shows how Terminal 3, which processes Indonesians returning from work abroad, is experienced by the returning emigrant and how that differs from that expected in the formal organization of the government bureaucracy.

The memo is a tool of data production that bridges data collection and data analysis. Chapter ten discusses "description" as a method of analysis that draws significantly on the practice of memoing while in the field (see Box 12.1). The memo is the researcher's partial reflection. You might write memos about how you operationalized your key variable, perhaps rethinking your assumptions. Memos might also reflect on the following indicative topics: Should you follow the convention for measuring "social capital" or do you think that social capital entails a broader range of activities that are better captured by reflecting more broadly on the sources of social networks? Have you gathered the data necessary to accommodate your rethinking of the operationalization of your variable, or do you have to proceed with a flawed operationalization. How will that affect your findings?

Blogging and writing "home" can offer you multiple imagined audiences for your reflections. By writing for multiple audiences you anticipate different concerns and starting points, as we explore further in Chapter thirteen on writing and publishing your research. In this way you enhance your ability to destabilize the power of your first thoughts, attend to the intersections of race, ethnicity, gender, sexuality, class and so on, notice relational subjectivities among interview subject-participants, and to situate and re-situate yourself and your research.

Tools for Practicing a Feminist Research Ethic in the Field

Whether your "field" is the Internet, statistical databases on developing countries, several multilateral government organizations, women's health

Box 12.1 Memo-writing

Kathy Charmaz (2006) offers a lot of guidance on how to write a memo, which is a titled and dated record of your analysis at one point in time.

Writing memos helps you to "stop and think about your data," to "develop your writer's voice and rhythm," to "spark ideas to check out in the field setting," to "discover gaps in your data collection," and among other things to link data-gathering with analysis.

We should "treat memos as partial, preliminary and provisional" (p. 84). Writing from the beginning of your research however, will inspire you to develop ideas in a narrative form and in some depth early on in the process.

Memos should be spontaneous and informal like writing a letter to a friend. Charmaz advises that you should adopt whatever method works for you in advancing your thinking as you write.

You may:

- Title your memo.
- Study your emerging data before memoing.
- Engage a category then brainstorm around it with the partial data you have collected; working towards defining the category – and its underlying and unstated assumptions.
- "[B]ring raw data into the memo" (Charmaz 2006: 82).
- Look for patterns and gaps in the data and use them to direct and focus further data collection.
- Use visual strategies (bolding, highlighting, capital letters) to emphasize ideas from the start and to prompt you to pursue them later.
- Consider observed relationships between ideas, concepts, stories, or narratives emerging in your data.
- Make comparisons of different data (Charmaz 2006: 82).
- Revisit and review your memos through the research process to identify areas you still need to explore or grapple with.

If memo-writing is difficult for you Charmaz (2006: 86-91) offers two prewriting exercises to help you get comfortable writing memos. They are "clustering" (drawing a visual diagram of relationships in your data and your project) and "free-writing" (2006: 72–95).

See also "Grounded Theory" in Chapter eleven and the practice exercise on the book's website, http://www.palgrave.com/methodology/doingfeministresearch.

advocacy groups cross-nationally, or a rural community in a foreign country you will be confronted by both anticipated and unanticipated deliberative moments in your research, especially in your data collection and generation, through which a feminist research ethic can guide you.

Ethics Statement

Most people associate ethics in research with a human subjects research ethics committee, an institutional ethics committee or *institutional review board* (IRB) of their institution or country. Your review board may not require an ethics statement in which you set out for yourself and your research team your general principles of ethical research. It is a way of organizing your ethical anxieties and creating for yourself and your team a compass. It can be a useful tool in introductions and getting permission to interview. It can also be an interesting conversation starter. Further, when something happens during research that gives you ethical pause, you can return to your ethics statement as a guide or for revision.

You may ask if the organization has its own ethics statement (Sapra 2009), you may encourage the organization to discuss the possible ethical dimensions of your project (Ackerly 2007), or you may write together a memo of understanding to set out your working relationship and mutual understanding. (For more on ethics and ethical review of research see Permission and Consent below and guiding materials on the book's website, http://www.palgrave.com/methodology/doingfeministresearch)

Making a First Impression

Making a good first impression is a foundational piece of trust. As we discuss in Chapter nine, most interviewers give great importance to trust; however, making a good impression is a tool for all researchers. You have *lots* of opportunities to make a first impression – on your colleagues, on your research assistants, on the librarian in the archive crucial to your research, on the person who runs the lunch room where you are conducting participant observation, on the shop keeper who later on introduces you to his cousin who is starting a non-government organization for human rights. You do not always know when you are making a first impression, so assume it is always.

Making a good first impression with research subject-participants can be difficult when one is a young woman who is often greeted by an interviewees' expression of shock that "she is the researcher?!" Many women researchers describe this happening most frequently when they were graduate students "studying-up" male elites and officials (Fernandez 2007; Hochstetler 2007; Ortbals and Rincker 2007). Gaining credibility with subject-participants and facilitators is thus especially important for young women and other researchers whose identity may seem "out of place" in their particular research field. Candice Ortbals (Ortbals with Rincker 2007: 20) argues that "presenting oneself as a professional is key." For instance, "professionalism in an interview requires both an energetic demeanor and professional attire – both of which present women with special challenges."

Following the adage, "when in Rome . . . " try to adopt the same standard of dress if not the same actual clothing as others in your research location. For women graduate students interviewing officials or observing elite forums I (Jacqui) recommend the navy blue suit as a way of keeping the focus on your questions or research and not on you personally. However, in some settings being pregnant – and therefore not being able to downplay your body – or being accompanied by children – may not be possible and may actually be to your advantage in establishing rapport and trust with research subject-participants. Meg Rincker (Ortbals and Rincker 2007: 21) comments that "being pregnant definitely proved to be a great icebreaker in Polish society," her research site. But it also meant she had to "explain to everyone – men and women – when her baby was due before getting into the meat of the interviews." Having a good, succinct explanation prepared can be helpful in such situations. Similarly, Aili Tripp (2002) describes how being accompanied by her child to interviews with women's organizations in Uganda increased the mutual rapport with her subject-participants and their acceptance of her presence as a researcher away from home but not family.

Of course, first impressions of you may be formed before anyone meets you. We have come across numerous instances of organizations and activists having terrible experiences with researchers – researchers taking data and not returning it, gathering findings and not sharing them, imposing their research team on a community without compensation for the extra burden that presence created often for the most marginalized. Bad research ethics by other researchers can be the first impression anyone has of you. When Sonalini Sapra went to India to study women's activism in environmental movement organizations, she heard of many such experiences because the organizations' past experience with researchers threatened her ability to do her work. It also prompted her to develop another research project on research ethics. Other feminist scholars have also found it challenging to go back into the field or have consciously decided not to revisit the same research site and question because a particular site has since become "saturated" with researchers from international organizations, NGOs, and governments organizations as well as from research universities.

Above all, if you are conducting interviews or participant-observing at a particular place and time be sure to make lots of time for travel to and arrival at your place of research. You can get lost and accidents can happen. One friend told a story of her experience of research at the European Commission in Brussels. Prior to her arrival she went to a nearby café to prepare for her meeting where someone spilt their cup of coffee on her completely spoiling her light colored dress. Fortunately she had just enough time to whip into a shop in the area and purchase a new outfit. She made her meeting with just a minute to spare. Horror stories "from the field" such as these remind us to take extra care with ourselves as well as our data. Make extra time to back up your data in case of its loss or of computer failure, to establish the location of your research meeting in advance, or to explain an obvious personal predicament to an interviewee. Carrying out your research with at least the appearance of ease can be important in making first impressions on subject-participants, facilitators, and ultimately the audiences for your research.

Sensitivity to Context

Always in the field you need to be sensitive to the context of your work. For some researchers, it is obvious that we always need to pay attention to context – "researchers must contend with political authoritarianism and violence," and often "deep cultural differences related to religion and . . . gender" (Clark 2006: 417). Our interview subject-participants and facilitators may be put at risk as a result of our research. By virtue of their political views, activists are often at risk; and some identity groups are always at risk (Mugisha and Mukasa 2008). For others, especially, as the novelty of research wears off and we are more comfortable in our research settings, we need to remind ourselves of our context. Cultural appropriateness – for instance whether to do handiwork while in meetings, whether to sit on the floor, whether to make eye contact, etc. – comes up in countless ways when you are doing research.

Sensitivity to context may mean changing the way you do or time your work. It may even mean changing your methods. Perhaps you do not do household surveys in the United States in the summer because response rates are historically low and skewed. Perhaps this means not doing long field stays in places where a natural disaster has just occurred, or maybe it means planning on staying there and using more ethnographic methods than you originally planned. In the example in Box 12.2 we see that not interviewing all subject-participants in a particular category or group would have unfairly advantaged some subject-participants or exposed a subset of participants interviewed to greater risks.

In a broad range of research designs a feminist research ethic requires us to pay attention to the way in which context can affect our work in transparent and subtle ways. Chapter ten and eleven (on grounded analysis) discuss how to pay attention to context and contextualization when analyzing the data you have collected from the field.

Timing

When should you do your research? Do you need to time it around an event? When is the optimal time to send out a survey and how long should one allow respondents to complete a survey? It is not often a good idea to conduct interviews or a survey during summer months at least in developed countries since you will not get a good sample, representative or not, when

> ## Box 12.2 Relationship between research subject-participants and non-participants
>
> During field testing for a study of microcredit programs, I (Brooke) discovered that a small amount of social capital accrued to those borrowers who participated in my interviews. Rather than interviewing a random selection of borrowers in a given location, I (Brooke) hired two research assistants and we interviewed every borrower of a given borrowing group. (The groups were determined with purposive sampling.) To the extent that social capital accrued to interview subject-participants by virtue of the interview, we wanted to distribute this evenly.
>
> The field testing also revealed that some of the organizations' employees were worried about repercussions of participating in the study. Consequently, we interviewed every employee of the branches where we conducted our research. To the extent that workers were nervous about negative repercussions associated having participated in the interviews, these could be assuaged if everyone in the bank participated anonymously (Ackerly 2005, 2007).

much of the population takes vacation. In developing countries where most people do not have the luxury of an extended holiday the considerations will be different. In Bangladesh, for instance, it is difficult to do survey research when the water is high and for reasons of sensitivity, certain research should not be done during food shortages. Obviously for those researchers working in conflict, disaster or post-crisis settings there is no good time to do research but the research may need to be done to affect crucial change and improvements in those settings (see Sriram *et al.* 2009).

Logistics

Developing contacts and arranging research requires attention to national and local cultural norms, but also attention to hierarchies, to norms of research, and to practical considerations such as access to mail, fax, email (all of which can change over time) in the place where you are working. Often the best tools for research in a given place are those available there. For example, in Bangladesh in 1993 there were cardboard boxes with a metal spring, perfect for keeping interview questionnaires clean and in order. On the other hand, we always travel with our own supply of batteries, and convertible electric plugs, and small appliance to boil water.

Social Networks

In Chapter six we argue that the researcher needs to sustain herself with social networks of individuals with a range of roles (see Box 6.2). If you do your research in multiple places, you will likely need to build these networks wherever you go.

When you are new to a place, you might gain knowledge about the reputation of researchers, context, logistics, etc. from a facilitator or gatekeeper or from your network. You may rely on one or more people to explain local logistics and their social norms to you. For this purpose many researchers seek out other researchers in their place of research. Because not all researchers share the same research ethic and because expatriate researchers may find each other in places where other expatriates – journalists, business people, government officials or contractors, or military personnel – congregate, you may or may not find that such circles are the most comfortable way to learn about local norms. Consider the reputational impact of the choices you make. A research site's being relatively crowded with researchers who have adopted similar methods for data collection may affect the data you are be able to collect. In that case it may be better to choose either another method or another research site. Such an instance may also be cause for collaboration.

One way to build social networks and supporters of your research may be to invite people to be part of your research. I (Brooke) hosted dinner parties during a Bangladesh research visit to introduce my new friends to my work, to ask for their cultural, development, and research sensitive reflections, to field test my focus group questionnaire and structure, and to role model for my research assistants how I wanted the focus groups to go. The guests knew the purpose of the invitation, we all had fun and strengthened our networks, and we gained important insights for the design of the focus group. Another way to strengthen your local networks and get key persons involved – and with a stake – in your research while in the field could be to present your research design, questions, and hypotheses at a meeting of an organization you are studying, or to a group who may have an interest in your study.

Techniques for Oral Histories, Interviews, and Some Surveys

When researchers who use interviews – whether surveys or in depth interviews – reflect on their method, they often mention the importance of establishing trust with research subject-participants (see also discussion of first impressions). Often decisions such as whether to use a voice recorder, what to wear, and when and where to conduct the interview, are justified in the context of the importance of trust between researcher and subject-participant or facilitator-participant. Give your interlocutor reason and opportunity to assess your character positively.

Be prepared. Make sure you have done some background research so that you don't ask questions that your interviewee has already published answers to. You might refer to these in the interview to help build the rapport with your subject-participant (Ray 1999: 172–3). Such preparation shows respect, which is fertile soil for gaining their trust and an important way of being attentive to relationships during research.

Sometimes, building trust with a subject-participant can begin prior to the interview. In correspondence via letter or electronically, you may explain your project, introduce your research team, and even obtain consent for the interview (particularly possible for elite interviews) so that by the time of the face to face interview much of the groundwork for a good interview has been laid. (See also "Permissions and Consent" below and the book's website, http://www.palgrave.com/methodology/doingfeministresearch, for sample email consent correspondence.)

Offer an appropriate, well thought out introduction to your project and the interview (it need not be lengthy, just good) that includes an explanation of how the interview will be used and the extent to which the interviewee can affect that use. Be prepared to answer a question about the impact of the study on the respondent, or those he or she cares about. Consider how you might overcome the problem, that may have been discovered during your field testing, of a subject-participants providing merely their organization's "official line" on a subject. This tendency may be a function of language or politics. If it is political, you might provide a fuller introduction to your project or a lesser one. Sometimes this problem may be dealt with by not having a recorder or by using one and providing the subject with the recording or transcript and the opportunity to edit her words. I (Jacqui) have had experiences where the elite interviewee, a government official, has explicitly stated that they will be able to give more fulsome answers if there is no voice recording. Focus groups or trust building public exercises before individual interviews can give subject-participants opportunities to express their concerns about the research, perhaps to tell stories of past researchers, and give them a chance to assess your character (Smith [1998] 1999).

Give the interview subject-participant authority and respect. This follows from the first dimension of a feminist research ethic of attending to epistemological authority, but it also is a way of attending to marginalization and silence, relationships, and of situating yourself, the researcher, always dependent on the participants in your project for the research. Participants often provide not only "data" but also analysis. I (Brooke) often begin an interview by telling the participant the role that they are playing in my research. For example:

"You are the first person I am interviewing."
"You are the most experienced person I have interviewed about this."

An introduction such as the following can also free the interview subject-participant to depart from the official line:

"In general, [the government, the party, the organization] says ..., but we are finding that our interviewees have a much broader range of views on [the issue at hand]. How do *you* think we should understand [the issue at hand]?"

By reiterating the authority of the participant to influence your thinking, and your own open-mindedness, you tell them and remind yourself of a feminist research ethic.

Gain permission for note-taking and recording. If you have already established some trust in the ways discussed above, it may be possible to ask for permission to use a recorder right away. In other contexts, particularly if there was no introduction prior to the interview or the subject-participant exhibited reticence up front such that you thought gaining permission for the interview was the most you could ask for as you started the discussion, you still might be able to get permission to record. After the conversation has begun try asking for permission in this way:... "You know, what you are telling me is so interesting and is really helping me to understand [the issue at hand] so well, would you mind if I recorded this?" Again, this shows the respect you have for the person and the *value* you place on the generosity of his time.

When your respondent has done her thinking while talking such that she has discovered her answer not just delivered it, you may want to ask her the question again perhaps in a slightly different way in order to give her the opportunity to state her view in its newly discovered completeness.

An interview is a conversation with a purpose (Mason 2002: 67). Your interviewee will likely try to determine your purpose which may or may not be a problem for your research. It certainly can be problematic if the subject-participant tries to give you *the* answer she thinks you want to hear, but it may not be problematic if the subject-participant tries to give you *the kind of* answer you want to hear. A participant who understands what you are trying to glean can offer rich examples and extensive reflection.

If you plan on using quotations to illustrate your data, once the interviewee has said something that seems important, perhaps she has discovered something upon reflection, offer her one more question on that topic so that she can articulate succinctly and carefully the idea she has discovered. This lets her be her best and will give you material you can quote.

Interviewing is a skill. It is one you need to train for, one you will improve, and one that will get rusty. All of my (Brooke's) worst interviews have been with people who were or whom I hoped to be friends. Sometimes this happens because I have been in a place for a while before I could schedule an interview and we become friends; it has also happened because I like the person so much, I forget myself and my purpose. In one case it affected the content of the interview. In another case, it did not affect the content of the interview, but rather because I was so excited (and understood exactly what she meant) that I did not offer her those questions that allowed her to restate her view in one coherent thought. Of course, there are a thousand ways to have a bad interview. To do good interviews, develop the skill and tend to it. It is more like a language than riding a bicycle, as use and study both strengthen the skill.

Instrument Development: for Interviews, Focus Groups, and Surveys

We could have discussed instrument development earlier in the book as it is a set of considerations that applies across a range of methods, but this discussion needed to take place after the introduction to each of the formats: interviews, focus groups, and surveys. There are two dimensions of questionnaire design and these apply across interview and survey methods. They are what questions to ask, and in what order to ask them. Developing these requires significant planning and reflection.

What question should you ask in order to have the subject-participant give the kind of answer you are looking for? In some fields, like social psychology, public opinion, and political behavior, a certain battery of questions for measuring certain variables and certain scaling (e.g., the five point scale between strongly agree and strongly disagree) have become routinized. Should you follow those batteries and scales that have been tested for approximating a certain concept that is important to your project or are you significantly reconceptualizing the concept or range such that that battery does not apply?

To avoid scripted answers, Elizabeth Bennion (2007: 22) describes how she deliberately asked US state legislators non-gender specific interview questions about "their issue priorities, bill sponsorship activity, interest group alliances, and observations about leadership styles and partisan relations" before she raises any questions specifically about gender even though her research question was primarily concerned with gender differences and gender dynamics in state legislatures. How do we find or create the most appropriate questions to gain good data on our specific research question? Reflection, social networks, and field testing are keys to developing these.

Don't reveal too much about how you are studying your interviews to your subject-participant. Certainly you want them to know what kind of answer you want – a yes or no answer versus a long answer, reflections from their own experiences or ideas that they have been told. But you do not want them to know your question or your order of questions in order to signal answers you might expect. For example Bennion's order of questions forces the legislator to reveal preferences before knowing the researcher's interest in gender. (Of course, in certain interview settings, the interviewer should expect that the content of the interview questions will be known prior to the interview for those interviewed later. Sometimes a subject-participant requests the questions in advance. And that too needs to be worked into the design.)

Avoid language that has been routinized in your context or that has come to assume one certain meaning from many, when that meaning needs to be studied not assumed. Ironically, I (Jacqui) found it was crucial not to use terms such as feminism and gender in my study of transformations in gender relations after socialism in order not to bias my subject-participants' responses (True 2003). This applies to all essentially contested concepts. Preliminary field work and field testing can help you determine what language – even ideas – have become routinized.

Plan your interview or questionnaire format so that it is doable in the time you imagine is appropriate being attentive to the value of your subject-participants' time.

Field Testing

In the discussion of documentation and social networks, we recommended field testing (or trialing). In order to be prepared for your work, field test everything you can. Make sure your voice recorder microphone (or smart pen – depending on what technology you use or can afford) works with ambient noise or that it can pick up sound from all directions – depending on what you need. Make sure you and your research team can operate all of your equipment without the manual (which will likely get lost). Some testing can be done under simulated conditions – like testing note-taking systems or equipment. Testing of interview format, survey questionnaires, and focus group techniques are more difficult to simulate without a closer proximity to the context of your research. I (Jacqui) always pilot my survey questionnaires with a selected group from the population, who are not so much representative but able to give timely feedback on the survey instrument and how it might be improved from the respondent perspective. This has proved tremendously helpful since one researcher can never think of all the relevant questions or of all the ways questions may be interpreted and misinterpreted. Having research assistants or collaborators can be helpful in field testing surveys also.

Field test your interviews for length of time and comprehensibility of the questions. If you are a student also get your supervisor and peers to check over your questions. You might change, eliminate, or add questions. If you are interviewing on a subject that is familiar to your respondents, they may be inclined to tell you what they tell everyone, or what their organization tells everyone. Field testing enables you to find language that doesn't trigger routine responses. For more on field testing and interview related-tools for field research, see Chapter nine (see also DeVault and Gross 2007; Grenz 2005; Presser 2005).

If your questions have never been asked before, field testing is important for helping you determine if your questions will enable you to interrogate concept you are studying. When Maria Stern started asking about security, women answered that they hadn't been beaten today. How could she ask the question so that women reflected on a less temporally bound, but no less pressing, security threat? (She could also have changed her research question to be about domestic violence in response to such a finding from her field testing. We discuss such choices in the formulating a research question in Chapter four.)

Every qualitative researcher we have asked has a question that enabled her to hone in on the thing or particular context she is studying for which she is proud. Here are some examples:

- Ask the subject-participant's view of a neighbor, not of herself.
- Ask about the traditions that the respondent's grandparents, parents, and nuclear family keep rather than asking the more general, "how progressive are you?"
- Ask not about feminism or equality and attitudes toward them, but whether the respondent has experienced "sexism" or not.

Do your best, especially if you or your research assistants have never used the methods of data production that you are using or you have not used these particular methods recently. Finally, and we don't usually call this "field testing," you will also need to discuss your coding scheme during the data collection phase of your research. How do you and your research team understand the key concepts that interest you? Grounded theory (see Chapter eleven) is an approach to analysis that invites the meaning of concepts to emerge through the research, but for other research designs you do not want meaning to shift across members of the research team. Therefore you will need systems to hold yourselves in dialogue around the meaning of the concepts that are central to your project.

Sharing Findings

In Chapter thirteen we discuss the importance of sharing your findings with research subject-participants. Sharing findings can also be a research method. By sharing findings we gain fresh perspective on our material. In one study of activists participating in an online working group, an activist said in subsequent personal correspondence that she had moderated her answer because of where she worked. Now that she has moved, she said she would describe the situation differently (Ackerly 2001). In Chapter three we discuss the deliberative moment that Rina Sen Gupta and Anne Marie Goetz provoke for themselves by sharing their preliminary findings from a study of credit programs and gender in a series of sessions with some organizations participating in the research. A woman at one of the organizations reflecting on their findings in one such session shared an insight with crucial theoretical import for the study. She reveals that gender had been co-opted to mean working with men or with men and women but without attending to the power dynamics in those relationships (personal anecdote; Goetz and Sen Gupta 1996). This example shows that there are real payoffs from sharing even your preliminary findings during data collection with subject-participants. Their insights and input can not only inform your interpretations and analysis of the data but also offer new perspectives that were not introduced as you collected the data and that you may not have considered otherwise. In this way feminist-informed research is an iterative process.

Tools for Practicing a Feminist Research Ethic in Your Research Relationships

Key Facilitators and Gatekeepers

In social research some people will have a great influence over your research. A feminist research ethic reminds you to pay attention to this influence. While these people are not part of your study and they may not appear in the methodology section of the article, report, or book your write, because they can have significant influence on your research, you need to reflect on the meaning of that influence. A key *facilitator* might help you find the right way of phrasing your questions. They are those people who assist us with our research by providing information, access, contacts, relevant contextualization, and so on. Facilitators often suggest how to handle the power dynamics in certain settings for instance. Similarly, a gatekeeper might introduce you to a range of potential interview subject-participants. The consequence of these introductions may be fabulous for your research. However, it may also be that prospective subject-participants have in common that they are known to the gatekeeper, which may introduce its own bias and perhaps a bias unable to be identified by you.

Facilitators and gatekeepers are often experts. From the point of view of ethical review boards, this "expertise" may make them not seem potentially "vulnerable." Though your ethical review board or committee may not focus on the status of your facilitator-participants or on the protections for these participants besides informed consent, a feminist research ethic requires you to consider these people in their contexts. More generally you should consider the role of all your research participants in your research project as Box 12.2 suggests. (For more on ethics see the book's website, http://www.palgrave.com/methodology/doingfeministresearch.)

A facilitator-participant may not be vulnerable; however, by participating in your research project, by informing you, by guiding you, he or she may change her own relationship to her community. Further, you need to be sensitive to the subtle ways in which he or she may have influenced your theoretical framework or research design. These reflections should be part of your process map (See the web exercise associated with Chapter 3, http://www.palgrave.com/methodology/doingfeministresearch).

Getting Introductions

Your reputation may be your most important asset in your research (Jamal 2006: 436). As noted above, another researcher's reputation may precede you and make it difficult to get the introductions that you need. Whether or not snowball sampling is your method of identifying subject-participants, you can use your social networks and snowballing to get introductions. Whatever methods you use to secure your introductions, reflect on the power dynamics of social life that become dimensions of your research through these methods of introduction.

Permission and Consent

For ethical and logistical reasons, most methods of data generation require you to get permission. This certainly applies to interview, focus group, and survey work. Depending on the work, you may need many kinds of permissions from organizations, governments, associations, other researchers, your thesis supervisor, your institutional ethics committee, and, of course, those who become your subject-participants. At our institutions, supervisors are accountable to the institutional ethics committee for the research of their graduate or postgraduate students. As such, if you are a student the process of gaining consent from your subject-participants will involve an additional step that involves developing credibility and mutual trust with your supervisor.

A feminist research ethic can help you reflect on the meaning of "consent" in the process of getting permission. Consider again its four dimensions:

1. the power of knowledge, and more profoundly, of epistemology;
3. boundaries, marginalization, and silences;
4. relationships and their power differentials; and
5. our own situatedness as researchers.

Let's start with the third. Getting permission is a social interaction that is part of building a relationship of trust. "Consent" is a form of permission that asserts that the relationship between the parties is one of freedom and equality. The person giving consent is not coerced into giving her consent by any power inequality between the researcher and subject-participants. Given the huge differences between researcher and subject-participants, no matter how we frame our work or want to imagine our relationships with our subject-participants, a feminist research ethic requires us to attend to the potential power dynamics among us and to attend to the research participants' context of relationships that may be sources of exploitable hierarchy or subtle coercion.

Some institutional review boards focus a lot on the conditions of consent and may be very good at helping you consider the ways in which a potential research participant may or may not be free to participate in your research. Other review boards focus on drafting a consent form that specifies full disclosure and protections, but – not appreciating the political dimensions of the social context in which consent is sought – may not *in fact* secure free consent. Consent granted under this gray meaning of consent may satisfy an institution's concerns about legal liability, but not a feminist researcher's concern about her own ethical accountability.

Reflecting on relationships and power alone is enough to throw into question the legitimacy of a consent framework for thinking about permission to do research. The other three dimensions of a feminist research ethic guide us in thinking about what to do about this. First, the power of epistemology: A consent document can read like an act of epistemological authority. Make clear to your subject-participants that it is an authority that your institution exercises over you, the researcher, and be clear what authority it gives the respondent (to say "no" for example). But don't limit the authority of the respondent to the terms of the consent form. This is another opportunity to explain to the respondent that they have the authority to decide what to tell you and what not to tell you, to interpret the implications of their ideas and how you the researcher should understand them. Perhaps you want to give them the authority to contact you about the research. Perhaps they should have the authority to contact a third party (such as an ethical review board) about your research. Even if your IRB requires you to follow "consent" protocols, you can challenge the epistemological power dynamic of the consent form by giving the potential respondent the information she would need to challenge your authority.

Institutional review boards often focus on the meaning of a "vulnerable" population, one whose ability to "consent" they anticipate will be constrained. Attentive to boundaries, marginalization, and silences, you recognize that some individuals who may not seem to be part of a recognized "vulnerable" group are in fact in relationships of power that condition their ability to "consent."

Finally, reflecting on your own situatedness as a researcher, on the context of your research, on the particularities of the power dynamics in which your research participants are living, you may be able to identify research design

---

Box 12.3 Consent and hierarchy

In one research design, I (Brooke) sought to interview everyone in a hierarchy, that is, the worker, the person to whom he reported, the person to whom he reported, all the way up the hierarchy to the founder and director of the organization. In retrospect this was a ridiculous aspiration, but at the time I naively thought it was possible. And it would have been possible, except that one person in the middle of the chain did not show up. When I told an insider-outsider of the organization what happened, he recommended that I send a formal letter to my funder who was also a funder of the organization.

Having cultivated my neutrality in order to get my interviewees to feel confident that their ideas would be protected and kept anonymous, I now needed to signal my place in the organization's political world. Without the advice of this insider-outsider, I would not have considered such a solution nor thought it appropriate. But the choice to use this political capital salvaged the research and the considerable inputs of the subject-participants already interviewed.

---

solutions to the problems of consent. Perhaps rather than telling their own stories, you could ask a respondent to tell the story of a larger unit, like her community or neighborhood. In Box 12.3 using one's political capital within the hierarchy of an organization, although a last resort, helped with gaining the consent of some non-responding subject-participants.

Rather than hiring research assistants to survey, you could also identify a marginalized portion of the population and hire them to do the survey, of their own group, or of the whole sample depending on your research. This approach follows the methodology of *"matching"* or *"twinning "* as it is called in Europe when an experienced research organization in one country partners with a less experienced organization in another country on a project of mutual interest. The idea here is to transfer technical know-how and expertise. Matching is described further in the section on research assistants and paraprofessionals.

Of course, you can reflect on your own situatedness alone; however, if you have ethical concerns, then it is appropriate to bring in interlocutors to help you think about the ethical dimensions of your project. These interlocutors may be those who are familiar with your kind of research and those who are not. The experience of being vulnerable that you will likely have while reflecting on the ethical dimensions of your field research will be a tool for reminding you to be attentive to the four dimensions of a feminist research ethic in your research design overall. (For more on ethical considerations see the book's website, http://www.palgrave.com/methodology/doingfeminist research.)

Research Assistants and Paraprofessionals

Your data could be collected by a range of sources. You could collect it all yourself. You might hire research assistants locally. Perhaps you are gathering data on health and nutrition and want to leave the community with the skill set of monitoring their own health and nutrition so you hire community members and train them as *paraprofessionals*. Perhaps you want to provide your facilitators with the means to represent their meaning and make use of facilitators' journals, photo diaries, voice and DVD recorders, or cameras. Perhaps you see a pedagogical opportunity in training students in a class to gather data. Perhaps you want the best trained and best qualified assistants. Jim Collins, author of *Good to Great*, is looking for four intangibles in his research assistants: "smart, curious, willing to death-march ('there has to be something in their background that indicates that they just will die before they would fail to complete something to perfection') and some spark of irreverence ('because it's in that fertile conversation of disagreement where the best ideas come, or at least the best ideas get tested')" (Bryant 2009: 6). Perhaps you have an opportunity to research collaboratively with your fellow students who with you are learning to become researchers and want to do so in a way that enables each to feel full participants and not being taken advantage of. Perhaps you see research as a collaborative endeavor leading you to take on collaborators, not just research assistants; perhaps you see research as a context for mentoring; perhaps you know students who need jobs. All have been bases for choosing research assistants and all create different challenges in research management.

You could subcontract some work, for example transcription of interviews, to a research company. You could hire your own students whom you have trained in the appropriate methods. Or, you could hire students who have training that complements your skill set. Note, observing at least one interview can make it much easier for a transcriber to understand what she or he is hearing.

For some research, the gender or race of your research assistants matter. Interviewer-respondent race matching is considered the standard methodology in social surveys today. Research findings on the effects of *race matching*, even *perceived* race of interviewer, have a long history. In the United States, survey questions about race, racial politics, identity, discrimination, prejudice, and the like are most sensitive to bias from non-race matching. Sensitivity to ethnicity, nationality, gender, religion, age, political affiliation or other politically important dimensions of identity, or what a respondent may perceive as identity, may be an important consideration in politically charged environments. Guided by a feminist research ethic you should learn to read the often overlapping "identity codes" in the field and encourage your research assistants to be mindful of them.

Considerations about *who* should collect your data are really considerations about who should *produce* or *co-construct* your data. Perhaps your research subject-participant requires another form of sensitivity to race and gender. Carol Swain, an African American, hired an Italian American professor to do her research on white nationalists in the United States (Swain 2002). As with every other methods choice, this one will affect your research profoundly and should be chosen guided by profound reflection about your project and how it might reproduce or challenge epistemologies, boundaries, subjectivities, and your self-understanding as a person who does research.

If you are a professor, or at the helm of a research team, in preparing research assistants, time yourself at the task assigned and expect them to take some multiple of that time to complete the task. Know what you are asking them to do exactly and give detailed, step-by-step instructions. When your research assistants perform tasks that you have never done, such as format texts for coding software, be sure to know what the work requires and how long it takes. Make sure you schedule time for shared reflection with your research assistants. By bringing them into the research process, they can "think like you" and therefore help you get better information. They also come to think like a researcher, and this is an important piece of professional development. With a team of researchers whose experiences, ethnicities, age, discipline, and language skills vary, you create opportunities for peer-to-peer learning and the development of each as a teacher and learner.

Translators and Translation

Feminists have written a lot about the challenges associated with translation and interpretation across language and cultural difference. These are related to the general challenge of mitigating the epistemological bias of the researcher (Bhavnani 1993; Chafetz 2004; Diamond 2006; Griffin and Braidotti 2002; Harding and Hintikka 1983; Krieger 2000; Longino 1994; Nagar 2002). However, we can attend to them in specific ways.

In the field of translation, "translation" refers to written text translated from one language to another, "interpretation" refers to spoken word translated and the speaker pausing until the translation is completed, and "simultaneous translation" or "simultaneous interpretation" refers to a translator speaking a second language at the same time that the speaker is speaking such that the speaker does not pause. This usually requires proper equipment and is ideal for large international meetings. It is very tiring work, is usually conducted orally, but a simultaneous translator could write or type the translation so as not to have an extra voice in the room and thus the method can be adapted usefully for interviewing.

Consider the desired population for your interview or survey. Is there language variability among your subject-participants? Will you use a common, likely colonial second language (e.g., English or French), attentive to different language abilities among respondents? If not, how will you handle translation?

There are different ways to work across multiple languages if you are not multilingual or have not acquired the necessary language skills yourself. You can have your questions translated and have your interviews conducted by research assistants familiar with the native language. This method is generally possible if you are working in one language at a time. You can translate your questions, conduct the interviews without understanding the speakers, and then have your interviews transcribed and translated. This method may be necessary if you are working in many languages in one place, for example at an international meeting. You can also work through an interpreter through simultaneous interpretation. In this method, the researcher can ask follow up questions and doesn't need to rely on the research skills of a native speaker, but the dynamic of a conversation is hard to sustain under these circumstances. In one context, I (Brooke) conducted interviews with a research assistant asking the questions and transcribing a simultaneous interpretation in English so that I could ask follow up questions. As a result, the interview proceeded without the time lag of normal interpretation. Such a combination of skills cannot be expected from inexperienced researchers.

Working with a translator or interpreter can provide additional opportunity for reflection about meaning. It can provide two sources of memory, which is particularly important if voice recording is not allowed. With an interpreter present, you may be able to achieve the gender balance or gender norms necessary for the research you are doing. A woman interpreter may enable a man to conduct an interview that he would otherwise not be able to do. I (Brooke) had a male and a female research assistant and used them interchangeably for some interviews, but judiciously for others.

Even if you are able to do your own translations, consider the logistical advantages of having someone else provide your translations. They could be done while you are doing something else, somewhere else.

Tools for Managing the Relationships in Research

As essential and integral to your research as translators, research assistants, and paraprofessionals can be, their presence creates a realm of power dynamics. There are the relationships between the researcher and subject-participant, between the subject-participants and research assistant, between the researcher and research assistant, between the researcher and paraprofessional, between the translator and researcher.

Some challenges associated with these might be characterized as management problems: how does the researcher get the RA, translator, interpreter, or paraprofessional to do the work necessary for the research in the way that is necessary for the research? If you do not have management and training skills, then you should be extra cautious about entering into such roles. If you are new to research and new to managing, it may be too much for you to take on two new roles at once.

Research assistants, translators, and interpreters can insert "noise," in the form of their own interpretation bias, into an interview and other interactions (see below). In statistical work, there are systems for assessing the personal differences among coders, inter-coder reliability (see Box 9.4). Qualitative researchers need to develop systems with a similar purpose for their projects.

Additionally, anyone working with you on your project can create reputational or political difficulties for you. Sonalini Sapra tells the story of participant observation at the beginning of which a translator (from a city) belittled the knowledge and expertise of the subject-participants who were rural grassroots environmental activists. The translator later came to know them as experts in part through Sapra's mentoring (2009). On one project, I (Brooke) had a research assistant who wanted to impress me by finding out information that workers were not sharing with other people. The challenge was to keep him interested in the project without having his curiosity make our host institutions uncomfortable. I had the added concern of not knowing how he would use the information.

Often the objectives of training and mentorship seem to require different practices toward research partners than the research might otherwise need were we not paying attention to power dynamics. If Sonalini had fired her translator on the spot, neither Sonalini nor the translator would have been able to learn about the work of the women from Zaheerabad. In another example, I (Jacqui) employed a local interpreter working for the New Zealand embassy in a foreign country in the Global South to help conduct interviews. This gave me a credible assistant and it also gave the individual woman some insight into some personally relevant gender issues that were the focus of the research, and how they were being treated by her government. Taking a cue from a New Zealand woman administrator working in the embassy who knew about the differential treatment in foreign embassies of local and home country staff, I wrote a letter to the male ambassador appreciating the woman's interpreting skills.

For one of my projects, I (Brooke) elected to send additional research assistants to do field work at an international meeting rather than going myself so that the graduate students could gain the experiences from independent research and problem-solving in the field. Additionally, this enabled some of those students to find the inspiration for their own dissertation work or to be able to contribute to a shared research project as contributors with unique insights. For that project, attention to multiplicity in research ethics was important. By each working on *their own aspect of our shared question* about research *for* social justice, they would develop leadership in thinking about these ethical questions and bring back diverse views.

Working with paraprofessionals enables much of the knowledge generated during research to remain in the community. That, in itself, is one way of attending to power dynamics, but we must be attentive also to the ways in which shifts in local power dynamics give some people more authority and expertise than they had before. In development organizations, paraprofessionals have been used for public health and education community-based work, for example for gathering nutrition and consumption information and disseminating health messages. This model can also be developed for research that is not directly tied to programmatic objectives.

Conclusion

The tools discussed in this chapter are resources that can be used in a wide range of circumstances. You will adopt and adapt them guided by your feminist research ethic and your research question.

Selected Sources for Further Reading

Chafetz, Janet Saltzman. 2004. "Some Thoughts by an Unrepentant 'Positivist' Who Considers Herself a Feminist Nonetheless." In *Feminist Perspectives on Social Research*, ed. Sharlene Nagy Hesse-Biber and Michelle L. Yaiser. New York: Oxford University Press, 320–9.

DeVault, Majorie, and Glenda Gross. 2007. "Feminist Interviewing: Experience, Talk, and Knowledge." In *Handbook of Feminist Research: Theory and Praxis*, ed. Sharlene Nagy Hesse-Biber. Thousand Oaks, CA: Sage, 173–97.

Mason, Jennifer. 2002. *Qualitative Researching*. London: Sage.

Presser, Lois. 2005. "Negotiating Power and Narrative in Research: Implications for Feminist Methodology." *Signs: Journal of Women in Culture and Society* 30, 4: 2067–90.

Smith, Linda Tuhiwai. [1998] 1999. *Decolonizing Methodologies: Research and Indigenous Peoples*. London: Zed Books.

Wolf, Diane L., ed. 1996. *Feminist Dilemmas in Fieldwork*. Boulder, CO: Westview Press.

Chapter 13

Writing and Publishing

Introduction

In this chapter we take up writing and publication in the broad sense of sharing your findings with other researchers, those affected by your research, and those who have contributed to it. In other words, with a great research project coming to completion, it is time to write up your findings for your field. Your "field" is the audience for your argument. Your field may be your professor, your class, your department, your discipline, others interested in the same question, others interested in related questions, or your aunt who has always wondered what interested you. You define your field and its boundaries. You may share your findings in a course paper, an article, a book, a research report, a presentation, an Op-Ed piece, a blog, a website, a video, etc. The possibilities are endless. We focus on the first three forms of writing for an academic audience, and give some attention to other forms of writing as a feminist research ethic guides us to consider these.

We approach academic writing and sharing of findings as another step in, not the conclusion of, the research process. Although research methods and analysis are crucial to the quality of the research findings, research is ultimately judged by the final written or presented product. That product must communicate clearly with your audience. Therefore, for academic work, innovation in writing style is not generally an effective use of your creativity. Better to use your creativity to make a compelling argument and more conventional norms of expository argumentation to convey it.

Feminists disagree about this. Some urge us to "mainstream" our writing style and choice of language (Joeres 1992). Others encourage the deconstruction of language norms through writing in order to provoke new thinking (Lather 2000). For the purposes of this book, we take the first view, cautiously, because certainly we value the insights gained from reading Lather (1991) and others who use the tools of deconstruction to challenge epistemological authority. A feminist research ethic invites us to appreciate our work as incomplete without the work of others and always in dialogue with and often building on our own and other feminist work. Presenting our work in written form is an important way of entering and sustaining feminist research dialogue.

As with every other step in the feminist research process, sharing our findings is a political opportunity and a feminist research ethic can guide us in that process. Here we return to the question, how is knowledge powerful? How do texts give meaning and legitimacy to particular sets of existing social and politics relations? Will the presentation of my knowledge/research findings contribute to social change or to legitimating existing social relations? Who is our research for? Is our work geared to an academic audience only? Are there implications that may be useful for the policy professional and for our subject-participants? When and how should we make arrangements to share those findings with non-academic as well as academic audiences? Attending to these questions, in this chapter we discuss putting our feminist research in its scholarly and political contexts in order to maximize its potential impact and its reception by multiple audiences. In addition, this chapter discusses how we might approach co-authorship and overcome writing blocks from a feminist perspective. We discuss the considerations of identifying appropriate venues for your scholarship. And we make the reader aware of the possibility of having our work used in unintended ways, even in ways opposed to our own politics (Khan 2005).

It may be obvious to you why your research project was feminist and why your question required feminist methods. It may be less obvious to you how a feminist research ethic can help you work through the writing process – that is the process of outlining your argument, anticipating your audience, working with co-authors, and overcoming writing blocks in order to share your findings. However, at each turn in the writing process a feminist research ethic can be as constructive and helpful as it is in the other phases of research. Ongoing self-reflection and the commitments to addressing power, boundaries, relationships and the situatedness of the researcher undergirding a feminist research ethic are valuable writing tools as well as valuable research tools. After setting out the basics of writing, we anticipate the more common dilemmas that we all face in writing, undergraduates and professors alike. Everyone has faced these challenges; some of us are more experienced at facing them down and working with students who face them.

Planning Your Argument

Having a clear sense of the structure of your paper, chapter, or book can greatly facilitate your writing process. There are two common ways to plan and organize an argument before you begin to write: *writing an abstract* and *outlining the argument.* I (Brooke) prefer the abstract method, because it helps me see the *reasoning* that holds the pieces of my argument together. I (Jacqui) prefer an outline complete with subheadings and approximate word counts for the sections. For shorter projects maybe only one is necessary. For longer projects abstracts and outlines can work together.

In the abstract approach to planning an article length argument, the abstract sets out the key pieces of the argument, the kind of evidence offered, and the relationship between the pieces of the argument. It is most helpful if the order of the argument in the abstract follows the order you plan to make the argument in the body of the essay. If it does not, then consider which ordering best makes your argument. This is your first deliberative moment in the writing process. You will have many more! After drafting each section of the argument, revisit your abstract. Are things going according to plan? Did you argue what you needed to in order to go on to the next piece in the argument? Should you revise your abstract?

The outline approach likewise provides many deliberative moments. This approach can be used in concert with the abstract or alone. For a basic outline, consider your argument. What are the parts of your argument? How do the parts fit together? Are they building blocks, that is, pieces that need to go first for other pieces to make sense? Are they pieces, as in a puzzle? An outline is a particularly good tool when you do not yet know how you will fit together the pieces of your argument. It lets you proceed, even when some of the big questions of your project are as yet unanswered. It is very satisfying to accomplish small writing tasks. The outline is an essential tool of

KEY CONCEPT

13.1 ABSTRACT

An abstract articulates the core thesis of an academic argument and gives an account of how the argument is put together, noting key examples or key moves in the argument as appropriate. An abstract is a common feature of a journal article.

Even if an abstract is not "required" for your publication, you may choose to write an abstract before you write the piece in order to be able to capture the key elements of and the structure of your argument in a paragraph. Abstracts are preferably one short paragraph, usually between 100 and 200 words long.

co-ordinating multiple authors and an important tool if you are going to work on your project over a long time during which you may forget all of the pieces of your argument. Further, it provides a structure for changing the structure of your argument as you write. When you discover that you need *to have already* made a certain piece of your argument for the present piece to make sense, you can go back, put in an outline heading for that piece (which you will write later) and continue with your present piece.

Another more contemporary method is to prepare a power point presentation on your argument. If you do this with *very sparse* use of text, this style of exposition encourages you to think about your thesis, the structure of your argument, and what your audience will find convincing.

Whichever method or methods you use to plan your argument, plan to write in drafts. Plan a first draft that is approximately one half the length that you anticipate your final argument will require. Upon rereading you will identify missing parts to your argument, the need for additional examples or discussions of certain literature. It is much easier to add these in than to add them in while having to take out other bits to make sure you achieve your desired length. Additionally, if you plan on multiple drafts, you can focus on one thing at a time, the substance of the argument first; style later.

We anticipate writing to be a dynamic rather than a linear process. Guided by a feminist research ethic, we encourage you to make and take the opportunities in the writing process (for instance if you come to what seems like a dead-end in the argument) to deliberate and reflect again on your data and consider possible alternative analyses and interpretations that can make sense of what you are finding.

Anticipating Your Audience

A writer needs to make choices about how to write and these choices must be *specific* to your audience. For example, some social scientists of the positivist approach follow scientific exposition in presenting their hypothesis and findings even when their actual research process did not follow this process. Such an exposition makes it difficult for others to learn from your methodology (because you have not shown your actual methodology). However, if this is the norm of your audience, then it may be the appropriate choice for you because it may lead to acceptance and easy readability.

Or, for a contrary example, for some audiences, following such a norm would make the reader suspicious of the credibility of the research. In a planning meeting for developing research on gender in contexts of crisis and recovery, scholars who were familiar with the complexities and nuances of gender in conflict settings in Africa were suspicious of scholars whose research questions were too narrowly focused on sexual trauma.

Who we intend our audience to be, that is, who we are writing for and who will likely read our research, should influence all aspects of our research process and not just our writing process at the end of this research. Critical theory reminds us that theory is always for someone and for some purpose regardless of whether the author is aware of it or not (Cox with Sinclair 1996); a feminist researcher always wants to be aware of who her analysis is for. It is highly likely feminist-informed research will be for multiple audiences since feminism did not emanate from any one scholarly discipline but from a broader social movement and is thus of interest to multiple disciplines and publics beyond the academy. Scholarly audiences are generally interested in theoretical purposes and conceptual breakthroughs whereas feminist audiences are more interested in understanding power dynamics in order to change them. Similarly, policymaking and advocacy audiences may also want to know about the practical and policy implications of your research findings. You need to anticipate (to the extent possible) how these difference audiences will hear and make sense of your research.

This chapter comes near the end of the book but it is nonetheless important to point out the ways in which attentiveness to audience is appropriate at each stage of the research and in each chapter of the book. It is much easier to publish your research if you have given substantial thought throughout the research process to its potential audiences. For instance, in thinking through the research process from a feminist perspective, as we discuss in Chapter three, you may discover that a collaborative research process with a co-author or co-researcher will help you to address the audiences you wish to reach. Collaboration across different expertise also shows that you can come to some consensus across fields thus enhancing the credibility of your research with your audience. In a unique example of such mutual learning, researchers from different disciplines (Maori Studies, Law, and Spanish Literature and Languages) collaborated on the translation and the presentation of Maori (Aotearoa-New Zealand) research about indigenous rights and biculturalism in three languages (Maori, Spanish, and English) at a United Nations conference on human rights in Chile. The aim was to show and inform the development of Latin American perspectives on indigenous rights and biculturalism (Lehman and Tomas 2006).

In Chapters four and five, as you considered the compelling research question that you wanted to investigate, you thought about the political world beyond academic disciplines in which you had situated your project. In conceptualizing your puzzle you were attentive to the literature with which your audience could be expected to be familiar. If you are writing for a course, this is the course material and other material your assignment encourages you to consider (generally other secondary sources not explicitly assigned in the course). When researching for academic audiences, this would be the literatures of disciplinary fields.

When writing up your research, similar considerations abide. You want to situate your project in literature that will contextualize your project in a way that your audience could understand. When writing for a course, do not write for your professor, but rather for someone else in the class or for a friend outside of the class who took it another year or who might take it in the future. When writing for an academic audience, you let them know that they *are* your audience by situating your project in literature that they recognize and (as necessary) other literature that you think they *should* become familiar with in order to understand your question or your approach to your question. For example, Brooke writes on the political theory of human rights. She situates her argument in the political theory that is familiar to academics working on human rights *and* she uses feminist theory and methodology which she argues are important resources for political theorists who are studying human rights.

Further, many feminists want their work to influence policy makers, donors, and non-scholarly audiences, such as NGOs. In these cases, you should familiarize yourself with the communication norms of those audiences. For most projects, we advise writing an academic piece first and then preparing a separate document, perhaps an opinion piece or report that is geared specifically to the non-academic audience. Your skill set and your context will determine what is best for you.

Note, writing for *any* audience is a particular skill. The more you write for that audience, the better you will be at writing for *that audience*. When you switch audiences, whether that is because you have switched disciplinary audiences for the same argument or you have switched topics and arguments, you will need to redevelop your writing skills for *this audience*.

From the point of view of a feminist research ethic, clarifying your relationship to each of the audiences to which your research aims to speak is crucial. Your positionality is not a matter of identity or of epistemic authority (Nagar 2002), but rather of relationship. A feminist research ethic requires us to attend to the situatedness of the researcher as it affects all parts of our research process, including our writing, because it is relevant and important to how we make our arguments and how they are evaluated.

You, as the author, need to discuss transparently the ethical relationships and choices that are raised by the presence of multiple audiences and in relation to them. For example, a feminist-informed researcher may recognize the subject-participants of his research not only as source of knowledge and data but also as audiences for it and explicitly note the choice to publish his research in ways that are accessible to them. For many feminist researchers the challenge is to "align our theoretical priorities with the concerns of marginalized communities whose struggles we want to advance" (Nagar 2002: 182; also Pratt 2002). This goal is both constrained and enabled by opportunities, norms, and values embedded in our academic institutions.

Guided by a feminist research ethic, writing and publishing your research in order to address multiple audiences may involve anticipating the appropriate time and venues for making your findings public. For example, it may involve early or partial publication of findings for non-scholarly audiences. Moreover, it may involve "workshopping" your research findings (by presenting your work in small, informal venues) or presenting them in report form so that they can be rapidly disseminated rather than prioritizing scholarly publishing in peer-reviewed journals which generally have longer time frames for dissemination. Finally, a feminist research ethic leads us to consider how our audiences will use our research and what is necessary to enable people to use it well. This involves, as we discuss later in this chapter, providing a context for readers to interpret the meaning and the limits of the implications of our findings. We have an ethical obligation to share our research and pass it along but also to guard against the potential misconstrual and misuse of our research.

Writing Style

Neither of us fancies herself an excellent writer. We work hard at our writing, particularly at making it vivid and jargon-free. How do we learn to write better? With the help of a thoughtful editor, and with exposure to good writing, and practice. Learning to write better is a field unto itself, one academics apparently don't avail themselves of often enough according to Helen Sword (2009), despite the fact that we generally teach writing in the political and social sciences.

From the famous, Strunk and White (1918) *Elements of Style* to the contemporary Helen Sword's *The Writer's Diet* (2007), we have been trying to learn to write more clearly, accessibly, and effectively. As much as we think that tastes have changed over the last century, these texts have remarkable similarity in their view of what makes good writing. The key point is that none of us is born with the ability to write. We work really hard at it. You can learn to write well. It is not a gift that you have or don't have.

This section follows our discussion of audience because writing in ways that engage your readers based on a clear understanding of who they are, will go a long way to ensuring that your research has an impact. The substantive content of your research findings and where you publish them is important. However, aesthetic merit also greatly adds to the impact of your study. Instructors are more likely to understand your ideas if you write clearly. Instructors are far more likely to assign your papers, articles, or books to students if the writing style is accessible and compelling; that is, likely to motivate students to read! Further, instructors also like to read and assign work that is a model of good writing.

> ## Box 13.1 Checklist for good writing
>
> Helen Sword (2009: 322) offers a helpful check list that is summarized here. Engaging books and papers all tend to have the following:
>
> 1. An interesting and concrete TITLE
> 2. An engaging OPENING PARAGRAPH
> 3. An ARGUMENT that anyone can follow.
> 4. Clear, JARGON-FREE prose.
> 5. A VOICE that is your own.
> 6. Relevance to multiple fields or disciplines.
> 7. Vibrant ILLUSTRATIONS, textual and visual.
> 8. ELEGENT sentences
> 9. ACTIVE verbs and concrete nouns
> 10. CREATIVE or IMAGINATIVE content and structure.

Our view is that feminist writing is good writing: accessible, vivid, and able to convey difficult concepts clearly (Joeres 1992). However, these commitments have to be balanced – some challenging ideas require provocative exposition (Lather 2007). The key is not to allow our language choices to render our work exclusionary, meant for a narrow audience as indicated by the requirements of familiarity with certain forms of jargon. Box 13.1 has a checklist for good writing.

The longer the project, the more important is its organizational structure. The longer the piece of writing the harder it is for author and reader to remember what piece of the argument goes where. Topic sentences help the reader – everyone hears this repeated in language arts instruction from about the age of nine. We are here to tell you that everyone, *especially the author*, needs topic sentences. The longer the project, the harder it will be for you to remember what you said where and in what order if you cannot rely on your topic sentences to recreate the general flow of the argument for you.

Making an Impact with Your Research

You can have an impact with your research through academic presentation and publishing, non-academic circulation of your ideas in non-academic publications, websites and other new media, and publicity. While guiding you in writing for these audiences is out of our area of expertise, we do think a feminist research ethic can guide your thinking about the choices you make regarding the circulation of your ideas and the concern you need to have with their potential misuse.

Identifying the Appropriate Venue for Your Scholarship

For students who do not intend to publish their scholarship, this section may not seem relevant. However, if you are considering writing an honors thesis or going to graduate school, some of the professional academic's considerations may be ones that deserve a bit of your attention too. Just as a professional academic must think about who her professional audience is, a student who aspires to continue her research needs to consider in which discipline and under whose mentorship her research can flourish.

Choosing an appropriate venue for publishing or presenting your research is crucial to maximizing its impact. Of course, the venue you choose depends on a range of factors. They might include what kind of audience you want to reach, that is does your project make a theoretical or a policy impact? Are your conversation partners other empiricists in your discipline or feminists in other disciplines? Additionally, you will need to consider as well as the speed of publication, the research expectations of your institution, the standards for obtaining an academic position or seeking promotions, and your own career trajectory more generally.

Over the last two to three decades feminist researchers have been increasingly successful in getting their message heard in academia and across societies (Cancian 1992: 634). This is in large part because they have published and presented in forums, journals, and publishing houses developed by feminists for feminists (Ackerly and True 2008a; under review). Similarly, the success of people of color and working class people in legitimating their perspectives has been encouraged by having publications that they control. Since feminist inquiry has burgeoned in so many fields, the publication of feminist work depends now on blind reviews from other feminist researchers. With plenty of exceptions, the early crisis of legitimacy for feminist scholarship (Spender 1981) has passed.

Today as a result of its success and the growth of a feminist-informed readership, mainstream journals and presses are relatively open to publishing feminist scholarship. There are therefore now more options for publication. How can a feminist research ethic help us to decide where to publish? A feminist research ethic cannot decide for you, but it can guide you in assessing the trade-offs of different venues. For example, if your research involves a collaborator or co-author, attending to that relationship, you may want to determine where you will publish before you embark on your project together. Your joint decision may involve compromise, such as publishing in an interdisciplinary journal if you are from different disciplines or it may involve publishing twice, once in each field alternating the lead authorship.

Other considerations have less to do with a research ethic and more to do with your professional goals for your scholarship. In deciding whether to publish your research in an edited volume or in a journal you will want to consider a number of factors. For instance, you may choose to publish in a disciplinary journal or edited collection if that will put your work squarely in a mainstream field, in relation to and in dialogue with others and requiring non-feminist scholars to consider your work when they might not if it were published in a specialist feminist journal outside their area of expertise. Journal articles are also often published faster than books. But you should notice the average turnaround rates of the journal and publication rate before you select the journal to which you submit your research article. The downside to choosing journal publication is that as well as situating your research within a disciplinary field you may have to adopt the often prescriptive format, literatures, data, methodology, and methods of the disciplinary journal.

You may prefer to publish in edited collections which may be more pluralistic in method and may be more easily accessed by non-academics. You may wish to consider shelf-life. Edited volumes disseminated in paperback are likely to have a longer shelf life than journal articles though they are not as easily found and circulated as journal articles by those with access to academic libraries and online journal services. You may choose a venue based on the quality of feedback you will receive through the peer review process. Informed by a feminist research ethic we face a tradeoff between seeking feminist-friendly publication outlets and the desire to break into venues where feminist impact has yet to be mainstreamed. The benefit of the latter decision is that if successful your work will probably get widely read and cited and potentially pave the way for other feminist work.

Finally, if you are seeking professional advancement within academe, you need to consider how the venues of your publications will be respected by those who hold the key to that advancement.

Sharing Your Findings with Non-Academic Audiences

While the focus of this chapter is publishing or presenting your particular research project for an academic readership, sometimes the political import of our findings or our own normative imperatives prompt feminists to write for a broader audience (Ehrenreich 2001; Murray 2008). A feminist research ethic that is self-reflexive about power relations in the broader world and the researcher's situatedness in those relations encourages the researcher to understand her research project as on-going, that is continuing through the dissemination of the research. Scholars have a responsibility to pass on their research findings to those who have shared their knowledge.

Further, those who study social injustice, have an obligation to enable their findings to be used by those who participate least in decision-making related to these questions. This is not to say that an academic needs to learn the additional skills necessary for disseminating her work. And yet, a feminist research ethic invites us to ask some questions about our work when we are at the stage of sharing our findings. Is our work geared to an academic audience only? Or are there implications that may be useful for the policy professional, activist or advocacy networks, or our subject-participants?

Taking up the responsibility to disseminate your research broadly, requires you to think about the implications of your research in different ways. How might my work be read by others? For example, whereas other International Relations scholars may be interested in the theoretical implications of my (Jacqui's) study of gender mainstreaming in global governance organizations for what it says about international cooperation among states, the transformation of the states-system, and the role of women or changing gender relations in these processes, a broader audience may be more interested in practically how these organizations can eliminate gender inequalities in the global economy and the best practices and models for doing so. From the perspective of a feminist research ethic it is crucial to try to address the concerns of both types of scholarly and non-scholarly audiences in order to maximize the impact of your research. Amartya Sen's work discussed in Box 13.2 shows how it is possible both to make a successful theoretical breakthrough and to bring about a major change in global policymaking.

Box 13.2 Sen's research with a policy impact

While most of us do good scholarship without becoming a Nobel Prize winner or changing the way governments do anything, the work of Amartya Sen, Economist and Philosopher, illustrates the impact that academic inquiry can have on global politics. In a 2004 interview with *Asia Society*, Amartya Sen comments on the importance of translating theory into actionable empirical analysis. The *Human Development Report* is an annual publication of the United Nations Development Program that puts Sen's theory of human capability into practice by giving us the data necessary to make cross-country comparisons of development as measured by the quality of life that citizens of each country are able to achieve through health, education, and income.

"Human development, as an approach, is concerned with what I take to be the basic development idea: namely, advancing the richness of human life, rather than the richness of the economy in which human beings live, which is only a part of it. That is, I think, the basic focus of the human development approach. It was pioneered by Mahbub ul-Haq and the first [*Human Development Report*] came out in 1990. Mahbub started working on this in the summer of 1989. I remember his ringing me in Finland where I was living at the time . . . When he called me in 1989, he told me that I was too much into pure theory and I should drop all that now ('enough is enough'), and that he and I should work together on something with actual measurement, actual numbers, and try to make an impact on the world." (Available on line.)

Sharing your findings with non-academic audiences at appropriate points in the research process is one approach to enhancing not only the impact but also the rigor of your research. A feminist research ethic requires us to consider when and how we should make arrangements to share findings and not to assume that this occurs only at the end of a research project. Moreover, when you decide to publish your research is a deliberative moment that should not create closure because your findings should always be open to critique and to shaping your next project.

One approach to sharing findings is to use a survey questionnaire early on in your research for guiding discussion with subject-participants about how your findings will be used and shared with the community (for instance, what format, what language/terms/jargon would be most useful for research participants' own purposes). You might ask whether there are times when you should share your incomplete data if subject-participants need it and if waiting for publication would negatively affect them. For example, your research on workers in a Mexican Maquiladora might contribute to lawsuits on the health of workers. (One graduate student used a Mexican lawyer to gain the community trust necessary to do his research on their health conditions and then refused to share his data with either the lawyer or the community.) At a minimum you will need to talk with your subject-participants or facilitators about what they need so that you can anticipate what they want in the way of presentation or publication of your research findings and design into your research schedule.

As we discussed in Chapters three and twelve in the context of Goetz and Sen Gupta's (1996) work, sharing initial findings with academic audiences close to the site of research if you are engaged in fieldwork research may bring benefits both to you and that community (Goetz 2001). Presenting your theoretical framework and research questions could animate their discussions and enrich your scholarship. It is also an opportunity for you to get important feedback on preliminary findings if you state explicitly that you are sharing them early precisely to get such feedback. In a dialogical way, this feedback and engagement can influence your interpretation of your findings and make them more relevant and interesting to others be they research participants, academics, or policymakers.

Sharing academic findings is not a substitute for other forms of responsible scholarship. As we discussed in Chapter three, giving something back to research participants may not involve sharing your research findings but rather responding to their needs and concerns in other ways, for instance, by training paraprofessionals, writing an op-ed piece, or fixing their generator. For example, I (Jacqui) conducted an organizational review for a gender specialist network I was studying in part to share the insights of my scholarly research in a way that would improve both the processes and visibility of the network in a larger political and institutional context. A participatory action researcher who goes to work with an indigenous community may find that they do not want another participant observation study but econometric research to support their political agenda.

Although sometimes, we might be able to identify a policy implication for our work *after* we have done the work, as we discuss above, considerations of audience should have a profound effect on research design. This may mean merely understanding how policymakers hear and make sense of research and altering our language, concepts, and writing format accordingly. However, it could also have an effect on every aspect of research design. Often the mixed format of a story or illustration combined with statistics and lucidly articulated analysis are the winning combination for policy relevance. Such an exposition requires a mixed method research approach.

It may be that we need to limit the use of the word "feminist" in our exposition. For example, during her tenure directing a social science research division of the United States federal government, Judith Auerbach (International Women's Health Coalition) deliberately avoided the term "feminism" and pitched feminist-informed ideas to appeal to the paternalism of lawmakers. In this way social scientists have been able to secure funding for feminist research that has directly influenced public policy. The guidelines of a feminist research ethic lead us to rigorous scholarship by any name.

We need not publish in non-academic venues for our academic scholarship to have a policy impact. Academic publishing and the scholarly community have an important role to play in advancing social and policy change. Take the example of the study on gender differences in natural disasters that we have cited in other contexts (Neumayer and Plümper 2007). The major finding of this study was that natural disasters lower the life expectancy of women drastically more than that of men, and as the disaster intensifies, so too does this effect. Women's lack of economic and social rights and resources relative to men makes them especially vulnerable to the effects of these disasters. The Women's Environment & Development Organization took this research on natural disasters and the connection to women's economic and social rights it revealed and used it to lobby the UN Human Rights Commission to anticipate and address gender issues in their policy-making on the impact of climate change. They were able to argue that the published academic study provided "definitive," peer-reviewed evidence of gender differences and on this basis bring about a policy change.

By contrast with the above example, publishing your results in the media and informing government policy before it has been peer reviewed holds risks and may not advance an advocacy or policy change agenda. Peer review enhances the credibility and political legitimacy of research. For example, the media often portrays research on climate change as going both ways but scholarly research is peer reviewed. Peer review enhances the credibility of your interpretation of the evidence on politically controversial topics such as climate change, natural disasters, the drivers of educational outcomes, and the benefits and costs of childcare.

Anticipating the Potential Use and Abuse of Your Research

Many of us are concerned at some time or another about what happens when we let go of our research findings by publishing or presenting them. Jennifer Bickham-Mendez and Diane Wolf remind us that: "[l]eaving the field does little to extricate you from the political implications of your research" (2007: 657). In an increasingly connected global world, research participants are more likely to have access to and to read our work and it is probable that our research will have a material impact on them. As feminist researchers we are often working in areas that are intended to benefit women so our criticism of these areas be they programs, organizations, groups, or movements could be construed as "anti-feminist," and be used to tarnish reputations, to deny funding, or to close them down. At the same time, feminist social science can be misappropriated in ways that bolsters existing stereotypes as in the case of popular psychology books (*Men are from Mars; Women are from Venus* . . .) that exaggerate scholarly claims and reinforce gender differences (Williams 2000: 11).

A feminist research ethic requires you to analyze how you want your findings to be used and how they might be used. The research project is not done if you do not think about the how the audience is going to use the findings. It is our ethical responsibility to consider self-consciously how we should present our findings given their possible impacts. Rather, than staking out critical distance from the ethical implications of our scholarship as Judith Butler once argued (Bell and Butler 1999), our ethical obligation is to figure our how to achieve critical distance, and a longer-term perspective about the implications of our work without denying that it will be used in the present.

In writing up your research we recommend that you explicitly engage with the question of the use of your research. You may want to discuss the legitimacy of using it to draw certain implications or make certain criticisms but not others given your study's particular research design. For example, research on the United Nations gender equality mainstreaming initiatives rather than judge these initiatives as wholesale failures or successes should identify the nature of that failure or success whether it lies in the concept of gender mainstreaming itself, the lack of funding, political commitment, or expertise (Snyder 2006). Criticism may be heard by policymakers in a way that bolsters arguments for the rejection of an approach or cancellation of a program when the actual full analysis does not support these conclusions.

A feminist ethical approach is to reform and rethink with a view to incremental change rather than change for its own sake or criticism with a broad brush since this often does not address underlying power relations and issues which are immune to the outward change of a policy, program, or institution. Consider the example of a collaborative feminist research project on social justice in education and how they addressed the potential impact of their critical evaluation of a program for pre-school children and mothers from low socio-economic groups:

> We all worried about how our writing would be used by policymakers and wondered how we could fairly construct a critique of the Head Start Transition program at a time when "the public sphere" was weak and when such a critique could be seen at best, as an "academic waste of time" and at worst, an invitation for "collusion with the Right" (Spatig *et al.* 2005: 108).

Given this self-reflection on the ways their criticism could be misconstrued in the public sphere with detrimental effects for a marginalized group, the research team decided to adopt the principle of "no harm." The focus of their evaluation was on constructive improvement: "How could we do something like this better? How can we learn from this?... It would be bad if [our papers were] used to say, 'Well, schools don't need social workers ... or 'We don't need to help families. We don't need to put money and effort into kids and families'" (Spatig *et al.* 2005: 108).

Another example of research collaboration illustrates how a feminist research ethic that calls you to think through the implications of the publication of research, in particular its potential negative impact on research participants, may mean you decide *not* to publish or even to do the research. Two feminist scholars worked on a research proposal to analyze and compare the impact of government policies designed to prevent sex trafficking in selected receiving countries. They chose not to further this project, however, when they realized that the public disclosure of information from research participants, "the trafficked women," could have a negative impact on migrant sex workers who actively seek to cross borders for work. State policies often fail to distinguish between voluntary and coerced trafficking and may aim to control all forms of prostitution with security and immigration policies.

Other ways to anticipate the use of your research and to prevent its abuse include the need to contextualize your criticism and be specific about its intent (to improve something specific such as an institutional practice) so that the criticism is taken in a constructive way. Highlighting the strengths as well as the weaknesses of the subject under analysis in a balanced way will also mean your findings are interpreted in a way that makes it possible to realize them in practice whether in the short or long term. There should be no surprises in your research process and write-up if you have kept people informed about how your analysis is evolving, shared findings, and received feedback along the way.

Feminist Co-authoring

As discussed in Chapter six, feminist co-authoring can be very rewarding, a way of surmounting some of the intellectual challenges of the most interesting feminist puzzles, and also a way of overcoming the isolation which sometimes leads to writing blocks. There are as many models of collaborative writing as there are co-authors. Note, we said that there were as many styles as co-authors – each participant in a collaboration participates as an individual, differently from her partner or partners. You will need to be self-conscious in the development of your style of collaboration and develop it uniquely for *each* partnership.

First, outline each partner's strengths and limitations. Note with which material each is most familiar. Note anticipated time constraints each will face. Consider other approaches to collaboration in which you share data and ideas, but write separately, perhaps yielding two articles one with each of you as lead author.

Second, outline the project. Work collaboratively through the plan for your argument (see above). What are the pieces that need to be argued? Who is best able to argue each piece in the sense of drafting its first version?

Third, work out your division of labor for each of the pieces. For example, for the first part of this book we outlined each chapter together. Each chapter then had an individual "first drafter" and the other wrote the second draft. Finally, we each edited and revised each chapter multiple times often in response to readers. For the second half of the book, we each organized the chapters we were "first-drafting" and then we followed the same procedure as the first half of the book. Some chapters (Chapter five, eleven, and one on feminist theory that ended up being too theoretical for this book) became too challenging for the first author to write alone. The second-drafter often significantly rewrote and reorganized a chapter.

Fourth, throughout the process, stay in touch. Be aware of the effort that the other is putting into the project. Discuss shifts in effort or intellectual direction as the writing proceeds. You may discover that your co-author wants to write a different paper, perhaps using the same data, and that you should really write separate projects in which you each acknowledge your intellectual debt to your partner. You may discover that your work schedules are incompatible and that one of you needs to "finish" the project without the other. All sorts of changes in your work plans and even the authorship of your research can be handled in a feminist way if both parties are attentive to the power dynamics of their relationship, to the ways in which *they* have co-constructed the boundaries of their project, to the relationship they have with one another *and* the multiple relationships that each has with others.

When you co-author, you develop a shared public identity, but this shared identity does not supplant your individual public identity. It is important to consider how you present your shared work to the world as this reflects on you individually and collectively. Give careful consideration to how you characterize your authorship. We are equal co-authors and have published together more than once. At one point we worried that because Ackerly comes first alphabetically, some audiences might think that Brooke was the lead author. However, we realized if we switched the author order on future scholarship (or on this book), it would throw into question how shared our effort is in our co-authorship. It is evenly shared.

Writing Blocks and Overcoming Them

There are *even more* reasons for writer's block than there are researchers. A given researcher may experience writer's block for so many reasons: fatigue, intellectual fatigue, struggles with a feminist research ethic (including a self-restraining caution about making knowledge claims), a fear of going outside disciplinary or an instructor's boundaries, trouble knowing your audience, trouble knowing yourself as an author, a desire to be closer to done than you are (and therefore not *wanting* to read new material that may make you change direction or rethink some of your arguments).

Fatigue is a common source of writer's block. It may not be the initial source, but the author confronted with a challenge distractedly stays up late with some form of modest entertainment and the chance at eight hours of sleep a night slips away. Whatever is the initial source of your writer's block, try to get eight or so hours of sleep. The brain vacation may be all your mind needs to face any problem afresh. Also, we are not nutritionists, but it is pretty obvious that if you feel healthy – because you are getting proper rest, nutrition, and exercise – you will write better. For Brooke the anti-writer's block regime is sleep, fruit and spinach smoothies for breakfast and lunch, and a 3 mile/5K run or walk per day. For Jacqui it is tea, more tea, rice crackers and pilates!

With projects that have been going on too long relative to your interest level, you may face intellectual fatigue no matter how exciting the topic. Your mind may have plenty of energy, but want to work on something else. For this problem, the trick is to make it fresh again. One possibility is to plan a project that requires multiple kinds of writing. For example, in their book, *Troubling with Angels* on women diagnosed with HIV/AIDS, Patti Lather and Chris Smithies experiment with multiple forms of text and knowledge in order to explore how these women fight, live, and die with the disease (Lather and Smithies 1997). They self-consciously weave into their analyses their own experiences as researchers and as women emotionally tied to the sufferings of sisters, mothers, wives, and lovers with HIV/AIDS. Their analyses are also interspersed with the women with HIV/AIDS' own words.

Finally, the reader is provided with statistics and fact boxes that put these women's words in context for a fuller understanding of the epidemic of HIV/AIDS as it affects women, its fastest growing population (see also Behar 1994 [2003]).

Or, you may refresh your interest in your writing by publishing online which may enable you to imagine your work for multiple audiences or reignite your writing style. Publishing online also provides many possibilities for experimenting with multiple texts. For example, *hypertext* is predicated on the view that the reader's relationship with a given text (such as a literary work or a work of reference) is not restricted to the linear reading of that text in a predetermined sequence. Its approach is non-linear, more akin to browsing and following up cross-references. With hypertext you can follow, and indeed create, diverse pathways through a collection of textual materials. Hypertext applications thus support a much more interactive relationship between the text and its readers. Reading is a method as readers can become authors of their own reading. Coffey *et al.* (1996) argue that hypertext allows researchers to reconstruct social worlds through multiple, coexisting representations: "The simultaneous availability of written text (including the ethnographer's own interpretations and commentary), visual and sound data permit[s] the reader to explore alternative and complementary modes of representation" (Coffey *et al.* 1996). Brooke is quite cautious about recommending this approach as she is more conservative and wonders if this may yield distraction rather than renewed focus on your project. But intellectual fatigue usually hits her quite close to the end of a project if at all. Jacqui recommends it though for those who get intellectual fatigue when they are still wrestling with an early draft, experimenting with online exposition and the use of hypertext may help you see your material anew.

You may also face writing blocks associated with your feminist reflection. For example, when there appears to be a lack of fit between your data and your concepts, you may feel your project has become unmoored and adrift. Even though as we argue in Chapter five, you know that your theoretical frameworks should not be fixed, perhaps you were finding them comfortable. The iterative feminist research process is particularly challenging because it prompts us to reflect continually and revise our frameworks. However, in addition to research collaboration, there are some good writers' tricks for overcoming blocks be they induced by sensitivity to our relationships with subject-participants or attentiveness to the power of epistemology and boundaries of inclusion and exclusion in research.

Many researchers confront writing blocks even after having spent considerable time researching and nearing the completion of a project. One of the reasons for these blocks is often our struggle with exercising the power (position) involved in representing subject-participants and what we have learned from them and the research process as we write up findings (Harding and Norberg 2005: 2012). A feminist research ethic reminds us that equal power does not define feminist-informed or any other research. But feminists especially struggle with issues of power (Gaskell and Eichler 2001). We exercise power as researchers when we decide to continue or end the research. Moreover, when we write or present our research we invariably control the presentation of the research (Wolf 1996: 2). However, we can also often reclaim power lost when researching elites or foreign cultural contexts in the writing process or share power in useful ways when we collaborate with other scholars with complementary knowledge.

One possible interpretation of a feminist research ethic is that it requires us to spend so much time and energy self-reflecting on potential epistemological, methodological, and other potential political failings of our research that we don't actually get going and do it. Actually, the political import of our work is better read as *a reason to get going* and get that work visible. Of course, you should address the concerns that you have identified in your own work. However, you cannot address those you have not identified. Do your work, get it done, and get feedback. Whether for an assignment or for professional publication, your scholarship is part of a larger field and can only contribute to that field if it is in circulation. You cannot improve the field by keeping your ideas to yourself. You have to risk criticism. You have to open your work up to how it might inspire others. And they can engage only with the work you share.

Or, you may be confident in your interpretation and its appropriate exposition, but consider that it requires you to go outside the norms that guide your mentor or colleagues. That is a tough one. First, are you sure? Or is that just an excuse? You need to write for an audience, if you want to change that audience's thinking on this matter; perhaps conforming to the norms of the audience *is* the best way to communicate effectively (see above). As we discussed in Chapter six, only you know your constraints and how external or self-imposed they are. Ultimately, you are the author of your argument, if the attempt to conform to constricting norms is preventing your exposition; perhaps the most effective strategy is to write for your desired audience using the norms of that audience. Such writing may be an incremental step toward your final product, or my lead you to shift your audience.

In addition to not wanting to write for your anticipated audience, another obstacle is *not knowing* your anticipated audience. A very common way that students try to deal with this problem is to ask for past papers written for the course. While your instructor may not want to share those with you (because they create another pedagogical problem), academics do deal with the audience problem by reading other articles published in their desired venue. To know your audience, you need to know what they are used to reading (and publishing). Now, mimicking these norms may not yield the most effective writing style by academic standards or what we like to read, but it will help you come to know the norms of your audience.

Maybe you know your audience, but you do not know yourself yet as an author of material *your audience should read*. Writing "has significance far greater than putting words on paper or on to the computer screen: It is a way of transforming ourselves into writers" (Grant and Knowles 2000: 8). Collectively imagining ourselves as writers in peer writing groups, in collaborative writing retreats, or in co-authoring relationships can help with becoming writers and with feeling at ease in the writing process. If participants are themselves writing for different audiences, such groups mitigate hierarchies of experience or status among participants. Therefore, we both have found such groups valuable when they are interdisciplinary, ideally of mixed rank and experience as well.

Perversely, some writer's block is born of a desire to be closer to done than you are. From this perspective, you don't want to read the background material that your research has revealed you need. Perhaps you don't want to recode some data or gather new data. Perhaps while you were starting your first teaching job, the field saw a burgeoning of new literature such that you need to reacquaint yourself with the field before finishing your book.

Box 13.3 contains some advice for overcoming writer's block.

Conclusion

Writing, presenting, and publishing your work are integral parts of the research process, which is always an evolving process. We should not short-shrift this process or think that the research is over before we have shared and disseminated our findings. Attending to the power of epistemology, to relationships, boundaries, and our situatedness as researchers requires us to approach writing and publishing in a self-conscious way and use it as an opportunity for making explicit these ethical commitments. Moreover, it is much easier to publish or present your work and you are more likely to overcome writing blocks and avoid dilemmas and surprises in the reception of your work if you think about the multiple audiences for whom it is intended and the impact you wish to have *from the outset* of your research project.

From a feminist perspective reflecting on these writing and publishing questions is particularly crucial since we need to be effective at communicating our theories and research to others if we are to accomplish our

Box 13.3 Advice for overcoming writing blocks

Which advice is right for you depends on what kind of block you are having.

Don't know where to start

- Write a letter or a memo rather than a chapter or article to your friend, mother, or research participants about your key findings. This will help you get to the point and break your internal resistance to writing.
- Use the 30 second "Elevator pitch" with a friend or colleague to explain the significance of your research question or thesis.
- Take a friend out for a walk, coffee, or ice cream. Tell the friend your idea and the key pieces of the argument. Too shy to do this? Go alone with a voice recorder.
- Take turns. Examining someone else's argument helps you practice the discipline of constructing a clear argument.

Easily distracted

- Put your tangential thoughts in a notebook without processing them or in another file to maintain your focus and avoid distractions when you are writing.
- Try writing first thing in the morning for an hour. If you are on a roll after an hour, keep at it. If you are not, go do something else, something that you find distracting like paying your bills, or something that will make your brain more chemically inclined toward thinking clearly like getting exercise (Talbott 2007).

Intimidated by your data

- Read your data, an inspirational piece of writing, a literature review that is illuminating for your question, or a book that follows a model or logical structure you might follow.
- More mature scholars can re-read their own work or their co-authors work in order to remind themselves that they have done it before.

normative goals of social and political change. Enhancing the accessibility and the relevance of feminist scholarship is a collective project which requires renewed commitment to research collaboration, to mentoring future generations of feminist researchers, and importantly, to hearing how others read our work in local and global activist and policy communities.

Selected Sources for Further Reading

Charmaz, Kathy. 2007. "What's Good Writing in Feminist Research? What Can Feminist Researchers Learn about Good Writing?" In *Handbook of Feminist Research: Theory and Praxis*, ed. Sharlene Nagy Hesse-Biber, New York: Sage, pp. 443–58.

Grant, Barbara and Sally Knowles. 2000. "Flights of Imagination: Academic Women Be(com)ing Writers." *The International Journal for Academic Development 5*, 1: 6–19.

Richardson, Laurel. 2000. "Writing: A Method of Inquiry." In *Handbook of Qualitative Research*, 2nd edn, eds. Norman K. Denzin and Yvonna S. Lincoln. Sage: New York: pp. 923–48.

Spatig, Linda, Kathy Seelinger, Amy Dillon, Laurel Parrott, and Kate Conrad. 2005. "From an Ethnographic Team to a Feminist Learning Community: A Reflective Tale." *Human Organization 64*, 1: 103–15.

Chapter 14

Conclusion: Feminist Research Ethic, Review, and Evaluation

Introduction

We have organized this book to help you through the process of research from coming up with a question, through research design, specification of methods, analysis, and write-up. Throughout our exposition, we have cautioned that this chronologically linear exposition is not typically the experience of most researchers or the process of most research projects. However, this linear organization has enabled us to help you meet the expectations of an academic audience using the tools of feminists who work within political and social science disciplines. We have shown that you can challenge many of the ontological and epistemological underpinnings of these disciplines by doing rigorous feminist research. Such a commitment to challenging norms where appropriate does not leave feminist work without standards of evaluation and guidelines for improvement.

During the writing of this book we shared chapters with many audiences. Some have asked us: "How do you know what is *good* feminist research?" The answer? *Critical evaluation.*

However, this answer begs the question of how we evaluate feminist research that challenges the norms of evaluation. A feminist research ethic may seem like a normative set of commitments, but each element, as we have been demonstrating throughout the book, gives us concrete suggestions for better research. We can evaluate feminist and other research based on how well it attends to the considerations raised by a feminist research ethic. These are not "different" standards than those used to assess other social and political science, but they are more specific standards and possibly more rigorous standards also.

Consider the kinds of evaluation to which we submit academic work: the proposal review (by an instructor or small committee, likely familiar with your field and your project); funding review (by a donor who may or may not be familiar with your field, but who is likely *not* familiar with your project); an ethical review (by an institutional review board or human

264

subjects research ethics committee, which is likely not familiar with your field or research question, but which is familiar with a range of methods and their ethical considerations); and finally peer review (which is done by people familiar with your field, but not your project). These are different audiences, yet for each, the challenge is to articulate the standards you have set for your project and how you have met them.

Certainly, a feminist research ethic can guide your reflections for improving your research, but we do not recommend that you organize the exposition of your project and defense of its question, research design, methods, and conclusions along the lines of the four aspects of a feminist research ethic. Rather, we recommend that you *organize* the defense of your project following the norms of your audience and use feminist reflection to guide your *content*. Some of these considerations may strike you or your audience as ethical and not methodological reflections, or as methodological, but not ethical; we argue that they are both.

As we have been sharing throughout the book, feminism can help us think about how we should understand the ethical relations of research. We have focused on the methodological implications of these considerations. Research takes resources not only to cover its expenses but also specifically resources in terms of the opportunity costs of the subject-participants. That is, if they were not participating in your research, your subject-participants would be doing something that *they* valued. Because research takes resources, we have an ethical obligation to do it well. Thus, many of our guidelines for evaluation are explicitly methodological.

However, when most researchers consider the ethical dimensions of their research, emerging norms in medical and social sciences research urge us to think about ethics through a relatively narrow lens of ethics, that is the lens of hierarchy and vulnerability between researcher and subject-participant.

Feminism and a feminist research ethic give a much fuller set of demands for good, ethical research. Feminism offers concrete guidelines for research. These are demanding, so demanding that some may prefer the question "how do you know good feminist research?" to remain rhetorical.

Feminism isn't rhetorical. It is hard, challenging social and political science.

Feminist Reflections on Conventional Ethics in Research

Because the most rigorous methods require us to pay careful attention to the ways in which researchers interact with participants in their research studies, good research requires considering all of the hierarchies of the research context. Reflecting on theories of freedom and agency encourages us to consider how the research design can both avoid exploiting and contribute to mitigating these hierarchies. This may require some exposition. The characterization of freedom as the essential quality of an autonomous person, and of consent or refusal as the essential act of a free person is a misguided common place concept in political theory, law, and research ethics review guidelines. From birth we are all vulnerable and dependent. With maturity we gain interdependence with the rest of our community, the boundaries of which can be broadly and narrowly understood. For all humans, vulnerability and interdependence vary over the life course. True, political theory and law have sought to characterize the human or the legal subject as someone autonomous as opposed to dependent, and if dependent, vulnerable. However, the reality is that, even when laws construct the legal subject in that way (as review board guidelines do), this dichotomous way of understanding individuality and humanity is inappropriate. Our research and our lived experience show us otherwise.

Is it possible to think about human agency in a more nuanced way, a feminist relational way, and *not* commit the egregious ethical violations or even mild ethical missteps that others have made? Yes, absolutely. Ethical reflection is not dependent on the notion of the individual as autonomous. In fact, an inaccurate characterization of the human condition is a poor foundation for ethical reflection. Rather, ethical reflection is about responsibility and humility. Ethical reflection in research is about the researcher developing and maintaining an ethical compass that informs and guides her decisions in anticipated and unanticipated dilemmas of research.

A feminist research ethic, as we have been developing and applying it in this book, has been developed through reflection on feminist research practices that go by many names, including transnational and global feminism (Ackerly 2000, 2008b; Ackerly and Attanasi 2009; Ackerly and True 2006, under review; True 2008c). It provides among other things a lens for thinking about the ways in which the notion of an autonomous agent as either vulnerable in need of paternalistic protection or able to consent freely to participate in research is too narrow a conception of what it means to be human.

When we consider gender centrally to any research question we notice first, that power functions in ways that often render its own exercise invisible. We notice that the acceptance of gender norms is a way of perpetuating gender hierarchy. We notice second, that researchers also participate in the construction of boundaries that conceal the exercise of power. If a research project cannot train local women as paraprofessionals to disseminate health messages while gathering health data because in the view of an ethical review board that would be making a "vulnerable" woman more vulnerable (by challenging community norms when leaving her family *bari* in Bangladesh to do her work for example), then our research would actually maintain her vulnerability. If by contrast we hire Masters' students from the cities to gather our data, then we are contributing to maintaining the view of village women as objects of study not agents of change in their own lives. Fundamentally, researchers must be able to design research projects that attend to hierarchy without exploiting hierarchies.

When researchers attend to gender we notice third, that our research and our presence as researchers can change relationships among community members, challenging or reinforcing hierarchies for example. *A priori* there is nothing more ethical in one or the other. Through ongoing conversation and imagination, researchers need to reflect on all of the relationships affected by our research. Reflection in this way will do some of the work that the risk and benefit analysis familiar to institutional research ethics processes promise to accomplish, but it will do much more as well. It will enable us to interpret the risks and benefits of research in the lives of subject-participants and all stakeholders in our research. In the remainder of this chapter we discuss the insights for evaluation and review as they are prompted by a feminist research ethic. On the book's website (http://www.palgrave.com/methodology/doingfeministresearch) we provide a concrete set of guidelines and reviewer questions for evaluating the quality of feminist research.

The Power of Knowledge, and more Profoundly, of Epistemology

Good feminist scholarship asks a research question that matters to those who participate in the research and are affected by the subject of inquiry. The "so what" or "why bother" questions of good feminist research puts the resources of research, the imbalance of authority associated with the ability to make and defend claims about what is "true," in the service of global justice (Ackerly and True under review). Make your "so what" discussion a good one.

Attending to the power of knowledge and norms about what is important to know means reading and citing a broad literature (as we discuss in Chapter four), not letting certain arguments get privileged merely because they are often present when someone takes up a topic such as yours. What *else* should you be reading?

In addition to acknowledging your debts, to certain literatures, acknowledge your intellectual debts to those works or authors who have had a significant influence on your thinking by naming or invoking them in your text. Acknowledge your conversation partners or research facilitators who may or may not be known to your audience but whose influence on your thinking would be invisible without your reference to them (see Box 14.1).

Finally, challenge norms of academic knowledge by sharing your findings with research participants, their communities, and the organizations who work with them as appropriate. This is one way and one part of appreciating the opportunity cost of your subject-participants *and* their organizations and communities.

Box 14.1 From our own experience: feminism as collaborative writing

Beginning when I (Jacqui) was a graduate student, the implicit practice I was taught was continually to recognize the contributions of others, to notice them as if in conversation with them, and to cite them. This is a feminist practice, and some students not familiar with feminism or appreciative of the collective nature of scholarship, may not understand the importance of extensive and thorough citation and literature review.

In this book, we model this practice often including citations where one might not have thought a reference necessary or including multiple citations where one might have thought one reference would suffice. These citations reflect as much our effort to model the importance of acknowledging our intellectual debts as our desire to invite the reader to engage with our interlocutors, and not just with us. A feminist research ethic and our account of it in this book is part of a collaborative field of knowledge, only a part.

Boundaries, Marginalization, Silences, and Intersections

Good feminist research pushes the boundaries of how other scholars have understood things. Be clear in your conceptualization of your research question, and be careful in your articulation of what would constitute an answer to that question. Take care with your research design, case selection, and operationalization of your variables so that you can be confident that your research will enable you to answer your question.

And then, be prepared to change your research question in light of your self-reflection during the research process. Over and over again, for different reasons, we see examples of a scholar who begins research with one question and discovers in the process that he was asking the wrong question. For those studying phenomena this is to be expected and delightful, a sign that you have done original research that has yielded findings rather than research that led you to findings that you anticipated. Of course, there is nothing wrong with good hypotheses and finding them supported. Hopefully, this happens with theoretically informed theory-testing research often. However, if you are theory-seeking, if you are looking to discover something, then if you knew what you would find before you got there, you have probably wasted your time and that of your subject-participants and their communities.

Relationships and their Power Differentials

Good feminist research attends to relationships among all research subject-participants and their associated power dynamics. This means developing ways to collaborate across potential hierarchies and learning to work democratically among peers. It also means negotiating the ethics of working with "shirkers," that is, classmates or co-authors who are not contributing as peers, or rogue research assistants. The example of the latter comes from Sapra (2009), described in *Tools for Managing the Relationships in Research* in chapter twelve, who tells the story of a translator who argued about points of substance with the women in a women's meeting that she was supposed to be observing and providing interpretation.

Conclusion

Following our view of the implications of feminist understandings of agency and vulnerability for research ethics, on the book's website (http://www.palgrave.com/methodology/doingfeministresearch) we offer feminist-informed guidelines that researchers and reviewers can use to evaluate their work. These guidelines integrate the methodological considerations of a feminist research ethic and feminist-informed reflection on conventional institutional research ethics processes.

We have written this book to promote and improve feminist research by foregrounding its intellectual architecture. A feminist research ethic inspires us to do rigorous, feminist-informed research that can make a significant difference to transforming persistent and egregious injustices around us.

Selected Source for Further Reading

Yanow, Dvora, and Schwartz-Shea, Peregrine. 2008. "Reforming Institutional Review Board Policy: Issues in Implementation and Field Research." *PS: Political Science and Politics* 41 (July): 483–94.

Bibliography

Ackerly, Brooke A. 1995. "Testing the Tools of Development: Credit Programs, Loan Involvement, and Women's Empowerment." *IDS Bulletin* 26, 3: 56–68.

Ackerly, Brooke A. 2000. *Political Theory and Feminist Social Criticism.* Cambridge: Cambridge University Press.

Ackerly, Brooke A. 2001. "Women's Human Rights Activists as Cross-Cultural Theorists." *International Feminist Journal of Politics* 3, 3 Autumn: 311–46.

Ackerly, Brooke A. 2005. "Is Liberalism the Only Way toward Democracy? Confucianism and Democracy." *Political Theory* 33, 4: 547–76.

Ackerly, Brooke A. 2007. "Sustainable Networking: Collaboration for Women's Human Rights Activists, Scholars, and Donors." In *Sustainable Feminisms: Enacting Theories, Envisioning Action,* ed. Sonita Sarker. Oxford: Advances in Gender Research, Elsevier 143–58.

Ackerly, Brooke A. 2008a. *Universal Human Rights in a World of Difference.* Cambridge: Cambridge University Press.

Ackerly, Brooke A. 2008b. "Feminist Methodological Reflection." In *Qualitative Methods in International Relations: A Pluralist Guide (Research Methods),* ed. Audie Klotz and Deepa Prakash, Basingstoke: Palgrave Macmillan, 28–42.

Ackerly, Brooke A., and Katy Attanasi. 2009. "Global Feminisms: Theory and Ethics for Studying Gendered Injustice." *New Political Science* 31, 4: 543–55.

Ackerly, Brooke A., and Jacqui True. 2006. "Studying the Struggles and Wishes of the Age: Feminist Theoretical Methodology and Feminist Theoretical Methods." In *Feminist Methodologies for International Relations,* ed. Brooke A. Ackerly, Maria Stern, and Jacqui True. Cambridge: Cambridge University Press, 241–60.

Ackerly, Brooke A., and Jacqui True. 2008a. "An Intersectional Analysis of International Relations: Recasting the Discipline." *Politics & Gender* 4, 1: 156–73.

Ackerly, Brooke A., and Jacqui True. 2008b. "Reflexivity in Practice: Power and Ethics in Feminist Research on International Relations." *International Studies Review* 10, 4: 693–707.

Ackerly, Brooke A. and Jacqui True. Under review. "Back to the future: Feminist Theory, Activism, and Doing Feminist Research in an Age of Globalization."

Ackerly, Brooke, Lyndi Hewitt, and Sarah VanHooser. 2009. "The Research Questions of Women's Movements." *Working Paper.*

Ackerly, Brooke A., Maria Stern, and Jacqui True. 2006. "Feminist Methodologies for International Relations." In *Feminist Methodologies for International Relations,* ed. Brooke A. Ackerly, Maria Stern and Jacqui True. Cambridge: Cambridge University Press, 1–15.

Agathangelou, Anna M., and L. H. M. Ling. 2004. "Power, Borders, Security, Wealth: Lessons of Violence and Desire from September 11." *International Studies Quarterly* 48, 3: 517–38.

Aggarwal, Ravina. 2000. "Traversing Lines of Control: Feminist Anthropology

Today." *The ANNALS of the American Academy of Political and Social Science* 571, 1: 14–29.

Aguilar, Lorena, and Itzá Castañeda. 2001. "About Fishermen, Fisherwomen, Oceans and Tides: A Gender Perspective in Marine-Coastal Zones." San Jose, Costa Rica: World Conservation Union.

Alker, Hayward R. 1996. *Rediscoveries and Reformulations: Humanistic Methodologies for International Studies*. New York: Cambridge University Press.

Andersen, Nils Akerstrom. 2003. *Discursive Analytical Strategies: Understanding Foucault, Koselleck, Laclau, and Luhmann*. Bristol: Policy Press.

Apodaca, Clair. 1998. "Measuring Women's Economic and Social Rights Achievement." *Human Rights Quarterly* 20, 1: 139–72.

Apodaca, Clair. 2000. "The Effects of Foreign Aid on Women's Attainment of Their Economic and Social Human Rights." *Journal of Third World Studies* 17, 2: 205–19.

Apodaca, Clair. 2009. "Overcoming Obstacles in Quantitative Feminist Research." *Politics & Gender* 5, 3: 419–26.

Archer, Margaret. 1995. *Realist Social Theory: A Morphogenetic Approach*. Cambridge: Cambridge University Press.

Archer, Margaret, Roy Bhaskar, Andrew Collier, Tony Lawson, and Alan Norrie, eds. *Critical Realism: Essential Readings*, New York: Routledge, 1998.

Atkinson, Rowland, and John Flint. 2001. "Accessing Hidden and Hard-to-Reach Populations: Snowball Research Strategies." *Social Research Update* 33: 1–4.

Attanasi, Katy. 2008. "South African Pentecostalism: Gendered Perspectives on Theology, Sexuality, and HIV/AIDS." Paper presented at American Academy of Religion, Chicago, November.

Auerbach, Judith. 2000. "Feminism and Federally Funded Social Science: Notes from Inside." *Annals of the American Academy of Political and Social Science* 571, 1: 30–41.

Austen, Siobhan, Therese Jefferson, and Vicki Thein. 2003. "Gendered Social Indicators and Grounded Theory." *Feminist Economics* 9, 1: 1–18.

Baglione, Lisa A. 2006. *Writing a Research Paper in Political Science: A Practical Guide to Inquiry, Structure, and Methods*. Belmont, CA: Thomson Higher Education.

Baker, Ella, and Marvel Jackson Cooke (1935). "The Bronx Slave Market." *Crisis* 42: 330–31, 40.

Baker, Sidney J. 1955. "The Theory of Silences." *Journal of General Psychiatry* 52: 145–67.

Barber, Elizabeth Waylan. 1994. *Women's Work: The First 20,000 Years: Women, Cloth, and Society in Early Times*. New York: Norton.

Barker, Drucilla K. 2005. "Beyond Women and Economics: Rereading 'Women's Work'." *Signs* 30, 4: 2189–209.

Barrett, Michele, and Anne Phillips (eds). 1992. *Destabalizing Theory: Contemporary Feminist Debates*. Cambridge: Polity, 201–19.

Barrientos, Stephanie. 2001. "Gender, Flexibility, and Global Value Chains." *IDS Bulletin* 32, 3: 83–93.

Barton, Allen H. 1958. "Asking the Embarrassing Question." *Public Opin Q* 22, 1: 67–8.

Bateson, Mary Catherine. 1989. *Composing a Life*. New York: Plume.

Bayard De Volo, Lorraine 2003. "Analyzing Politics and Change in Women's Organizations." *International Feminist Journal of Politics* 5, 1: 92–115.

Bazely, Patricia. 2007. *Qualitative Data Analysis with Nvivo.* London: Sage.

Behar, Ruth. 1994 [2003]. *Translated Woman: Crossing the Border with Esperanza's Story*, 2nd edn. Boston: Beacon Press.

Behar, Ruth, and Deborah A. Gordon (eds). 1996. *Women Writing Culture.* Berkeley, CA: University of California Press.

Bell, Vikki, and Judith Butler. 1999. "On Speech, Race and Melancholia: An Interview with Judith Butler." *Theory, Culture and Society* 16, 2: 163–74.

Benhabib, Seyla. 1986. "The Generalized and the Concrete Other: The Kohlberg-Gilligan Controversy and Feminist Theory." *Praxis International* 5, 4: 402–24.

Benmayor, Rita. 1991. "Testimony, Action Research, and Empowerment: Puerto Rican Women and Popular Education." In *Women's Words: The Feminist Practice of Oral History*, ed. Sherna Berger Gluck and Daphne Patai. New York: Routledge, 159–74.

Bennett, Andrew, and Colin Elman. 2006. "Qualitative Research: Recent Developments in Case Study Methods." *Annual Review of Political Science* 9: 455–76.

Bennion, Elizabeth. 2007. "Sitting Down for Sexual Harassment." *American Political Science Association Women and Politics Section Newsletter* 18, 1 (Summer): 22–3.

Benson, Koni, and Richa Nagar. 2006. "Collaboration as Resistance? Reconsidering the Processes, Products, and Possibilities of Feminist Oral History and Ethnography." *Gender, Place and Culture* 13, 5: 581–92.

Berg, Bruce L. 2004. *Qualitative Research Methods for the Social Sciences.* Boston: Pearson.

Berman, Jacqueline. 2003. "(Un)Popular Strangers and Crises (Un)Bounded: Discourses of Sex Trafficking, the European Political Community and the Panicked State of the Modern State." *European Journal of International Relations* 9, 1: 37–86.

Bhavnani, Kum-Kum. 1993. "Tracing the Contours: Feminist Research and Feminist Objectivity." *Women's Studies International Forum* 16, 2: 95–104.

Bickham-Mendez, Jennifer, and Diane Wolf. 2007. "Feminizing Global Research/Globalizing Feminist Research: Methods and Practice under Globalization." In *Handbook of Feminist Research: Theory and Praxis*, ed. Sharlene Nagy Hesse-Biber, Thousand Oaks, CA: Sage, 651–62.

Blakeslee, Ann M., Caroline M. Cole, and Theresa Conefrey. 1996. "Constructing Voices in Writing Research: Developing Participatory Approaches to Situated Inquiry." In *Ethics and Representation in Qualitative Studies of Literacy*, ed. Peter Mortensen and Gesa E. Kirsch. Urbana, Ill: NCTE, 134–52.

Bleiker, Roland. 1997. "Forget IR theory." *Alternatives* 22, 1: 57–85.

Bleiker, Roland. 2000. *Popular Dissent, Human Agency and Global Politics.* Cambridge: Cambridge University Press.

Bleiker, Roland. 2003. "Learning from Art: A Reply to Holden's: 'World Literature and World Politics.'" *Global Society* 17, 4: 415–28.

Borooah, Vani K., and Patricia M. McKee. 1994. "Modelling Intra Household Income Transfers: An Analytical Framework with an Application to the U.K." In *Taxation, Poverty, and Income Distribution*, ed. John Creedy. London: E. Elgar.

Bourdieu, Pierre. 2001. *Masculine Domination*. Cambridge: Polity Press.

Bourque, Susan C., and Jean Grossholtz. 1974. "Politics as Unnatural Practice: Political Science Looks at Female Participation." *Politics and Society* 4, 2: 225–66.

Bowker, Lee, "Publishing Feminist Research: A Personal Note by Lee H. Bowker." In *Feminist Perspectives on Wife Abuse*, ed. Kersti Yllo and Michele Bograd. New York: Sage.

Bowles, Gloria, and Renate Klein, eds. 1983. *Theories of Women's Studies*. London: Routledge & Kegan Paul.

Brady, H. E. 2003. *Models of Causal Inference: Going Beyond the Neymen–Rubin–Holland Theory*. Presented at Annual Meeing of the Midwest Political Science Association, Chicago.

Brines, Julie. 1994. "Economic dependency, gender and the division of labor at home." *American Journal of Sociology* 100, 3: 652–88.

Brisolara, Sharon, and Denise Seigart. 2007. "Participatory and Action Research and Feminisms: Toward a Transformative Praxis." In *Handbook of Feminist Research: Theory and Praxis*, ed. Sharlene Nagy Hesse-Biber. Thousand Oaks, CA: Sage, 297–326.

Bristow, Ann R., and Jody A. Esper. 1984. "A Feminist Research Ethos." *Humanity and Society* 8 (November): 489–96.

Bryant, Adam. 2009. "For This Guru, No Question Is Too Big." *The New York Times*, May 24: 1, 6.

Burnham, Peter, Karin Gilland, Wyn Grant, and Zig Layton-Henry. 2004. *Research Methods in Politics*. New York: Palgrave Macmillan.

Burns, Nancy. 2005. "Finding Gender." *Politics and Gender* 3, 1: 137–41.

Butler, Judith. [1990]1999. *Gender Trouble: Feminism and the Subversion of Identity*. New York: Routledge.

Cancian, Francesca M. 1992. "Feminist Science: Methodologies That Challenge Inequality." *Gender & Society* 6, 4: 623–43.

Cancian, Francesca M. 1996. "Participatory Research and Alternative Strategies for Activist Sociology." In *Feminism and Social Change: Bridging Theory and Practice*, ed. Heidi Gottfried. Urbana and Chicago: University of Illinois Press, 187–205.

Cantillon, Sara, and Brian Nolan. 2001. "Poverty within Households: Measuring Gender Differences Using Non-Monetary Indicators." *Feminist Economics* 7, 1: 5–23.

Caprioli, Mary. 2000. "Gendered Conflict." *Journal of Peace Research* 37, 1: 51–68.

Caprioli, Mary. 2003. "Gender Equality and State Aggression: The Impact of Domestic Gender Equality on State First Use of Force." *International Interactions* 29, 3: 195–214.

Caprioli, Mary. 2004. "Feminist IR Theory and Quantitative Methodology: A Critical Analysis." *International Studies Review* 6, 2: 253–69.

Caprioli, Mary. 2009. "Making Choices." *Politics & Gender* 5, 3: 426–31.

Caprioli, Mary, and Mark A. Boyer. 2001. "Gender, Violence, and International Crisis." *The Journal of Conflict Resolution* 45, 4: 503–18.

Caprioli, Mary, and Kimberly Lynn Douglass. 2008. "Nation Building and Women: The Effect of Intervention on Women's Agency." *Foreign Policy Analysis* 4, 1: 45–65.

Caprioli, Mary, Valerie M. Hudson, Rose McDermott, Bonnie Ballif-Spanvill, Chad F. Emmett, and S. Matthew Stearmer. 2008. "The WomanStats Project Database:

Advancing an Empirical Research Agenda." *Journal of Peace Research* 46, 6: 839–51.

Carapico, Sheila. 2006. "No Easy Answers: The Ethics of Field Research in the Arab World." *PS, Political Science & Politics* 39, 3: 429–31.

Carli, Linda.L. 1990. "Gender, Language, and Influence." *Journal of Personality and Social Psychology* 59: 94: 1–51.

Carr, Marilyn, ed. 2004. *Chains of Fortune: Linking Women Producers and Workers with Global Markets*. London: Zed Books.

Chafetz, Janet Saltzman. 2004. "Some Thoughts by an Unrepentant 'Positivist' Who Considers Herself a Feminist Nonetheless." In *Feminist Perspectives on Social Research*, ed. Sharlene Nagy Hesse-Biber and Michelle L. Yaiser. New York: Oxford University Press, 320–9.

Chambers, Robert. 1994. "Participatory Rural Appraisal (PRA): Challenges, Potentials and Paradigm." *World Development* 22, 10: 1437–54.

Chambers, Robert. 1997. *Whose Reality Counts? Putting the First Last*. London: Intermediate Technology Development Group.

Charmaz, Kathy. 2006. *Constructing Grounded Theory: A Practical Guide through Qualitative Analysis*. London; Thousand Oaks, CA: Sage.

Charmaz, Kathy. 2007. "What's Good Writing in Feminist Research? What Can Feminist Researchers Learn about Good Writing?" In *Handbook of Feminist Research: Theory and Praxis*, ed. Sharlene Nagy Hesse-Biber, Thousand Oaks, CA: Sage, 443–58.

Childs, Sarah. 2002. "Conceptions of Representation and the Passage of the Sex Discrimination (Election Candidates) Bill." *Journal of Legislative Studies* 8, 3: 90–108.

Childs, Sarah. 2004. *New Labour's Women MPs*. London: Routledge.

Childs, Sarah. 2006. "The Complicated Relationship between Sex, Gender and the Substantive Representation of Women." *European Journal of Women's Studies* 13, 1: 7–21.

Childs, Sarah, and Julie Withey. 2004. "Women Representatives Acting for Women: Sex and the Signing of Early Day Motions in the 1997 British Parliament." *Political Studies* 52, 3: 552–64.

Childs, Sarah, and Julie Withey. 2006. "The Substantive Representation of Women: The Case of the Reduction of VAT on Sanitary Products." *Parliamentary Affairs* 59, 1: 10–23.

Chin, Christine B. N., and James H. Mittelman, 1997. "Conceptualising Resistance to Globalization." *New Political Economy* 2, 1: 25–37.

Clark, Cindy, Ellen Sprenger, Lisa Vaneklasen, and Lydia Alpízar Durán. 2006. *Where Is the Money for Women's Rights?* Washington, DC: Just Associates.

Clark, Janine A. 2006. "Field Research Methods in the Middle East." *PS: Political Science & Politics* 39, 3: 417–24.

Clarke, Adele. 2003. "Situational Analyses: Grounded Theory Mapping After The Postmodern Turn." Special Issue on Theory and Method. *Symbolic Interaction* 26, 4: 553–76.

Clarke, Adele. 2005. *Situational Analysis: Grounded Theory after the Postmodern Turn*. Thousand Oaks, CA: Sage.

Coffey, Amanda, Beverley Holbrook, and Paul Atkinson. 1996. "Qualitative

Data Analysis: Technologies and Representations." *Sociological Research Online* 1, 1.

Cohn, Carol. 2006. "Motives and Methods: Using Multi-Sited Ethnography to Study US National Security Discourses." In *Feminist Methodologies for International Relations*, ed. Brooke Ackerly, Maria Stern and Jacqui True. Cambridge: Cambridge University Press, 91–107.

Confortini, Catia. 2006. "Galtung, Violence, and Gender: The Case for a Peace Studies/Feminism Alliance." *Peace and Change* 31, 3: 333–67.

Confortini, Catia. 2009. *Imaginative Identification: Feminist Critical Methodology in the Women's International League for Peace and Freedom (1945–1975)*. PhD Dissertation. School of International Relations, University of Southern California.

Cooke, Bill, and Uma Kothari. 2001. *Participation: The New Tyranny?* New York: Zed Books.

Cooke, Miriam, and Angela Woollacott, eds. 1993. *Gendering War Talk*. Princeton, NJ: Princeton University Press.

Corbin, Juliet and Anselm Strauss. 1990. *Basics of Qualitative Research Techniques and Procedures for Developing Grounded Theory* (first edition). London: Sage.

Cornwall, Andrea. 2003. "Whose Voices? Whose Choices? Reflections on Gender and Participatory Development." *World Development* 31, 8: 1325–42.

Cosgrove, Lisa. 2003, "Feminism, Postmodernism, and Psychological Research." *Hypatia* 18, 3: 85–112.

Cox, Robert W., with Timothy S. Sinclair. 1996. *Approaches to World Order*. Cambridge: Cambridge University Press.

Crawley, Heaven. 1998. "Living up to the Empowerment Claim? The Potential of PRA." In *The Myth of Community: Gender Issues in Participatory Development*, ed. Irene Guijt and Meera Kaul Shah. New Delhi: Vistaar Publications, 24–34.

Crenshaw, Kimberle Williams. 1989. "Demarginalizing the Intersection of Race and Sex." *The University of Chicago Legal Forum*: 139–67.

Crenshaw, Kimberle Williams. 1991. "Mapping the Margins: Intersectionality, Identity Politics, and Violence against Women of Color." *Stanford Law Review* 43: 1241–99.

Crenshaw, Kimberle Willams. 2002. "Gender-Related Aspects of Race Discrimination." United Nations DAW, PHCHR, UNIFEM, Background Paper for the Expert Meeting November 21–24, Zagreb, Croatia.

Currie. 1999. "Gender Analysis from the Standpoint of Women: The Radical Potential of Women's Studies in Development." *Asian Journal of Women's Studies* 5, 3: 99–144.

Currier, Carrie Liu. 2007a. "Bringing the Household Back In: The Restructuring of Women's Labor Choices in Beijing." *American Journal of Chinese Studies* 14(1): 61–81.

Currier, Carrie Liu. 2007b. "Redefining 'Labor' in Beijing: Women's Attitudes on Work and Reform." *Asian Journal of Women's Studies* 13(3): 71–108.

D'Costa, Bina. 2003. *The Gendered Construction of Nationalism: From Partition to Creation*. PhD Dissertation. Canberra: Australian National University.

D'Costa, Bina. 2006. "Marginalized Identity: New Frontiers of Research for IR?" In *Feminist Methodologies for International Relations*, ed. Brooke Ackerly, Maria Stern and Jacqui True. Cambridge: Cambridge University Press, 129–52.

D'Costa, Bina. 2010. *Nationbuilding, Gender and War Crimes in South Asia.* London: Routledge

Davies, Hugh, and Heather Joshi. 1994. "Sex, Sharing and the Distribution of Income." *Journal of Social Policy* 23, 3: 301–40.

Davis, James W. 2005. *Terms of Inquiry: On the Theory and Practice of Political Science.* Baltimore: Johns Hopkins University Press.

Della Porta, Donatella, and Sidney Tarrow eds. 2005. *Transnational Protest and Global Activism.* New York: Rowman and Littlefield.

Denzin, Norman K., and Yvonna S. Lincoln. 2005. "Introduction: The Discipline and Practice of Qualitative Research." In *The Sage Handbook of Qualitative Research*, ed. Norman K. Denzin and Yvonna S. Lincoln. Thousand Oaks, CA: Sage, 1–32.

DeRiviere, Linda. 2006. "A Human Capital Methodology for Estimating the Lifelong Personal Costs of Young Women Leaving the Sex Trade." *Feminist Economics* 12, 3: 367–402.

DeVault, Majorie L. 1990. "Talking and Listening from Women's Standpoint: Feminist Strategies for Interviewing and Analysis." *Social Problems* 37, 1: 96–116.

DeVault, Marjorie L. 1999. *Liberating Method: Methodologies that Challenge Inequality.* Philadelphia: Temple University Prress.

DeVault, Majorie, and Glenda Gross. 2007. "Feminist Interviewing: Experience, Talk, and Knowledge." In *Handbook of Feminist Research: Theory and Praxis*, ed. Sharlene Nagy Hesse-Biber. Thousand Oaks, CA: Sage, 173–97.

Development. 48, 2 2005. Special Issue "The Movement of Movements."

Dever, Carolyn. 2004. *Skeptical Feminism: Activist Theory, Activist Practice.* Minneapolis: University of Minnesota Press.

Diamond, Lisa M. 2006. "Careful What You Ask For: Reconsidering Feminist Epistemology and Autobiographical Narrative in Research on Sexual Identity Development." *Signs* 31, 2: 471–91.

Dietz, Mary G. 2003. "Current Controversies in Feminist Theory." *Annual Review of Political Science* 6: 399–431.

Du Bois, W. E. B. 1956. *Black Reconstruction: An Essay toward a History of the Part Which Black Folk Played in the Attempt to Reconstruct Democracy in America, 1860–1880.* New York: S. A. Russell.

Dwyer, Daisy Hilse, and Judith Bruce. 1988. *A Home Divided: Women and Income in the Third World.* Stanford, CA: Stanford University Press.

Ehrenreich, Barbara. 1999. "Fukuyama's Follies: So What If Women Ruled the World? Men Hate War Too." *Foreign Affairs* 78, 1: 118–29.

Ehrenreich, Barbara. 2001. *Nickel and Dimed: On (Not) Getting by in America.* New York: Metropolitan Books.

Ellis, Carolyn, and Arthur Bochner, 2000. "Autoethnography, Personal Narrative, Reflexivity: Researcher as Subject." In *Handbook of Qualitative Research*, 2nd edn., ed. Norman K. Denzin and Yvonna S. Lincoln. Sage: New York, 733–68.

Elshtain, Jean Bethke. 1981. *Public Man, Private Woman: Women in Social and Political Thought.* Princeton, NJ: Princeton University Press.

Elshtain, Jean Bethke. 1987. *Women and War.* New York: Basic Books.

Emerson, Robert, Rachel Fretz, and Linda Shaw. 1995. "Processing Fieldnotes: Coding and Memoing." In *Writing Ethnographic Fieldnotes*. Chicago: UC Press: 142–68.

Enloe, Cynthia. [1989] 1990. *Bananas, Beaches & Bases: Making Feminist Sense of International Politics*. Berkeley, CA: University of California Press.

Enloe, Cynthia H. 2004. *The Curious Feminist: Searching for Women in a New Age of Empire*. Berkeley, CA: University of California Press.

Erlandson, David A., E. L. Harris, B. L. Skipper, and S. D. Allen. 1993. *Doing Naturalistic Inquiry: A Guide to Methods*. Newbury Park, CA: Sage.

Eschle, Catherine, and Bice Maiguashca. 2007. "Rethinking Globalised Resistance: Feminist Activism and Critical Theorising in International Relations." *The British Journal of Politics and International Relations* 9, 2: 284–301.

Evans, Peter B., Peter J. Katzenstein, James C. Scott, Atul Kohli, Susanne Hoerber Rudolph, Adam Przeworski, and Theda Skocpol. 1996. "The Role of Theory in Comparative Politics." *World Politics* 48, 1: 1–49.

Fausto-Sterling, Anne. 2000. *Sexing the Body: Gender Politics and the Construction of Sexuality*. New York: Basic Books.

Favret-Saada, Jeanne. 1980. *Deadly Words: Witchcraft in the Bocage*. Cambridge and New York: Cambridge University Press.

Feliciano, Cynthia, Belinda Robnett and Golnaz Kolmaie. 2009. "Gender Racial Exclusion Among White Internet Daters." *Social Science Research* 38, 1: 39–54.

Fernandez, Sujatha. 2007. "Gender and Fieldwork." *APSA Women and Politics Section Newsletter* 18, 1: 23.

Ferree, Myra Marx. 2009. "Inequality, Intersectionality and the Politics of Discourse: Framing Feminist Alliances." In *The Discursive Politics of Gender Equality: Stretching, Bending and Policy-Making*, ed. Emanuela Lombardo, Petra Meier and Mieke Verloo. New York: Routledge (EU Series), 86–104.

Fine, Michele, Lois Weiss, Linda Powell Pruit, and April Burns eds. 2004. *Off–White: Readings on Power, Privilege and Resistance*. 2nd edn. New York: Routledge.

Fletcher, Catherine, Rebecca Boden, Julie Kent and Julie Tinson. 2007. "Performing Women: The Gendered Dimensions of the UK New Research Economy." *Gender, Work and Organization* 14, 5: 433–52.

Folbre, Nancy. 1984. "Household Production in the Philippines: A Non-Neoclassical Approach." *Economic Development and Cultural Change* 32, 2: 303–30.

Fonow, Mary Margaret, and Judith A. Cook. 1991. *Beyond Methodology: Feminist Scholarship as Lived Research*. Bloomington, IN: Indiana University Press.

Fonow, Mary Margaret, and Judith A. Cook. 2005. "Feminist Methodology: New Applications in the Academy and Public Policy." *Signs: Journal of Women and Culture* 30, 4: 2295–301.

Frey, Ada Freytes, and Karina Crivelli. 2007. "Women's Participation in Argentina's Picketing Movement: Accomplishments and Limitations in the Redefinition of Feminine Roles." *Journal of Developing Societies* 23, 1–2: 243–58.

Friedman, Elisabeth J. 2000. *Unfinished Transitions: Women and the Gendered Development of Democracy in Venezuela, 1936–1996*. University Park, PA: Pennsylvania State University Press.

Gadamer, Hans-Georg. 1989. *Truth and Method*. New York: Crossroad.

Gallie, W. B. 1962. "Essentially Contested Concepts." In *The Importance of Language*, ed. Max Black. Englewood Cliffs, NJ: Prentice-Hall.

Gardner, Katy. 1991. *Songs at the River's Edge: Stories from a Bangladeshi Village*. London: Virago.

Gardner, Katy. 1995. *Global Migrants, Local Lives: Travel and Transformation in Rural Bangladesh*. Oxford: Oxford University Press.

Garwood, Shae, 2005. "Politics at Work: Transnational Advocacy Networks and the Global Garment Industry." *Gender and Development* 13, 3: 21–33.

Gaskell, Jane, and Margrit Eichler. 2001. "White Women as Burden: On Playing the Role of Feminist 'Experts' in China." *Women's Studies International Forum* 24, 6: 637–51.

Gatenby, Bev, and Maria Humphries. 2000. "Feminist Participatory Action Research: Methodological and Ethical Issues." *Women's Studies International Forum* 23, 1: 89–105.

Gear, Sasha. 2005. "Rules of Engagement: Structuring Sex and Damage in Men's Prisons and Beyond." *Culture, Health & Sexuality* 7, 3: 195–208.

George, Alexander L. and Andrew Bennett. 2005. *Case Studies and Theory Development in the Social Sciences*. Cambridge, MA: The MIT Press.

Gilgun, Jane F., and Laura McLeod. 1999. "Gendering Violence." *Studies in Symbolic Interactionism* 22: 167–93.

Gills, Barry K. ed. 2000. *Globalization and the Politics of Resistance*. New York: St. Martin's Press.

Gilmore, Leigh. 2005. "Autobiography's Wounds." In *Just Advocacy?: Women's Human Rights, Transnational Feminisms, and the Politics of Representation*, ed. Wendy S. Hesford and Wendy Kozol. New Brunswick, NJ: Rutgers University Press, 99–119.

Gluck, Sherna Berger, and Daphne Patai, eds. 1991. *Women's Words: The Feminist Practice of Oral History*. New York: Routledge.

Goertz, Gary. 2006. *Social Science Concepts: A User's Guide*. Princeton, NJ: Princeton University Press.

Goetz, Anne Marie. 2001. *Women Development Workers: Implementing Rural Credit Programmes in Bangladesh*: New Delhi: Sage.

Goetz, Anne Marie, and Rina Sen Gupta. 1996. "Who Takes the Credit? Gender, Power, and Control over Loan Use in Rural Credit Programs in Bangladesh." *World Development* 24, 1: 45–63.

Goldstein, Joshua S. 2001. *War and Gender: How Gender Shapes the War System and Vice Versa*. Cambridge: Cambridge University Press.

Grant, Barbara. 2006. "Writing in the Company of other Women: Exceeding the Boundaries." *Studies in Higher Education* 31, 4: 483–95.

Grant, Barbara, and Sally Knowles. 2000. "Flights of Imagination: Academic Women Be(com)ing Writers." *The International Journal for Academic Development* 5, 1: 6–19.

Green-Powell, Patricia. 1997. "Methodological Considerations in Field Research: Six Case Studies." In *Oral Narrative Research with Black Women*, ed. Kim Marie Vaz. Thousand Oaks, CA: Sage, 197–222.

Grenz, Sabine. 2005. "Intersections of Sex and Power in Research on Prostitution: A Female Researcher Interviewing Male Heterosexual Clients." *Signs: Journal of Women in Culture and Society* 30, 4: 2091–113.

Griffin, Gabriele, and Rosi Braidotti. 2002. *Thinking Differently: A Reader in European Women's Studies*. London: Zed Books.

Guevarra, Anna Romina. 2006. "The Balikbayan Researcher: Negotiating

Vulnerability in Fieldwork with Filipino Labor Brokers." *Journal of Contemporary Ethnography* 35, 5: 526–51.

Guijt, Irene, and Meera Kaul Shah, eds. [1998] 1999. *The Myth of Community: Gender Issues in Participatory Development.* New Delhi: Vistaar Publications.

Hall, Nina, and Jacqui True. 2009. "Gender Mainstreaming in a Post-Conflict State: Toward a Democratic Peace in Timor Leste." In *Gender and Global Politics in Asia-Pacific*, ed. Katrina Lee Koo and Bina D'Costa. Basingstoke: Palgrave Macmillan, 159–74.

Han, Jongwoo, and L. H. M. Ling. 1998. "Authoritarianism in the Hypermasculinized State: Hybridity, Patriarchy, and Capitalism in Korea." *International Studies Quarterly* 42, 1: 53–78.

Hansen, Lene. 2006. *Security as Practice: Discourse Analysis and the Bosnian War.* London: Routledge.

Haraway, Donna. 1988. "Situated Knowledges: The Science Question in Feminism and the Privilege of Partial Perspective." *Feminist Studies* 14, 3: 575–99.

Harding, Sandra G. 1987. *Feminism and Methodology: Social Science Issues.* Bloomington, IN: Indiana University Press.

Harding, Sandra. 1991. *Whose Science? Whose Knowledge? Thinking from Women's Lives.* Ithaca: Cornell University Press.

Harding, Sandra. 2000. "Feminist Philosophies of Science." *APA Newsletter on Feminism and Philosophy* 99, 2: online.

Harding, Sandra G., and Merrill B. Hintikka, eds. 1983. *Discovering Reality: Feminist Perspectives on Epistemology, Metaphysics, Methodology, and Philosophy of Science.* Dordrecht, Holland: D. Reidel.

Harding, Sandra, and Kathryn Norberg. 2005. "New Feminist Approached to Social Science Methodologies: An Introduction." *Signs: Journal of Women in Culture and Society* 30, 4: 2009–15.

Harding, Susan Friend. 2000. *The Book of Jerry Falwell: Fundamentalist Language and Politics.* Princeton, NJ: Princeton University Press.

Hartmann, Heidi and Roberta Spalter-Roth. 1996. "Small Happinesses: The Struggle to Integrate Social Research with Social Activism." *Feminism and Social Change: Bridging Theory and Practice*, ed. Heidi Gottfried. Champaign, IL: University of Illinois Press, 206–24.

Hashemi, Syed M., Sidney Ruth Schuler, and Ann P. Riley. 1996. "Rural Credit Programs and Women's Empowerment in Bangladesh." *World Development* 24, 4: 635–53.

Hawkesworth, Mary. 2005. "Engendering Political Science: An Immodest Proposal." *Politics & Gender* 1 , 1: 141–56

Hawkesworth, Mary E. 2006. *Feminist Inquiry: From Political Conviction to Methodological Innovation.* New Brunswick, NJ: Rutgers University Press.

Henderson, Frances B. 2009. "'We Thought You Would Be White': Race and Gender in Fieldwork." *PS: Political Science & Politics* 42, 2: 291–4.

Henry, Marsha. 2007. "If the Shoe Fits: Authenticity, Authority and Agency in Feminist Diasporic Research." *Women's Studies International Forum* 30, 1: 70–80.

Herndl, Diane Price. 2006. "Our Breasts, Our Selves: Identity, Community, and Ethics in Cancer Autobiographies." *Signs* 32, 1: 221–45.

Hesse-Biber, Sharlene Nagy, ed. 2007. *Handbook of Feminist Research: Theory and Praxis.* Thousand Oaks, CA: Sage.

Hesse-Biber, Sharlene Nagy, and Deborah Piatelli. 2007. "From Theory to Method and Back Again: The Synergistic Praxis of Theory and Method." In *Handbook of Feminist Research: Theory and Praxis*, ed. Sharlene Nagy Hesse-Biber. Thousand Oaks, CA: Sage, 143–53.

Hesse-Biber, Sharlene Nagy, and Michelle L. Yaiser. 2004. *Feminist Perspectives on Social Research*. New York: Oxford University Press.

Hesse-Biber, Sharlene Nagy, Christina K. Gilmartin, and Robin Lydenberg. 1999. *Feminist Approaches to Theory and Methodology: An Interdisciplinary Reader*. New York: Oxford University Press.

Hewitt, Lyndi. 2008. "Feminists and the Forum: Is It Worth the Effort?" *Societies Without Borders* 3, 1: 118–35.

Hewitt, Lyndi. 2009. *The Politics of Transnational Feminist Discourse: Framing across Differences, Building Solidarities*. PhD Dissertation, Sociology, Vanderbilt University, Nashville.

Hill, Linda, and Nancy Kamprath. [1991] 1998. "Beyond the Myth of the Perfect Mentor: Building a Network of Developmental Relationships." *Harvard Business School*. paper no. 9-491-906.

Hirschmann, Nancy J. 2003. *The Subject of Liberty: Toward a Feminist Theory of Freedom*. Princeton, NJ: Princeton University Press.

Hochschild, Arlie Russell. 1997. *The Time Bind: When Work Becomes Home and Home Becomes Work*. New York: Metropolitan Books.

Hochstetler, Kathy. 2007. "Gender, Age and Fieldwork." *APSA Women and Politics Section Newsletter*. 18, 1: 22–3.

hooks, bell. 1984. *Feminist Theory: From Margin to Center*. Boston: South End Press.

Hootman, J. L. 2006. "Feminist Methodologies for Critical Researchers: Bridging Differences (Review)." *Choice* 43, 10: 1864.

Hoover, Kenneth, and Todd Donovan. 2008. *The Elements of Social Scientific Thinking*. Belmont, CA: Thomson Wadsworth.

Htun, Mala. 2005. "What It Means to Study Gender and the State." *Politics & Gender* 1, 1: 157–66.

Huntington, Samuel P. 1991. *The Third Wave: Democratization in the Late Twentieth Century*. Norman: University of Oklahoma Press.

International Women's Health Coalition, Annual Report, 2000. 2000. "Equality Now!". http://www.equalitynow.org/reports/annualreport_2000.pdf [accessed 2.9.2010].

Jacoby, Tami. 2006. "From the Trenches: Dilemmas of Feminist IR Fieldwork." In *Feminist Methodologies for International Relations*, ed. Brooke Ackerly, Maria Stern and Jacqui True. Cambridge: Cambridge University Press, 153–73.

Jamal, Amina. 2006. "Gender, Citizenship, and the Nation-State in Pakistan: Willful Daughters or Free Citizens?" *Signs* 31, 2: 283–304.

Jayaratne, Toby Epstein, and Abigail J. Stewart. 1991. "Quantitative and Qualitative Methods in the Social Sciences: Current Feminist Issues and Practical Strategies." In *Beyond Methodology: Feminist Scholarship as Lived Research*, ed. Mary Margaret Fonow and Judith A. Cook. Bloomington: Indiana University Press, 85–106.

Joachim, Jutta. 2003 "Framing Issues and Seizing Opportunities: The UN, NGOs, and Women's Rights." *International Studies Quarterly* 47, 2: 247–74.

Joeres, Ruth-Ellen Boetcher. 1992. "Editorial: On Writing Feminist Academic Prose." *Signs* 17, 4: 701–4.

Johnson, James. 2002. "How Conceptual Problems Migrate: Rational Choice, Interpretation, and the Hazards of Pluralism." *Annual Review of Political Science* 5, 1: 223–48.

Johnson, Janet. 2007. "Gendering Fieldwork." *APSA Women and Politics Newsletter* 18, 1: 21–2.

Kantola, Johanna. 2008. "'Why Do All the Women Disappear?' Gendering Processes in a Political Science Department?" *Gender, Work & Organization* 15, 2: 202–25.

Kanuha, Valli Kalei, Patricia Erwin, and Ellen Pence. 2004. "Strange Bedfellows: Feminist Advocates and U.S. Marines Working to End Violence." *AFFILIA* 19, 4: 358–75.

Karraker, Mary M. Wilkes, and Barbara Elden Larner. 1984. "Sociology and Women: Building Toward the New Scholarship." *Humanity and Society* 8 (November): 497–506.

Katzenstein, Mary Fainsod. 1998. *Faithful and Fearless: Moving Feminist Protest Inside the Church and the Military.* Princeton, NJ: Princeton University Press.

Katzenstein, Peter, and Rudra Sil, eds. 2008. *The Contributions of Eclectic Theorizing to the Study and Practice of International Relations.* Oxford: Oxford University Press.

Kaufman-Osborn, T. 2006. "Gender Trouble at Abu Ghraib?" *Politics & Gender* 1, 4: 597–619.

Keck, Margaret E., and Kathryn Sikkink. 1998. *Activists Beyond Borders: Advocacy Networks in International Politics.* Ithaca, NY: Cornell University Press.

Keohane, Robert O. 1998. "Beyond Dichotomy: Conversations between International Relations and Feminist Theory." *International Studies Quarterly* 42, 1: 193–8.

Kesby, Mike. 2005. "Retheorizing Empowerment-through-Participation as a Performance in Space: Beyond Tyranny to Transformation." *Signs* 30, 4: 2037–65.

Khan, Shahnaz. 2005. "Reconfiguring the Native Informant: Positionality in the Global Age." *Signs* 30, 4: 2017–35.

King, Gary, Robert O. Keohane, and Sidney Verba. 1994. *Designing Social Inquiry: Scientific Inference in Qualitative Research.* Princeton, NJ: Princeton University Press.

Kinsella, Helen M. 2005. "Securing the Civilian: Sex and Gender in the Laws of War." In *Power in Global Governance*, ed. Michael Barnett and Raymond Duvall. Cambridge: Cambridge University Press.

Kirsch, Gesa E. 1999. *Ethical Dilemmas in Feminist Research: The Politics of Location, Interpretation, and Publication.* Albany, NY: State University of New York Press.

Kirsch, Gesa E. and Peter Mortenson. 1999. "Toward an Ethics of Research". Pp. 87-103. In Gesa E. Kirsch, *Ethical Dilemmas in Feminist Research: The Politics of Location, Interpretation, and Publication.* Albany, NY: State University of New York Press.

Kirshner, Jonathan. 1996. "Alfred Hitchcock and the Art of Research." *PS: Political Science and Politics* 29, 3: 511–13.

Knopf, Jeffrey W. 2006. "Doing a Literature Review." *PS: Political Science and Politics*, 39, 1: 127–32.

Krieger, Nancy. 2000. "Passionate Epistemology, Critical Advocacy, and Public Health: Doing Our Profession Proud." *Critical Public Health* 10, 3: 287–94.

Kronsell, Annica. 2006. "Methods for Studying Silences: Gender Analysis in Institutions of Hegemonic Masculinity." In *Feminist Methodologies for International Relations*, ed. Brooke Ackerly, Maria Stern and Jacqui True. Cambridge: Cambridge University Press, 108–28.

Krook, Mona Lena. 2009. *Quotas for Women in Politics: Gender and Candidate Selection Reform Worldwide.* New York: Oxford University Press.

Krook, Mona Lena, and Jacqui True. Forthcoming. "Rethinking the Life Cycles of International Norms: The United Nations and the Global Promotion of Gender Equality." *European Journal of International Relations.*

Lakatos, I. 1970. "Falsification and the Methodology of Scientific Research Programmes." In *Criticism and the Growth of Knowledge*, ed. I. Lakatos, pp. 91–196. Cambridge: Cambridge University Press.

Lamott, Anne. 1994. *Bird by Bird: Some Instructions on Writing and Life.* New York: Pantheon Books.

Larner, Wendy, and Maria Butler. 2005. "Governmentalities of Local Partnerships: The Rise of a Partnering State in New Zealand." *Studies in Political Economy* 75, Spring: 79–101.

Larner, Wendy, and David Craig. 2005. "After Neoliberalism? Community Activism and Local Partnerships in Aotearoa New Zealand." *Antipode, Working the Spaces of Neoliberalism, Special Edition* 37, 3: 402–24.

Lather, Patti. 1986. "Research as Praxis." *Harvard Educational Review* 56, 3: 257–76.

Lather, Patricia Ann. 1991. *Getting Smart: Feminist Research and Pedagogy with/in the Postmodern.* New York: Routledge.

Lather, Patti. 2000. "Responsible Practices of Academic Writing: Troubling Clarity." In *Revolutionary Pedagogies: Cultural Politics, Instituting Education, and the Discourse of Theory*, ed. Peter Pericles Trifonas. New York: Routledge/Falmer, 289–311.

Lather, Patricia Ann. 2007. *Getting Lost: Feminist Efforts toward a Double(D) Science.* Albany: State University of New York Press.

Lather, Patricia Ann, and Chris Smithies. 1997. *Troubling the Angels: Women Living with HIV/AIDS.* Boulder, CO: Westview Press.

Leavy, P. 2000. Feminist Content Analysis and Representative Characters. [70 paragraphs]. *The Qualitative Report* [On-line serial], 5(1/2). http://www.nova.edu/ssss/QR/QR5-1/leavy.html.

LeClere, Felicia B., Richard G. Rogers, and Kimberley Peters. 1998. "Neighbourhood Social Context and Racial Differences in Women's Heart Disease Mortality." *Journal of Health and Social Behaviour* 39: 91–107.

Lehman, Kathyrn, and Nin Tomas. 2006. "Presentation on Indigenous Human Rights in English, Spanish and Maori" at the International Globalisation, Human Rights and Indigenous Peoples Conference, CEPAL, Santiago, Chile.

Lennie, June, Caroline Hatcher, and Wendy Morgan. 2003. "Feminist Discourses of (Dis)Empowerment in an Action Research Project Involving Rural Women and Communication Technologies." *Action Research* 1, 1: 57–80.

Lieberman, Evan S. 2005. "Nested Analysis as a Mixed-Method Strategy for Comparative Research." *American Political Science Review* 99, 3: 435–52.

Lister, Pam Green. 2003. "Feminist Dilemmas in Data Analysis: Researching the Use of Creative Writing by Women Survivors of Sexual Abuse." *Qualitative Social Work* 2, 1: 45–59.

Lombardo, Emanuela, and Petra Meier. 2006. "Gender Mainstreaming in the EU: Incorporating a Feminist Reading?" *European Journal of Women's Studies* 13, 2: 151–66.

Lombardo, Emanuela, Petra Meier, and Mieke Verloo eds. 2009. *The Discursive Politics of Gender Equality: Stretching, Bending and Policy-Making*. New York: Routledge (EU Series).

Longino, Helen. 1994. "In Search of Feminist Epistemology." *The Monist* 77, 4: 472–85.

Lykes, M. Brinton, and Erzulie Coquillon. 2007. "Participatory Action Research and Feminisms." In *Handbook of Feminist Research: Theory and Praxis*, ed. Sharlene Nagy Hesse-Biber. Thousand Oaks, CA: Sage, 297–326.

Lynch, Michael. 2000. "Against Reflexivity as an Academic Virtue and Source of Privieged Knowledge." *Theory, Culture & Society* 17, 3: 26–54.

MacKinnon, Catharine A. 1989. *Toward a Feminist Theory of the State*. Cambridge, MA: Harvard University Press.

Macleod, Arlene Elowe. 1991. *Accommodating Protest: Working Women, the New Veiling, and Change in Cairo*. New York: Columbia University Press.

Maguire, Patricia. 1987. *Doing Participatory Research: A Feminist Approach*. Amherst, MA: Center for International Education, School of Education, University of Massachusetts.

Mahoney, J. 1999. "Nominal, Ordinal and Narrative Appraisal in Micro-Causal Analysis." *American Journal of Sociology* 104(4): 1154–96.

Mahmood, Saba. 2005. *Politics of Piety: The Islamic Revival and the Feminist Subject*. Princeton, NJ: Princeton University Press.

Maiguashca, Bice. 2006. "Making Feminist Sense of the 'Anti-globalisation Movement': Some Reflections on Methodology and Method." *Global Society*, 20, 2: 115–36.

Man Ling Lee, Theresa. 2007. "Rethinking the Personal and the Political: Feminist Activism and Civic Engagement." *Hypatia* 22, 4: 163–79.

March, James G., Lee S. Sproull, and Michal Tamuz. 1991. "Learning from Samples of One or Fewer." *Organization Science* 2, 1: 58.

Marchand, Marianne, and Anne Sisson Runyan, eds. 2000. *Gender and Global Restructuring: Sites, Siting and Sightings*. New York: Routledge.

Marsh, David, and Gerry Stoker, eds. [1995] 2002. *Theory and Methods in Political Science*. New York: Palgrave Macmillan.

Mascia-Lees, Frances, Patricia Sharpe, and Colleen Ballerina Cohen. 1989. "The Postmodernist Turn in Anthropology: Cautions from a Feminist Perspective." *Signs* 15(1): 7–33.

Mason, Jennifer. 2002. *Qualitative Researching*. London: Sage.

Maynard, Mary, and June Purvis. 1994. *Researching Women's Lives from a Feminist Perspective*. London; Bristol, PA: Taylor & Francis.

Mazur, Amy G., and Dorothy McBride. 2006. "The RNGS Dataset: Women's Policy Agencies, Women's Movements and Policy Debates in Western Post Industrial Democracies." *French Politics* 4, 2: 209–36.

Mazurana, Dyan. 2004. *Women in Armed Opposition Groups Speak on War,*

Protection, and Obligations under International Humanitarian and Human Rights Law. Geneva Call and the Program for the Study of International Organization, University of Geneva: Geneva.

Mazurana, Dyan. 2006. *Women in Armed Opposition Groups in Africa and the Promotion of International Humanitarian and Human Rights Law*. Geneva Call and the Program for the Study of International Organization(s), University of Geneva: Geneva.

McCall, Leslie. 2005. "The Complexity of Intersectionality." *Signs: Journal of Women in Culture and Society* 30, 3: 1771–800.

McCammon, Holly J., Soma Chaudhuri, Lyndi Hewitt, Courtney Muse, Harmony Newman, Carrie Smith, and Teresa Terrell. 2008. "Becoming Full Citizens: The U.S. Women's Jury Rights Campaigns, the Pace of Reform, and Strategic Adaptation." *American Journal of Sociology* 113, 4: 1104–47.

McIntosh, Peggy. 2003 [1988]. "White Privilege and Male Privilege: A Personal Account of Coming to See Correspondences through Work in Women's Studies." In *Feminist Legal Theory: An Anti-Essentialist Reader*, ed. Nancy E. Dowd and Michelle S. Jacobs. New York: New York University Press, 63–72.

McWilliam, Erica. 1997 "Performing between the Posts: Authority, Posture and Contemporary Feminist Scholarship." In *Representation and the Text: Reframing the Narrative Voice*, ed. W. G. Tierney and Y. S. Lincoln. Albany: SUNY Press, 219–32.

Meernik, James. 1996. "United States Military Intervention and the Promotion of Democracy." *Journal of Peace Research* 33, 4: 391–402.

Mendoza, Breny. 2002. "Transnational Feminisms in Question." *Feminist Theory* 3, 3: 295–314.

Mills, Mary Beth. 2005. "From Nimble Fingers to Raised Fists: Women and Labor Activism in Globalizing Thailand." *Signs: Journal of Women in Culture and Society* 31, 1: 117–44.

Miraftab, Faranak. 2004. "Can You Belly Dance? Methodological Questions in the Era of Transnational Feminist Research." *Gender, Place and Culture: A Journal of Feminist Geography* 11, 4: 595–604.

Mohanty, Chandra Talpade. 1991. "Under Western Eyes: Feminist Scholarship and Colonial Discourses." In *Third World Women and the Politics of Feminism*, ed. Chandra Talpade Mohanty, Ann Russo and Lourdes Torres. Bloomington: Indiana University Press, 51–77.

Moon, Katharine H. S. 1997. *Sex among Allies: Military Prostitution in U.S.–Korea Relations*. New York: Columbia University Press.

Mosse, David. 1994. "Authority, Gender and Knowledge: Theoretical Reflections on the Practice of Participatory Rural Appraisal." *Development and Change* 25, 3: 497–525.

Mugisha, Frank, and Victor Juliet Mukasa. 2008. "Uganda: LGBT Arrested at International HIV/AIDS Meeting." In *International Gay and Lesbian Human Rights Commission*.

Murray, Anne Firth. 2008. *From Outrage to Courage: Women Taking Action for Health and Justice*. Monroe, ME: Common Courage Press.

Nagar, Richa. 2002. "Footloose Researchers, 'Traveling' Theories, and the Politics of Transnational Feminist Praxis." *Gender, Place and Culture* 9, 2: 179–86.

Narayan-Parker, Deepa. 2005. *Measuring Empowerment: Cross-Disciplinary Perspectives*. Washington, DC: World Bank.

Neuman, W. 1997. *Social Research Methods: Qualitative and Quantitative Approaches*. Needham, MA: Allyn & Bacon.

Neumann, Iver B. 2008. "The Body of the Diplomat." *European Journal of International Relations* 14, 4: 671–95.

Neumayer, Eric, and Thomas Plümper. 2007. "The Gendered Nature of Natural Disasters: The Impact of Catastrophic Events on the Gender Gap in Life Expectancy, 1981–2002." *Annals of the Association of American Geographers* 97, 3: 551–66.

Nielsen, Joyce McCarl, Robyn Marschke, Elisabeth Sheff, and Patricia Rankin. 2005. "Vital Variables and Gender Equity in Academe: Confessions from a Feminist Empiricist Project." *Signs* 31, 1: 1–28.

Oakely, Ann. 1972. *Sex, Gender and Society*. London. Maurice Temple Smith Ltd.

Okin, Susan. 1991. *Justice, Gender, and the Family*. New York: Basic Books.

Okin, Susan Moller. 1992. "Gender, the Public, and the Private." In *Feminism and Politics: Oxford Readings in Feminism*, ed. Anne Phillips. Oxford: Oxford University Press, 116–41.

Olesen, Virginia L. 2000. "Feminisms and Qualitative Research at and Into the Millennium." In *Handbook of Qualitative Research*, 2nd edn. ed. Norman K. Denzin and Yvonna S. Lincoln. Sage: New York.

Ortbals, Candice D., with Meg Rincker. 2007. "Gender and Fieldwork: Special Considerations and the Occasional Advantage." *APSA Women and Politics Section Newsletter* 18, 1: 20–1.

Ortbals, Candice D, and Meg E Rincker. 2009a. "Fieldwork, Identities, and Intersectionality: Negotiating Gender, Race, Class, Religion, Nationality, and Age in the Research Field Abroad: Editors' Introduction." *PS: Political Science & Politics* 42, 2: 287–90.

Ortbals, Candice D., and Meg E. Rincker. 2009b. "Embodied Researchers: Gendered Bodies, Research Activity, and Pregnancy in the Field." *PS: Political Science & Politics* 42, 2: 315–19.

Parisi, Laura. 2009. "The Numbers Do(n't) Always Add Up: Dilemmas in Using Quantitative Research Methods in Feminist IR Scholarship." *Politics & Gender* 5, 3: 410–19.

Parpart, Jane L. 2000. "The Participatory Empowerment Approach to Gender and Development in Africa: Panacea or Illusion?" Occasional Paper, Centre for African Studies, University of Copenhagen.

Paxton, Pamela. 2000. "Women's Suffrage in the Measurement of Democracy: Problems of Operationalization." *Studies in Comparative International Development* 35: 92–111.

Peterson, V. Spike. 1992. *Gendered States: Feminist (Re)Visions of International Relations Theory*. Boulder, CO: Lynne Rienner.

Phipps, Shelley A., and Peter Burton. 1995. "Social/Institutional Variables and Behaviour within Households: An Empricial Test Using the Luxembourg Income Study." *Feminist Economics* 1, 1: 151–74.

Poe, Steven C., Sabine C. Carey, and Tanya C. Vazquez. 2001. "How Are These Pictures Different? A Quantitative Comparison of the US State Department and

Amnesty International Human Rights Reports, 1976–1995." *Human Rights Quarterly* 23, 3: 650–77.

Popper, Karl F. 1959. *The Logic of Scientific Discovery*. London: Hutchinson.

Pratt, Geraldine, 2002. "Collaborating Across Our Differences." *Gender, Place and Culture* 9, 2: 195–200.

Presser, Lois. 2005. "Negotiating Power and Narrative in Research: Implications for Feminist Methodology." *Signs: Journal of Women in Culture and Society* 30, 4: 2067–90.

Przeworski, Adam, and Frank Salomon. 1995. *The Art of Writing Proposals: Some Candid Suggestions for Applicants to Social Science Research Council Competitions*. New York: Social Science Research Council.

Ragin, Charles. 1987. *The Comparative Method: Moving Beyond Qualitative and Quantitative Strategies*. Berkeley and Los Angeles: University of California Press.

Ragin, Charles C., and Howard Saul Becker. 1992. *What Is a Case?: Exploring the Foundations of Social Inquiry*. Cambridge: Cambridge University Press.

Rahmani, Ladan. 2005. *The Politics of Gender in the United Nations Human Rights Treaty Bodies*. Sydney, Australia: University of Sydney. PhD Dissertation.

Ramazanoğlu, Caroline, and Janet Holland. 2002. *Feminist Methodology: Challenges and Choices*. Thousand Oaks, CA: Sage.

Ray, Raka. 1999. *Fields of Protest: Women's Movements in India*. Minneapolis, MN: University of Minnesota Press.

Reid, Graeme, and Liz Walker. 2005. "Editorial Introduction: Sex and Secrecy: A Focus on African Sexualities." *Culture, Health & Sexuality* 7, 3: 185–94.

Reinharz, Shulamit. 1992. *Feminist Methods in Social Research*. New York: Oxford University Press.

Reinharz, Shulamit and Rachel Kulick. 2007. "Reading Between the Lines: Feminist Content Analysis into the Second Millennium." In *Handbook of Feminist Research: Theory and Praxis*, ed. Sharlene Nagy Hesse-Biber. New Delhi: Sage, 257–75.

Rice, Carla. 2009. Imagining the Other? Ethical Challenges of Researching and Writing Women's Embodied Lives." *Feminism and Psychology* 19, 2: 245–66.

Richardson, Laurel. 1997. *Fields of Play: Constructing an Academic Life*. New Brunswick, NJ: Rutgers University Press.

Richardson, Laurel. 2000. "Writing: A Method of Inquiry." In *Handbook of Qualitative Research*, 2nd edn, ed. Norman K. Denzin and Yvonna S. Lincoln. Thousand Oaks, CA: Sage, 923–49.

Richardson, Laurel. 2007. "Reading for Another: A Method for Addressing Some Feminist Research Dilemmas." In *Handbook of Feminist Research: Theory and Praxis*, ed. Sharlene Nagy Hesse-Biber, Thousand Oaks, CA: Sage, 459–67.

Ridgeway, Cecilia L.. 1982. "Status in Groups: The Importance of Motivation." *American Sociological. Review* 47: 76–88

Risman, Barbara J. 2004. "Gender as a Social Structure: Theory Wrestling with Activism." *Gender & Society* 18, 4: 429–50.

Robinson, Fiona. 2006. *Methods of Feminist Normative Theory: A Political Ethic of Care for International Relations*. Cambridge: Cambridge University Press.

Rose, Gillian. 1997. "Situating Knowledges: Positionality, Reflexivities and other Tactics." *Progress in Human Geography* 21, 305–20.

Ross, Karen. 2000. "Unruly Theory and Difficult Practice: Issues and Dilemmas in.

Work with Women Politicians." *International Feminist Journal of Politics* 2, 3: 319–36.

Roth, Benita. 2004. *Separate Roads to Feminism: Black, Chicana, and White Feminist Movements in America's Second Wave.* Cambridge; New York: Cambridge University Press.

Rothman, Barbara Katz. 2005. "Pushing Them Through." *Chronicle of Higher Education* 52, 4: C2.

Ruddick, Sara. 1989. *Maternal Thinking: Towards a Politics of Peace.* Boston: Beacon Press.

Ryan, Gery W., and H. Russell Bernard. 2000. "Data Management and Analysis Methods." In *Handbook of Qualitative Research*, 2nd edn, ed. Norman K. Denzin and Yvonna S. Lincoln. Thousand Oaks, CA: Sage. 769–802.

Saegert, Susan. 2006. "Building Civic Capacity in Urban Neighborhoods: An Empirically Grounded Anatomy." *Journal of Urban Affairs* 28, 3: 275–94.

Sampaio, Anna, and Hermanas En La Lucha. 2004. "Transnational Feminisms in a New Global Matrix." *International Feminist Journal of Politics* 6, 2: 181–206.

Sanbonmatsu, Kira. 2004. *Where Women Run: Gender and Party in the American States.* Ann Arbor: University of Michigan Press.

Sangari, Kumkum, and Sudesh Vaid. 1989. *Recasting Women: Essays in Colonial History.* New Delhi: Kali for Women.

Sapiro, Virginia. 1981. "Research Frontier Essays: When Are Interests Interesting? The Problem of Political Representation of Women." *The American Political Science Review* 75, 3: 701–16.

Sapiro, Virginia. 1998. "Feminist Studies and Political Science – and Vice Versa." In *Feminism and Politics*, ed. Anne Phillips. Oxford: Oxford University Press, 67–90.

Sapra, Sonalini. 2009. *Participatory Democracy and Social Justice: The Politics of Women's Environmental Action in India.* PhD Dissertation, Political Science, Vanderbilt University, Nashville TN.

Savery, Lynn. 2006. *Engendering the State: The International Diffusion of Women's Human Rights.* New York: Routledge.

Sax, Linda J., Linda Serra Hagedorn, Marisol Arredondo, and Frank A. Dicrisi III. 2002. "Faculty Research Productivity: Exploring the Role of Gender and Family-Related Factors." *Research in Higher Education* 43, 4: 423–46.

Schwedler, Jillian. 2006. "The Third Gender: Western Female Researchers in the Middle East." *PS, Political Science & Politics* 39, 3: 425–31.

Scott, Joan W. 1992. "Experience." In *Feminists Theorize the Political*, ed. Judith Butler and Joan W. Scott. New York: Routledge, 22–40.

Sedgwick, Eve Kosofsky. 1990. *Epistemology of the Closet.* Berkeley, CA: University of California Press.

Seguino, Stephanie. 2002. "Gender, Quality of Life, and Growth in Asia 1970–90." *The Pacific Review* 15, 2: 245–78.

Sen, Amartya. 2004. "Amartya Sen: A More Human Theory of Development." In *Asia Society*.

Shapiro, Ian. 2005. *The Flight from Reality in the Human Sciences.* Princeton, NJ: Princeton University Press.

Silliman, Jael Miriam, Marlene Gerber Fried, Loretta Ross, and Elena R. Gutiérrez. 2004. *Undivided Rights: Women of Color Organize for Reproductive Justice.* Cambridge, MA: South End Press.

Silvey, Rachel. 2007. "Unequal Borders: Indonesian Transnational Migrants at Immigration Control." *Geopolitics* 12, 2: 265–79.

Skinner, Tina, Marianne Hester, and Ellen Malos, eds. 2005. *Researching Gender Violence: Feminist Methodology in Action.* Devon, UK: Willan Publishing.

Smith, Dorothy E. 1987. *The Everyday World as Problematic: A Feminist Sociology.* Boston, MA: Northeastern University Press.

Smith, Linda Tuhiwai. [1998] 1999. *Decolonizing Methodologies: Research and Indigenous Peoples.* London: Zed Books.

Snarr, C. Melissa. 2009. "Waging Ethics: Living Wages and Framing Public Religious Ethics." *Journal of the Society of Christian Ethics* 29, 1: 69–86..

Snow, David, and Robert D. Benford. 1988. "Ideology, Frame Resonance, and Participant Mobilization." In *International Social Movement Research*, ed. Bert Klandermans, Hanspeter Kriesi and Sidney Tarrow. Greenwich, CT: JAI Press, 197–217.

Snyder, Margaret. 2006. "Unlikely Godmother: The United Nations and the Global Women's Movement." In *Global Feminism: Transnational Women's Activism, Organizing, and Human Rights*, ed. Myra Marx Ferree and Aili Mari Tripp. New York: New York University Press, 24–50.

Spatig, Linda, Kathy Seelinger, Amy Dillon, Laurel Parrott, and Kate Conrad. 2005. "From an Ethnographic Team to a Feminist Learning Community: A Reflective Tale." *Human Organization* 64, 1: 103–15.

Spelman, Elizabeth V. 1988. *Inessential Woman: Problems of Exclusion in Feminist Thought.* Boston, MA: Beacon Press.

Spender, Dale. 1981. "The Gatekeepers: A Feminist Critique of Academic Publishing." In *Doing Feminist Research*, ed. Helen Roberts. Routledge: London, 186–202.

Spender, Dale ed.1983. *Feminist Theorists: Three Centuries of Women Intellectual Traditions.* London: Women's Press.

Spender, Dale, with Cherie Kramarie eds. 1993. *The Knowledge Explosion: Generations of Feminist Scholarship.* New York: Athene Series, Teachers College Press.

Sprague, Joey. 2005. *Feminist Methodologies for Critical Researchers: Bridging Differences.* Walnut Creek, CA: AltaMira Press.

Sriram, Chandra Lekha, John C. King, Julia A. Mertus, Olga Martin Ortega, and Johanna Herman, 2009. *Surviving Field Research: Working in Violent and Difficult Situations.* New York: Routledge.

Stacey, Judith. 1999. "Ethnography Confronts the Global Village." *Journal of Contemporary Ethnography* 28, 6: 687–97.

Stacey, Judith, and Barrie Thorne. 1985. "The Missing Feminist Revolution in Sociology," *Social Problems* 32: 301–16.

Staeheli, Lynn A., and Richa Nagar. 2002. "Feminists Talking across Worlds." *Gender, Place and Culture* 9, 2: 167–72.

Stake, Robert E. 2005. "Qualitative Case Studies." In *The Sage Handbook of Qualitative Research*, ed. Norman K. Denzin and Yvonna S. Lincoln. Thousand Oaks, CA: Sage, 443–66.

Stanley, Liz. 1984. "Should 'Sex' Really be 'Gender' or 'Gender' Really be 'Sex'?' In *Applied Sociology*, ed. R. Anderson and W. Sharrock. London: Allen & Unwin.

Stanley, Liz. 1995. *Sex Surveyed, 1949–1994: From Mass-Observation's "Little Kinsey" To the National Survey and the Hite Reports.* Bristol, PA: Taylor & Francis.

Steinberg, Ronnie J. 1990. "Social Construction of Skill: Gender, Power and Comparable Worth." *Work and Occupations* 17, 4: 449–82.

Steinbugler, Amy, Julie Press, and Janice Dias. 2006. "Gender, Race and Affirmative Action: Operationalizing Intersectionality in Survey Research." *Gender and Society* 20, 6: 805–25.

Stern, Maria. 2005. *Naming Security – Constructing Identity: "Mayan Women" in Guatemala on the Eve of "Peace."* Manchester, UK: Manchester University Press.

Stern, Maria. 2006. "Racism, Sexism, Classism and Much More: Reading Security-Identity in Marginalized Sites." In *Feminist Methodologies for International Relations*, ed. Brooke Ackerly, Maria Stern and Jacqui True. Cambridge: Cambridge University Press, 174–97.

Stimson, James. nd. "Professional Writing in Political Science: A Highly Opinionated Essay." Unpublished Manuscript, 1–14.

Strunk, William, and E. B. White. 1918. *Elements of Style*. Geneva, NY: W. P. Humphrey.

Sturgeon, Noël. 1997. *Ecofeminist Natures: Race, Gender, Feminist Theory, and Political Action*. New York: Routledge.

Su, Fubing. 2006. "Gender Inequality in Chinese Politics: An Empirical Analysis of Provincial Elites." *Politics and Gender* 2, 2: 143–63.

Sullivan, Barbara. 2003. "Trafficking in Women. Feminism and New International Law." *International Feminist Journal of Politics* 5, 1: 67–91.

Sullivan, Shannon, and Nancy Tuana. 2007. *Race and Epistemologies of Ignorance*. Albany: State University of New York Press.

Swain, Carol M. 2002. *The New White Nationalism in America: Its Challenge to Integration*. Cambridge: Cambridge University Press.

Sword, Helen. 2007. *The Writer's Diet*. Auckland: Pearson Publishers.

Sword, Helen. 2009. "Writing Higher Education Differently: A Manifesto on Style." *Studies in Higher Education* 34, 3: 319–36.

Sylvester, Christine. 1993. "Homeless in International Relations? Women's Place in Canonical Texts and Feminist Reimaginings." In *Reimagining the Nation*, ed. Adam Lerner and Marjorie Martin. London: Open University Press, 76–97.

Sylvester, Christine. 1994. *Feminist Theory and International Relations in a Postmodern Era*. Cambridge: Cambridge University Press.

Sylvester, Christine. 2006. "Bringing Art/Museums to Feminist International Relations." In *Feminist Methodologies for International Relations*, ed. Brooke A. Ackerly, Maria Stern and Jacqui True. Cambridge: Cambridge University Press, 201–20.

Talbott, Shawn M. 2007. *The Cortisol Connection: Why Stress Makes You Fat and Ruins Your Health – and What You Can Do About It*. Alameda, CA: Hunter House.

Talley, Heather Laine. 2008. *Face Work: Cultural, Technical, and Surgical Interventions for Facial "Disfigurement."* PhD Dissertation, Vanderbilt University.

Tarrow, Sidney G. 2005. *The New Transnational Activism*. New York: Cambridge University Press.

Taylor, Verta. 1999. "Gender and Social Movements: Gender Processes in Women's Self-Help Movements." *Gender & Society* 13, 1: 8–33.

Taylor, Verta, and Leila J. Rupp. 2005. "When the Girls Are Men: Negotiating

Gender and Sexual Dynamics in a Study of Drag Queens." *Signs: Journal of Women in Culture and Society* 30, 4: 2115–39.

Thompson, Susan, and Penelope Barrett. 1997. "Summary Oral Reflective Analysis: A Method for Interview Data Analysis in Feminist Qualitative Research." *Advances in Nursing Science* 20, 2: 55–65.

Tickner, J. Ann. 1992. *Gender in International Relations: Feminist Perspectives on Achieving Global Security*. New York: Columbia University Press.

Tickner, J. Ann. 1997. "You Just Don't Understand: Troubled Engagements between Feminists and IR Theorists." *International Studies Quarterly* 41, 4: 611–32.

Tinker, Irene. 1990. *Persistent Inequalities: Women and World Development*. New York: Oxford University Press.

Tong, Rosemary. 1998. *Feminist Thought: A More Comprehensive Introduction*, 2nd edn. Colorado: Westview Press.

Trachtenberg, Marc. 2006a. "Working with Documents." In *The Craft of International History: A Guide to Method*. Princeton, NJ: Princeton University Press.

Trachtenberg, Marc. 2006b. *The Craft of International History: A Guide to Method*. Princeton, NJ: Princeton University Press.

Tremblay, Manon. 2007. "Democracy, Representation, and Women: A Comparative Analysis." *Democratization* 14, 4: 533–53.

Tripp, Aili Mari. 2002. "Combining Intercontinental Parenting and Research: Dilemmas and Strategies." *Signs: A Journal of Women in Culture and Society*. 27, 3: 794–811.

Tronto, Joan. 2006. "Is Peace Keeping Care Work?" Paper presented at Annual Meeting of the American Political Science Association, Philadelphia, PA, August 31, 2006.

True, Jacqui. 2003. *Gender, Globalization, and Postsocialism: The Czech Republic After Communism*. New York: Columbia University Press.

True, Jacqui. 2008a. "Global Accountability and Transnational Networks: The Women Leaders Network and Asia Pacific Economic Cooperation." *Pacific Review* 21, 1: 1–26.

True, Jacqui. 2008b. "Gender Mainstreaming and Regional Trade Governance." In *Global Governance: Feminist Perspectives*, ed. Shirin Rai and Georgina Waylen. Basingstoke: Palgrave, 129–59.

True, Jacqui. 2008c. "The Ethics of Feminism." In *Oxford Handbook of International Relations*, ed. Christian Reus-Smit and Duncan Snidal. Oxford: Oxford University Press.

True, Jacqui. 2008d. *Independent Assessment of the ECOTECH Implementation of APEC Working Groups and SOM Taskforces: Gender Focal Point Network*. APEC Secretariat, Singapore, May, pp. 60.

True, Jacqui. 2009a. "Feminism." In *Theories of International Relations*, ed. Scott Burchill, Richard Devetak, Andrew Linklater, Matthew Paterson, Christian Reus-Smit and Jacqui True. New York: Palgrave Macmillan, 213–34.

True, Jacqui. 2009b. "Gender Mainstreaming in International Institutions." In *Gender Matters in Global Politics*, ed. L. J. Shepherd. New York: Routledge.

True, Jacqui. 2009c. "Trading-in Gender Equality: Gendered Meanings in EU Trade Policies." In *The Discursive Politics of Gender Equality: Stretching, Bending and Policy-Making*, ed. E. Lombardo, P. Meier and M. Verloo. New York: Routledge (EU Series), 118–34.

True, Jacqui, and Charlie Gao. 2009. "National Identity in a Global Political Economy". In *New Zealand Government and Politics*, 5th edn, ed. R. K. Miller. Melbourne: Oxford University Press.

True, Jacqui, and Michael Mintrom. 2001. "Transnational Networks and Policy Diffusion: The Case of Gender Mainstreaming." *International Studies Quarterly* 45, 1: 27–57.

Truong, Thanh Dam, Saskia Wieringa, and Amrita Chhachhi. 2007. *Engendering Human Security: Feminist Perspectives.* London: Zed Books.

United Nations (1995) *Beijing Declaration and Platform for Action*, New York: United Nations.

VanHooser, Sarah. 2009. *Freedom Means.* Unpublished doctoral dissertation. Vanderbilt University.

Vargas, Virginia. 2005. "Feminisms and the World Social Forum: Space for Dialogue and Confrontation." *Development* 48, 2: 107–10.

Verloo, Mieke. 2005a. "Displacement and Empowerment: Reflections on the Concept and Practice of the Council of Europe Approach to Gender Mainstreaming and Gender Equality." *Social Politics: International Studies in Gender, State and Society* 12, 3: 344–65.

Verloo, Mieke. 2005b. "Mainstreaming gender equality in Europe: A critical frame analysis." *Greek Review of Social Research* 117 (B): 11–35.

Verloo, Mieke. 2006. "Multiple Inequalities, Intersectionality and the European Union." *European Journal of Women's Studies* 13, 3: 211–28.

Vickers, Jill. 2006. "Some Methodological and Conceptual Issues in Connecting Feminisms with Nationhood and Nationalisms." *International Feminist Journal of Politics* 8, 1: 84–109.

Visweswaran, Kamala. 1994. *Fictions of Feminist Ethnography.* Minneapolis: University of Minnesota Press.

Wapner, Paul. 2000. "The Normative Promise of Nonstate Actors: A Theoretical Account of Global Civil Society." In *Principled World Politics: The Challenge of Normative International Relations*, ed. Paul Wapner and Lester Edwin J. Ruiz. Lanham, MD: Rowman and Littlefield.

Waylen, Georgina. 2010. "Democracy, Democratization and Gender." In *The International Studies Compendium Project*, ed. Robert Denemark *et al.* Oxford: Wiley-Blackwell.

Ward, Kathryn B. and Linda Grant. 1991. "Co-authorship, Gender and Publication among Sociologists". In *Beyond Methodology: Feminist Scholarship as Lived Research*, ed. Mary M. Fonow and Judith A. Cook. Bloomington: Indiana University Press, 248–64.

Weatherall, Margaret, and Jonathan Potter. 1992. *Mapping the Language of Racism.* New York: Columbia University Press.

Weeks, Gregory. 2006. "Facing Failure: The Use (and Abuse) of Rejection in Political Science." *PS* 39, October: 879–82.

Weldes, Jutta. 2006. "High Politics and Low Data: Globalization Discourses and Popular Culture." In *Interpretation and Method: Empirical Research Methods and the Interpretive Turn*, ed. Dvora Yanow and Peregrine Schwartz–Shea. Armonk, NY: ME Sharpe, 176–86.

Weldon, Laurel. 2006. "The Structure of Intersectionality: A Comparative Politics of Gender." *Politics and Gender* 2, 2: 235–48.

Williams, Christine L. 2000. "Preface." *The ANNALS of the American Academy of Political and Social Science* 571, 1: 8–13.

Wilson, Ara. 2004. *The Intimate Economies of Bangkok: Tomboys, Tycoons, and Avon Ladies in the World City.* Berkeley: University of California Press.

Winter, Nicholas W. J. 2008. *Dangerous Frames: How Ideas about Race and Gender Shape Public Opinion.* Cambridge: Cambridge University Press.

Wolf, Diane L. 1996. "Situating Feminist Dilemmas in Fieldwork." In *Feminist Dilemmas in Fieldwork*, ed. Diane L. Wolf. Boulder, CO: Westview Press, 1–55.

Wolf, Margery. 1992. *A Thrice-Told Tale: Feminism, Postmodernism, and Ethnographic Responsibility.* Stanford: Stanford University Press.

Women for Women International. 2008. *Women Afghanistan Update.* http://www.womenforwomen.org/global-initiatives-helping-women/support-women-afghanistan-update.php [accessed 12.2.2009].

Worell, Judith. 2000. "Feminism in Psychology: Revolution or Evolution?" *The ANNALS of the American Academy of Political and Social Science* 571: 183–96.

Wylie, Alison. 2002. *Thinking from Things: Essays in the Philosophy of Archaeology.* Berkeley, CA: University of California Press.

Yanow, Dvora. 2006a. "Thinking Interpretively: Philosophical Presuppositions and the Human Sciences." In *Interpretation and Method: Empirical Research Methods and the Interpretive Turn*, ed. Dvora Yanow and Peregrine Schwartz-Shea. Armonk, NY: M. E. Sharpe, 5–26.

Yanow, Dvora. 2006b. "Neither Rigorous Nor Objective? Interrogating Criteria for Knowledge Claims in Interpretive Science." In *Interpretation and Method: Empirical Research Methods and the Interpretive Turn*, ed. Dvora Yanow and Peregrine Schwartz-Shea, Armonk, NY: M. E. Sharpe, pp. 67–88.

Yanow, Dvora. 2006c. "Reading as Method: Interpreting Interpretations." *Interpreting Method.* Prepared for the workshop on Political Ethnography: What Insider Perspectives Contribute to the Study of Power University of Toronto, October 26–28.

Yanow, Dvora, and Peregrine Schwartz-Shea eds. 2006. *Interpretation and Method: Empirical Research Methods and the Interpretive Turn.* Armonk, NY: M. E. Sharpe.

Yuval-Davis, Nira. 2006a. "Human Rights/Women's Rights and Feminist Transversal Politics." In *Global Feminism: Transnational Women's Activism, Organizing, and Human Rights*, ed. Myra Marx Ferree and Aili Mari Tripp eds New York: New York University Press, 275–95.

Yuval-Davis, Nira. 2006b. "Intersectionality and Feminist Politics." *European Journal of Women's Studies* 13, 3: 193–209.

Zalewski, Marysia. 2006. "Distracted Reflections on the Production, Narration, and Refusal of Feminist Knowledge in International Relations." In *Feminist Methodologies for International Relations*, ed. Brooke A. Ackerly, Maria Stern and Jacqui True. Cambridge: Cambridge University Press, 42–61.

Zerubavel, Eviatar. 1999. *The Clockwork Muse: A Practical Guide to Writing Theses, Dissertations, and Books.* Cambridge, MA: Harvard University Press.

Zippel, Katherine. 2004. "Transnational Advocacy Networks and Policy Cycles in the European Union: The Case of Sexual Harassment." *Social Politics* 11, 1: 57–85.

Index of Names

Index of Subjects

analysis and 187, 189, 201
defined 32
relationships with non-participant
226
trust and 223ff
Subjectivity 18
defined 23
see also Positionality
Supervisor
making the most of 107, 142
significance of 104, 105
Survey research 7
techniques for 227ff

Theoretical framework 91ff
Theoretical methodology 6
Theoretical reflection 79
Theory, constraints on 115F
Theory-seeking research 78, 80ff
Theory-testing research 78, 80ff
challenges of 84
Timing 225–6
Transdiciplinarity *see*
Multidisciplinarity
Translation 238ff
Translators 32, 34–5, 238ff
Transnational feminism, defined 15ff

Transparency 45
Trialing *see* Field test
Triangulation 127
Twinning *see* Matching

Unit of analysis 123ff, 217

Validity 202
Variability 137, 154, 189
Variable, dependent 154ff
Variables 10, 141, 147
independent 147
Variance *see* Variability

Website, use of 5, 68, 95, 123, 138,
222, 223, 228, 233, 234, 236, 269
Workshopping 44
Writing 49, 106–7, 197ff, ch. 13
passim
checklist for 249
deliberative moments and 244ff
learning to 248
Writing blocks, overcoming 243,
258ff
Writing process, grounded theory and
207
Writing style 248ff